1995

THE HUMAN RELATIONS OF ORGANIZATIONS

THE HUMAN RELATIONS
OF ORGANIZATIONS

Harold W. Berkman
University of Miami

Linda L. Neider
University of Miami

KENT PUBLISHING COMPANY

A Division of Wadsworth, Inc.
Boston, Massachusetts

LIBRARY
College of St. Francis
JOLIET, ILLINOIS

Editor • *Rolf A. Janke*

Production Editor • *Marianne L'Abbate*

Interior Designer • *Vanessa Piñeiro*

Cover Design • *Hannus Design Associates*

Production Coordinator • *Marcia A. Locke*

Kent Publishing Company
A Division of Wadsworth, Inc.

Printed in the United States of America
1 2 3 4 5 6 7 8 9 — 91 90 89 88 87

Library of Congress Cataloging-in-Publication Data

Berkman, Harold W.
    The human relations of organizations.

    Includes bibliographies and index.
    1. Psychology, industrial. 2. Organizational behavior. I. Neider, Linda L., 1953–   . II. Title.
HF5548.8.B393 1987   658.3   86–18573
ISBN 0–534–07410–3

For Rose and Abel   *To my mother, Rosemary*

—HWB   *—LLN*

ABOUT THE AUTHORS

Harold W. Berkman (Ph.D., St. John's University) is currently Associate Dean of Graduate Business Programs and Research Administration and Professor of General Business, Management, and Organization. Dr. Berkman has written fifteen books in the fields of management and marketing. His books have been adopted for classroom use by colleges and universities in the United States, Canada, Australia, Europe, and the Orient. In addition, he has contributed a number of scholarly articles to various journals. He serves as Executive Vice President and Director of the Academy of Marketing Science and is the founder of the *Journal of the Academy of Marketing Science.* In 1983, Dr. Berkman was the first recipient of the World Marketing Congress Award for leadership and scholarly contributions to the field of marketing. He has been involved in various research projects and has served as a consultant to firms marketing services, retailing, consumer goods manufacturing, and publishing. Before entering academia, Dr. Berkman was a successful corporate executive and entrepreneur.

Linda L. Neider is currently the Chairperson of the Department of General Business, Management, and Organization in the School of Business Administration at the University of Miami. Dr. Neider received her Ph.D., M.B.A., and M.A. degrees from the State University of New York at Buffalo. She has published numerous articles in the areas of organizational behavior and human resources management, and has served as a consultant for a variety of companies on productivity improvement. Dr. Neider has received the University of Miami's Outstanding Teacher Award, and has been cited in the 1985 volume of *Outstanding Young Women of America,* and the 1985 premier edition of *Who's Who and Why of Successful Florida Women.* She is a member of the Academy of Management and the American Psychological Association.

v

Note to the Student

Dear Student,

    If you winced when you learned the price of this textbook, you are experiencing what is known as "sticker shock" in today's economy. Yes, textbooks are expensive, and we don't like it anymore than you do. Many of us here at Kent have sons and daughters of our own attending college, or we are attending school part time ourselves. However, the prices of our books are dictated by the cost factors involved in producing them. The costs of paper, designing the book, setting it in type, printing it, and binding it have risen significantly each year along with everything else in our economy. You might find the following table to be of some interest.

Item	1967 Price	1986 Price	The Price Increase
Monthly Housing Expense	$114.31	$686.46	6.0 times
Monthly Automobile Expense	82.69	339.42	4.1 times
Loaf of Bread	.22	1.00	4.6 times
Pound of Hamburger	.39	1.48	3.8 times
Pound of Coffee	.59	2.45	4.2 times
Candy Bar	.10	.40	4.0 times
Men's Dress Shirt	5.00	25.00	5.0 times
Postage	.05	.22	4.4 times
Resident College Tuition	294.00	1,581.00	5.4 times

    Today's prices of college textbooks have increased only about 2.8 times 1967 prices. Compare your texts sometime to a general trade book, i.e., a novel or nonfiction book, and you will easily see significant differences in the internal design, quality of paper, and binding. These features of college textbooks cost money.

    Textbooks should not be looked on only as an expense. Other than your professors, your textbooks are your most important source for what you hope to learn in college. What's more, the textbooks you keep can be valuable resources in your future career and life. They are the foundation of your professional library. Like your education, your textbooks are one of your most important investments.

    We are concerned, and we care. Please write to us at the address below with your comments. We want to be responsive to your suggestions, to give you quality textbooks, and to do everything in our power to keep their prices under control.

Wayne Barcomb

Wayne A. Barcomb
President

Kent Publishing Company
20 Park Plaza
Boston, MA 02116

TO THE STUDENT

Ask any executive about the biggest challenge facing businesspeople today, and the answer will be the same: people problems. Whether it's unmotivated employees, uncooperative colleagues, or unfair bosses, the most frequent source of complaint in any organization is the sheer difficulty of working with other human beings.

This book is about the human side of organizations. It was written to help you understand why people behave the way they do on the job. In some of the examples, you'll probably recognize people you've worked with or for—and maybe even yourself—for this book offers more than just theoretical concepts. It gives you practical knowledge that can be applied in the real world of business. Specifically, the book offers you:

1. Sound principles that explain why people in organizations behave the way they do.

2. An understanding of the ideas behind many management techniques; you can learn to apply them more effectively and to respond constructively when they are applied to you.

3. Selected applications of theory and research to people problems you are likely to encounter on the job.

4. The challenge of working out your own answers to some case study problems in human behavior within the organization.

5. The opportunity to learn how some chief executive officers have solved human relations difficulties in their own organizations.

Before you begin your first assignment, take a minute to look through the book and familiarize yourself with its features. Note "On the Job" that begins and "On the Job Revisited" that ends each chapter; the

Managerial Dialogues; and the boxes that shed additional light on currently hot topics. Get in the habit of using the outline at the beginning of each chapter to guide your reading and notetaking and the summary at the end to check your comprehension. See for yourself how this book can make your human relations course more interesting, more challenging, and ultimately more successful for *you*.

TO THE INSTRUCTOR

Our objective in writing this text was simply to build up a knowledge of human relations concepts, drawing from all relevant disciplines, and to show students how that knowledge is and can be used to solve real-world business problems. Because human relations is an interdisciplinary course, it poses special problems for instructor and student alike. It is manifestly impossible to provide simultaneously a complete background in sociology, psychology, anthropology, social psychology, and organizational theory in the space of only one textbook. Yet it is important for students to understand the differences in point of view of each of the varied disciplines that contribute knowledge of human behavior within the organization. We have tried to solve this problem by eliminating the jargon and special terminology that is unique to each field and concentrating on the principles that may be generalized to fit different situations.

More importantly, we have chosen to concentrate on practical applications wherever possible. The text is crammed with examples and illustrative vignettes. We have tried to introduce a concept and then immediately illustrate it with a practical example, which helps teach the concept and simultaneously gives the student some concrete suggestions for using their knowledge in real-world situations. We recognize that students want not just conceptual understanding but the advantage of practical mastery. The features of this textbook are all designed to help the student achieve that practical mastery of human relations concepts.

READABILITY

Although nearly every textbook begins with a claim that it is particularly readable, the low level of readability remains the most frequent criticism of most texts, from instructors and students alike. A quick browse through this text will reveal a style that is closer to conversation than "textbookese." Concepts are defined in simple terms, without relying on the jargon of any particular discipline. Copious examples reinforce and illustrate the concepts to make them easier to grasp, and examples come from the real world that students are likely to be familiar with—fast-food chains, telephone sales work, teaching—rather than the rarefied world of the Fortune 500. We hope you'll even enjoy the occasional outburst of a sense of humor!

ON THE JOB

Each chapter begins with a problem in human relations. The opening text describes the basic situation and outlines the areas of focus. The new material introduced in the chapter then suggests ways to think about the problem and possible solutions. The case also is discussed at the end of the chapter (On the Job Revisited), sometimes with answers, sometimes with more questions, sometimes with a different way to think about the situation.

These practical examples demonstrate to the student that the material in the text has relevance and can be used to solve the problems that arise on the job. Thus, they are another tool for learning the basic concepts that lead to practical mastery.

MANAGERIAL DIALOGUE

Perhaps the most unusual feature of the text is the inclusion of Managerial Dialogues. These sections are based on interviews with a number of well-known chief executive officers, such as Harold Geneen, Mary Kay Ash, and Admiral Inman. These successful executives speak directly about the human relations problems they have faced in the course of their careers and the ways they have tried to solve them. Each interview relates *directly* to the material contained in a specific chapter, and the effect is like sitting down with a wise and experienced counselor. The Managerial Dialogues help students see that the concepts in the text are not divorced from the real world of corporate success or failure, but rather are an integral part of being a manager in a business organization.

HUMAN RELATIONS APPLICATIONS

Another element that helps the student use basic concepts to achieve practical mastery is the feature called Human Relations Applications. This section lists the most important concepts introduced in each chapter. Every concept is then given a practical application. The text provides students with the direct and concrete links between theory and applications in a form that is easy to comprehend and to study. This is just one more way to emphasize that the ultimate goal of any course in human relations is to help the students solve problems on the job.

ACKNOWLEDGMENTS

We would like to thank the following reviewers for their valuable contributions in catching errors, expanding our viewpoint, and sometimes pushing us just a little further down the road to excellence: Don W. Kassing, Western State College; Robert J. Kroll, Rock Valley College; Jim Lee Morgan, West Los Angeles College; Jeffery D. Stauffer, Ventura College; Fred Sutton, Cuyahoga Community College; and Al Travers, Indiana Vocational Technical College.

Special thanks are due to the chief executive officers who graciously agreed to share their views and expertise with our readers; we learned that it is true that the more important people are, the more willing they are to be helpful. Thanks, too, to Dick Westlund for his hard work and reportorial skills that add so much to the Managerial Dialogues.

We thank researcher Donna Chang for her uncanny ability to locate the unfindable. Christina Foo put all the material on diskette, as well as handled typing and permissions, with skill and aplomb. Other members of our department at the University of Miami have kindly let us share ideas with them and contributed personal insights: Carl McKenry, Harold Strauss, Bob Hannan, and Ed Sofen.

BRIEF CONTENTS

P A R T   1   **BASIS OF HUMAN RELATIONS: PEOPLE AT WORK   1**

CHAPTER 1   The Work Place of the Future   3
CHAPTER 2   Behavior and Personality   38
CHAPTER 3   Communication and Perception   63
CHAPTER 4   Employee Needs, Social Relationships, and Motivation   89
CHAPTER 5   Employee Attitudes and Job Satisfaction   116

P A R T   2   **THE ORGANIZATIONAL ENVIRONMENT   137**

PART 2

CHAPTER 6   Organizational Patterns and Views on Design   139
CHAPTER 7   Groups in the Organization   168
CHAPTER 8   Participation and Productivity   195

P A R T   3   **ORGANIZATIONAL PROCESSES   223**

CHAPTER 9   The Role of the Manager in the Organization   225
CHAPTER 10   Leadership   257
CHAPTER 11   Evaluating Subordinates: Performance Appraisal and Discipline   287
CHAPTER 12   Managing Conflict   311
CHAPTER 13   Improving the Quality of Working Life   335

PART 4   **MANAGING THE ORGANIZATION IN A CHANGING SOCIETY   359**

CHAPTER 14   Managing Change   361
CHAPTER 15   Corporate Culture   381
CHAPTER 16   Social Responsibility and the Organization   404

CASES FROM THE CONSULTANT'S IN-BASKET   427

APPENDIX A   Journal/Magazine Review   457

APPENDIX B   Suggested Readings   466

GLOSSARY   482

INDEX   487

CONTENTS

P A R T   1   **BASIS OF HUMAN RELATIONS: PEOPLE AT WORK   1**

1   THE WORK PLACE OF THE FUTURE   3

ON THE JOB . . .   4

When the Future Comes, Will We Recognize It?   4
Will We Recognize Ourselves?   5

    Trends in the work force   5
    Social trends of the present and future   9
    Values will be different   10
    Trends in organizations   17

The Revolution in Technology   19

MANAGERIAL DIALOGUE Admiral B. R. Inman   22

    Technology is as old as humankind   23
    The industrial revolution   24
    Technological innovation   26
    The rise of computers   27
    Managing technological change   28

Jobs of the Future   30
What About Your Own Future?   33

ON THE JOB REVISITED . . .   35

Summary   35
Human Relations Applications   36
Discussion Questions   36
Notes   37

2 BEHAVIOR AND PERSONALITY 38

CHAPTER 2

ON THE JOB . . . 39

What Is Personality? 40

How Does Personality Develop? 42

  According to Freud 42
  The learning theorists: How do we learn to behave? 46
  Is a personality greater than the sum of its traits? 49

Nature Versus Nurture: Which Is It? 50

Personality and Behavior on the Job 51

  The type A/type B personality 51

MANAGERIAL DIALOGUE George R. Wackenhut 52

  Internal/external control 54
  Machiavellianism 54

Personality and Prejudice 57

  The causes of prejudice 57
  Prejudice leads to discrimination 58

ON THE JOB REVISITED . . . 60

Summary 61
Human Relations Applications 61
Discussion Questions 61
Notes 62

3 COMMUNICATION AND PERCEPTION 63

ON THE JOB . . . 64

Everybody Talks About Communication, but They're Still Confused 65

The Process of Communication 65

  How does communication happen? 66
  Patterns of communication 67

Problems of Communication 71

  Perceptual barriers 71
  Physical barriers 73
  Semantics 75
  Sociopsychological barriers 76

Effective Communication 78

  Message sending 78
  Listening and receiving 79

Staying alert to nonverbal communication   81
Encouraging more effective communication   83

MANAGERIAL DIALOGUE Peter Storer   84

ON THE JOB REVISITED . . .   86

Summary   86
Human Relations Applications   87
Discussion Questions   87
Notes   88

4 EMPLOYEE NEEDS, SOCIAL RELATIONSHIPS, AND MOTIVATION   89

ON THE JOB . . .   90

Why Work?   90
Theories About Motivation   91
Content theories of motivation   92
Process theories of motivation   99

Using Motivation As a Manager   103
Job enrichment   103

MANAGERIAL DIALOGUE George W. Jenkins   104

Participation   107
Cafeteria incentive plans   107
Flextime   110
Behavior modification   111

ON THE JOB REVISITED . . .   113

Summary   113
Human Relations Applications   114
Discussion Questions   114
Notes   114

5 EMPLOYEE ATTITUDES AND JOB SATISFACTION   116

ON THE JOB . . .   117

Everybody Has an Attitude   117
What Are Attitudes?   117
What attitudes do for the individual   118
Opinions, beliefs, and values   119
Changing attitudes   120
Three-component attitude model   120

Attitudinal Effects on Behavior   122

    Consistency of attitude   123
    Attitudes and job satisfaction   124
    Postitive and negative attitudes   124

MANAGERIAL DIALOGUE M. Anthony Burns   125

    The relationship between job satisfaction and performance   130

Measuring Attitudes Toward the Job   130

    Survey design   131
    Administration issues   133
    Survey feedback   134

ON THE JOB REVISITED . . .   134

Summary   134
Human Relations Applications   135
Discussion Questions   135
Notes   136

P A R T   2   THE ORGANIZATIONAL ENVIRONMENT   137

6   ORGANIZATIONAL PATTERNS AND VIEWS ON DESIGN   139

ON THE JOB . . .   140

What Is an Organization?   141

    An organization pursues goals   141
    Defining profits   142
    The structure of the organization   143
    Formal structure   144
    Organizational design   144

MANAGERIAL DIALOGUE William Schaefer   148

Classical Organization Theory   154

    Frederick W. Taylor   155
    Henri Fayol   156
    Max Weber   157
    Evaluating classical theory   159

Humanistic Organization Theory   160

    Chester Barnard   160
    Chris Argyris   161
    Rensis Likert   161
    Evaluating humanistic theory   163

ON THE JOB REVISITED . . . 166

Summary 166
Human Relations Applications 166
Discussion Questions 167
Notes 167

7 GROUPS IN THE ORGANIZATION 168

ON THE JOB . . . 169

Working Together Means Forming Groups 170
The Informal Group 170

    The peer group 171
    The task-oriented peer group 172

How Do Groups Help? 176

    How the work group helps the individual 176
    How the work group helps the larger organization 179

MANAGERIAL DIALOGUE Janet Chusmir 180

Understanding Behavior in the Group 183

    Norms 183
    Sanctions 184
    Learning the norms 185

Deviance 186

    Causes of deviance 187
    Deviance within the organization 188
    Controlling deviance on the job 189

The Manager's Role in Small Work Groups 191
The Small Group and Organizational Conflict 191

ON THE JOB REVISITED . . . 192

Summary 192
Human Relations Applications 193
Discussion Questions 194
Notes 194

8 PARTICIPATION AND PRODUCTIVITY 195

ON THE JOB . . . 196

Participation Is the Key to Productivity 197
Economic Productivity 197
The Concept of Participation 198
Participation Should Be Linked to Productivity 199

Using Controls for Increased Productivity   200
    Traditional approaches   201
    Modern theory   201
    Workers' reactions   201

Supportive Management   202
    The role of the organization   204

MANAGERIAL DIALOGUE Frank Perdue   205

    The role of the labor union   207

Delegating Control   208
    Consultive management   209
    Suggestion programs   209
    Democratic management   210
    Economic participation and democratic management   211
    Multiple management   211

Stages of Participation and Delegation   211
How Much Participation Is Appropriate?   213
Quality Control Circles   215
    Japanese methods   216
    Quality control circles in American businesses   218

ON THE JOB REVISITED . . .   218
Summary   219
Human Relations Applications   219
Discussion Questions   220
Notes   220

PART 3   ORGANIZATIONAL PROCESSES   223

9   THE ROLE OF THE MANAGER IN THE ORGANIZATION   225
ON THE JOB . . .   226
A Good Manager Plays the Role   228
What Is a Role?   229
    Are role players born or made?   229
    Never underestimate the power of the individual   230

Defining the Managerial Role   232
MANAGERIAL DIALOGUE Harold Geneen   233

Leader   235
Executive   236
Negotiator   237
Developer   237
Innovator   239
Human being   239
The Mintzberg model   239

Role Strain and Role Conflict   241

A manager faces conflicting demands   241
A manager must satisfy many people   242
Resolving role conflict   243

The Special Role of the Woman Manager   244

The stereotypes and the realities   244
Overcoming the barriers   247
The managerial woman   249

Demands of the Outside Environment   250

ON THE JOB REVISITED . . .   253

Summary   254
Human Relations Applications   255
Discussion Questions   255
Notes   255

10   LEADERSHIP   257

ON THE JOB . . .   258

Leadership   260
Leaders Are Made, Not Born   260

MANAGERIAL DIALOGUE George E. Johnson   262

Managers versus leaders   263
Can leadership be developed?   265

What Does a Leader Do?   266

The executive function   266
Other leadership functions   268
How should a leader behave?   269

How Does a Member Become a Leader?   271

Personal qualifications   271
Situational factors   272
Formal versus informal leadership   273

How Does a Leader Exercise Control? 276

Power and authority 277
Other means of control 278

New Views of Leadership 279

Blake and Mouton's Managerial Grid 279
Hersey and Blanchard's situational leadership model 281
House's path-goal theory 283

ON THE JOB REVISITED . . . 284

Summary 284
Human Relations Applications 285
Discussion Questions 285
Notes 285

11 EVALUATING SUBORDINATES: PERFORMANCE APPRAISAL AND DISCIPLINE 287

ON THE JOB . . . 288
Evaluating Workers Is Tough 288
The Evaluation Process 288

Evaluations are necessary 289

MANAGERIAL DIALOGUE Judith Berger 290

Legal aspects of performance appraisals 292

Evaluation Tools 293

Three ways of measuring individual employee performance 294
Evaluations by comparison with other employees 300
Errors and problems with evaluation tools 301
Minimizing appraisal errors and problems 303

Conducting Appraisal Sessions 304

Giving performance feedback 304
Structuring the appraisal interview 306
Dealing with the problem employee 307

ON THE JOB REVISITED . . . 308

Summary 308
Human Relations Applications 309
Discussion Questions 309
Notes 309

12 MANAGING CONFLICT 311

ON THE JOB . . . 312

Conflict Is Inevitable 313
What Is Conflict? 314
Why Conflicts Arise 317
Goals and Conflict 318

Conflicting expectations 319
Job assignments create conflicts 321

The Personal Nature of Conflict 322

Satisfying needs 323
Frustration 323

Psychological Reactions to Conflict 324

Defense mechanisms 324
Aggression 325
Substitution reactions 325
Avoidance mechanisms 326
Personal styles of handling conflict 327

Consequences of Conflict 328

Negative effects 328

MANAGERIAL DIALOGUE Norman R. Weldon 329

Positive effects for the individual 331
Positive effects for the organization 332

ON THE JOB REVISITED . . . 333

Summary 333
Human Relations Applications 333
Discussion Questions 334
Notes 334

13 IMPROVING THE QUALITY OF WORKING LIFE 335

ON THE JOB . . . 336

What Does "Quality of Working Life" Mean? 337
The First Concern about QWL 337
Finding Out What QWL Really Is 340

MANAGERIAL DIALOGUE Mary Kay Ash 341

Organizational Stress 342

Organizational stressors 343
Consequences of excessive stress 347

Coping with Job Stress 349

> Organizational methods 349
> Individual methods 353

Promoting the Health and Safety of Employees 353
Other QWL Programs 355

ON THE JOB REVISITED . . . 355

Summary 356
Human Relations Applications 356
Discussion Questions 357
Notes 357

P A R T 4   **MANAGING THE ORGANIZATION IN A CHANGING SOCIETY 359**

14 MANAGING CHANGE 361

ON THE JOB . . . 362

Change Can Be Threatening 363
Resistance to Change 364

> Why resistance occurs 365

MANAGERIAL DIALOGUE Jane Campbell Cousins 366

> Reducing resistance to change 367
> Diagnosing obstacles to change 370

The Stages of Change 371

> Unfreezing stage 371
> Changing stage 371
> Refreezing stage 372

Selecting a Change Approach 373

> Top-down change 373
> Bottom-up change 374
> Shared responsibility 375
> The people who make the changes 375

The Organizational Development Approach to Change 376

ON THE JOB REVISITED . . . 378

Summary 378
Human Relations Applications 379

Discussion Questions   379
Notes   380

15   CORPORATE CULTURE   381

ON THE JOB . . .   382

What Is Corporate Culture?   383
Corporate Culture Determines Productivity   384
Bureaupathology: A Corporate Illness   385
Matching Your Personality to a Corporate Culture   386

Dress codes   387
Status symbols   389

Types of Corporate Culture   390

IBM   390
PepsiCo   391
J.C. Penney   391
Looking for a way to classify corporate cultures   392

Is There an Ideal Corporate Culture?   395

The Japanese system   395
What creates excellence?   396
A closer look at successful corporate cultures   397

MANAGERIAL DIALOGUE Thomas J. Peters   398

How to Change the Corporate Culture   399

Role modeling   400
Positive reinforcement   400
Make employees feel important   401

ON THE JOB REVISITED . . .   401

Summary   402
Human Relations Applications   402
Discussion Questions   402
Notes   403

16   SOCIAL RESPONSIBILITY AND THE ORGANIZATION   404

ON THE JOB . . .   405

What Does a Business Owe the Community?   406
Defining Social Responsibility   407
Pursuing Purely Economic Goals   410
The Case for the Separation of Business and Social Welfare   410

The Pragmatic Approach to Social Responsibility   412
    Can companies be both socially responsible and profitable?   413
MANAGERIAL DIALOGUE James W. McLamore   414
    Deregulation and social responsibility   416
    How can social responsibility be measured?   418
An Activist View of Corporate Responsibility   420
Social Responsibility and People in the Organization   421

ON THE JOB REVISITED . . .   422

Summary   423
Human Relations Applications   423
Discussion Questions   424
Notes   424

CASES FROM THE CONSULTANT'S IN-BASKET   427

APPENDIX A   Journal/Magazine Review   457

APPENDIX B   Suggested Readings   466

GLOSSARY   482

INDEX   487

THE HUMAN RELATIONS
OF ORGANIZATIONS

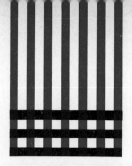

BASIS OF HUMAN RELATIONS: PEOPLE AT WORK

PART 1

CHAPTER 1
The Work Place of the Future

CHAPTER 2
Behavior and Personality

CHAPTER 3
Communication and Perception

CHAPTER 4
Employee Needs, Social Relationships, and Motivation

CHAPTER 5
Employee Attitudes and Job Satisfaction

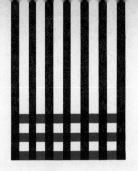

THE WORK PLACE OF THE FUTURE

CHAPTER 1

ON THE JOB . . .

WHEN THE FUTURE COMES, WILL WE RECOGNIZE IT?

WILL WE RECOGNIZE OURSELVES?

    Trends in the Work Force
    Social Trends of the Present and Future
    Values Will Be Different
    Trends in Organizations

THE REVOLUTION IN TECHNOLOGY

    Technology Is As Old As Humankind
    The Industrial Revolution
    Technological Innovation
    The Rise of Computers
    Managing Technological Change

JOBS OF THE FUTURE

WHAT ABOUT YOUR OWN FUTURE?

ON THE JOB REVISITED . . .

SUMMARY

HUMAN RELATIONS APPLICATIONS

DISCUSSION QUESTIONS

NOTES

MANAGERIAL DIALOGUE: Admiral B. R. Inman

ON THE JOB

When Suzy Smith walked into the factory, she didn't know what to expect. She'd heard all about working for the General Motors assembly division from her dad. With two years at her community college under her belt, she was ready to take her place on the line.

But what Ms. Smith saw threw her for a loop. Dozens of industrial robots, lots of flashing video display terminals, conveyor belts on all sides—and not one person in sight. She saw the sign "Production Control Office" and walked through the door. There, Henry Warren greeted her by name. He told her that he would be her new supervisor. Since this was her first day on the job, she'd spend her shift reading manuals. Tomorrow she'd be quizzed on her responses.

Much to Ms. Smith's surprise, her assembly line job required her to think! After fourteen years of school, she had hoped to throw away her textbooks. Instead, there was more of the same. "Even graduate school wouldn't be this hard," she thought to herself around midnight as she paged her way through the GM manuals. "I was hoping for an ordinary nine-to-five job that I could forget when I left the plant,"she told her boyfriend the next day. "I wonder if they make jobs like that anymore."

Ms. Smith's frustrations only increased in the next few weeks. There was so much to learn about statistics, parts inventories, and computer control systems that it cut her free time, and she had to drop out of her scuba diving classes—something that made her boyfriend angry. Somehow, though, she absorbed the technical manuals and began to understand what was happening in the assembly line control room.

Six months later, Warren called Ms. Smith into his office and told her he wanted to promote her to shift foreman. But first, she'd have to spend six weeks in Detroit learning the latest control room technology. That evening as she had dinner with her boyfriend, she wondered what direction to take.

If you were Ms. Smith, what would you do?

WHEN THE FUTURE COMES, WILL WE RECOGNIZE IT?

What kind of society will we have in the twenty-first century? What kind of work will we be doing? Our society is undergoing some dramatic changes. Our values are in the process of being transformed, and the kinds of work we do may be revolutionized. In this chapter, we will examine three broad movements that are shaping the organization of the future. By following our society's changes in demographics, values, and technology, we will have at least a glimpse of the organization of the future. Some of the following questions will be addressed:

What will the work force of the future be like?

Will the change in life-styles bring a change in the way we look at work?

Will the technological revolution continue? Will it change the way we do our work in the future?

How will *you* fit into the work place of the future?

WILL WE RECOGNIZE OURSELVES?

A number of changes are now taking place in American society that will affect our life-styles, our job choices, our careers, and the organizations for which we will work. The most basic changes in society are demographic—changes in population patterns and family trends. In turn, these demographic changes affect society's values. A society in which teenagers are the largest population group is likely to be different in its organizations, values, and life-styles than one in which senior citizens make up the largest component. In similar fashion, a nation such as Japan, which is primarily made up of one ethnic group, is likely to have organizations that differ from those of the United States, which is rich in ethnic diversity.

"The work force of the future will be older, more skilled . . . and you'll see more women at every level of the organization."

Trends in the Work Force

Working from U.S. Census Bureau reports and other statistical information, researchers have pinpointed the demographic trends that are affecting our society and our business organizations.

An aging work force.   As we move closer to the twenty-first century, our work force will be graying. During the 1970s, the typical worker was just entering the labor pool, perhaps getting his or her first job. The labor force of the 1980s is full of middle-aged workers, and the first two decades of the twenty-first century will be dominated by older workers and retirees (see Figure 1.1; Table 1.1).

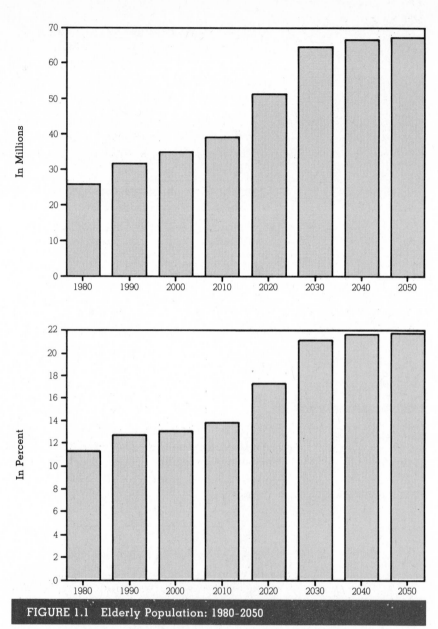

FIGURE 1.1   Elderly Population: 1980–2050

Source: Courtesy of the American Demographic Institute.

TABLE 1.1 Projected Number and Proportion of Persons Aged 65 Years and over in the U.S. Population: 1980-2050

| Year | Population[a] | | |
	Age 65+	Total	Percentage age 65+
1980	25,714	227,704	11.29
1990	31,697	249,657	12.70
2000	34,921	267,955	13.03
2010	39,196	283,238	13.84
2020	51,422	296,597	17.34
2030	64,580	304,807	21.19
2040	66,988	308,559	21.71
2050	67,412	309,488	21.78

[a]In millions.

Source: Bureau of the Census, Current Population Reports, Series P-25, No. 952. Washington, DC, May 1984.

Recent federal legislation raising the mandatory retirement age from 65 to 70 years and passage of the Age Discrimination in Employment Act are clear signs that politicians are already responding to this population trend. Business organizations appear to be slower to recognize this change. Career paths in organizations, training programs for new employees, the types of benefits offered—all these will have to change dramatically as the average employee grows older.

Coupled with the graying of the American work force will be a decline in the number of entry-level workers. This may be good news for young people just entering the job market. Corporate needs for rookies may induce more high school graduates to join the job market immediately without going to college. It may also mean higher turnover among new employees, who suddenly find themselves in demand. On the other hand, entry-level workers may find it tougher to move ahead. Mid-level management posts will be oversupplied with experienced workers and supervisors. New workers may therefore spend proportionately more of their time in a subordinate position than their parents did.

This combination of demographic trends—more older workers and fewer younger ones—is likely to spur efforts to restrain older employees and keep them on the job longer than in the past. Managers, often much younger than their workers, will have to deal with a work force that may be less agile and grow fatigued more quickly than in the past. There may also be a gap in opinions and values between the "oldsters" and the "newsters" in sports, politics, and life-styles.

More women in the work force.   Over the last two decades there has been an across-the-board rise in the number of women joining the American work force. Regardless of age or family circumstances, more and more women are working outside the home, sometimes by choice, sometimes by necessity. During the 1970s, a record 12,000,000 women entered the work force. During the 1980s, that number is expected to rise to 16,500,000. About 45 percent of all mothers with children under school age are now employed, and an even larger percentage of women with school-age children are working.

Women are making inroads even in jobs traditionally held by men. The U.S. Bureau of Labor Statistics reported that in 1980, more than 5,500,000 women were working in blue-collar jobs, many wearing hard hats and safety shoes. Reasons for this female surge into the work force are varied. Better education and the desire to use that knowledge are important. The increase in the number of women heading households as a result of divorce, and the subsequent need for many of these women to work, is another factor. Smaller families and the need to supplement family income because of inflation undoubtably also play a role. Interestingly, the rise in female participation in the work force appears to be occurring throughout the industrial world. A 1984 report by the International Labor Organization found that in most countries, female participation rose from about 45 percent in 1960 to 85 percent in 1980. Federal statistics indicate that 47 percent of the American work force will be female by 1995.

Rise of the white-collar worker.   There has been a marked shift in the kinds of jobs Americans hold. White-collar jobs are booming, while blue-collar positions are steady at best and declining in some years. Managers and professionals outnumber unskilled laborers five to one. Teachers outnumber production workers in the chemical, oil, rubber, plastic, paper, and steel industries combined. Peter Drucker, one of the country's most prominent management experts, projects that blue-collar jobs will follow the pattern of agricultural jobs and shrink to a tiny percentage of the work force. Unskilled factory workers, meat packers, tobacco workers, and elevator operators, for example, have been almost totally replaced by machines. Even factory management positions have been affected. Routine decisions about inventory levels, distribution procedures, and other middle-management chores can be worked out by computers, which can be programmed to combine sophisticated economic and behavioral theory with such mathematical techniques as operations research and systems analysis.

The decline in blue-collar jobs, however, has been accompanied by an increase in productivity. In other words, fewer workers are producing about the same amount of goods. Manufacturing output as a percentage of the gross national product has been stable for decades: 24.5 percent in 1950; 23.3 percent in 1960; 24.1 percent in 1970; and 23.8 percent in 1984. The United States appears to be in no danger of losing its industrial base. As happened to American agriculture, higher output can be achieved with fewer workers.

The types of factory jobs are also changing. General Motors is projecting that skilled tradespeople, who made up 16 percent of the auto giant's work force in the mid-1980s, will compose up to 50 percent of the work force by the year 2000. According to one expert, this is what the factory of the future may look like:

> *The scope of typical production jobs—once just above the level of sweeping and cleaning—will be broad. Nearly everyone in the plant will be comfortable in accessing computerized information and inputting commands as well as data. . . . These workers will be monitors more than doers, troubleshooters more than fixers, and information manipulators rather than object manipulators.* [1]

Information workers are already the largest occupational group in the nation. They are predicted to make up 70 percent of the work force by 1990 and 80 percent by 2000. The increased demand for such employees will promote the concept of continuing education programs, often financed by the employer. A shortage of specialists in some areas may lead to greater use of outside consultants and more competition in the hiring of experienced personnel.

Social Trends of the Present and Future

In addition to the demographic trends directly affecting the work place, a number of social trends will also have a broad impact on the business organization of the future.

More two-income families.   With the rise in female participation in the work force comes an increase in the number of two-income families. During the decade ending in 1978, the number of two-income families in America grew by 25 percent, and that trend is continuing. Two-income couples generally have more education than their traditional counterparts. There are also significant ethnic differences: the number of two-income families was higher for blacks than for whites, while Hispanics had the lowest number.

Postponement of marriage. Marriage is still the most popular institution in the United States. Americans regularly tell surveyors that a happy marriage and a good family are the most important aspects of life. A 1980 study found that more than 90 percent of American youth plan to marry—a proportion that hasn't changed since 1960. The same study also found that Americans are putting off their wedding plans for a few years. In the 1980s, the median first-marriage age for white women was 23 years. During the "baby boom" years of the late 1940s and 1950s, the median age was 20 years, whereas during the late 1970s, the marriage age was 22 years.

More singles in society. The percentage of single adults in America has risen sharply over the past few decades. In 1960, for instance, 64 percent of women aged 20 to 24 years were married and living with their husbands. In 1982, that figure dropped to 39 percent. A higher divorce rate, the postponement of marriage, and a drop in remarriage rates have combined to increase the number of single-person households. Single living is particularly common among adult black Americans—fewer than half of black women aged 30 to 54 years were married and living with their husbands in 1982.

Both young people and their parents are growing more tolerant of remaining single. A survey in 1976 found that only a third of all Americans would disapprove of a decision by someone to remain single—a dramatic change since 1957, when 50 percent said they would disapprove.

More unmarried adults are also living together. From 500,000 persons cohabiting in 1970, the number climbed to close to 2,000,000 in just over a decade, according to demographic experts. Researchers are not certain whether the increase is due to the general postponement of marriage or whether cohabitation is simply becoming a more acceptable lifestyle.

"Changing social values will alter the way we look at our work and the organizations that employ us."

These social changes are important to the study of the business organization because they affect the external environment in which it operates and the needs and values of its members.

Values Will Be Different

Changes in social values often accompany changes in population patterns, life-style, and technology. Which comes first—the changes in the environment or the changes in values—is a question best left to philosophers. In this section, we will examine how changes in American society and advances in technology accompany changing values in regard to work and organizations.

Researchers surveying the American public have identified several new directions in value orientation.[2]

From work to leisure.   America developed its farms, its factories, and its technology through a belief in the value of hard work—a value that has been declining in importance for several decades. Perhaps the growing affluence of society has diminished the drive to work hard. For whatever reason, the work week has been growing shorter, sabbaticals have become more common, and part-time jobs are growing in popularity. Yet the puritan work ethic remains a strong ground swell in America. A recent study of leisure time shows that six out of ten Americans say that leisure time is best spent on "constructive" activities, that people have a responsibility to help others, and that work should have a higher priority in a person's life than leisure.[3]

In certain segments of our economy, particularly high-technology industries in California, Arizona, Texas, Massachusetts, and Florida, the sixteen-hour working day is alive and well. When employees have an active stake in a company—perhaps a share of ownership or profits—and they see that their hard work can directly increase their economic well-being, they are willing to forgo some leisure time. This is particularly true when the work they are doing is absorbing in its own right.

One change in the puritan work ethic is that Americans are no longer willing to delay their gratification; they are eager for pleasure for its own sake. This has spurred industries ranging from consumer credit ("Buy now, pay later") to gourmet foods and the home improvement industry.

From conformity to individualism.   Americans have always valued individuality, and perhaps never more than at the present time. In the 1950s, the baby boom generation, reared in the shadow of the atom bomb, demanded security and social conformity. The generation that came of age in the 1960s reacted against the suburban stereotype and spawned political radicals and hippies. Since the 1970s, extremists on both sides of many social questions have learned to live with each other. This has resulted in a growing acceptance of personal choice in clothing, life-styles, and careers. The move toward personal choice also embraces the idea that an individual can be creative on or off the job.

From independence to interdependence.   Coupled with the support of individual values comes a realization that everyone in modern society depends on others. Sales managers are intensely aware that they depend on the production line to make the widgets they sell. A beautician may depend on clients' word-of-mouth to promote business. The challenge of foreign competition—particularly Japan—may have contributed to the awareness of interdependence. Other social movements, such as the anti–drunk driving campaign of the mid-1980s and the moves of many states to raise the drinking age, suggest that we are more aware of the impact one person can have on an interdependent society.

These three trends in values, which emerged in the 1960s and 1970s, remain strong in our society. Other commentators have noticed new trends of the 1980s that help to change the landscape of American values, one of which is *voluntary simplicity.* No longer is increased consumption considered a good in itself. Instead, there is a "back to basics" move reflected in the rise in generic foods and drugs and inexpensive commuter automobiles and the failure of some luxury products (e.g., quadrophonic stereos, home computers) to reach a mass market. Voluntary simplicity has its roots in the ecological movements of the 1970s, when more people became aware that natural resources are limited. The two gasoline crises of the 1970s fueled the drive toward voluntary simplicity, as did the recession of the early 1980s. Handmade items, finds from garage sales, and a subscription to *Workbench* in some circles have become better gifts for friends than the latest trinket from Bloomingdales.

Another new value is *self-fulfillment.* The goods and services people now purchase are meaningful in themselves, rather than just symbols of conspicuous consumption. Diet and health programs, exercise equipment, perfumes, and massages are typical of the self-fulfilling purchases Americans are now making.

The area of values and life-styles (VALS) is currently the focus of much research. The most widely used VALS typology identifies nine different groups, based on attitudes, activities, needs, and hopes, that can provide "value futures" for social planners who need to predict changing values in the population at large. The key applications of VALS in the area of human resources are:

1. Developing recruitment strategies, matching individuals to jobs.
2. Designing benefits attractive to employees with different life-styles.
3. Career planning.
4. Selecting leaders able to build teams from diverse personnel.
5. Sales training to identify life-style types and hence improve sales productivity.[4]

Table 1.2 summarizes the VALs types.

TABLE 1.2   Values and Life-Styles Types

Percentage of Population	Personality Type	Values and Life-Styles	Demographics	Buying Patterns	Discretionary Income (000)
	Need-driven				
4	*Survivors*	Struggle for survival Distrustful Socially misfitted Ruled by appetites	Poverty-level income Little education Many minority members Live in city slums	Price dominant Focused on basics Buy for immediate needs	$ 459,703
7	*Sustainers*	Concern with safety, security Insecure, compulsive Dependent, following Want law and order	Low income Low education Much unemployment Live in country as well as cities	Price important Want warranty Cautious buyers	2,199,413
	Outer-directed				
38	*Belongers*	Conforming, conventional Unexperimental Traditional, formal Nostalgic	Low to middle income Low to average education Blue-collar jobs Tend toward noncity living	Family Home Fads Middle and lower mass markets	43,902,318
10	*Emulators*	Ambitious, show-off Status conscious Upwardly mobile Macho, competitive	Good to excellent income Youngish Highly urban Traditionally male but changing	Conspicuous consumption "In" items Imitative Popular fashion	12,278,533
20	*Achievers*	Achievement, success, fame Materialism Leadership, efficiency Comfort	Excellent incomes Leaders in business, politics, etc. Good education Suburban and city living	Give evidence of success Top of the line Luxury and gift markets "New and improved" products	159,836,799

TABLE 1.2 *(continued)*

Percentage of Population	Personality Type	Values and Life-Styles	Demographics	Buying Patterns	Discretionary Income (000)
	Inner-directed				
3	*I-am-me*	Fiercely individualistic Dramatic, impulsive Experimental Volatile	Young Many single Student or starting job Affluent backgrounds	Display one's taste Experimental fads Source of far-out fads Clique buying	12,300,781
5	*Experiential*	Drive to direct experience Active, participative Person-centered Artistic	Bimodal incomes Mostly under 40 Many young families Good education	Process over product Vigorous, outdoor sports "Making" home pursuits Crafts and introspection	17,348,446
11	*Societally conscious*	Societal responsibility Simple living Smallness of scale Inner growth	Bimodal low and high incomes Excellent education Diverse ages and places of residence Largely white	Conservation emphasis Simplicity Frugality Environmental concerns	50,497,709
2	*Integrated*	Psychological maturity Sense of fittingness Tolerant, self-actualizing World perspective	Good to excellent incomes Bimodal in age Excellent education Diverse jobs and residential patterns	Varied self-expression Aesthetically oriented Ecologically aware One-of-a-kind items	8,000,000

Source: Arnold Mitchell, *Consumer Values: A Typology.* Menlo Park, CA: SRI, 1978. Updated to 1983, SMRB/VALS, the Conference Board. By permission of the Values and Lifestyles (VALS)™ Program, SRI International, Menlo Park, CA.

Lower expectations mean that Americans are no longer convinced that their standard of living will be higher than that of their parents. The uncertainty of the economic world of the 1980s—with dramatic boom and bust industries, high interest rates, and worldwide trade competition—appears to have shaken traditional American confidence in the future. Difficulties in obtaining promotions, in purchasing a single-family home, in getting a fulfilling job all appear to have reduced expectations.

The increase of women in the work force has left many men and women with less free time. Both husband and wife find their weekends are spent buying groceries, repairing the car, or running errands—chores that once might have been performed by the nonworking wife. The time squeeze is reflected in the rise of convenience foods, convenience stores, and shopping centers.

"Expect the worker of the future to be more mature."

As the American population grows older, tastes will also mature. Demand for t-shirts and bikinis may be expected to drop. Golf may enjoy a resurgence, while tennis declines. Along with a difference in consumption patterns, an older population is likely to hold more conservative political and social values. (See Table 1.3 for a recent profile of U.S. moral values.) This may affect our political organizations as well as the ways our organizations conduct business. Older Americans are more concerned with risk than are youth, since they generally have more to

TABLE 1.3   Profile of Moral Values

Traditional Norms	
Statement	Percentage in agreement
1. Would still have children if they "had it to do over again"	90
2. Feel use of hard drugs is "morally wrong"	87
3. Feel it's up to parents to educate teenagers about birth control	84
4. Feel "mate swapping" is "morally wrong"	81
5. Disapprove of married women having affairs	79
6. Disapprove of married men having affairs	76
7. Agree that a woman should put her husband and children ahead of her career	77
8. Want their children to be better off and more successful than parents are	74
9. Agree that it's best to "demand a lot" from children; they have to "do their best to get ahead"	57
10. Feel "it's more important for a wife to help her husband's career than to have one herself"	55
11. Believe that "strict, old-fashioned upbringing and discipline" are still the best ways to raise children	51

TABLE 1.3 *(continued)*

Changes in Social Norms

Statement	Year		Percentage in agreement
1. Disapprove of a married woman earning money if she has a husband capable of supporting her	1938		75
	1978		26
2. Four or more children is the ideal number for a family to have	1945		49
	1980		16
Two children is the ideal	1936		29
	1980		51
3. For a woman to remain unmarried she must be "sick," "neurotic" or "immoral"	1957		80
	1978		25
4. Would vote for a qualified woman nominee for president	1937		31
	1980		77
5. Condemn premarital sex as morally wrong	1967		85
	1979		37
6. Favor decision making abortion up to three months of pregnancy legal	1973		52
	1980		60
7. Agree that both sexes have the responsibility to care for small children	1970		33
	1980		56
8. Approve of husband and wife taking separate vacations	1971		34
	1980		51
9. Agree that "hard work always pays off"	1969		58
	1976		43
10. Agree that "work is at the center of my life"	1970		34
	1978		13
11. Would go on working for pay even if they didn't have to	1957	(Men)	85
	1976	(Men)	84
	1957	(Women)	58
	1976	(Women)	77
12. Increase in level of anxiety and worry among young Americans 21–39 years of age	1957		30
	1976		49
13. Agree that "the people running the country don't care what happens to people like me"	1966		26
	1977		60
14. Agree that they "can trust the government in Washington to do what's right"	1958		56
	1978		29
15. Experience a "hungering for community"	1973		32
	1980		47

TABLE 1.3 (continued)

Traditional Norms		
Statement		Percentage in agreement
16. Americans with a "sour grapes" outlook on life	1970 1980	38 19
17. Agree that it is morally acceptable to be single and have children	1979	75
18. Agree that interracial marriages are not morally wrong	1977	62
19. Agree that it is not morally wrong for couples to live together even if they are not married	1978	52
20. Agree that they would like to return to standards of the past relating to: —sexual mores —"spic and span" housekeeping —women staying home and only men working outside the home	1979	21

Source: Daniel Yankelovich, *New Rules: Searching for Self-Fulfillment in a World Turned Upside Down*. A Bantam Book, published by arrangement with Random House, Inc., © May 1981, p. 87. Reprinted by permission.

lose. Managing personal risk may be a far-reaching concern of the future.

Trends in Organizations

These broad changes in society's values are reflected in the values of the work force and the organization. Two positive trends are associated with our new working environment:[5]

1. There will be a dramatic growth in the amount of discretion or control that people have in their jobs. Fewer people will have narrowly focused jobs, such as the traditional assembly line worker, and more people will have jobs that force them to think and make decisions.

2. There will also be a growth in the inner-directed value of expressivism, a desire to live in closer harmony with nature and with other people. Rather than working for survival or to accumulate material goods, more people will be working for reasons of personal growth and self-development.

During the 1970s, the catchword used to describe the psyche of the worker who was perceived as being dominated by powerful computers was *dehumanized.* Popular authors like Charles Reich and Theodore Roszak found hope for the good life only outside the technological system and viewed current business organization with despair over the dehumanization wrought by technocracy, agent of the corporate state. Reich stated it strongly:

> *Technology and production . . . pulverize everything in their path—the landscape, the natural environment, history and tradition, the amenities and civilities, the privacy and spaciousness of life, much beauty, and the fragile slow-growing social structure that binds us together. Organization and bureaucracy, which are an application of technology to social institutions, increasingly dictate how we shall live our lives, with the logic of organization taking precedence over any other values. . . . The essence of the corporate state is that it is relentlessly single-minded, it has just one value, the value of technology as represented by organization, efficiency, growth, progress.*[6]

In the 1980s, the mood among writers on the subject of technology is more optimistic. No longer are computers the soulless, giant creations of a machinelike corporate data processing environment. Instead, they are user friendly, ready to perform a secretary's most boring chores, a salesperson's routine calculation, or a middle manager's monthly budget without a groan. Americans are finding that computers can provide more interesting, less routine work. Once a secretary had to spend hours retyping a letter to correct one mistake; now it may take only a few moments on the word processor. Once sending a letter to a branch office on the West Coast took three days; now it may take three minutes using telecommunications equipment.

The accelerating growth in technology has touched nearly half of all Americans, and contrary to once-popular notions, many of the changes have been favorable. In a recent study, about 44 percent of the American work force said they have already experienced significant technological change on the job. About three-fourths of those said the changes made their work more interesting, and more than half said the changes had given them more independence.[7]

It is fortunate that the new technology—from automatic teller machines to dedicated word processors—is making jobs more interesting, because Americans are becoming more demanding of their jobs. For instance, families traditionally have adapted their schedules to the needs of the work place, but a recent study shows such an acceptance of night-shift work, weekend work, and split days off is on the decline. Concerns about family needs, particularly child-care arrangements, are becoming paramount:

> *Although American family members favor virtually any form of help for working parents, they are most enthusiastic about flexibility in the schedules of working parents. According to the report, 85 percent of the family members surveyed feel it would be a good thing for families if "employers made it easier for working parents to arrange their jobs around their children." Among those respondents identified as human resource executives and union leaders, majorities of 86 and 87 percent, respectively, agreed. Those identified as family traditionalists agreed by a margin of 75 percent, and 94 percent of the feminists wanted to see an increase in flexible, family-oriented scheduling.* [8]

"Technology has the potential to make jobs more interesting and workers more involved in what they are doing."

No longer is a steady income enough to ensure the worker's dedication and involvement. Now the "expressivist" worker demands that the job satisfy needs of belonging to a team and working for personal growth. Given the proper situation—a group of computer specialists charged with creating a new machine—the dedication of these expressivist workers is overwhelming. Given the wrong situation—an old-fashioned office clerical pool—the dedication is nonexistent.

Creating that dedication and desire to work hard will be the challenge of the manager of the twenty-first century. With all the distractions and leisure time options available to workers, it may be tougher than ever. Yet, this task fundamentally will be no different than it was thousands of years ago. (See the box on pages 20–21 that describes a GM automobile plant of the future.)

THE REVOLUTION IN TECHNOLOGY

Technology, in the broadest sense, is the human creation of physical systems that create work. Some definitions of technology emphasize its effect on the attempt to control nature and the environment; other definitions focus on technology as the processes by which things are done or made by humans. Some interesting views on one subject of technology

THE SATURN PLANT: THE WORK PLACE OF THE FUTURE?

"GM is mapping out in an experimental way a whole range of new initiatives they'd like to see implemented elsewhere. . . . If the production techniques are successful, within five to 10 years you are looking at a smaller industry as they diffuse through other auto companies."

Because union influence traditionally has been measured by union muscle—the size of membership and ability to shut down production during a strike—it seems clear that Saturn will be as profound a catalyst for union change as it is for management.

In fact, it may be difficult to tell the Saturn autoworkers from the managers under the new UAW-Saturn contract.

Workers and managers alike will peer into computer screens for sensitive financial data. Autoworkers will be responsible for meeting production and quality schedules and performing on budget, tasks accorded only to managers now. Saturn workers will hold their own meetings, if they want, keep their own records and help select fellow workers. Everyone at Saturn will eat in the same cafeteria, park in the same lot, use the same entrances. No one will punch a time clock.

It will be a system "that doesn't exist anywhere in the world, not even in Japan," said Joseph Malotke, UAW staff member and liaison between the union and GM on the Saturn project. "We wanted to get rid of the differences between people, the different ways they're treated now."

How fast the work-together attitude has grown in both union and management circles surprises even retired UAW President Douglas Fraser.

"If anybody had told me . . . that these things would occur, 10 years ago, I'd have said they were crazy," he said. "When you look where we have come from when individual workers had no dignity, when we couldn't challenge a decision. Here we are helping make the decisions. It's a dramatic change.

"It seems [management] has at long last realized what I knew 30 years ago. Men and women in factories are intelligent and they can make a contribution if you let them."

Alfred Warren Jr., GM vice president of industrial relations, said: "We have been accused many, many times in the past of paying the highest wages in the country and getting the least for it. We paid for hands and feet, as one union leader put it, and we simply seemed to ignore that there was anything above the neck. We're trying to change that."

Besides the novel treatment of Saturn workers in day-to-day operations, the contract breaks new ground in work practices, pay, job security, disciplinary procedures, hiring and training.

Saturn workers will be part of work units of six to 15 people. Each unit will have a member serving as the union representative, but that person also will be a working participant in the unit. The system eliminates the union shop committee in traditional plants where committee members, paid by the company, work full time on union matters.

One Saturn worker will represent the union on a committee that will oversee the day-to-day operation of the plant. A top UAW official also will have a seat on another committee that will determine long-term strategy.

There will be no rules specifying work practices, unlike at traditional plants. Work unit members will determine job assignments among them selves, rather than having management tell them what to do. Consensus decision-making will be stressed.

Members of the work units will monitor health and safety issues, do housekeeping in their work areas, maintain and repair equipment. All of that is unheard of in conventional plants.

Saturn's job classifications will be cut from the traditional 100 or more to one for unskilled workers and three to five for skilled employees.

All workers will be salaried, with the hourly pay rate figured as an annual salary in an effort to eliminate a distinction that exists now between white- and blue-collar employees. Saturn auto-workers will receive overtime pay, however, like workers in traditional plants.

Saturn workers will receive additional cost-of-living adjustments, performance and atten-dance bonuses and profit sharing, which could

boost their earnings above those at conventional plants. Saturn workers could receive less than their counterparts at other plants if perfor-mance, quality and profits are below expectations.

Most Saturn workers will receive blanket job security, a policy that states: "Saturn will not lay off Saturn members except in situations arising from unforeseen or catastrophic events or severe economic conditions." The UAW, through its seat on the Saturn strategic advisory committee, will have a say in whether conditions are dire enough to warrant the layoffs.

Workers may get a chance to establish flexi-ble work hours and to rotate between morning and afternoon shifts. A medical clinic is planned on the site.

Source: Extracted from Knight-Ridder News Service, *Miami Herald* (July 28, 1985), p. F-2.

and the organization of the future are expressed by Admiral Inman in the Managerial Dialogue on pages 22–23.

Thousands of years ago, the chief technological skill humans needed was wielding an animal bone to kill prey more efficiently. With the advent of civilization came an era when reading and writing skills were essential. The Industrial Revolution ushered in another age—that of production machinery. People who understood, designed, and repaired machines prospered with the times. The Industrial Revolution also brought about the modern assembly line, which rewarded workers who were obedient and able to dull their senses to survive the mono-tony.

Now we are in the midst of another great technological revolution—the age of information. Computers coupled with new communication techniques are reshaping our working world once again. Workers who understand information as a product, who can process the words or numbers needed by modern business managers, will flourish in this new environment. As in other technological ages, there will be casualties, and one of the aims of this chapter is to ensure that you will not be among them.

Managerial Dialogue

"Workers of the future will be hired for their output and brains."

Admiral B. R. Inman, USN (retired), president and chief executive officer of Microelectronics and Computer Technology Corporation

MCC is a joint research venture formed by several U.S. corporations in the computer and micro-electronics industry.

Will robots run our nation's factories in another decade? Will our white-collar offices filled with managers, salespersons, and secretaries disappear? What types of new jobs will be created by onrushing technology?

Admiral B. R. Inman spends much of his time wrestling with questions like these. As president of Microelectronics and Computer Technology Corporation (MCC), Inman directs the Austin, Texas, firm's attempts to size up the future. "Workers of the future will be hired for their output and their brains, not to put in office hours," Inman says. Much of the new technology—computers and telecommunications devices particularly—are strong decentralizing forces, allowing more and more workers to do their jobs away from the traditional office. For instance, according to Inman, the research department of the Federal Reserve Bank in Atlanta has an automated data base stored in a mainframe computer. Workers in that department can tap information from their work stations (called *desks* just a decade ago). They can also reach that data base through their personal computers at home, from the lightweight portables they carry when they travel, or from the transportable computers they can check out from the office.

What such a computer-intensive organization gains is more productivity. On the other hand, it's hard to escape from a 24-hour-a-day job. According to Inman, the decentralizing trend of the new technology is counterbalanced by the social life of the office. "The human animal likes to interact with other people. With the new technology, how do you not lose the personal contact in the process?"

The spread of computers is giving new shape to many offices. In many businesses, the "open architecture" of clustered working areas separated by partitions allows groups of employees to use their new electronic tools more effectively.

"Within the office itself, we're going to see more buildings designed to assist the flow of information," Inman asserts. That information flow from office to office will be enhanced by electronic mail and message capability. Rather than playing "telephone tag," two people who want to talk to each other can leave messages at convenient times. "And you will have a choice of when you want to commit a message to paper."

For companies spread across several time zones—or for salespeople constantly on the road—electronic mail and teleconferences (a meeting of people in different locations) offer better use of time. No need to spend thousands of dollars and lose several days to fly a dozen key executives from New York to Los Angeles for a quarterly meeting, when a satellite-assisted teleconference might cost $200 and take two hours. The new technology will make more demands on workers in the organizations of the future, Inman believes. There will be a need for employees who are both more highly educated and more self-reliant. Working at home, for instance, requires "enhanced degrees of personal responsibility." Adds Inman, "We will need a work force that has a broader education. Not computer nerds, but people who can deal with automated factories and offices." While some writers speculate that such trends could create sharper divisions in American society, Inman feels that "it clearly has the potential of doing the exact opposite—if we carry through national commitment to bring the blue-collar work force up." Computers are not complex machines anymore, and each year they become friendlier to employees.

Inman sees an increase in service industries and a rise in white-collar employment over the next decade. Among the growth industries will be telecommunications, microelectronics, aerospace, energy, materials processing, and biotechnology. "Even agriculture and energy will increasingly be high-tech industries," he states.

Inman believes that young people are entering the work force at the right time. The next ten to fifteen years will be strong ones for the U.S. economy. "If we devise policies to modernize our older industries, there will be a broad growth in our economy," says Inman, "If not, there will still be economic growth, but at a slower rate."

Technology Is As Old As Humankind

Homo sapiens, at whatever point one sets the origin of the species, also has distinctively been *Homo faber,* or man the maker. Anthropologist L. S. Leakey dug up a number of stone tools made by prehistoric toolmakers and demonstrated their efficiency. They still served quite adequately to kill animals and dress their skins for wearing. The first technological revolution, however, occurred with the establishment of the irrigation civilizations in Mesopotamia, Egypt and the Indus Valley, and finally, in China about 7,000 years ago. This agricultural technology gradually yielded a regular production of surplus food that brought about not only organized trade with money, credit, law, merchants, and transport, but also the standing army. These innovations naturally led to the separation of people into social classes: the producers or farmers, the traders, the protectors or military, and to keep order, the governing body, a class with a corner on knowledge and, for several centuries, on religion as well. While this reorganization of human groups from tribes into city-states did enhance the concept of the individual, the existence of Egypt's great pyramids, constructed by hundreds of thousands of slaves, reminds us of the mixed nature of technology's blessings.

The groundwork for the next technological revolution, the age of machines, was laid in the Middle Ages. Although gunpowder and printing certainly rank foremost among the systems humans devised to work for them, the technology of exploration that took Europeans to the New World also contributed largely to the development and establishment of modern economic, political, social, and industrial organizations.

America was not only a source of abundant raw materials, it was also a wide-open market. Each new colony rendered the new European nation-states more powerful. Such strong governments could then apply pressures (taxes, jails) that would keep laborers at work when and where the governments deemed their national interest most affected. The decline of the feudal system shoved many people into the cities, increasing the trend toward urbanization. Iron and steel production also increased as a result of more efficient technologies of manufacture. Both guns and plows exerted their respective forces on human life. In the history of technology, the sixteenth, seventeenth, and early eighteenth centuries were a time of setting up the scenery and trotting out the opening acts.

The Industrial Revolution

The main act, accompanied by the steam engine, the railroad, and later, the gasoline internal combustion engine and electricity, began its long run in the 1750s, primarily in Great Britain. Central to the drama at that time was the idea that humans and nature contend, that to go forward humans must conquer and rule natural forces and must bend nature's energies to their will. Clearly, such a notion provoked dispute, and by the mid–nineteenth century, many voices decried the quality of life produced by the technology of machine labor. The philosopher Rousseau yearned for man's return to nature. The fear of the dehumanizing and alienating consequences of technology so loudly voiced in the 1960s and 1970s is by no means new.

The question of why the Industrial Revolution came about when and where it did can be left to historians. The dramatic changes in the relationship of humans to machinery, however, do show how technology shapes a society. James Watt and his steam engine cannot be considered the cause of the sweat shop and child labor, but the application of new power sources to production did stimulate a burst of consequences— social, economic, and political.

When the United States underwent its great commercial and industrial expansion about a century ago, a number of factors came together. New agricultural equipment dramatically increased farm productivity.

"The Industrial Revolution made work more efficient . . . and workers more alienated from their tasks."

An expansive banking system created liquid assets, the capital necessary to pay for the new industrial machinery. Lack of enough native-born labor spawned the great immigration of the late 1800s, as millions of Europeans arrived on our shores. New transportation networks, primarily railroads, rivers, and roads, led to the development of markets for mass-produced goods. Raw materials were plentiful. Inventive force and entrepreneurial force came together simultaneously.

Americans felt a strong desire for material betterment, acclaimed social mobility, and willingly embraced new techniques to advance material betterment, all of which helped create a new organization: the factory. The keynote of the factory system, as of all technology, is efficiency. For the sake of efficiency, humans had to behave as if they were interchangeable parts of the machines with which they worked. Mass production demanded an assembly line technique.

Some socioeconomic consequences of the factory system belied its benefit. The idea of free competition enabled factory managers and owners to hire laborers at the lowest wages, and many workers merely traded rural starvation for dreary urban subsistence. Poet William Blake saw factories as "dark Satanic mills," and novelist Charles Dickens dwelt at length on the violations of human dignity he saw in most working persons' lives. It seemed to Karl Marx and Friedrich Engels that only the factory owners benefited from the differentiation and specialization of tasks and the enslavement to cash incomes that the factory system imposed on workers. No longer producing for themselves such necessities as food, clothing, and shelter, families were forced to purchase these items from outside sources.

Increases in production built up the wealth and power of the nation as a whole, while a working class made ends meet in squalor or landed in debtor's prisons and poorhouses. Critics believed that economic growth, a goal based on developing in the population a style of behavior that would enhance production capacity, had unwarranted ascendance over the goal of human welfare.

Politically, the factory system provided a rationale for absolute government: the most efficient government is that which governs most. The Communist Manifesto sets forth the bitterest depiction of industrialization:

Owing to the extensive use of machinery and to division of labor, the work of the proletarians has lost all individual character, and, consequently, all charm for the workman. He becomes an appendage of the machine, and it is only the most simple, most monotonous, and most easily acquired knack that is required of him.

Modern industry has converted the little workshop of the patriarchal master into the great factory of the industrial capitalist. Masses of laborers, crowded into the factory, are organized like soldiers. As privates of the industrial army they are placed under command of a perfect hierarchy of officers and sergeants. The more openly this despotism proclaims gain to be its end and aim, the more petty, the more hateful, and the more embittering it is.[9]

The pessimism of that view of technology was strongly countered by Adam Smith, advocate of free enterprise. He believed that in a capitalistic economy, an "invisible hand" is continually working for the good of the public.[10] That is, for a business to remain competitive, it must produce goods and services that satisfy society's needs. Further, a competitive organization must deal fairly with the public to remain in business. Competition for labor means that companies will treat their employees fairly.

On the sunny side of the factory system and profit motive stood Robert Owen's mill community, New Lanark, in Scotland. His great contribution to innovation in the economic sphere was the idea that labor need not be exploited to produce profit. In fact, he made a goodly sum from his textile mills. Sad to say, he went on to wilder schemes like New Harmony, Indiana, and the Grand National, England's first nationwide trade union, both of which were unqualified failures. "Man," said Owen, "is the creature of circumstance." He proved that man could shape circumstances, however, for the good of workers.

Another optimist in the dawn of the industrial age was Count Claude Henri de Saint-Simon, who envisioned that government should be economic rather than political and, in particular, should reward the members of a society according to their productive contribution. He felt that such a plan would redistribute wealth and put it into the hands of the active toilers rather than into the pockets of idle investors.

By the end of the nineteenth century, the machine had become the dominant image of the day. The American Henry Adams became the dynamic symbol of a frighteningly incomprehensible and accelerating force. England's Prince Albert, on the other hand, opened the great international exhibition of 1851 with the prediction that technology would "tend rapidly to accomplish that great end to which all history points—the realization of the unity of mankind."

Technological Innovation

America has a long history of technological innovation. From Samuel Morse's telegraph in 1844 to Alexander Graham Bell's telephone in 1876,

Americans have led the way toward better communications. Henry Ford's assembly line in Dearborn, Michigan, has been well chronicled as the symbol of the modern industrial age.

Less well known is another significant American contribution to early twentieth century technology: the research laboratory. It features the union of science and technology in a new kind of institution, one in which large numbers of scientists and mathematicians cooperate and work side by side with engineers and technicians to provide an industry with useful knowledge ranging from basic research into the laws of nature to simple quality controls for current products. Thomas Edison's laboratory at Menlo Park, New Jersey, and C. P. Steinmetz's General Electric laboratory in Schenectady, New York, set a pattern followed by most major governmental and industrial research centers today. Rising from this new type of work—research and development—came innovation.

"American workers have always been quick to embrace technological innovations."

Innovation stands apart from invention primarily in method. Systematic research supplants the "flash of genius," and a new product or process is derived from the patient trial-and-error working out of solutions to specified problems. An excellent example is Edison's failure to turn out a workable electric light by the method so often depicted in the form of a suddenly glowing light bulb over someone's head. He found himself forced to define the qualities needed in a filament and then to test systematically some 1,600 different materials. That and other problems compelled Edison to use a large number of highly trained assistants, that is, a research team. Although they are highly skilled and trained, workers engaged in testing in a research laboratory still bear some resemblance to people working on an assembly line.

The Rise of Computers

The latest technological revolution got underway in the mid-1940s with the first modern computers. Big, expensive, clumsy devices by today's standards, ENIAC, UNIVAC, and IMB's Mark I were pace-setting machines. The development of complex switching and storage devices that used the speed of electricity to solve mathematical problems signaled the age of cybernation. Inventors soon were able to write more complex programs to tell computers how to solve more difficult problems. Subsequent inventions, such as the transistor, integrated circuits, and microchips, multiplied the abilities of these primitive computing machines.

The nature and organization of work have changed forever since the IBM-built Harvard Mark I began clicking away in August 1944. The classic assembly line began heading for the museum, where it will one day reside alongside the cotton gin and the steam engine.

Nowadays, in a Bendix Corporation plant, which turns out disk brake parts, twenty-five different machining operations are performed along 230 feet of line without human intervention. A single person at a console monitors the scene. One worker visits the room evey half hour where rolls of rubber are vulcanized and turned into belts for Goodyear. Five hundred people in 100,000 windowless square feet watch for the quality of the dyes at a plant, where thousands upon thousands of dozens of Hanes pantyhose are produced each year.

The name for the marriage of computers and automation is *cybernation* (from the Greek word for *steerman*). Norbert Weiner derived this term for the study of the processes of intercommunication between persons and machines. A cybernetic goal-oriented activity is determined by the system's ability to adjust its behavior to correct for any discrepancy between "where it is" and "where it wants to go." Note that the human element is now simply a portion of the entire system.

For the human element, the rise of computers is as likely to mean freedom from routine chores as it is to mean a ticket to the unemployment line (for further details, see the box on page 29). Computers have opened the door to many to work at home or to start a new business outside the corporate world.

Managing Technological Change

Because the organization of the future will have to contend with the broad demographic changes in society, the changes in social values, and the rise of computer-based technology, it is likely that the responsibilities, duties, and schedules of its workers will be revised. Consider these examples:

A company scheduling workers into a four-day, forty-hour week can employ more people and put them in more productive shift patterns. The workers then gain a long weekend or its three-day equivalent for leisure and pleasure. A Volkswagen agency near Boston is using such a system in its service department, which stays open from 7:00 A.M. to 10:00 P.M., six days a week.

A number of hospitals in southern Florida, unable to recruit enough nurses for weekend shifts, revised working schedules so that a nurse who worked twenty-four hours on a weekend (two 12-hour shifts) would be paid for a full thirty-six-hour week and get five days off in return.

Supermarket chains based in Ohio, New Jersey, and California now stay open all the time—twenty-four hours a day. The cost of remain-

DOES TECHNOLOGY REALLY CREATE JOBS?

David Birch, the Massachusetts Institute of Technology researcher who first measured the role of small companies in creating jobs, recently turned his computer's attention to the role of high technology in job creation. Does high tech create jobs or doesn't it, Birch asked the machine, and if it does create jobs, how does the process work?

His conclusion, in general, is that technology itself creates relatively few jobs. It is the intelligent use of technology—which he lumps under the "innovation" rubric—that generates employment.

High technology, you might say, is a lot like potatoes. Potato farming employs a few people in a few places, and relatively few new jobs are going to open up in potato farming in the next decade or so. On the other hand, while potato farming is not a large industry in Manhattan these days, there is a bar in the SoHo area that serves the best hot, homemade potato chips you have ever washed down with a beer. In fact, innovative entrepreneurs from Key West, Fla., to Seattle employ hundreds of thousands of people to make and sell French-fried and baked potatoes, and some really creative genius not long ago launched a whole new restaurant concept based on doing things with potato skins.

In other words, potato farming by itself will never amount to much more as an industry; it is what creative people do with the potato that makes it important. And that, Birch found, is the way it is with technology, too.

High tech accounts for only 2.8% of the jobs in the United States and, Birch projects, high tech per se will contribute only 5% of the net new jobs created in the United States during this decade. However, innovation—the use of technology to create either new or replacement goods or processes—can drive the U.S. economy forward and keep it competitive in world markets.

From the numbers his computer generated, Birch, director of MIT's Program on Neighborhood and Regional Change, draws several general conclusions.

- Cities and states should stop chasing high-tech businesses and concentrate instead on creating the kind of environment that fosters creative thinking in all kinds of industries. "There is no need" Birch says, "to produce technology to reap its benefits." You can buy it, like New Yorkers buy potatoes.

- Most innovation does not create new products; rather, it involves finding a better and, often, more efficient way of doing something—making steel, for example. While innovation is absolutely essential to keep American steel companies in business, it is just as essential to find something else for laid-off steel workers to do. If we don't, organized steel workers facing unemployment won't allow innovation to go forward, and eventually the United States will be out of the steel business altogether.

- In addition to products and processes, innovation involves the replacement of old corporations with new ones. One-third of the companies on the *Fortune* 500 in 1970, Birch notes, were not on the list in 1981. This is not an argument against relying on big business, says Birch. Rather, as "we attempt to make it easier for our larger companies to compete in world markets, we must simultaneously create a very fertile soil in which to grow their replacements."

ing open the extra hours is marginal, and customers can enjoy the added convenience.

The assembly line jobs of the future may very well be performed by robots, freeing human operators to perform more complex activities. Hitachi, for example, advertises that its robots can quickly switch from welding to machine repair or to materials handling jobs.

If a current shift in values makes money an insufficient cause for working, what other rewards are taking its place? A number of U.S. companies are experimenting with status and self-esteem as rewards. Managers are beginning to open new lines of communication with their subordinates and to assign them more responsibility. A shape cutter at Donnelly Mirrors of Holland, Michigan, one of the companies that has gone furthest in this direction, stated: "We work as teams, decide our own goals—we're really involved in making the decisions. If everyone doesn't work, we can't make it, so we have a meeting and talk it over." A wax assembler at Precision Castparts Corporation of Portland, Oregon, adds, "You don't have anyone hovering over you. We can make decisions. Now there's more responsibility on the individual."[11]

In addition to improving communication and assigning more responsibility to employees, some corporations are combatting the stifling effects of dead-end jobs by opening the way to job shifts and advances within the organization. Openings anywhere in the firm are advertised first to other employees. At Polaroid, for example, a job opening at one level may result in at least three moves within the company before a newcomer is brought in further down the ladder.

Such a policy creates more chances for experienced production workers to move upward to supervisory positions. Texas Instruments sends out a monthly "want ad" newspaper listing new job openings at all of its plants. Such companies as First National City Bank, General Mills, and Equitable Life Insurance have set up training centers for lower-level white-collar employees to enable employees who wish to move up to get the necessary training and education. One of the largest programs is that of First National City Bank, with more than 6000 persons each year taking courses at a center staffed by sixty-five instructors and $800,000 of teaching equipment.

"The future will bring new work schedules, new responsibilities, and new opportunities for self-expression and fulfillment."

JOBS OF THE FUTURE

The butcher, the baker, and the candlestick maker will still have a spot in the organization of the future, as so will the gene splicer, the hologram designer, and the C-code compiler. But major companies, and perhaps even entire industries that have provided employment to millions, will decline, and new ones will spring up to take their place. Consider these news items:

> A high-tech answering machine known as *voice mail* is expected to emerge as a $1 billion per year market by the end of the decade and cut down on the amount of time a typical office worker spends on the telephone (from Reuters News Service, October 10, 1984).

> A couple of Ivy League professors have developed a computer program that resembles an ordinary video game. The difference is that it also helps companies save money by making their truck deliveries more efficient (from *The Wall Street Journal,* October 19, 1984).

> General Motors is experimenting with bacteria that eat paint solvents at its Corvette assembly plant in Bowling Green, Kentucky. The bacteria feed on spray paint solvents that otherwise would pollute the air or water (from *The Wall Street Journal,* October 26, 1984).

> Two University of Miami industrial engineers are attempting to give robots the senses of touch and sight, making them smarter and more useful in the marketplace (from a university news release, November 13, 1984).

When you try to imagine the typical American worker of the twenty-first century, what image comes to mind? Back in the mid-1800s, your great-great-grandparents probably pictured the typical American worker as a proud farmer standing alongside his wife in the great wheat fields of the Midwest. If you asked your parents, they probably would tell you about the assembly line worker standing in one of Henry Ford's auto plants near Detroit or the secretary who took dictation, wrote letters, and filed sales reports all day for her boss. Nowadays, the typical American worker probably has a college degree and is working in the information business. Once the province of librarians, authors, and researchers, the information business has mushroomed to include economists, demographers, computer repairmen, and telephone switchboard operators.

The rise of computers is perhaps the most significant trend as we look at jobs of the future. From microcomputers to minicomputers to mainframes, computers and computer-driven technology have advanced mightily in the 1980s. Design firms are using computer-assisted design and manufacturing techniques to draw architectural plans for businesses, houses, and assembly lines. News reporters write their stories on video display terminals, advertising salespeople produce their ads on graphics terminals, and computerized typesetters can produce an entire page at a time. The savings in labor and in paper are immense. Corporations with offices scattered throughout a state or region routinely send data on sales, expenses, and profits back and forth through computers networked over dedicated telephone lines or through portable modems.

It's no wonder that computer science remains a popular college major and that computer courses are among the most frequent offerings of educational institutions throughout the nation. Persons who can understand computers and use them as tools of the modern information age have a giant head start over those unfortunates who suffer from "computerphobia." Yet the overall growth of the computer industry will include plenty of casualties along the way. The shakeout of the mid-1980s in the personal computer industry, which claimed Victor, Osborne, Gavilan, and other manufacturers, was most likely only the first setback. The fortunes of Apple, IBM, Radio Shack, and others are likely to rise and fall as new products are released and the marketplace changes directions.

A second trend that will affect jobs of the future is the deregulation of major industries. Begun during the Carter administration and continued under President Reagan, federal policy has been to encourage free market forces in industries rather than government intervention. Starting with the airline and the trucking industries, deregulation has continued in the 1980s in communications and financial services. Industries once noted for their protected status now face intense competitive pressures. At the same time, new opportunities have led to the growth of other companies, such as regional airlines and long-distance communications.

This trend is perhaps most evident in the banking industry, which for five decades after the Great Depression was well watched and guarded by federal regulatory agencies. That protection is fast disappearing, and the forces of competition are changing the way banks do business. For years, banks have provided the same level of service to all customers, regardless of the size of their bank balances. But deregulation has led to increased bank service charges and thus a fundamental change in the way banks treat the American public. Now, big depositors are being wooed by low charges and extra service, while ordinary customers probably will continue to pay more fees and get less service.

"The future looks bright, but the pattern of jobs and careers is shifting."

Deregulation of the airline industry led to the development of smaller carriers, many of which have experienced soaring profits. Deregulation in banking may have the opposite effect: major banks may use their muscle to acquire a disproportionate share of the market. In all deregulated industries, however, the odds are that individual firms will experience periods of instability as they adjust to their new environment.

The future looks bright for another mushrooming American industry: *communications*. The 1984 breakup of American Telephone and

Telegraph signaled new opportunities for many competitors and the prospects of jobs in many of the smaller firms that moved to capitalize on a perceived market opening. A host of new technologies—long-distance communications, business telephone systems, satellite communications, voice mail, electronic post offices, and fiber optic cables—are already providing jobs to tens of thousands of workers. This is another area where near-term corporate instability may be expected, but long-run prospects for individual career growth look promising.

Health care is another industry that will be providing an increasing share of jobs in the future. The longer life span of Americans, the larger number of senior citizens, and the national concern with fitness and nutrition all indicate continued growth for the health care industry. As in banking and transportation, however, shifting federal policies are creating new problems for existing institutions and new opportunities for others. Many hospitals, for instance, are finding their profits cut as private industry and the federal government use insurance payments as a device to keep rates down. On the other hand, outpatient clinics, home health care agencies, and other innovative firms are booming as more patients are treated outside the traditional hospital setting.

To sum up, the economic future of America looks strong for the next generation, but the pattern of jobs and careers is shifting. Many once-profitable corporations will fold, while others spring up. It will not be a time that favors timid job seekers, anxious to cut their risks. Adventuresome souls, willing to take a chance to achieve greater personal or financial success, may find it an era to their liking.

WHAT ABOUT YOUR OWN FUTURE?

However interested in the subject of future trends we may be, the subject that really rivets our attention is not so much the world's, but our own future. We want to know not just what the work place of the future will be like, but how we personally will fit into it. Will it be easier or harder for us to get a job? Will our job be more interesting than it used to be? Are we more or less likely to be successful in our chosen line of work?

Since you are reading this textbook, it can be concluded that you have already taken the first step toward preparing yourself to succeed in the marketplace of the future: you have decided to take college courses in business to learn the skills you will need for eventual success. In this textbook, you will have the opportunity to learn the basic principles of human relations and to master their practical applications. As the future beckons, you should be ready.

In Chapter 4, you will learn what motivates the worker of tomorrow and some surprising facts about what will not. Chapter 2 tells you how to recognize personality traits that affect everyone, including yourself, on the job and why personality is one factor that is not likely to change dramatically in a short period. In Chapter 10 you will learn what makes certain people in the organization become leaders and others followers, and Chapter 11 will give you some concrete ideas about how performance is going to be measured in organizations of the future.

The specific topic of change within the organization is covered thoroughly in Chapter 14; read it to find out why people resist change, even when it improves the quality of their working lives. Chapter 15 discusses the subject of corporate culture, which can help members of an organization adapt to change or encourage them to view it fearfully. Chapter 16 focuses on an area that is particularly affected by changing attitudes toward work and working—corporate social responsibility. As you will see, changes in the values and beliefs of American society have brought a real change in the way we define the ideal relationship between a business and the larger community.

A topic hardly discussed a decade ago is now the focus of an entire chapter: the quality of working life. Once thought to be inevitably grim, life at work now calls forth major efforts at improvement. Experts discovered that one of the most effective ways to improve an organization is to change its very structure, as discussed in Chapter 13.

As a manager of the future, you have much to anticipate. You probably will work for a company that is more responsive to employee needs and desires than it used to be. Your job will be structured to give you more responsibility and more satisfaction. You will be encouraged to participate more than were your predecessors. The employees you will manage will be better educated, better motivated, and more diverse and will have different emotional needs. The computer age can provide you with new and better ways to measure performance and to see where it needs to be improved; it can also provide training and help employees do their jobs more effectively, at their own time and pace. On the other hand, it may make supervision even more difficult, and in some cases, it has the negative effect of intimidating people who haven't yet become computer-literate.

The longer you look into the future, the more you recognize that it will be a mixture of problems and solutions, challenges and opportunities, the good and the bad. The best way to prepare yourself for it is to learn all you can about today and tomorrow.

ON THE JOB
REVISITED . . .

Suzy Smith, who is considering whether to accept a promotion that will interfere with her personal life as well as her personal values, is in a classic job dilemma. She may find that she prefers a carefree life-style over a demanding job as a supervisor; she may choose not to risk her relationship with her boyfriend by flying off to Detroit for six weeks; or she may decide to put the job first and experience the satisfaction of hard work. Whatever her decision, Ms. Smith's situation illustrates that behind all the high-technology flash and glitter, the working world of the future may not be much different from today.

SUMMARY

Our society is undergoing dramatic changes in population patterns, life-styles, and values. Combined with a revolution in technology, our work places are likely to be transformed by the time the twenty-first century arrives. Demographic changes in population patterns and family trends are occurring in our society. In turn, these changes affect social values. Combined with the revolution in technology, these forces are already shaping the organization of the future.

Researchers have identified several demographic trends affecting our society: an aging work force and a decline in the number of entry-level workers, an across-the-board rise in women joining the work force, and a marked increase in white-collar jobs, with information workers already the largest occupational group in the nation. In addition, a number of social trends will also have a broad impact on the organization of the future: more two-income families, delayed marriages, more singles.

Changes in social values often accompany changes in population patterns, life-style, and technology. Researchers surveying the American public have found a number of new directions in value orientation: from work to leisure, from puritanism to hedonism, from conformity to individualism, and from independence to interdependence. Other researchers have found new value trends in the 1980s: a move toward voluntary simplicity, self-fulfillment, lower expectations, a lack of time, and a maturing of tastes.

Dramatic growth is expected in the amount of discretion or control that people have in their jobs. Fewer people will have narrowly focused jobs, and more people will have jobs that force them to think and to make decisions. There will also be a growth in the inner-directed value of expressivism, a desire to live in closer harmony with nature and with other people.

America is undergoing a new technological revolution with the rise of computers and communication systems. The first technological revolution occurred 7,000 years ago; the next, during the Industrial Revolution, which replaced our agrarian economy with the factory. The last has been under way since the introduction of the ENIAC computer in the mid-1940s. Business applications of technology have included mass production and the research laboratory. Human relations implications have centered around the fact that mass production makes blue-collar workers a mere part of the manufacturing process, extensions of machinery.

The organization of the future likely will be forced to revise the responsibilities and duties of its workers, as many companies are doing today, to more closely match their employees' values and life-styles. In addition, the technological revolution is likely to spawn new industries while existing ones suffer.

As we look at job trends, the rise of the computer is perhaps the most significant. The computer will bestow jobs, and it will take them away in patterns as yet unestablished. A second trend that will affect jobs of the future is the deregulation of major industries—transportation, banking, and communications. Health care is another industry that will be providing an increasing share of jobs in the future.

Overall, the economic future of America looks strong for the next generation, but the pattern of jobs and careers is shifting.

HUMAN RELATIONS APPLICATIONS

Conclusion 1: The work force of the future will differ from the present and the past in terms of value orientation and demographics.
Application: Jobs of the future will need to be designed for older, more skilled employees who have come to appreciate and desire more leisure time.

Conclusion 2: Current and future organizations must learn to manage high levels of technological change, particularly in the area of computer information systems.
Application: Jobs in the organizations of the late 1980s and 1990s will require workers who are adept at monitoring and troubleshooting complex information systems.

DISCUSSION QUESTIONS

1. How will the demographic trend of an aging work force affect future work place life?
2. What is meant by the "value of expressivism"?

3. How has technological change affected workers' responsibilities, duties, and schedules? Provide examples.

4. Explain how deregulation will affect jobs of the future.

5. What major industries appear to have the most promising future employment opportunities? What types of employees do you think will be
hired in such industries?

NOTES

1. Homer J. Hagedorn, "The Factory of the Future: What About the People?" *Journal of Business Strategy* 5 (Summer 1984), p. 39.

2. Harold W. Berkman and Christopher Gilson, *Consumer Behavior:
Concepts and Strategies.* Boston: Kent Publishing Co., 1981,
pp. 106–108.

3. John C. Pollock, "A Rebirth of American Craftsmanship," *Industry
Week* (June 11, 1984), p. 37.

4. Arnold Mitchell, "Styles in the American Bullring," *Across the Board,*
(March 1983), p. 51.

5. Daniel Yankelovich and John Immerwarhr, "The Emergence of
Expressivism Will Revolutionize the Contract Between Workers and
Employers," in *Work in the 21st Century.* Alexandria, VA: American
Society for Personnel Administration, 1984, pp. 13–15.

6. Charles A. Reich, "The Greening of America," *New Yorker* (September 26, 1970), p. 42.

7. Yankelovich and Immerwahr, "The Emergence of Expressivism,"
p. 15.

8. "Work and the Fabric of Family Life," *Management Review* (July
1981), p. 55.

9. Karl Marx, *Capital, the Communist Manifesto and Other Writings,*
Max Eastman, ed. New York: Carlton House, 1932, p. 328.

10. J. C. Williams, A. J. DuBrin, and H. L. Sisk, *Management and Organizations,* 5th ed. Cincinnati: South-Western Publishing, 1985,
pp. 53–54.

11. Judson Gooding, "The Frayed White Collar," *Fortune* (December
1970), p. 81.

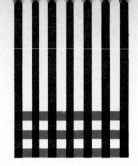

BEHAVIOR AND PERSONALITY

C H A P T E R 2

ON THE JOB . . .

WHAT IS PERSONALITY?

HOW DOES PERSONALITY DEVELOP?

    According to Freud
    The Learning Theorists: How Do We Learn to Behave?
    Is a Personality Greater Than the Sum of Its Traits?

NATURE VERSUS NURTURE: WHICH IS IT?

PERSONALITY AND BEHAVIOR ON THE JOB

    The Type A/Type B Personality
    Internal/External Control
    Machiavellianism

PERSONALITY AND PREJUDICE

    The Causes of Prejudice
    Prejudice Leads to Discrimination

ON THE JOB REVISITED . . .

SUMMARY

NOTES

HUMAN RELATIONS APPLICATIONS

DISCUSSION QUESTIONS

MANAGERIAL DIALOGUE: George R. Wackenhut

ON THE JOB . . .

Wendy Withers looked around her advertising agency and realized she had a problem. Her photographer, Willie Brown, was in a slump. For six weeks Willie had produced stellar photographs of new buildings, new products, and new company officials—the raw material needed by her copywriters to churn out the attractive, creative ads that had made Withers a success in her business. But in the last week, Brown had arrived late at two assignments and then ruined several rolls of film. On top of that, he was generally down in the dumps.

Tomorrow would be an important day for the agency. The president of Soft Soap and Lather was to arrive for a full day of photographic sessions. If the photos came out well, Withers could almost be assured of landing the $2 million account; if not, Soft Soap would certainly find another agency. In an attempt to figure out what might be wrong with her photographer, Withers sat down with Bruce Epstein, the production coordinator, who made out most of the photo assignments.

"Bruce, what's wrong with Willie?" Withers asked. "He started off fine, but lately something's the matter. We can't afford to blow the big Soft Soap session tomorrow. What's going on?"

Epstein scratched his beard. "He told us he's a professional photographer. Maybe he's not. I gave him his assignments each morning in writing, in plenty of time for him to set up his gear. If he's a professional, that should be enough. I don't have time to worry about all the details, I've got half a dozen ad writers who are constantly sending me their rough drafts, ideas, and slogans. I've got to pull the jewels out of the rubbish. Why don't you talk to Willie? I've just about had it with him."

Withers thought for a minute, then replied. "I think talking with Willie would be great, but I'm leaving in ten minutes for another ad presentation and I won't be back until tomorrow. I want this cleared up, so you should talk to Willie after lunch.

"When Willie joined our firm, you spent a lot of time with him explaining our procedures and looking at his photographs. I haven't seen you do that very much lately. Just remember that everybody is different. You work best when I leave you alone. Willie may have a different personality. You handle this as you see fit—just make sure Willie is ready to do his best tomorrow."

If you were Epstein, what would you say to Willie after lunch?

WHAT IS PERSONALITY?

Individuals differ greatly in the way they behave in everyday situations. Some are caring and sensitive, others are selfish and insular; some are outgoing and social, others are shy and reserved; some are aggressive, others are passive. The word we generally use to describe an individual's collection of such behavior traits is *personality*.

For decades, people who studied business organizations seemed to think personality was something you left at home when you headed for the office in the morning. They could design an organization chart with neat boxes describing each person's responsibilities and duties, but they never made allowances for the fact that the people who occupy these boxes have distinct personalities that are likely to affect the way they carry out their jobs. For example, one branch manager of a big city bank may have a breezy, informal personality; she kids with the tellers and encourages loan officers to stop by her desk and chat whenever they have a question. Imagine the shock that one of these loan officers is in for when she is transferred to another branch, with a manager who is very formal and reserved; he doesn't see anyone without an appointment and still refers to the secretary who's been with him for twenty years as "Mrs. Williams."

In real life, jobs are not held by faceless bureaucrats, but by humans, each with a unique personality that influences the way he or she performs the job. To be a good supervisor, subordinate, or colleague, you have to understand what personality is and how it affects behavior on the job.

This chapter will address some of the following issues and questions about behavior and personality:

What are the key factors that make up an individual's personality?

Are there certain types of personality traits that are related to putting more effort into a job?

How is personality developed? Is it influenced by one's genes? One's parents? One's friends?

Since it is probably impossible to find two people who behave exactly the same, we know immediately that personality implies uniqueness. Further, if you were to observe someone day in and day out, you would probably perceive clear-cut consistencies in their behavior. You notice that when you talk to Sam at 9:30 A.M., he snaps your head off, but when

"There are as many different personalities as there are human beings; personality is unique."

you have to get back to him at 3:30 P.M., he is friendly and cooperative. The next morning, he ignores your smiling greeting, only to buy you a cup of coffee when the snack cart comes by at 11:00 A.M. Eventually your observations form a consistent pattern, and you realize that Sam is the kind of guy who is extremely grouchy for the first few hours of the morning. Now that you know about that aspect of his personality, you make sure never to discuss anything important with Sam before 10:30 A.M.

Thus, there are two immediate characteristics of personality: uniqueness and relative stability. The term *relative stability* is used because, even if a trait seems quite consistent over time, it is always possible that something could change that trait temporarily. Sam might open his morning paper to discover that he has won $1,000 in the state lottery; this news would probably bring a smile to his face, even though it's only 9:03 A.M. The next morning, however, his grumpiness undoubtedly will return.

Therefore, we can define *personality* as a unique combination of traits and characteristics that results in behaviors that are relatively stable over time. Other aspects of personality are:

1. Personality is an organized whole.

2. Personality appears to be organized into patterns that are observable and measurable to some degree.

3. Although there is a biological basis to personality, it is also a product of social and cultural environment.

4. Personality has superficial aspects, such as attitudes toward being a team leader, and a deeper core, such as sentiments about authority or the protestant work ethic.

5. Personality involves both common and unique characteristics. Every person is different from every other person in some respects and is similar in other respects.

There seems to be a permanent fascination with the notion that individual personalities can be classified into types. Systems have been devised to classify personalities on the basis of people's handwriting, the shapes of their heads, the organ of the body by which they are dominated, and the constellations in the sky at the time they were born. So far, none of these systems have been scientifically accepted. A modern-day version of the attempt to classify personalities uses the computer to develop trait inventories (see the box on page 42). Employers may use such inventories to screen job applicants.

PEOPLE AND INNOVATIONS: PSYCH SHOP

Has inventory buildup got you down? Are your suppliers supplying you with nothing but grief? Maybe it is time to check out the shopping mall shrink.

The idea comes from Laguna Beach, Calif.— surprise, surprise—where psychologist Martine J. RoBards and her husband, David Hardin, a management consultant, have opened the first in what they hope will be a nationwide chain of "psych shops" located in shopping malls. It is called The Human Equation Ltd. and offers everything from sessions in "holistic architec-ture" to computer-assisted psychological screening.

"The computerized test saves time and money," says RoBards. Conventional therapy "may take several weeks or even months. . . . We cover that ground in an hour." Which leaves plenty of time to pick up a quick hamburger, or get your poodle groomed, or whatever.

Source: *Inc.* (October 1983), p. 43. Reprinted by permission. Copyright © 1983 by INC. Publishing Company, 38 Commercial Wharf, Boston, MA 02110.

HOW DOES PERSONALITY DEVELOP?

Personality theories attempt to explain and understand how certain consistent forms of behavior are developed and can be predicted over time. Three of the more popular views of personality development are

1. Freudian and sociopsychoanalytic
2. Learning theory
3. Trait

Each of these major orientations will be described.

According to Freud

"Freud thought personality was the outcome of a constant battle among the three aspects of the human mind: id, ego, and superego."

One of the most widely discussed and influential views of personality development was suggested by Sigmund Freud. Although it is not possible to do justice to his insights in a few short textbook pages, his main contributions revolve around two key topics: the structure of personality and the psychosexual stages of development.

Structure of personality. Freud believed that the behavior displayed by any individual is a function of the interaction that occurs between the three main components of personality. A young executive who has spent weeks formulating a new strategic plan for his department is told by his boss that the plan is premature and poorly conceived. One part of the executive would like to make a nasty face at his boss and tell him what he can do with his opinion. Another part tells him that he must respect authority and accept his boss's opinion. A third part attempts to balance the first two feelings. In the end, the executive responds to his boss by saying, "Let's discuss the specific aspects of the plan you think are poorly conceived, so I can go back to the drawing board and revise them."

The *id* represents the part of the executive that wants immediate satisfaction in this situation—making a face and suggesting an anatomically impossible action. According to Freud, this is the first aspect of personality to develop in a child. Additionally, it is the main energy source of personality. The id might best be conceptualized as a spoiled child. It wants immediate gratification and responds angrily to anyone who stands in the way.

In reality it is rarely possible to achieve instant gratification. Thus, a second element of the personality develops—the *ego.* The ego attempts to balance the impulsive, pleasure-seeking desires of the id with reality. Telling your boss to shove it might feel good for a moment, but it could also lead to the loss of your job. The ego thus pushes the executive to respond in a mature way by asking his boss for specifics on where the plan went wrong. In fact, ego is sometimes considered to be the chief executive officer of the personality because it controls our actions, selects aspects of the environment to respond to, and decides which of the id's instructions it will satisfy.

Freud considered the *superego,* the last of the three components of personality to develop, as the moral aspect of our being. It continually pushes us in line with those traditional values and cultural mores passed on to us by our family and society. The superego of our irate executive tells him to "respect authority" and be submissive.

According to Freud, the superego is in a constant battle with the id. The id strives solely for pleasure and immediate satisfaction of needs, while the superego continually tries to inhibit such impulses and persuade us to behave like paragons of virtue. The ego has the sometimes difficult job of mediating between the pleasure instincts of the id and the stringent moralistic goals of the superego. This continual struggle and mediation, according to Freud, plays an essential role in the stages of personality development.

Stages of development. Freud maintained that during childhood we all go through four stages of development. If a child experiences frustration and anxiety at any one of these stages, there will be noticeable effects on the personality of the adult.

During the first year of infancy, a baby is in the oral stage, when such activities as sucking, eating, and swallowing are most vital. Excessive anxiety at the oral stage will fixate the personality to a pattern of talkative, passive, greedy, and selfish behavior. Years two and three of infancy compose the anal period. Strains and difficulties in the process of being toilet-trained will predispose the child to develop as stubborn, authoritarian, scrupulously neat, and stingy. During years four and five, the child enters the phallic stage, with a primarily sexual focus. Boys supposedly fantasize about sex with their mothers (the so-called Oedipus complex), and girls entertain fantasies of sex with their fathers. Freud theorized that fixation at this state would lead to abnormal attitudes toward the opposite sex or deviant attitudes toward authority. Finally, the genital stage arrives, during which the child shifts from self-centeredness to awareness of others, interest in the outside world, and normal socialization. According to the dictates of society, the person is attracted to the opposite sex, takes up a career, and starts a family of his or her own.

Freud believed that all the traits and behaviors we display as adults could be traced back to these early stages of development. Specific personality characteristics are the result of the ways in which the ego resolves struggles between the id and the superego components of our personality. An executive fixated at the oral stage, for example, may display the personality characteristic of being overly gullible.

Later additions to Freud's theories.   Many of Freud's disciples expanded on his original theories to include other personality dimensions. (See Table 2.1 for a summary of significant theories based on the Freudian perspective). Karen Horney viewed the child's development in social interaction as a prime determinant of personality. She classified individuals into three general orientations: compliant, detached, and aggressive. Compliant individuals need to be accepted, loved, and appreciated. They will subordinate themselves to others to avoid conflict and gain companionship. The compliant person is a conformist. The detached individual wants to remain free from obligations and dependence on others. People of this type consider themselves intelligent and rational and believe that they possess talents that should be recognized and applauded. Self-sufficiency is a high-ranking value. The aggressive individual competes to gain prestige, success, excellence, and admiration. Such a person values strength and power and, while seeing others as competitors, manipulates people to reinforce his or her own self-image. This kind of individual believes that everyone else also operates on the basis of self-interest alone.

TABLE 2.1   Other Theories Influenced by Freud

Theorist	Major Ideas/Views
Carl Jung	Human beings possess a permanent store of memories passed on by their ancestors, the collective unconscious. This contains archetypes, symbols that appear over and over again in art, literature, mythology. (Superman, the wicked witch from *the Wizard of Oz,* and Darth Vader from *Star Wars* are examples.) Human beings are born as either introverts, who are primarily concerned with the self, or extroverts, who are more concerned with the outside world.
Erik Erikson	At each stage of development, there is a crisis or conflict. The way in which this is resolved determines the kind of person we become. For example, in the first stage (sensory stage), we learn feelings of trust or mistrust. If our mother is kind and dependable, we learn trust; if she is unkind and undependable, we learn mistrust.
Erich Fromm	Society is seen as an attempt on the part of people to resolve the basic contradiction of human nature; we are part of nature but also separate from it. In contrast to animals, we have needs aside from basic physiological drives. In particular, we have needs for identity. A number of basic personality types exist: receptive type, marketing type, and productive type.
Harry Stack Sullivan	This theory stresses the importance of interpersonal relationships. Our interactions with others are a major determinant of our personality. We pass through a series of stages (infancy, childhood, juvenile, preadolescence, early adolescence, late adolescence, maturity). In each, we learn to play specific roles (e.g., bully, good boy/girl, clown) and to interact with others. Our personal problems arise because other persons create them for us by what they do or fail to do.

Source: Robert A. Baron, *Behavior in Organizations.* Boston, MA: Allyn & Bacon, 1983, p. 92.

Like Freud, Horney believed that the strategy a child finds most successful for dealing with parents, peers, and authorities will lead to the adoption of similar adult responses. Eventually an individual becomes better skilled in some strategies than in others, and one of the three personality types emerges.

Using Freud's theories.   Freud's theories of personality and behavior emphasize that much of what we do is unconscious. We usually are not totally aware of our reasons for behaving in particular ways. As a member of a business organization you may, through an understanding of such theories, develop a more objective view of the causes of your colleague's behavior. You can thus do a better job of interpreting the behavior of your bosses, and you may be able to assist subordinates in becoming aware of and changing their own behavior. People usually do not feel a need to change their behavior until they become consciously aware of the fact that it is not particularly effective.

An understanding of Freud's theories also helps us to realize that many important aspects of personality are formed in early life and may be quite difficult to change later. Thus, it is especially important to match job openings with appropriate candidates. Good initial selection may be much more valuable than performance appraisals or job training programs, since it is extremely difficult to create permanent behavior change.

The Learning Theorists: How Do We Learn to Behave?

The learning theorists' view of personality contends that behavioral patterns are based on each individual's unique set of experiences. Behavior is learned through daily experience. How does such learning take place?

Classical learning views.   The three generally recognized essentials of the learning process are *drives, cues,* and *reinforcement.* A *drive* is an arousal mechanism that causes an individual to act. Primary drives include such physiological motivators as hunger, sex, and the avoidance of pain. Secondary drives are acquired through previous learning and reflect social and cultural influences on the individual. Examples are the desire for prestige and the need for affection. A *cue* is any stimulus found in the individual's environment that can trigger a drive. An advertisement is a cue intended to induce a drive to purchase the product or service in the person who sees the cue. A *reinforcement* serves as a reward for some response and reduces an individual's drive. For instance, a hungry animal may be rewarded for some activity by being fed, while a hard-working employee may be rewarded by an increase in salary.

Learning takes place when an individual who wants to satisfy needs or reach certain goals responds to specific cues in the environment. Because the responses are strengthened when reinforcement occurs, the individual learns to repeat the response when faced with a similar cue.

Personality, according to leading theorists, is the sum of response habits learned over time. As responses to environmental cues are rewarded,

"People don't change their behavior until they realize it is not getting them what they want."

"An individual's personality is the sum of a lifetime of learning."

they become part of an individual's behavioral repertoire. Personality is developed by the continuous association of some stimulus from the environment with the desired response.

Learning is thus largely social, and the society in which a person lives will play a part in determining which personality traits will be learned. For example, an American boy who shows a strong spirit of competition with other boys on his baseball team will be rewarded by the approval of his coach, his parents, and his teammates. His competitiveness will be reinforced and will therefore become an important and prominent aspect of his personality. A young Japanese boy who showed the same sort of competitiveness might be reprimanded by his coach, urged by his parents to learn to cooperate with the other boys, and disliked by his teammates until he began to show signs of a change toward greater teamwork. Since his competitiveness was punished, he will probably learn to keep it under control, and it will not be a noticeable part of his adult personality. Table 2.2 sums up some of the differences in American, European, and Japanese societies that will lead individuals in each of these societies to develop somewhat different personalities.

The guiding premise of learning theorists was to consider only those aspects of behavior that could be scientifically observed. This limitation

TABLE 2.2 Attitudes Toward Competition in Three Different Cultures

Nature and Effect of Competition	Typical American Viewpoints	Typical European Viewpoints	Typical Japanese Viewpoints
Nature of competition	Competition is a strong moral force: it contributes to character building.	Competition is neither good nor bad.	There is conflict inherent in nature. To overcome conflicts, many must compete, but man's final goal is harmony with nature and his fellowman.
Business competition compared	Business competition is like a big sport game.	Business competition affects the livelihood of people and quickly develops into warfare.	The company is like a family. Competition has no place in a family. Aggressive action against competitors in the marketplace is in order for the survival and growth of the company.

TABLE 2.2 *(continued)*

Nature and Effect of Competition	Typical American Viewpoints	Typical European Viewpoints	Typical Japanese Viewpoints
Motivation	One cannot rely on an employee's motivation unless extra monetary inducements for hard work are offered in addition to a base salary or wage.	A key employee is motivated by the fact that he has been hired by the company.	Same as the European viewpoint.
Reward system	Money talks. A person is evaluated on the basis of his image (contribution) to the company. High tipping in best hotels, restaurants, etc., is expected.	An adequate salary, fringe benefits, opportunities for promotion, but no extra incentives—except in sales. Very little tipping (service charge is included in added-value tax).	Same as the European viewpoint.
Excessive competition	Competition must be tough for the sake of the general welfare of society. No upper limit on the intensity and amount of competition is desirable.	Too much competition is destructive and is in conflict with brotherly love and Christian ethic.	Excessive competition is destructive and can create hatred. Only restrained competition leads to harmony and benefits society.
Hiring policy	Aggressive individuals who enjoy competition are ideal employees. Individuals who avoid competition are unfit for life and company work.	Diversity of opinion. How competitiveness or aggressive behavior of an individual is viewed varies with national ideology and the type of work. In England, it is not a recommendation to describe a job applicant as being aggressive.	Individuals are hired usually not for specific jobs but on the basis of their personality traits and their ability to become an honorable company member. Team play and group consensus are stressed.

Source: Hugh E. Kramer, "Concepts of Competition in America, Europe, and Japan," *Business and Society* (Fall 1977), pp. 22–23.

was a reaction on the part of many experimental psychologists to what they perceived as the theoretical excesses of Freudian psychology with its blatantly unmeasurable concepts. The ideal for these learning theorists was rigorous empirical control. Research results tended to be confined to the responses of laboratory animals.

In more recent years, learning theorists have broadened their focus. One example is the social learning theory of personality. Consider the behavior of different people at a cocktail party. Some may feel at ease in such situations, approaching strangers cordially and introducing themselves. They have a high expectancy, based on past experiences, that when they approach people in a friendly way, they will be treated well. Other individuals may feel quite insecure in such a situation. They seem to expect that when they introduce themselves to a stranger, the response will be "Buzz off!" In other words, individuals have different expectations regarding the outcomes of their behavior. It is also important to note that people differ in the value that they attach to the responses of others. Some people are badly shaken by rejection, whereas others may not care how people respond to them. A cool stare may make one person decide never to attend another cocktail party, while a second person might not even notice it. Obviously, they will have two entirely different social learning experiences.

Using learning theory.   Learning theory clearly has contributed a great deal to our understanding of behavior. A number of organizations have applied learning theory concepts as motivational techniques in the form of behavior modification strategies (see Chapter 4). Many of these programs have been very successful.

There are, however, a number of criticisms of the learning approach to understanding personality development. For one, the essential element in most theories of this kind is that an environmental stimulus causes a particular behavioral response, even though there are numerous situations in which external stimuli cannot be found to account for behavior. What environmental stimulus, for example, occurs to prompt someone to write a poem or to try solving a challenging puzzle?

Additionally, the learning view of human development emphasizes that any learning or behavior that takes place occurs on the basis of reinforcement. Such a perspective does not recognize internal sources of reward or motivation for behavior. For example, the starving free-lance writer is certainly not receiving reinforcement for his or her writing efforts; however, the writing behavior continues because of the writer's internal needs to produce such products.

Is a Personality Greater Than the Sum of Its Traits?

The trait perspective recognizes that behavior may be the result of hereditary factors as well as environmental elements. *Traits* can be defined as the attributes that predispose a person to function in a certain way and identify him or her as a given person. Trait theorists contend that certain universal or common traits are possessed by people who share similar social experiences while other, unique traits apply to a particular person. Some of these traits are environmentally learned, whereas others are determined genetically. Most are the result of an interaction between the two.

A few of the major personality factors are displayed in Table 2.3. As you can see, these represent a broad range of elements, including such characteristics as assertiveness versus humility and stable versus emotional. Many such factors have been included in personality inventories used for management selection.

The trait perspective in personality research and conceptualizing is important for a number of reasons. If we can identify specific traits that individuals possess, we should be able to predict their behavior more accurately. Knowing that a colleague shows high levels of assertiveness, for example, gives us some indication of her behavior in a sales position. In addition, if we understand the behavioral elements linked to specific traits, we can devise organizational training sessions or modeling programs designed to reinforce particular types of traits.

NATURE VERSUS NURTURE: WHICH IS IT?

"Is a baby born with a personality of its own?"

Think for a few minutes about your own ideas of personality and human development. Are people born with particular traits or instincts that guide their behavior, or do environment and culture mold personality? Which perspective makes more sense to you and why? This is an important issue for future managers. If people are born with certain traits and

TABLE 2.3 Major Personality Factors Identified by Cattell	
Common Labels	
1. Outgoing/reserved	**7.** Venturesome/shy
2. More intelligent/less intelligent	**8.** Tender-minded/tough-minded
3. Stable/emotional	**9.** Suspicious/trusting
4. Assertive/humble	**10.** Imaginative/practical
5. Happy-go-lucky/sober	**11.** Shrewd/forthright
6. Conscientious/expedient	**12.** Apprehensive/placid

Source: R.B. Cattell, *The Scientific Analysis of Personality.* Chicago: Aldine, 1966, p. 365.

innate characteristics, then businesses must develop finely tuned selection techniques to hire employees who have the traits associated with high performance. If, on the other hand, people are molded by experiences, then businesses should put a greater emphasis on training programs to develop the type of employees they need.

The issue of nature versus nurture is hardly new. Early Christian philosophy, for example, contended that all humans were born evil, with original sin. Another medieval view was that all people were born with a depraved little man (the *homunculus*) in their heads. The homunculus constantly pushed people toward evil actions, and only strict punishment by parents could control him. On the other side, John Locke, a British philosopher, contended that a child is born with a blank slate for a mind. The experiences that a child faces are the sole molders of character.

Most experts now agree that nature and nurture are inseparable in their effect on personality development. It is inappropriate to ask which one plays a dominant role in determining behavior, since the two are linked. Each person starts out with certain predispositions, but it is the effects of experience that either bring out or suppress these traits. Therefore, predicting a co-worker's behavior requires an understanding of that person's unique attributes as well as of the experiences that can develop such attributes. Training methods and valid selection tools are *both* necessary for achieving high performance in the business organization.

PERSONALITY AND BEHAVIOR ON THE JOB

Certain personality characteristics have been found to be related to on-the-job behavior and have been the focus of considerable research. They are also frequently the focus of interest on the part of employers hiring new workers. In the Managerial Dialogue on pages 52–53, George Wackenhut speaks frankly about the way he sizes up a job applicant's personality.

The Type A/Type B Personality

Look around your classroom. Do you see fellow students who are continuously tapping their pens on their desks or moving their feet nervously? They may very well be type A personalities. Such people possess a spectrum of traits that might best classify them as workaholics. (See Table 2.4 on page 54 for a summary of Type A traits.) They generally complain

Managerial Dialogue

"If you diligently apply yourself, you'll find success."

George R. Wackenhut, president of the Wackenhut Corporation

The Wackenhut Corporation provides security systems and services around the world.

George Wackenhut believes that certain types of behaviors lead to success in the business world. Things like hard work, sincerity, and making a good impression still matter. "I believe that outstanding success in any area can be achieved only through single-minded dedication and personal sacrifice. If you diligently apply yourself, you'll find success." Wackenhut has been president of the Wackenhut Corporation, which provides security systems and services around the world, since 1958. During that time he's had occasion to observe many different types of employee behavior. "I look for a person with a solid personality," Wackenhut says. "His demeanor and the manner in which he presents himself are important. In a field manager, I look for someone with a sales personality—not necessarily sales experience, but sales personality—being outgoing. I like to hire someone who's had some business experience too, because after all, we're a business." The former FBI agent has strong feelings about first impressions, also. "First impressions are lasting. If you make a bad first impression, it's hard to overcome. If you make a good first impression, it's hard to kill."

Each potential manager is interviewed by several managers in Wackenhut's upper echelon. Then, each manager completes a form evaluating that person on a scale of one to five in certain areas. In Wackenhut's experience, after a new employee comes on board, his or her behavior probably won't change much. "Their behavior stays with them. Sometimes it changes, or our perception of their behavior changes. Those that are good, though, generally stay good. Other times, people change when they're given the opportunity to express themselves.

"For example, we had a man who was a full colonel in the military with no business experience, who didn't do well at several jobs. We gave him command experience at the Savannah River nuclear plant where we have 700 people. He did a bang-up job at that." Wackenhut believes employees want guidance and a certain amount of restrictions, but they don't want to be stifled. His company maintains a program to identify good performers and match them with the right positions. "We have what we call our skills inventory, which is a listing of names and backgrounds, so if opportunities in those areas develop, we've got someone to call upon. Those who look like they deserve a bigger opportunity are called upon when the opportunity presents itself."

Because of the nature of his business, Wackenhut hires numerous employees from the military and law enforcement agencies. Does he find them all to be autocratic types?

"That's a very interesting question. As far as I have ever categorized them, I'd have to say no. But perhaps I only see one side because so many of our top people are military or law enforcement.

"There are some that remain too military. In the military, it's a matter of taking and giving orders and saying 'yes, sir.' In the business world, it's different.

"There was one manager who kind of lost sight of the troops. There was lack of communication—a 'do it this way or else' approach. We had to point out to the top man that these were not military people, they could leave the job. He opened a hotline into his office, made some other changes, and things worked out pretty well."

Is there a difference in the behavior of those in the military and those in law enforcement?

"They strike me all as being men's men. But outside that . . . maybe the military are a little more demanding in their approach."

Is leadership in the corporate world similar or different from that in the military?

"I think that there's less room for individual thinking in the military than in the business world. But there's certainly a thread of similarities. Leadership on the front lines—that always works best. And you lead by example. If you want everybody else to work hard, you've got to work hard yourself."

Wackenhut probably would not disagree with the theory that employers hire persons similar to themselves. An interviewer remarked that he would be surprised to find anybody working at Wackenhut with long hair, with a beard, or without a tie.

Said Wackenhut with a laugh, "If you find anyone like that, let me know."

little about work and work to complete tasks swiftly even when no time pressures are imposed by others. Additionally, they seem to feel most comfortable in organizations characterized by high performance standards. In contrast, the person with a Type B personality is far more easygoing, relaxed, and social. An estimated 40 percent of the general population can be classified as Type A and 60 percent as Type B.[1]

Although the Type A personality may seem like the ideal employee, there is a clear liability to such traits. In one study, Type A managers were found to have significantly higher blood pressure and cholesterol levels than did Type B managers; further, they were more than twice as likely to suffer heart attacks and other cardiac problems.[2] As if the medical prob-

TABLE 2.4   Characteristics of the Type A Personality
Always moves, walks, and eats rapidly
Feels impatient with the pace of things; hurries others; dislikes waiting
Does several things at once
Feels guilty when relaxing or doing nothing for several hours a day
Tries to schedule more and more in less and less time
Uses Type A nervous gestures (such as clenched fist, banging hand on table)
Does not have time to enjoy life

Source: Meyer Friedman and Ray Roseman, *Type A Behavior and Your Heart.* New York: Alfred A. Knopf, 1974.

"The Type A is usually not a team player but performs best in solitary tasks with tight deadlines."

lems weren't bad enough, Type A's are also characterized by impatience, aggressiveness, and irritability, all of which may cause conflict with fellow workers. Identifying employees as Type A or B may help to place them in appropriate organizational positions. Type A's apparently work best in jobs requiring deadlines, and Type B's seem to work better on team tasks and jobs requiring complex judgment.

Internal/External Control

Another way of classifying personality type is based on an individual's belief about the amount of control he or she has over the events of life. Those who believe in internal control think that their own decisions and actions will influence what happens to them. Those who believe in external control think that situations occur because of fate or events over which they have little or no influence. Table 2.5 summarizes the differences between internals and externals. Julian Rotter, a social learning theorist, is most widely known for developing both the concept of locus control and a questionnaire to measure such personality traits.

As you might suspect, the organizational behavior of employees who believe in internal control differs from those who believe in external control. Specifically, internals have been found to have higher motivational levels than externals. They earn more money, hold jobs with higher status, and are more likely to advance in the hierarchy at faster rates than are externals.[3] Further, employees tend to rate supervisors who are internals as significantly higher in persuasiveness and more influential than externally inclined supervisors.[4]

Machiavellianism

Although the Machiavellian type of personality has been researched extensively in recent years, the concept was first explained in the sixteenth

TABLE 2.5 Some Ways in Which Internals Differ from Externals

Information processing	Internals make more attempts to acquire information, are better at information retention, are less satisfied with amount of information they possess, are better at utilizing information and devising processing rules.
Job satisfaction	Internals are more satisfied, less alienated, and less rootless.
Self-control and risk behavior	Internals exhibit greater self-control, are more cautious, engage in less risky behavior.
Expectancies and results	Internals see stronger relationship between what they do and what happens to them, expect working hard leads to good performance, feel more control over how to spend time, perform better.
Preference for skill versus chance achievements	Internals prefer skill-achievement outcomes; externals prefer chance achievements.
Use of rewards	Internals are more likely to use personally persuasive records and power bases and less likely to use coercion.
Response to others	Internals are more independent, more reliant on own judgment, and less susceptible to influence of others; they resist subtle influence attempts and are more likely to accept information on merit rather than prestige of source.
Leader behavior	Internals prefer participative leadership; externals prefer directive.

Source: J. R. Schermerhorn, J. G. Hunt, and R. N. Osborn, *Managing Organizational Behavior,* 2nd ed. New York: John Wiley & Sons, 1982, p. 109. Reprinted by permission.

century writings of Niccolò Machiavelli. His book *The Prince* describes the personality profile of an ideal ruler: a person who successfully manipulates others to achieve his own goals. Some of Machiavelli's suggestions:

"It is better to be feared than loved."

"Humility not only is of no service, but is actually harmful."

"Princes should . . . keep in their own hands the distribution of favors."

As shown in Table 2.6, questionnaires have been developed to assess Machiavellian tendencies. High scorers are extremely effective at mani-

TABLE 2.6   The Short Form of the Machiavellian Scale

Indicate your reactions to each of the statements shown below by circling one number for each. If you agree strongly with a given statement circle 5; if you agree, but to a lesser extent, circle 4, and so on.

	Disagree			Agree	
	Lot	*Little*	*Neutral*	*Little*	*Lot*
1. The best way to handle people is to tell them what they want to hear.	1	2	3	4	5
2. When you ask someone to do something for you, it is best to give the real reason for wanting it rather than giving reasons which might carry more weight.	1	2	3	4	5
3. Anyone who completely trusts anyone else is asking for trouble.	1	2	3	4	5
4. It is hard to get ahead without cutting corners here and there.	1	2	3	4	5
5. It is safest to assume that all people have a vicious streak and it will come out when they are given a chance.	1	2	3	4	5
6. One should take action only when sure it is morally right.	1	2	3	4	5
7. Most people are basically good and kind.	1	2	3	4	5
8. There is no excuse for lying to someone else.	1	2	3	4	5
9. Most men forget more easily the death of their father than the loss of property.	1	2	3	4	5
10. Generally speaking, men won't work hard unless they're forced to do so.	1	2	3	4	5

Source: R. Christie and F. L. Geis (eds.), *Studies in Machiavellism*. New York: Academic Press, 1970. Reprinted by permission.

pulating and influencing others. They are much more believable liars than are those who score low.[5] They use ingratiation tactics, particularly with their superiors, to achieve their goals. They tend to isolate themselves emotionally from their co-workers and are guided more by their heads than their hearts in making decisions. A number of consulting firms currently offer training sessions designed to increase the understanding of and ability to use Machiavellian tools.

PERSONALITY AND PREJUDICE

One personality trait that has special implications for on-the-job behavior is prejudice. *Prejudice* means making judgments about people and situations on the basis of preexisting attitudes and opinions—quite literally, prejudging. The office manager who decides where to buy new typewriters by comparing prices and services of a number of different suppliers is making a rational judgment based on the evidence he or she has about each different firm. The manager who rejects one supplier because the company is owned by Koreans—"you can't trust Orientals"—and another because "Jews will always get the better of you when you negotiate price" is acting on prejudice. The manager has no experience with either firm in question but has arrived at a conclusion based on insufficient evidence.

We tend to think of prejudice as a feeling against a person or group, but prejudice can also operate in favor of a group or ethnicity or race. For example, a personnel manager who attended Tulane University might have a prejudice in favor of job applicants who also attended Tulane, or the chief of a construction crew may hire only Italians in the belief that they are the strongest workers.

The Causes of Prejudice

"Prejudice is easily learned . . . but unlearning it can be very difficult."

Most studies agree that prejudice is *learned.* Parents who are prejudiced against blacks raise children who grow up to be prejudiced against blacks. Once a prejudice is learned, it is extremely difficult to unlearn. Even direct experience with people who disprove the mistaken stereotype doesn't necessarily eliminate prejudice; the person may be viewed as an exception that does nothing to disprove the rule.

Some prejudice is purely a personal response to past experience. For example, when an Irish contractor takes the money to build on a new bedroom to the house but never turns up to do the work, members of the bilked family may respond by developing a prejudice against Irish contractors. But most prejudice is a result of long-term socialization by family, peers, and even institutions such as school or church. A white child growing up in a racially mixed city may be warned by parents not to bring home a black friend, cautioned by playmates never to venture into a black neighborhood, and taught at school that "they" are different from "us." Thus, the child's prejudice against black people is learned from and supported by the environment.

Sociologists note that prejudice is particularly likely to develop when people of different races or ethnic backgrounds are in competition with one another for jobs, housing, and opportunities for advancement. The person most likely to develop strong prejudice is one with relatively low social status, low income, and a low level of education. In other words, prejudice may serve as a sort of defense, a way of blaming someone else for the things that go wrong and a chance to feel superior to members of the supposedly inferior group.

Prejudice of any sort—against blacks, Vietnamese, the elderly, or Baptist—runs counter to the noble ideals most people would like to live up to. Yet it is an undeniable fact that has long existed, and continues to exist, despite all efforts to the contrary. For many workers it will be an issue on the job. No matter what the company's official position, there will be prejudiced bosses, co-workers, and subordinates. You may find that you have to deal with prejudiced colleagues, that you have become the victim of someone's prejudice, or that you recognize in yourself a tendency to respond with prejudice rather than a careful examination of the facts in the particular case at hand.

Prejudice Leads to Discrimination

Prejudice is a feeling, a way of looking at the world. Like many opinions and attitudes, it is extremely difficult to change. Although a company can try to create an environment that discourages the expression of prejudice, there is probably little it can do to change prejudiced feelings on the part of its employees.

The company does have a real responsibility in the area of discrimination. *Discrimination* refers to the actions that are taken against the object of prejudice. For example, a supervisor may feel that Mexican-American workers are likely to be lazy, frequently absent, and generally low in productivity. As long as this is simply a feeling, it is merely a case of prejudice and something that the company can do little about. If the supervisor acts on this prejudice and refuses to hire Mexican-Americans, or promptly invents reasons for firing any Mexican-American who is assigned to the department, then the supervisor is guilty of discrimination and the company legally is required to intervene. In the last several decades, legislation has been passed that makes it illegal for businesses to discriminate against minorities (as defined, the term includes working women) in either hiring or compensation. A worker who can prove to the satisfaction of a court that he or she was passed over for employment (or promotion) on the basis of race, age, religion, or sex can win a large settlement. Table 2.7 summarizes the major pieces of legislation in this area.

"Companies are now expected to treat all employees as equals, discriminating neither for nor against any particular group."

TABLE 2.7 Summary of Discrimination Legislation

Legislation	Jurisdiction	Prohibitions
Civil Rights Act, Public Law 88–352 (1964)	Employers with 25 or more employees; also covers labor unions.	Discrimination with respect to color, national origin, race, religion, and sex
Equal Employment Opportunity Act (1972) (Amendment to Title VII of the Civil Rights Act)	Most employers with more than 15 employees.	Same as Civil Rights Act.
Age Discrimination in Employment Act (1967, amended in 1978)	Employers with more than 25 employees.	Age discrimination in employment decisions concerning individuals between 40 and 70 years old.
Executive Order 11246 [sec. 201(1)] 1965; amended by Executive Order 11375, 1966.	Federal contractors and subcontractors with contracts exceeding $50,000 and 50 or more employees.	Discrimination in employment decisions with respect to color, national origin, race, religion, and sex.
Vocational Rehabilitation Act (1973)	Government contractors and federal agencies.	Discrimination in employment decisions against people with physical and/or mental handicaps.
Pregnancy Discrimination Act of 1978 (Amendment to Civil Rights Act, Public Law 95–555	Same as Civil Rights Act.	Discrimination on the basis of pregnancy, childbirth, or related medical conditions in benefit administration and other employment decisions.

Source: Adapted from J. Klotchman and L.L. Neider, "EEO Alert! Watch Out for Discrimination in Discharge Decisions," *Personnel* (January–February 1983), pp. 60–66. Reprinted by permission of the publisher, from *Personnel,* January–February 1983 © 1983 American Management Association, New York. All rights reserved.

Fifteen years ago, it was not sufficient for a company merely to refrain from discrimination against minorities; it had to bend over backward to recruit and promote a certain percentage of minority workers. In the 1980s, however, there seems to be a growing consensus that such tokenism is not the most effective way for corporations to address the problem of discrimination. The corporation may be better served by initiating training programs to bring minority workers up to the general standard by donating money to minority institutions to improve education, or by providing more opportunities for learning experiences such as apprenticeship programs. In its hiring and compensation activities, however, the corporation is expected to treat all people as equals, which means not turning down qualified applicants because they are members of a minority group as well as not choosing a minority worker over more qualified applicants who are not minorities.

The laws regarding discrimination grow even more complicated, perhaps because the task of trying to legislate in this area of human behavior is virtually impossible. A manager who is strongly prejudiced against Mexican-Americans can probably find a way to exercise discrimination, no matter what the law says. It may be illegal to refuse to hire them because of race, but the supervisor can find some other reason; this one is too inexperienced, that one doesn't know enough English, a third has inadequate references.

The environment of the organization may be able to accomplish what the laws cannot. Top management as well as subordinates can make it clear that it discourages prejudice and discrimination, however subtly it is expressed. Fairness remains one of the most consistently held values in our society, and whatever the sociological reasons for the continued existence of prejudice, most people are willing to agree that it should be curbed when it leads to unfairness.

ON THE JOB REVISITED . . .

Bruce Epstein called photographer Willie Brown over to his desk after lunch. "Willie, I'm not one to throw a lot of praise around. I figure that doing a good job has its own reward. But I want to tell you that some of the photos you've taken in the past were absolutely brilliant: colorful, well-lit, pleasant backgrounds. I don't understand why you've been having such a hard time the past two weeks."

Brown responded, "Well, Bruce, I take good photographs when I'm feeling good and bad photographs when I'm feeling bad. When I started here, you made me feel like I was important, a part of the team. You also gave me some freedom in how I set up my photographs. Now I feel like I'm just part of the assembly line, you tell me what to do and when to do it."

Said Epstein, "Let's make a deal then, starting with tomorrow's Soft Soap session. I'll tell you when the client is coming in and what he or she has in mind. You tell me how you think we should photograph the subject. Then when you show me your prints, I'll tell you what I think—good or bad."

Brown replied, "You've got a deal. I'm feeling better already. I know tomorrow's photographs will be fine."

SUMMARY

This chapter attempted to help you understand the importance of the employees' personalities. We started off by looking at specific theories on how personality is developed: Freudian views, learning theory, and trait approaches. Next we described the nature versus nurture controversy, a controversy that can never be fully resolved. We then discussed some of the specific types of traits that organizational researchers have studied, specifically, the Type A/Type B dichotomy, Machiavellianism, and locus of control. Finally, we discussed the problems of prejudice and discrimination.

HUMAN RELATIONS APPLICATIONS

Conclusion 1: Many times people are unaware of the underlying reasons for their behavior.

Application: An effective supervisor tries to help employees to become aware of the reasons behind their behavior so that they can work in more productive ways.

Conclusion 2: Personality is formed by the interaction of genetic characteristics and learning experiences.

Application: To facilitate high levels of employee performance, organizations must spend time to develop valid selection devices and effective training methods. Selection instruments are used to hire or promote individuals with those personality traits found to predict high levels of performance. Training can be used to help change employees' behavior patterns to fit organizational needs.

Conclusion 3: A number of personality characteristics have been found to be related to on-the-job behavior.

Application: Supervisors should understand such traits as the Type A personality, Machiavellianism, internal locus of control, and prejudice in order to better match employees with job requirements and demands.

DISCUSSION QUESTIONS

1. Describe the similarities and differences among Freudian, learning, and trait views of personality development.
2. Do you feel that we are born with certain personality traits or that one's personality is molded by learning experiences? Defend your viewpoint.

3. What is Machiavellianism? Do you think it is ethical for organizations to develop training programs to teach this trait? Why or why not?

4. Describe the relationship between prejudice and discrimination. What actions can top management take to prevent discrimination from occurring?

NOTES

1. R.A. Baron, *Behavior in Organizations.* Boston: Allyn & Bacon, 1983, p. 98.

2. J.C. Quick and J.D. Quick, *Organizational Stress and Preventive Management.* New York: McGraw-Hill, 1984, p. 65.

3. P.J. Andresani and C. Nestel, "Internal-External Control as a Contributor to and Outcome of Work Experience," *Journal of Applied Psychology* 61 (1976), pp. 156–165.

4. A.L. Johnson, F. Luthans, and H.W. Hennessey, "The Role of Locus of Control in Leader Influenced Behavior," *Personal Psychology* 37 (Spring 1984), pp. 61–75.

5. F.L. Geis and T.H. Moon, "Machiavellianism and Deception," *Journal of Personality and Social Psychology* 41 (1981), pp. 766–775.

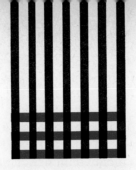

COMMUNICATION AND PERCEPTION

CHAPTER 3

ON THE JOB . . .

EVERYBODY TALKS ABOUT COMMUNICATION, BUT THEY'RE STILL CONFUSED

THE PROCESS OF COMMUNICATION

    How Does Communication Happen?
    Patterns of Communication

PROBLEMS OF COMMUNICATION

    Perceptual Barriers
    Physical Barriers
    Semantics
    Sociopsychological Barriers

EFFECTIVE COMMUNICATION

    Message Sending
    Listening and Receiving
    Staying Alert to Nonverbal Communication
    Encouraging More Effective Communication

    ON THE JOB REVISITED . . .

SUMMARY

HUMAN RELATIONS APPLICATIONS

DISCUSSION QUESTIONS

NOTES

MANAGERIAL DIALOGUE: Peter Storer

ON THE JOB . . .

When Hugh Dickson graduated from college with his computer science degree, he couldn't wait to go to work for Big Orange Computers, an unconventional chain of computer retail stores. During his last semester, Dickson had talked with John Gentry, a Big Orange regional sales manager and college recruiter. Gentry told Dickson that if he joined Big Orange he'd be working for the most idealistic computer retailer around. The company had special discounts for students, teachers, and senior citizens. Each store offered the services of a "computer counselor" who followed each customer home, helped the customer set up the computer, and then provided several hours of free training.

Most important of all was the Big Orange policy: if a customer's computer stopped working during the first year, Big Orange would replace the computer for free, no questions asked. The defective computers, once repaired, were donated to schools or other needy organizations. As a result of these well-publicized policies, Big Orange had risen to become the third largest computer retail chain in the country.

"When you work for Big Orange, you're working for a company that really cares about its customers," Gentry had told Dickson. "If you care about people and how they can use computers, we want you to work for us. If you're not truly a people person, we don't want you—go work for our big competitors."

Dickson became a sales trainee for Big Orange that summer. He completed the company's six-week sales training school in California, then went to work as a salesperson for the Big Orange store in his hometown. Dickson worked hard and sold a lot of computers his first month. All was going well until he met the store's owner at a company-sponsored party.

"Glad to meet you, Hugh," said Lowry West, the store owner. "I hear you've already beaten your quota for the first month. That's good work. Just make sure that nobody checks the serial numbers of the computers too closely, we don't want any of our customers finding out they're buying broken down machines instead of the new ones they order," West added with a smirk.

Dickson didn't enjoy the rest of the party. In fact, he hardly slept that night thinking about West's remarks. In the morning as he drove to work, Dickson was still unsure of his course of action. If you were Dickson, what would you do?

EVERYBODY TALKS ABOUT COMMUNICATION, BUT THEY'RE STILL CONFUSED

Members of business organizations often feel cast adrift in a sea of communication—endless memos, garbled telephone communiqués, letters to interpret and answer, and face-to-face messages from superiors and subordinates. There seems to be little argument that corporate communications are in a state of some disrepair and that managers increasingly are faced with the imperative of improving channels of communication or sinking into the wreckage of misunderstood messages.

The way we perceive the world and communicate in response is based on the simple process of observing, sending, and receiving. When the barriers to perceptual problems and the principles of good communication are understood, people are in a much better position to make sense out of their daily information barrage. This chapter will look at some of the following issues:

What is the problem with traditional communication systems in the organizational hierarchy?

How does an "open door policy" encourage communication?

Why do psychologists find the major barrier to effective communication at the receiving end?

What do sociopsychological problems contribute to faulty communication?

What makes a good communication?

What are some of the perceptual problems that occur to prevent effective communication?

To what extent should people rely on informal communication patterns?

At a time when many corporations are striving to improve their communication systems, these questions merit immediate and careful consideration.

THE PROCESS OF COMMUNICATION

Communication has taken on so much importance that few of us fail to understand the meaning of the term. *Communication* is basically the process of transmitting and receiving information. From the human relations viewpoint, communication is perhaps the major goal of every chapter in this book. To be productive, a corporation needs cooperation from every one of its members. They need to know the organization's goals, its rules, and its regulations. They need to be motivated, to feel a sense of participation. They must coordinate their work with that of colleagues, superiors, and subordinates. All of these tasks require constant, effective, and clear communication.

"Communication is basically a process of give and take."

How Does Communication Happen?

In the first step, we become aware of some environmental stimulus. We interpret the stimulus and then decide on the appropriate way of responding or communicating. This initial process is called *perception*. After we have interpreted a particular stimuli, we *formulate* a message about it. This message is then sent through a channel of communication to the recipient. He or she *decodes* the message, which then becomes another stimulus and starts the whole process over again.

Figure 3.1 shows the steps involved in one such process. Ann, a supervisor, observes that one of her employees, Dave, is late for work again. She interprets this stimulus as indicating that Dave doesn't care much about his job. As a result, she develops the idea for a message to Dave to convey her feelings. She then transmits the message directly to her subordinate: "If you're late again, I'm going to put a record of it in your personnel file, Dave." Dave decodes the message to mean that Ann wasn't considerate enough to ask him for an explanation of his lateness. Dave's decoding of the message is the start of a new perceptual process. If Dave decides to respond to Ann, he will go through the same steps and two-way communication is achieved.

The communication between Ann and Dave was neither clear nor effective. Ann leapt to an unwarranted conclusion about Dave's feelings, and her subsequent remark was based on this conclusion. Instead of telling Dave that she was upset by his constant tardiness, Ann issued a threat based on her assumption that the lateness meant that Dave didn't care about the job. Dave responded to the threat by interpreting it as hostility rather than a supervisor's natural concern about productivity. Dave received a message—"Ann is trying to be tough on me"—that Ann didn't intend to send. Meanwhile, the message Ann wanted to send—"Your tardiness is too frequent"—was ignored, and the chances are good that this misunderstanding is about to go from bad to worse, as Dave feels defensive and reacts angrily.

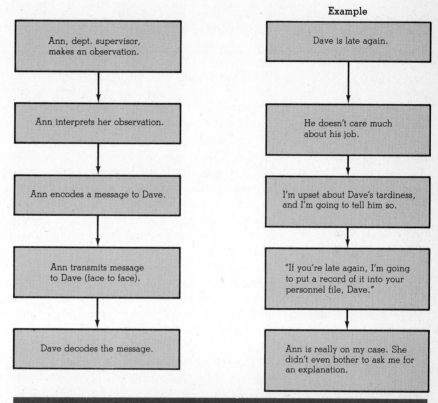

Example

Ann, dept. supervisor, makes an observation.	Dave is late again.
Ann interprets her observation.	He doesn't care much about his job.
Ann encodes a message to Dave.	I'm upset about Dave's tardiness, and I'm going to tell him so.
Ann transmits message to Dave (face to face).	"If you're late again, I'm going to put a record of it into your personnel file, Dave."
Dave decodes the message.	Ann is really on my case. She didn't even bother to ask me for an explanation.

FIGURE 3.1   The Perception/Communication Process

Any act of communication is really a two-way relationship between the sender and the receiver. Bosses cannot give a command unless they have a subordinate who is able to receive it. People often view the channels of communication as a top-to-bottom hierarchy of command, but in fact, for every communication sent downward, there is a reaction sent back up. Moreover, a large number of communications always bypass the best-planned theoretical organizational charts.

Patterns of Communication

Communication in a business organization can be either formal or informal. Most management training concentrates on formal communication, but informal communication can be just as powerful an influence on the well-being of an organization and the people who work in it.

Formal communication.   The two-way circle model of communication seems the most applicable to formal communication within the business organization. This model includes the typical hierarchy of authority, yet it assumes that interaction occurs between each link in the chain. In other words, an open channel of interaction exists between line worker and foreperson; foreperson and superintendent; superintendent and plant manager; plant manager and board of directors. Of course, there may be individual variations in the pattern. People, unlike charts they are placed on, often do not behave in an organizationally approved way, but communications commonly follow the prescribed pattern.

A corporation's board of directors may recommend on the basis of a report, that a certain alloy be used in the production of steel parts. The board will pass this information to the purchasing agents and inform plant managers as well. The managers, in conjunction with their subordinates in engineering, production, sales, and public relations, carry the information to its final conclusion—a change in production. The traditional downward chain of communication is a result of the delegation of authority and responsibility in the creation of a formal organizational structure. In its most simplified state, a supervisor simply says to an employee, "Here's what I want done. Here's how to do it. Now do it."

The obvious disadvantage of a strictly downward-oriented channel of communication is that it assumes that one person will talk and the other merely listen. The lack of feedback can make it hard to correct mistakes and misunderstandings. This authoritarian type of communication can lead to dissatisfaction and resentment on the part of subordinates. On the other hand, a tightly knit formal delegation of authority from top to bottom is sometimes a very effective means of coordination, so long as each member in the overall linkage is sufficiently motivated to perceive and carry out his or her assigned task. If this is the case, then the organization has a direct and immediate way of relaying information to each level of employment.

Formal organizational charts may also provide a way for information to travel between equally ranked individuals or groups in order to ensure coordination. The head of production is generally in close contact with the head of sales, so that each person can balance supply with demand, and the head of sales, in turn, is in close touch with the accounting department to ensure that prospective clients can pass credit checks. Yet much of the horizontal communication within a company takes place informally rather than formally.

Informal communication.   Employees who have no obligation to communicate with one another on the job may do so for purely personal

> *"The typical organizational chart draws a picture of a downward communication process in which the boss is the sender and the subordinate is the receiver."*

reasons. For example, the head of the personnel department and the head of public relations might happen to commute on the same train or car pool. Even though these two executives have little formal communication, they may relay much information through their after-hours contact. Suppose, for instance, that the personnel director tells the public relations head that large numbers of assembly line workers will soon be laid off. This information may serve as a clue that certain products will be dropped from the line, and the public relations head may thus begin outlining a program to handle the change before he hears about it officially.

This informal communication is often called the *grapevine*. The basic reasons for informal communication have been studied from a variety of cultural, social, historical, and psychological perspectives, and it boils down to this: people at all levels of employment need to communicate with one another on more than just a work-related level. For that reason alone, communication takes on a multidimensional form. An example of a grapevine at work is diagrammed in Figure 3.2.

Upward communication. In response to the inclination of workers to seek communication in many directions, organizations may set up formal channels whereby workers can communicate upwardly. Thus, information that otherwise would have been confined to informal channels can be used to aid the organization.

One form of upward communication is called an *open door policy.* This policy theoretically allows an employee to bypass his or her supervisor and communicate directly with a higher, more influential managerial official. Other forms of upward communication include suggestion boxes, labor-management councils, and other mutual consultative programs.

When workers have grievances, upward informal communication typically makes that known long before the union formally contacts its managerial counterparts. Although we often think of the grapevine as conveying distorted information, this actually is not the case. One study found, for example, that over 82 percent of such information is accurate.[1] For instance, suppose the employees in one department of a large corporation feel that their hourly quotas have been unfairly increased. These workers air their discontent to the foreman. At lunch he may mention their reaction to the new quotas to his immediate supervisor, who in turn will meet with the plant manager in conference later that afternoon. By the time union officials meet with the personnel director to protest, management may be prepared to negotiate a compromise or alternative rating system. It is common to find that many communications travel faster through informal channels.

"The grapevine is not only very active, it is also astonishingly accurate."

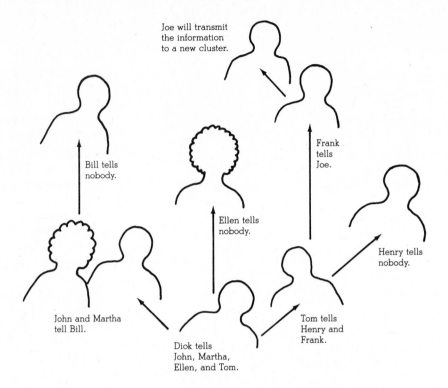

Joe will transmit the information to a new cluster.

Bill tells nobody.

Frank tells Joe.

Ellen tells nobody.

Henry tells nobody.

John and Martha tell Bill.

Dick tells John, Martha, Ellen, and Tom.

Tom tells Henry and Frank.

The Organization Grapevine Operates in Clusters Rather Than a Straight Line

FIGURE 3.2 The Grapevine at Work

The grapevine will always exist because it is based on personal relationships within the organization. Personal relationships are sometimes based on joint membership in some other organization or group, or they may stem from common membership in the same minority ethnic group, racial group, or religious group. They may also come into being between dating partners, relatives, or neighbors. Finally, close relationships can occur because of personal preferences based on work capacity; for example, an employee may bypass formal channels because she feels that the person designated to handle the problem is not as able as another person who is not in the direct chain of command.

PROBLEMS OF COMMUNICATION

Communication and its associated problems require a multidimensional outlook. In this section, we will examine four general problem areas: perceptual issues, physical issues, semantic issues, and sociopsychological issues. Each may be linked to the others.

Perceptual Barriers

Most of us automatically assume that our view of reality is accepted by others. After all, we believe that these are the *facts*. We "know" our boss is a lousy manager or that the company will move to New Jersey next year or that the new automated tellers have too many bugs. Frequently, however, it turns out that other people don't agree. Someone else in the department thinks your boss is a poor communicator, but a great organizer and canny entrepreneur, and thus rates her effectiveness more highly than you do. Your friend down the hall is certain the company is not moving to New Jersey, but to a cheaper building in Manhattan because he places a different interpretation on the memos that have circulated and the bits of evidence that have been fed into the grapevine. Someone in the accounting department "knows" the automated tellers have been a success because they've already paid for themselves in increased transactions, and the accountant is not impressed by your knowledge of the high level of customer complaints.

"What we are sure we 'know' is just our personal version of reality."

To prevent such problems, it helps to understand some of the more common barriers to agreement about perceptions. We will discuss three of these barriers: selective perception, stereotyping, and self-fulfilling prophecies.

Selective perception.   Those of you who have had the experience of living in a college dormitory probably have become very adept at *selective perception,* which is the tendency to listen to selected parts of a message and block out other information. When you study in a crowded, noisy dormitory, you learn to block out much of the commotion in order to concentrate. Sometimes selective perception is necessary to deal with the environmental stimuli that continually bombards us, but it can also block out important information.

A practical illustration of this problem can be seen in the following example. How many F's do you count in the following phrase?

> *Fouled up files are the result of foolish neglect, and finished files are the result of scientific study coupled with the experiences of many years.* [2]

You should have counted a total of nine F's. Most people, however, ignore the three F's in *of* because they have unconsciously assumed that all F's will be at the beginning of words, not the end. Once the reader decides that only first letters are important, that's all he or she will perceive.

Selective perception can lead to problems in communication. Since perceptions are shaped by experience and educational background, organizations are usually filled with employees who have enormous differences in their selective perspectives. Research and development employees, for example, tend to focus on innovations in product design. Production managers focus on monitoring costs and production schedules. Such differences between these functional areas in terms of the types of things they each believe are important or unimportant can lead to major communication difficulties.

Stereotyping.   Another type of perceptual barrier to effective communication occurs when we form judgments about people based on impressions we have about a group to which they belong. Such impressions are called *stereotypes.* Stereotypes may be generally accurate. For example, the stereotype that a black employee earns less than a white employee is supported by current statistics, which means it applies to the majority of cases; it is the average. A problem occurs when we move from that fact-supported generalization to the next step of believing that it must apply to everyone: *every* black employee is poorer than any white employee. That belief is inaccurate and offensive.

Stereotypes cause problems when either of two mistakes is made: (1) ignoring that there are individual differences within a group (e.g., believing that all men have lower verbal skills than women) or (2) holding faulty beliefs about the characteristics of an entire group (e.g., all professional football players are rich). Because of these problems we sometimes ignore the uniqueness of individuals. This creates a bias in the way we respond and communicate with them. Stereotypes with respect to race, sex, age, and physical characteristics can often have disastrous effects in the form of discrimination in organizations.

Self-fulfilling prophecies.   A *self-fulfilling prophecy* occurs when people behave in the manner that they believe is expected by others. A new, very young assistant is hired by the personnel department on the basis of her excellent skills, but the person she will work for takes one look at her and decides she is too immature to behave responsibly. At first the assistant will struggle to prove herself. She will offer to work late to finish an important job, to which her boss will sarcastically say, "Oh, I couldn't ask you to give up your big date." She is careful to restrict her personal phone calls, but when her boss hears her calling another employee by her first name, he jumps to the conclusion that she's talking to a friend rather than transacting business with a colleague and reprimands her for wasting time. If the assistant stays with such a boss, the chances are good that she will stop trying hard to act professional and start acting like the immature person he believes her to be.

A supervisor's expectations about employees can have major effects on their behavior. Earlier in the chapter we discussed an interaction between a supervisor, Ann, and her employee, Dave, who came in late. Ann's interpretation of Dave's behavior (e.g., "He doesn't care about his job") could very well lead to a self-fulfilling prophecy. Dave will begin to understand this perception and believe that it is useless to try to change his supervisor's mind by making a greater effort to be on time. The situation may then lead to other behaviors on Dave's part that reinforce Ann's idea that he no longer cares about his work.

Ideally, we should all form positive expectations about our co-workers, so that they will be encouraged to live up to them. However, few of us are capable of such ideal behavior. When something goes wrong, we tend to jump to the conclusion that someone else is careless or inept or unable to handle the work load. These assumptions all to often become self-fulfilling prophecies, but if you understand the problem, you can often interrupt the cycle.

Physical Barriers

"Sometimes the physical barriers between senders and receivers are so great they prevent communication."

At the heart of many communication problems is the unalterable fact that societal and business-related organizations have become increasingly large and diffuse. Ford Motor Company started as a centralized organization, wherein every part for the production of automobiles was relegated to other companies in the same general area. Today Ford has assembly plants in many countries and has diversified production and investments far beyond its original function of manufacturing passenger cars.

With expansion, many corporations find themselves faced with basic physical communication problems stemming from environmental factors that limit or prohibit effective information flow. The most obvious barrier is geographic distance. Even with advanced coast-to-coast or transcontinental telephones and data banks, the organization suffers

JUST PHONE MY COMPUTER

Gordon Matthews is a tall, trim Texan with eclectic tastes—fine wine, classical music, and the Dallas Cowboys. An inventor and entrepreneur, he has been described as "a technical Renaissance man." One day in 1978, however, he found himself up to his neck in trash.

At the time, he was senior vice-president of Action Communications Systems—a company he had founded—and he was visiting a plant owned by one of his customers, Johns-Manville Corp. (now called *Manville Corp.)* "I spotted a trash bin, maybe 10 feet long, 3 feet wide, and 5 feet deep," he recalls. "It was full of memos and letters. I don't normally go through trash bins, but I did that day." Each piece of paper, he realized, had cost Johns-Manville about $8. Then, after performing its function, the scrap had promptly been thrown away.

As he stood there amid the trash, he was struck by the waste and inefficiency of most methods of corporate communication, especially telephone calls. "I was never able to reach people when I needed them," he says. "I thought, if I could design a computer that you could call from any telephone in the world, at any time, and send voice messages to anyone you wanted to . . . that would be a neat system."

Now, five years later, voice messaging—also known as electronic voice mail—accounts for sales of some $20 million to $30 million per year, with analysts predicting a $1-billion market before the end of the decade. The leader in the field is VMX Inc. (the letters stand for voice message exchange), headed by Gordon Matthews.

Meanwhile, all kinds of companies have been discovering that voice messaging can save them time and money. As is generally the case with new office automation, major corporations including

3M, Corning Glass Works, American Express, and Westinghouse Electric were the first to benefit. Lately, however, smaller businesses have begun using voice messaging as well. Some have set up their own in-house systems; examples include Bain & Co., management consultants, and Infotron Systems Corp., a data-communications company. In addition, service bureaus are springing up in cities from Atlanta to Los Angeles, allowing other small businesses—such as Chicago Tube & Iron Co.— to take advantage of voice messaging without having to shoulder the hardware costs, which average about $300,000.

Voice messaging works by transforming a computer into what is, in effect, the cleverest and most versatile answering machine imaginable. By dialing a special number, a caller can leave a message up to three minutes in length for any other person on the system; the caller's voice, digitally recorded by the computer, can be retrieved by the recipient at any time. Using a variety of touch-tone instructions, callers or recipients can get messages to do everything short of turning cartwheels. The computer can be directed to deliver the message at a given time, date, and place (". . . To Mr. Jones at his Los Angeles office, on Wednesday at 1 p.m. . . ."), or to alert an entire department (". . . For everyone in sales . . ."). A message can be edited, added on to, and rerouted (". . . Bob, I thought you might want to hear what Bernie had to say about the ROI . . ."). Like a taped message, an electronic voice message can be run in reverse, stopped, saved, or erased.

The advantages are enormous. Communication takes place the first time, every time. Unlike electronic mail, which requires keyboards and modems, all you need is a telephone. Time zone differences become irrelevant. (One multinational uses voice messaging to deliver its New York–generated telephone correspondence to its San Francisco office after 11 P.M., minimizing long distance charges.) A call-answering option allows outsiders—a company's customers, for example—to leave messages (but not to retrieve them). What is more, the entire system is simple, unthreatening, and unobtrusive.

The disadvantages are minimal, according to people who use voice messaging. Messages cannot (as yet) be indexed, which would make scanning them easier, and there is no hard-copy printout.

John Hynes, project manager of telemarketing development for Hoffmann-LaRoche, the pharmaceutical giant, pays voice messaging the supreme compliment: He does not talk about it.

He believes that the less his competitors know, the better. The company now uses voice messaging as "the primary line of communication" for its 1,800 employees, 80 percent of them in sales. "The overall productivity on the part of the people has increased," Hynes observes cryptically, declining to reveal the specific figures.

Smaller companies find the system no less appealing, although most remain with a service bureau for economic reasons. Says an account executive with a public relations firm, "We're a service industry, but I can go out of town, and my clients won't even know that I'm not around . . . which is great."

Source: *Inc.* (November 1983), pp. 44–45. Reprinted by permission. Copyright © 1983 by INC. Publishing Company, 38 Commercial Wharf, Boston, MA 02110.

from time lags and information disorder. As the box on pages 74–75 shows, one entrepreneur has jumped in to offer a solution.

Part of this problem is a result of the less personal nature of any organizational network, where face-to-face contacts are not always possible. However, as we shall see in the following section, even close contact between organization members does not remove all of the pitfalls in a communicative process.

Semantics

Semantics is the science of word meaning. Words are symbols, and many communication problems arise when people interpret these symbols differently. For instance, suppose a person meets an old classmate and exclaims in happy surprise, "Harry, you dirty dog!" In this context, the word *dog* has positive connotations, implying perhaps that Harry is a likeable rogue. However, if the two men discuss a new car on the market and agree that the car "is a real dog," then the meaning is quite different. Language and the way it is employed are often very subjective. Even people who are fairly skilled at sentence structure and word meanings may sometimes find that other people misconstrue their messages. Part of the problem is due to the diversity of language. There are at least twenty-eight separate meanings for each of the 500 most-used words in the English language. A word like *dog* can refer to an animal, a personal characteristic, someone's physical appearance, a weather condition, or any of several other definitions.

Much of the communication within an organization is oral. One study noted that top-level executives typically spend 75 percent of their work day in oral communications.[3] In addition, managers must deal directly with superiors and subordinates. The interpretation of their messages will be largely dependent on the education and ethnic or regional origin of their listeners. They should not convey messages in a manner either too far above or too far below their listener's comprehension because either extreme may arouse resentment.

Written communication can also cause problems. No matter how clear and incisive a letter or memo seems, it cannot impart a message with all the nuances present in personal contact. Unfortunately, top executives in a large corporation simply do not have the time to speak personally to every subordinate about daily information. The speediest way to address all subordinates is by memo, but by writing memos, top executives lose the immediate reactions of subordinates. They may neither understand nor agree with the memo, but the form of communication precludes quick interactions.

Moreover, the actual contents of a letter or memo often serve as a barrier to effective communication. One common problem can be found in wording. Writers sometimes use technical words or jargon that they understand but that may be unfamiliar to many of their readers. The sheer number of words in a letter also may act as a barrier. People sometimes mistakenly assume that if they write long messages, the message will contain more meaning, while the opposite is usually true. A wordy communiqué is more apt to be confusing and dull than a concise, clearly worded form.

"The best form of communication is always short and direct. More words may just add more confusion.

Sociopsychological Barriers

One major theme in communication studies is that a good listener is a major necessity of good communication. Listening seems like a simple task, even a passive state, yet several emotional and social factors can intervene to block proper receiving. According to psychotherapist Carl Rogers, one problem is the tendency to evaluate. He states, "The major barrier to mutual interpersonal communication is our very natural tendency to judge, to evaluate, to approve (or disapprove) the statement of the other person or the other group."[4]

People in business organizations make business-related decisions from information passed on to them by other people. Although none of us is capable of always acting as dispassionate receivers, without careful listening, we sometimes miss the content of speech altogether. If one communicates about a subject that arouses strong feelings, it's even more likely that listeners will be distracted from careful listening by their tendency to evaluate what they think they are hearing. A casual observer can plainly see that when two people are engaged in a heated argument, neither party is listening to what the other is saying. In fact, such debates often deteriorate into shouting matches, with each person attempting to drown out the other person's speech. The communicative process of sending and receiving information is completely lost. In a lesser sense, many of our day-to-day encounters take on features of argument or debate. The tone usually is not so hostile, but if the topic engenders emotions, we tend to be more interested in convincing than in listening.

This argumentative means of communication formerly was considered an appropriate form of downward communication. According to the traditional managerial concept, the main objective in communication was for Supervisor A to convince Subordinate B that Viewpoint C was correct. The problem inherent in this outlook was that the subordinates were not always willing to accept a manager's solutions. This conflict can lead to a chain reaction of negative feelings and blocked communications. When A approaches B with an idea, A is naturally certain that his reasoning is correct. If B objects, A simply overrides his arguments. The end result of such a dogmatic approach is mutual antagonism and distrust. Supervisor A may feel that B is dense or obstinate for refusing to grasp the rightness of his reasoning. On the other hand, B probably will be frustrated at not having the opportunity to express her outlook. Over an extended period, this mutually suspicious view will be exacerbated by one-way communications and stifled responses.

"A good boss doesn't argue with subordinates. Instead, he or she attempts to foster two-way communication."

Although most corporations no longer believe that one-way communications are the best means of relaying information, they still may lack an organization-wide network to facilitate better communication. It is one thing to state that an open door policy is in effect at all levels and quite another to make it work. Employees can sense whether their attempts to relay information are taken seriously.

Despite the emphasis placed on equality in our society, we all agree that in reality people differ in many respects. These differences can block the flow of information in several ways, because personal characteristics often carry over into the work situation. Each worker brings a certain social and psychological perspective to a job. Personality traits (discussed in Chapter 2) affect people's views of their work, supervisors, and organization.

Perhaps the most important consideration for every member of the organization is that of social status. Within the corporation, work-related position usually determines an individual's social status. This creates obvious obstacles in communication. From the low-level employee's point of view, lack of status and personal worth dull the motivation to interact. The higher-status employee may realize that his or her position calls for less rather than more interaction with employees of lower status. The result of this twofold problem is poor communication.

In many respects, business organizations are a reflection of the larger society within which they exist. The use of charts, programs, and managerial training programs helps to emphasize supportive techniques. As long as society equates status and prestige with work position, however, even the most progressive organizations can only partially offset such attitudes. Even so, there are ways to encourage fuller communications among all levels of employees.

EFFECTIVE COMMUNICATION

The process of communication actually requires only three major actions: perception, sending, and receiving. Now we shall examine in more detail the processes that occur during accurate and meaningful communication.

Message Sending

The first step in any communicative process is the origin of the message. Expressing a thought effectively is not always a simple task. Some messages are based on complex, abstract ideas that are hard to verbalize in any form. Because misunderstanding by the receiver can distort a message beyond recognition, the message must be geared to the audience. The motto of a message sender should be "think before you speak."

A manager who must inform employees of a layoff or disciplinary action often finds it difficult to choose the right words. The correct semantics and vocabulary are important. Because a manager uses words—either spoken or written—to accomplish the organization's goals, it is especially vital to understand the importance of correct word usage. Tact is important too, but under certain circumstances clarity must override congeniality.

Emotions exert considerable influence on message sending. The sender's emotional state affects the message sent; a person's immediate state of mind is reflected in his or her speech and physical actions. An individual who is angry may betray a calm voice with clenched fist, furrowed forehead, or even a rather jerky body motion. All of us are at least subconsciously aware of these clues, and we react to the whole person, not just the voice. This is not to say that a message sender can, or should, mask his or her emotions completely, even if such a performance were possible. But an awareness of the part the emotions play in the overall message-sending process can be helpful in sending a clear message.

After the message is carefully thought out and encoded into the proper verbal and emotional tone, the message sender must decide on the best channel of communication. Either formal or informal channels may seem appropriate; the form used largely depends on the situation or message content. The sender should choose the proper time and atmosphere to deliver the information. If an employee wishes to pass on work-related data to a colleague, he or she should pick a period of the day when the person has some slack time. By correct timing, the message sender can be assured that his or her listener will not be distracted by noise or interruptions. The content of a message that requires concentration, questioning, or two-way planning must be afforded an adequate amount of time.

"Problems arise when a communication involves two talkers . . . and no listeners."

Listening and Receiving

The process of listening and receiving is merely one more step in the total message-sending process. Good communication relies on careful listeners who concentrate on the topic. Some of the rules of good listening are summarized in Table 3.1. One study has shown that, although most people have the ability to retain well over half of the messages they receive, they actually retain only 25 percent. Still another study charted the decrease of information retention from the board of directors in a corporation to the lowest-level employees and found that it was diluted from 100 percent down to 20 percent.[5]

If Carl Rogers's assumptions about effective listening are correct, then we can assume that when receiving messages, a good listener remains objective. The evaluative process is necessary, but a person must grasp the topic before he or she can judge it. Rogers noted that especially in emotion-laden communications, there was a tendency to send instead of receive. In such instances, Rogers recommended that each party be required to listen to the other, restate his or her immediate argument, and

> **TABLE 3.1   Ten Commandments of Effective Listening**
>
> 1. *Stop talking!*
>   You cannot listen if you are talking.
>   Polonius *(Hamlet):* "Give every man thine ear, but few thy voice."
>
> 2. *Put the talker at ease.*
>   Help him feel that he is free to talk.
>   This is often called a *permissive environment.*
>
> 3. *Show him that you want to listen.*
>   Look and act interested. Do not read your mail while he talks.
>   Listen to understand rather than to oppose.
>
> 4. *Remove distractions.*
>   Don't doodle, tap, or shuffle papers.
>   Will it be quieter if you shut the door?
>
> 5. *Empathize with him.*
>   Try to put yourself in his place so that you can see his point of view.
>
> 6. *Be patient.*
>   Allow plenty of time. Do not interrupt him.
>   Don't start for the door or walk away.
>
> 7. *Hold your temper.*
>   An angry man gets the wrong meaning from words.
>
> 8. *Go easy on argument and criticism.*
>   This puts him on the defensive. He may "clam up" or get angry.
>   Do not argue; even if you win, you lose.
>
> 9. *Ask questions.*
>   This encourages him and shows you are listening.
>   It helps to develop points further.
>
> 10. *Stop talking!*
>   This is first and last, because all other commandments depend on it.
>   You just can't do a good listening job while you are talking.
>
>   Nature gave man two ears but only one tongue, which is a gentle hint
>   that he should listen more than he talks.

Source: Keith Davis, *Human Behavior at Work.* New York: McGraw-Hill, 1972, p. 396. Reprinted by permission.

then proceed onward to state his or her own position. An emotional argument might sound like this:

> Alice: How can you expect anyone to come to this restaurant if we don't start doing some advertising? Your stinginess is ruining our business.
>
> Dana: That's a laugh! What's the point in advertising a restaurant that serves nothing but frogs garnished with peaches or peaches garnished with frogs? The problem here is your cooking!

This difficult problem of the poor business at the Frog and Peach might be discussed more effectively in this manner:

> Alice: As I see it, the main cause of our slow business here at the Frog and Peach is that we are not using advertising to attract new customers to the restaurant.
>
> Dana: You think our problem is that we don't use advertising to find new customers. I disagree. In my analysis, our primary problem is that the menu is too limited. We should offer something besides frogs and peaches.

The advantage of this pattern of exchange rests on the basis of mutual comprehension. Each speaker has to listen because he or she is expected to reiterate the colleague's message. Moreover, increased concentration and understanding on the part of the listener may lead to greater personal empathy with the speaker. Heightened understanding and empathy seem to be a natural result of good listening. The ability or willingness to stand in someone else's shoes gives the listener a deeper understanding of the original thought processes that took place within the sender's mind. It also helps the listener make a sound evaluation of the concept under discussion.

S. I. Hayakawa, a communications expert, has noted that empathy may require some courage. People who allow themselves to become involved in deep personal interactions run the risk of being changed when they enter the thought process of another person (like "Star Trek's" Mr. Spock in the mind-meld). From a humanistic vantage point alone, such a risk may seem worthwhile and could broaden one's outlook and depth. Unfortunately, managers may very well face a dilemma as empathy for other members of the organization increases. The needs of superiors, subordinates, and colleagues may conflict with the performance of one's own work role and the achievement of career success.

Improving the listening process may involve learning new skills. A number of organizations encourage employees to attend communication seminars to help them learn to communicate more effectively. Such seminars typically include exercises and hints on how to improve listening ability as well as message sending.

Staying Alert to Nonverbal Communication

Words, however carefully chosen and listened to, are only one element in the total act of communication. As the old saying goes, "Actions speak louder than words," and sometimes the nonverbal element of a communication is more important than the words themselves. *Nonverbal com-*

munication is defined as all behavior expressed consciously or unconsciously, performed in the presence of others, and perceived either consciously or unconsciously. Some examples of nonverbal communication include foot tapping, constantly looking at a watch, making eye contact, leaning forward in the chair, and moving papers around on a desk. If you go into your boss's office for a discussion of your suggestion of a new procedure, and she leans back in her chair, shuffles papers around while you are talking, and looks at her watch every few minutes, you can conclude that she is not very interested in your proposal.

Learning to understand nonverbal communication can help decipher the message that is actually being sent. An employee who says he agrees to a change of work assignment may give you nonverbal clues, such as refusing to meet your gaze or sitting in a "closed" posture with arms defensively crossed over his chest, that tells you his agreement is mere lip service. To get his genuine agreement, you will have to find out his unspoken objections and resolve them.

Of course, it is also important to check yourself to see what kind of nonverbal messages you are sending. Failure to arrive at a meeting on

TABLE 3.2 Types of Nonverbal Communication

Basic Types	Explanation and Examples
Body motion, or kinesic behavior	Gestures, facial expressions, eye behavior, touching, and any other movement of the limbs and body
Physical characteristics	Body shape, physique, posture, body or breath odors, height, weight, hair color, and skin color
Paralanguage	Voice qualities, volume, speech, rate, pitch, nonfluencies (saying "ah," "um," or "uh"), laughing, yawning, and so on
Proxemics	Ways people use and perceive space, including seating arrangements, conversational distance, and the "territorial" tendency of humans to stake out a personal space
Environment	Building and room design, furniture and other objects, interior decorating, cleanliness, lighting, and noise
Time	Being late or early, keeping others waiting, cultural differences in time perception, and the relationship between time and status

Source: Adapted with permission from Dalmar Fisher, *Communication in Organizations,* New York: West Publishing Co., 1981, page 120. Copyright © 1981 by West Publishing Company. All rights reserved.

time may send a message that is interpreted as meaning, "I didn't think this meeting is very important." Acting distracted, even when you have a lot of things on your mind, sends the message that you are not directing your full attention to the matter at hand (even though you are telling your customer that he or she is your top priority). Table 3.2 summarizes the various types of nonverbal communication and makes a good starting point for learning about the subject.

Encouraging More Effective Communications

Effective communication must start somewhere, and managers must take the responsibility for encouraging better communications. One executive who takes this responsibility very seriously is Peter Storer, chief executive officer of the communication company that bears his name. He is profiled in this chapter's Managerial Dialogue on pages 84–85.

One way in which a manager can sometimes improve communication is to restructure formal channels and allow informal channels more leeway. Organizational consent and cooperation usually limit large-scale changes of this sort, but most managers have some degree of autonomy, even within restrictive corporations.

There are a number of ways in which a manager can open up a dialogue with employees. Having and encouraging the use of an open door policy is one. Allowing employees the opportunity to participate in decisions that affect them is another. For workers to feel the need or desire to communicate formally with managers, they must believe that the topic is worthwhile. Communication channels may also be strengthened when a manager knows how to give good feedback to an employee. Table 3.3 gives several hints on how feedback should be given.

TABLE 3.3 Rules for Giving Feedback to a Subordinate

1. Be specific and give examples of recent behavior.
2. Make sure you are being *descriptive* concerning particular actions. Don't start name-calling.
3. Give feedback at a time when you and your subordinate are alone. Never give feedback in front of other subordinates.
4. Make sure your feedback is constructive and designed to help your subordinate improve.
5. Be prepared. Check your facts out thoroughly before giving someone feedback.

"A manager should be more concerned with the accuracy of a communication than with the channel it goes through."

We communicate most frequently and intimately when a feeling of trust and friendship is involved. This principle holds true even within the business organization. Thus, managers may not always adhere to the official channels of communication, emphasizing instead informal information exchanges with the people to whom they feel the closest. This deviance from the formal rule may result in increased worker participation, productivity, and morale.

A related phenomenon can also emerge to strengthen communications. By being in close touch with workers, a manager is in a position to restrain certain information, such as unfounded rumors and distortions of facts. Information may flow freely through informal channels, but its nature is often more detrimental than the slower, more truthful version within the formal communication network. A manager capable of talking and empathizing with his or her employees has opportunities to intervene, correct, and interpret the information that flows through informal channels.

Managerial Dialogue

"How important is a company's internal communications system? Absolutely essential."

Peter Storer, former president and chief executive officer of Storer Communications, Inc.

How important is a company's internal communications system? "Absolutely essential," says Peter Storer, president and chief operating officer of Storer Communications, one of the nation's biggest cable TV operators and the owner of seven television stations. "It's the only way a successful organization can be run." Storer has both a formal and an informal communications network to deal with the problems and opportunities of being in two related, but competitive, businesses at the same time. On one side of the company is the cable TV division. That division faces a highly regulated but unstable environment dominated by high capital costs, local rules that vary from suburb to suburb, and rapidly changing technology.

With close to 500 franchises scattered throughout the nation, Storer uses geography to organize this half of the company. A systems manager is assigned an area with 50,000 to 75,000 subscribers that may include one or many cable TV franchises. The systems managers report to three regional managers based in Phoenix, Atlanta, and Washington, DC. In turn, the regional managers report to the home office in Miami.

The other half of the company is the broadcast TV division, which operates in an older and more stable environment. The general managers of each of the seven TV stations report to one vice president at the home office.

Storer Communications is one of the nation's biggest cable TV operators.

"Our real problem is that we've got close to 5,000 employees scattered in groups of 500 to three people across the country," says Storer. Storer Communications deals with that diversity in two ways—a formal reporting system and an informal feedback system.

"We get profit and loss reports from everybody every month," Storer says. "In addition, we get an operating memo every month dealing with sales, programs, news, and technical information."

That flow of upward information is usually enough for the broadcast TV division, but not for the cable TV half. Regional managers meet monthly at the home office to go over profit and loss statements and discuss operations. Minutes of those meetings are distributed throughout top management. Storer Communications has put together a large policy book to guide members of its far-flung corporate world . "That's the bible for the people in the field. It deals with company cars, vacations, etc.," explains Storer. A manager of a half a dozen employees, for instance, might face a sudden personnel problem with absenteeism or drug abuse that is outside his or her normal range of experience. The policy book can provide the rules to follow in such a situation.

The company publishes a quarterly newsletter for all employees to bring them up to date on policy matters. In addition, perhaps because it is in the visual communications business, Storer produces a monthly half-hour TV show for its employees. These shows can be shown live or taped for later use. "That's proved very efficient for getting communications out fast to the field," Storer says, "and because they are visual, the shows have more impact than a written memo." While the upward communications are largely written, the downward channels—aside from the newsletter and TV shows—are mostly oral, according to Storer. An executive reading a monthly report is far more likely to call than to send the writer a note.

Storer adds, "Our downward communications tend to be 85 to 90 percent oral. We try to keep as little in writing as possible. Frankly, that's done to expedite matters."

Other types of organizational communications are important to Storer. With a sharp split between the divisions—and the fast pace of the cable market—Storer Communications must cultivate lateral communications among managers. "We have an annual meeting of the whole management staff, the top sixty-five managers, and go over broad policies. Then we have individual cable and broadcast TV meetings." In addition, informal gatherings of managers are arranged, particularly at trade conventions. "We encourage social things to engender rapport between both sides—cribbage, golf, tennis—so managers can get to know each other one on one. We have worked particularly hard on this issue of communication between the divisions. As to Storer Communications' overall approach: "Our philosophy is to keep very tight reporting and financial controls, particularly in cable, and then rely on oral reporting [to convey] what the business is really doing."

The organization, for its part, is largely responsible for encouraging the restructuring or restraint of information. Although there are limits to its capacity for directly influencing informal flows, an organization is in the position to strengthen the general communicative process by making the channels of communication clear and ensuring that they support the lines of power and authority.

ON THE JOB REVISITED . . .

Hugh Dickson wasn't sure whether Big Orange Computers was the idealistic company he thought he had joined or a predatory firm hiding behind the best public relations campaign around. Because he knew he had to believe his own sales pitch to be an effective seller, that morning, instead of going out on the floor, Dickson went into the repair section in back. He checked the serial numbers and jotted them down on a piece of paper. All the rest of the week, as he sold new computers, he checked the serial numbers against his slip. None of them appeared.

That Saturday, Teil Sweeney, the store manager, asked Dickson to accompany her on a charitable outing; they were going to give five repaired computers to a small private school that couldn't afford to buy its own. Dickson pulled out his piece of paper, and the serial numbers matched up.

"I'm glad to see this company really does do the right thing," Dickson told Sweeney. "At that party last weekend, West said some things that knocked the wind out of me. I thought Big Orange was a criminal outfit, if you can believe that."

"Oh, don't believe anything the owner says," Sweeney replied. "Didn't anybody tell you he's a joker? He loves shaking up people and watching their reactions. He says it's a relief from the constant 'nice guy' image he presents to the world. We all kid around with him, too. You'll have to learn when to take us seriously and when not to!"

SUMMARY

Communication and perception are interrelated processes. The perceptions that we form influence the way in which we communicate with others. Communication is closely aligned with an organization's success and is as important as any psychological or sociological determinants of behavior. Channels of communication may be formal, as in the typical hierarchy of authority, or informal, as expressed in horizontal communication between co-workers. A tightly knit formal pattern may be effective when each member in the linkage is motivated to perceive and carry out his or her assigned tasks. Informal communication is particularly important to the organization because people of all levels need to communicate with each other about more than work-related matters. A common informal pattern is the ever-present grapevine. Problems associated with communication may be traced to physical barriers when organizations are large and diffuse, to semantic barriers when people interpret words and symbols differently, and to sociopsychological barriers when receiving functions are blocked by poor listening and other factors. Other problems in communication occur because of such perceptual barriers as stereotypes, self-fulfilling prophecies, and selective perception. Effective communication involves both proper message sending and careful listening. Organizations may improve their communication systems by restructuring channels, encouraging informal dialogues, and training their supervisors in effective communication skills.

HUMAN RELATIONS APPLICATIONS

Conclusion 1: Communication difficulties can be eased by understanding some of the major barriers to communication flow—perceptual, semantic, physical, and sociopsychological problems.

Application: Effective supervisors know that their perceptions of reality are not always the same as their subordinates. They also realize that it is good communication technique to pay attention to semantic differences and to encourage feedback from the receiver. Fostering effective communication on the job may also require arranging the physical work environment so that employees will feel able to communicate freely.

Conclusion 2: Good communication relies on effective listening skills.

Application: Listening skills can be improved through supervisory training programs. Removing distractions, being patient and nonevaluative, and acting and *being* interested are all techniques that assist in developing such skills.

DISCUSSION QUESTIONS

1. What are the key differences between formal and informal communication networks? Which of the two do you believe is a more expedient way of conveying information? Explain.

2. Give an example of a self-fulfilling prophecy. How can this type of phenomenon be used to a manager's advantage?

3. What are the key elements involved in good communication?

4. If you were to design a training program to improve employees' listening skills, what key principles or ideas would you try to teach?

NOTES

1. E. Walton, "How Efficient Is the Grapevine?" *Personnel* 28 (1961), pp. 45–49.

2. This exercise was taken from D. L. Costley and R. Todd, *Human Relations in Organizations,* 2nd ed. New York: West Publishing Co., 1983, p. 81.

3. John R. Hinrichs, "Communications Activity of Industrial Research Personnel," *Personnel Psychology* (Summer 1964), p. 199.

4. Carl E. Rogers, "Barriers and Gateways to Communications," *Harvard Business Review* (July–August 1952), p. 29.

5. P. V. Lewis, *Organizational Communications: The Essence of Effective Management.* Columbus, OH: Grid Publishing Co., 1980, p. 146.

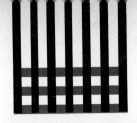

EMPLOYEE NEEDS, SOCIAL RELATIONSHIPS, AND MOTIVATION

CHAPTER 4

ON THE JOB . . .

WHY WORK?

THEORIES ABOUT MOTIVATION

    Content Theories of Motivation
    Process Theories of Motivation

USING MOTIVATION AS A MANAGER

    Job Enrichment
    Participation
    Cafeteria Incentive Plans
    Flextime
    Behavior Modification

    ON THE JOB REVISITED . . .

SUMMARY

HUMAN RELATIONS APPLICATIONS

DISCUSSION QUESTIONS

NOTES

MANAGERIAL DIALOGUE: George W. Jenkins

ON THE JOB . . .   Leo Keaton was the 24-year-old leader of a local chapter of the Boys Club in a Cape Cod town. He enjoyed his weekends helping troubled teenage boys, and he found it more rewarding than helping his father run the family's paint store.

Keaton normally arranged recreational activities for the boys on weekends, but every now and then Keaton would find various tasks for the boys to do. Just before Labor Day weekend, the town supervisor asked Keaton if the boys would work on a special project. Since the supervisor was expecting a large crowd of tourists to visit the town and its beaches, he asked Keaton if he and the boys would consider helping to clean up the main beach.

Once before, during the summer, Keaton had asked the boys to get involved in a cleanup program picking up roadside litter. That weekend, there was a low turnout of boys and Keaton had to do more yelling and scolding than he liked. The last thing Keaton wanted was to be considered a harsh disciplinarian.

That night, he talked to his wife about the problem.

Leo: Well, I've got to get the fellows out to clean up the beach tomorrow. I think they'll hate every minute of it.

Lisa: It's not the worst thing in the world. It's probably good that they begin to learn about responsibility now. After all, they shouldn't be led to believe that anyone can make a mess wherever he chooses without having to worry about cleaning it up.

Leo: Yeah, I know. But somehow I just wish I could make it even a little bit more enjoyable for them. These are good kids, and they deserve something more than picking up careless people's trash.

If you were Keaton, what would you do?

WHY WORK?

What is it that really motivates people to work well? Is it money? Status? Power? What about the desire to find self-fulfillment or self-expression through a job?

During the past decade or so, attitudes toward work in the United States have changed dramatically. In place of the "hard work as its own reward" philosophy once associated with American capitalism, we find the abbreviated work weeks and a growing dissatisfaction with the rewards of labor. This rejection of the traditional work ethic applies to blue-collar workers as well as to white-collar workers and professionals.

For many organizations, the problem of motivation is now a critical one and the crisis does not seem likely to subside within the next generation of management. Managers must search for new, more relevant ways to motivate their subordinates, and perhaps themselves as well. This chapter considers the problem of motivation, including questions such as:

What did Pavlov's salivating dogs tell us about human motivation?
What do workers consider the most important motivators?
What methods do managers find most effective in overcoming problems of motivation?
What types of people are motivated to achieve?

The primary goal of managers is influencing the behavior of subordinates in order to achieve predetermined goals. Managers must motivate their workers. This is not a simple task. A manager cannot make one correct analysis and then expect workers always to react with increased production or job satisfaction, or both. Motivating workers to do their best to achieve the goals of the organization requires that superiors closely evaluate the employees' changing response and behavior patterns. In this way they can arrive at a better understanding of the motivating forces behind employees' actions. In addition, since most managers are also subordinates in the organizational chain of command, they can use their knowledge of motivation to deal effectively with the boss.

THEORIES ABOUT MOTIVATION

How do you motivate people to behave the way that you desire? People have been interested in this question for centuries. There are lots of theories, but most of them can be divided into two major classifications: content theories and process theories. *Content theories* attempt to define the motives that drive us in organizational settings and in daily life. The works of Maslow and McClelland, for example, are content theories. *Process theories* attempt to explain how a manager can produce a motivated state in an employee. Expectancy theory, drive reinforcement theory, and goal setting theory are typical examples in this category.

Content Theories of Motivation

Perhaps the best known and most widely cited theory of motivation is that of psychologist Abraham Maslow.

"Everybody wants something . . . you just have to find out what it is."

Maslow's theory.   Maslow focused on human needs, ranging from the basic physical requirements up to the complex need for self-actualization, and he ranked the needs in order of priority:

1. Physiological needs
2. Safety and security needs
3. Love and belonging needs
4. Esteem and status needs
5. Self-actualization and self-fulfillment needs.

See Figure 4.1 for an illustration of Maslow's hierarchy of human needs. Maslow's theory implies that both psychological and social forces will produce motivation. Maslow suggests that basic physical needs (food, water, shelter) are not a motivating force in highly technological societies such as ours. Since American workers are assured of wages that will cover the costs of the necessities for survival, their primary concern will

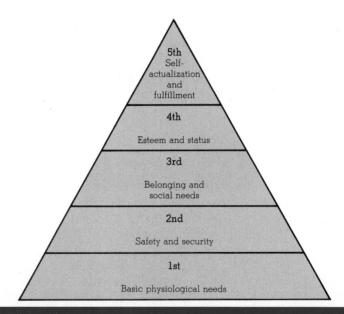

FIGURE 4.1 Maslow's Hierarchy of Human Needs

not be with these physical needs but instead with higher needs, such as group acceptance or status.

On the other hand, managers should not be too quick to discard money as a motivator. It may not be needed to meet physical needs, but many of the higher-order needs require money for their pursuit. For example, the man with status needs might fulfill them by purchasing expensive hand-tailored suits in London or having all his shirts custom-made. The drive for self-actualization might prompt one executive to join an exclusive tennis club, another to long for a weekend house in the country where she can garden and bake her own blueberry muffins. Incentive plans based purely on the chance to increase income (such as the one discussed in the box on this page) may well appeal to employees because they want to meet needs ranked high on Maslow's list.

Many employees will best be motivated by needs that are not directly related to money. For example, unionized workers have often been willing to give up raises, or even take pay cuts, to achieve job security. This need for security might be due in part to the desire for a continuing salary, but psychologists suggest that it also comes from subconsciously seeing the organization as a family and identifying the boss as a father image

GETTING MOTIVATED: INCENTIVE PLANS

A lot of people say money doesn't motivate, but I found myself grabbing for the phone as soon as it rang," says Catherine Hessinger, a travel agent who became the office quick draw when given the chance to earn a bonus. After three fiscal quarters, Hessinger added $3,000 to her salary, making her one of the top producers at Topaz Travel Inc., a $30-million company based in Framingham, Mass.

More and more companies in every business sector, including the penny-pinching travel industry, are seeing incentive plans as the key to motivation. Incentives are particularly suitable when the company's emphasis is on service, notes Mark Murray, an account manager with Hewitt Associates, a compensation and benefits consulting firm in Wellesley, Mass., who is designing a bonus system for a jewelry manufacturer's order

takers. Incentives can work well in any field, however, so long as management is clear about what sort of performance it wants to reward.

Susan Cornnell, Topaz Travel's director of agency affairs, wanted to encourage her agents to provide extra services to customers. In most travel bureaus, agents are looked upon as "maintenance personnel," those who service the accounts generated by commissioned outside salespeople; rarely are they rewarded for bringing in additional revenue. Cornnell decided to correct the imbalance. "We realized compensation in the industry as a whole was pretty abysmal," she says, "but I felt raising [agents'] salaries alone wasn't enough."

of sorts. Security thus depends on continuing to belong within the safety of the family.

No matter what type of work a person performs, personal self-esteem is important to motivation. All employees try to seek self-confidence and achievement through their work. Even tasks requiring little manual dexterity or intelligence can inspire workers to do their best if they make them feel that they are truly accomplishing something worthwhile. For example, an ardent ecologist will gladly stuff envelopes and type mailing labels at Greenpeace, because of a deep belief in its goal of saving the whale.

The social psychologist, with an orientation toward groups rather than individuals, emphasizes needs that are higher in Maslow's ranking of sources of motivation. A worker frequently tries to satisfy psychological needs through interaction with other members of the business organization. For example, one secretary might be motivated by a desire to feel accepted by others in the secretarial pool, while another might want to win praise for typing speed and accuracy.

A manager must try to understand both the individual and his or her relationship to the group in order to determine motivation and, ultimately, to increase production. For example, managers should be informed about the existence of work groups and learn their rules and goals. Ideally, they should also know when employees have formed relationships that are not based on their work. The extra dimension of such relationships—between golf partners, for instance, or fellow members of the League of Women Voters, or lovers—can create additional psychological and social motivations. These may either coincide or conflict with the individuals' work relationships.

In interpreting Maslow's theory, all organization members need to remember several points. There are always some people who rank their needs differently. An extreme example of this is the person who places creative expression before basic physiological needs; the "starving artist" is a case in point. To a lesser extent, many people show need satisfaction that is not structured according to the sequence suggested by Maslow. Moreover, one's need doesn't necessarily have to be completely satisfied in order to move on to a need on another level. An individual may forgo complete satisfaction of financial or emotional security when he or she quits one job and moves to a more challenging position that pays less.

The astute organization member should also be prepared to deal with fellow members who are discouraged or fearful about looking for satisfaction of higher-level needs. A person with a history of chronic unemployment often ends up satisfying only lower-order needs. Conditioned to struggle for mere survival, he or she can no longer conceive of employment as anything but a means of acquiring food, shelter, and security. People with limited abilities or education and individuals who have lived through long periods of mass unemployment or social disintegration may all be motivated primarily by the need for food, shelter, clothing, and safety and may never try to satisfy higher-level needs. Further, anyone who works for an organization with international connections must take note that Maslow's ranking may not be valid in all cultures. Recent research, in fact, indicates that needs may not be activated in the same sequence for people from non-Western backgrounds.[1]

Finally, in using Maslow's hierarchy, one must keep in mind that people within a single group can be at various need levels. (Figure 4.2, based

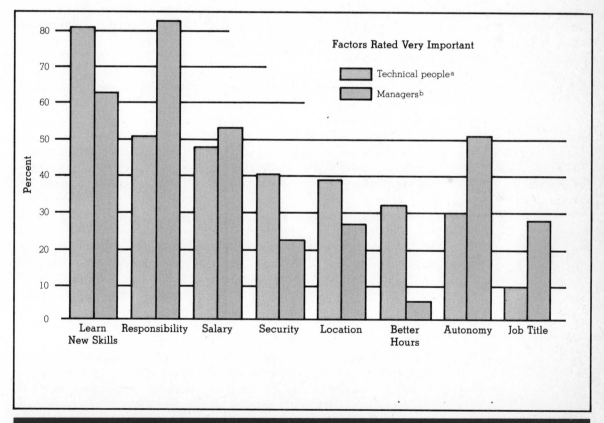

FIGURE 4.2   Priorities in Choosing a Job: Technical Innovators Versus Managers

Source: Data collected by Columbia University and BusinessWeek. BusinessWeek (February 20, 1984), p. 72. Reprinted from the February 20, 1984, issue of BusinessWeek by special permission. © 1985 McGraw-Hill, Inc.

on a recent study conducted jointly by *Business Week* and Columbia University, shows how two groups of employees—technical workers, who were mainly computer designers, and managers—differed in the types of needs they had.) One real estate salesperson may be motivated by a desire for status, wanting to handle only expensive homes in prestigious locations. Another in the same office may be motivated primarily by the need for financial security and may be willing to hustle to make any deal that will bring in a commission. This difference in motivation is a problem in their relationship as colleagues; each is convinced that the other is ruining the agency's business by working that way. Of course, it is also a problem for the manager/owner, since the two brokers will respond very differently to any incentive the manager tries to establish.

"It may be possible to teach the drive for achievement."

McClelland's theory.   Another important content theory of motivation was put forth by David McClelland. His early work and major contribution have been concerned with one particular type of need—the need to achieve.

During our educational experiences, we learn that people differ greatly in their needs to excel in particular fields: one student is content merely to pass, while another lives in fear of the B that could destroy a straight A average. McClelland was interested in studying the characteristics associated with people who seem driven to achieve excellence. To do this, he used a research technique that involved showing people ambiguous pictures and then asking them to write stories about what they thought was going on in the photos. This is called a *projective technique,* because psychologists believe we tend to project aspects of our own personalities into the stories we write about these vague situations. Another example of a projective technique is the famous—or infamous—inkblot test, which uses, instead of a photograph, a suggestive blotch of ink on paper that can form different images to different viewers.

A photograph similar to those used in McClelland's test (also called the *thematic apperception test,* or *TAT*) is shown in Figure 4.3. It's a picture of a man sitting at his desk, looking at several snapshots of children. Participants were asked to write a story about what they felt was going on in this photograph. People classified as high achievers might write stories like this: "The executive is trying to work out alternative solutions to an important product-pricing decision. Right now he is thinking about the pros and cons of some of those alternatives." Someone not particularly motivated by the need to achieve might write: "The executive is bored to death with all the paper work he's doing. Right now he's thinking that it's almost 5:00 P.M. and he'll soon be able to go home and relax with his wife and kids."

FIGURE 4.3 Thematic Apperception Test

Based on studies of the responses to such stories and to a variety of other types of experiments, McClelland found that several characteristics were associated with high achievers:

1. They enjoy being in situations in which they have individual responsibility for their actions.

2. They do best in situations that have challenging but achievable goals.

3. They need to receive feedback concerning their performance.

A TRUE ACHIEVER

Stephen G. Wozniak co-founded Apple Computer Inc., but his heart was not really in it. All he wanted to do was design computers. A self-taught computer engineer, Wozniak dropped out of college and worked as an electronics technician at Hewlett-Packard Co. in the early 1970s. A few years later, along with his friend Steven P. Jobs, now Apple's chairman, he masterminded the first commercially successful personal computer, the Apple II. "Basically, I didn't want to start Apple. I changed my mind because my best friend [not Jobs] called up and said, 'You could be an engineer and stay an engineer or be an engineer and get rich.' And I decided that was a reason for starting a company."

Money, however, is not the prime motivator for creative technicians, Wozniak claims. "An engineer has got to feel something's important or it's not motivating." Wozniak left Apple in 1981, primarily because he could no longer maintain full control over his projects as the company grew. "I need to be able to focus on one goal for months without interruptions," he says. "The company growing didn't really suit my style."

Last year, though, Apple persuaded Wozniak to return by promising him total control over new projects. His mandate: to design complete new machines and additional features for older models. He also hopes to bring back an entrepreneurial spark to Apple. "Most of the people now at Apple created the Apple III and Lisa [computers], both of which fell far short of their expected revenues," Wozniak says. As a result, these designers have become "demotivated." That happened, he says, because "engineers who are outstanding have a strong motivation to prove that they are capable and that their ideas are good."

Source: *Business Week* (February 20, 1984), p. 67. Reprinted from the February 20, 1984, issue of *Business Week* by special permission. © 1984 by McGraw-Hill, Inc.

Generally, people with such needs are found in entrepreneurial roles or positions in which they have a good deal of autonomy and control over their environment. The box on this page provides a glimpse of one such person, Stephen Wozniak, co-founder of Apple Computer.

McClelland has also been involved in research concerning two other needs: the need for affiliation (relationships with others) and the need for power (controlling and influencing others). Individuals with high needs for affiliation will do best in work settings that allow them to interact extensively with other employees and clients. They are usually very effective "team players." Although one would expect that individuals with high needs for power would be good managers, some research indicates that such needs could lead to an extremely autocratic management style that clearly is not effective in all situations. In fact, one study indicated that the highest performing companies in their sample were led by individuals with high needs for achievement and moderate needs for power.[2]

Is achievement something that can be taught? McClelland concluded that the answer was yes. Much of his recent work has been devoted to stimulating the needs for achievement in managers from a variety of cultural backgrounds. If, as he contends, the need for achievement is positively related to a country's level of economic development, then training people to become high achievers is obviously an important social goal.

Process Theories of Motivation

Unlike content theories of motivation, process theories do not try to identify or rank needs that employees consider important. Instead, they are concerned with explaining how the process of motivation takes place. How can the adept manager stimulate an employee to put forth maximum effort? There are three major theories in this area—stimulus-response theory, expectancy theory, and goal setting theory—each of which will be discussed.

Stimulus-response model. Ivan Pavlov pioneered the stimulus-response model that is now used for both objective and subjective psychological studies. Although his work generally is associated with psychology, Pavlov was not a psychologist but a physiologist. Pavlov conducted an experiment in which he measured the saliva flow (the response) of a dog in response to food (the stimulus). This famous test included first a ringing bell and then the appearance of food. The dog began to associate the bell with food, so that eventually it would salivate in response to the ringing bell even before any food arrived. However, if over a period of time, food failed to appear after the bell rang, then the dog ceased to salivate in response to the bell alone.

The *primary stimulus* in this experiment was food, but the same response of salivation could be induced by a *secondary stimulus,* the bell. Pavlov conditioned the dog to respond to the bell through positive or negative reinforcement. When the dog heard the bell, salivated, and was rewarded with food, the dog's original response received positive reinforcement. But if the dog's salivation to the bell was not rewarded by food, then eventually the learning process associated with positive reinforcement would become extinct; the dog would then cease responding to the bell with salivation.

Although Pavlov's original studies dealt only with simple behavioral responses of animals, the methodology he used can be carried over to the studies of more subjective responses conducted by behavioral psychologists. Probably the best-known behaviorist following in the Pavlovian tradition is B. F. Skinner, who devised experimental studies with animals and humans to determine the extent of what he called *respondent behavior.*

Respondent behavior is defined as an organism's reaction to external stimuli. Closely related to it is *operant behavior,* or a movement instrumental in changing the environment. For instance, a person who touches a hot stove flinches and pulls away in a respondent manner.

According to both Pavlov and Skinner, motivation is the predisposition within the individual that arouses, sustains, and directs behavior. In the business world, motivation can thus be interpreted as a spontaneous or calculated response to elements of the personal or work-related environment. For example, the distribution of pay envelopes could be considered a kind of stimulus, analogous to the food in Pavlov's experiment. Many companies pay their employees once a week so that they can continually reinforce the association of monetary rewards (the stimulus) and hard work (the response). Where workers can be assumed to be highly motivated by other rewards, as is generally the case with executives, the importance of this association lessens, so that they usually are paid only once or twice a month.

The stimulus-response model of motivation has been popularized in many companies through the use of behavior modification programs. Moreover, it has certain implications for effective management in general:

1. The key to such programs is to work with observable behavior.

2. A manager needs to pinpoint the types of behavior wanted from the workers and then to "stamp it in"—reward the behavior to give it positive reinforcement, so that the workers will repeat it in the future. Such reinforcement ideally must come as soon as possible after the behavior has occurred to make sure that employees understand what they must do to be rewarded. Waiting for six months until the next review period to point out a serious performance problem makes for very ineffective management.

Expectancy theory of motivation. The expectancy theory of motivation was the first applied to work by V. H. Vroom, in his now classic book *Work and Motivation* (New York: John Wiley & Sons, 1964). The theory views employees as rational decision makers who choose courses of action based on the outcomes expected from various behaviors. It is a choice model that tries to predict how much effort an employee is likely to put into a job.

Expectancy theory contends that work motivation is determined by the perceptions people have regarding two kinds of relationships. One is the link between effort (or behavior) and performance, while the other is

"Motivation depends on the employee's belief in a link between performance and reward."

the link between performance and reward. A motivated employee believes that a high level of effort will lead to a high level of performance, which then will be linked to rewards viewed as desirable.

Expectancy is defined as an employee's subjective estimate as to whether or not a certain effort will lead to a particular level of performance. Expectancy can be mathematically quantified. For example, it might be given a value of zero if an employee believes it is impossible to achieve a particular performance level. On the other hand, expectancy might be + 1 for a worker who felt that there was no doubt at all about achieving a particular performance target. Note that these estimates are based on the employees' own views of their ability and experience levels.

Instrumentality is the subjective estimate an employee makes concerning the likelihood that a particular performance level or target will lead to various types of work outcomes, such as promotions, pay increases, and stress. Instrumentality is a measure of employees' views of the work environment. It can quantify their expectations of rewards and punishments.

The term *valence* is used in expectancy theory to measure the attractiveness of certain work outcomes to the employees. If a particular outcome (such as stress) is very undesirable, it might be given a value of − 1. If an outcome is highly attractive, such as a promotion, it would be given a value of + 1. Although nearly everyone would prefer promotion to stress, some outcomes are given different values by different employees. For example, an employee for whom family life is both very important and very rewarding might give an outcome of spending nights away from home a − 1 valence rating. Conversely, a single employee who just ended a relationship might see that outcome as a chance to have new experiences and meet new people; thus, the valence value might be + 1.

There are some very practical implications of expectancy theory. Specifically, an effective manager has three jobs to do in motivating subordinates:

1. Make sure that subordinates believe that putting effort into their jobs will lead to high performance. Employees should have clear-cut information concerning the duties they have and the way performance is defined in the company. A manager may need to spend time training or coaching some employees to instill confidence that their efforts will lead to high performance.

2. Make it clear to subordinates that high performance in the company is linked to the types of outcomes they want.

3. Investigate the needs employees have so as to pinpoint the outcomes that should be linked to high performance levels. If money has va-

lence of $+1$ to subordinates, a monetary incentive program linked to performance targets might help in the motivation process (providing, of course, that expectancy and instrumentality relationships are clear).

The expectancy theory of work motivation requires managers to understand the needs of each of their subordinates. In some respects, it is similar to stimulus-response theory in suggesting that reinforcers (outcomes) must be linked to desired behavior (performance) in order to reproduce that behavior in the future.

"Employees who set goals for themselves need to be given accurate feedback about how well they are achieving those goals."

Goal setting.   A third process theory of motivation has been put forth by Edwin Locke. This view contends that setting goals has a dramatic effect on performance. People do their best work when they clearly understand their targets or goals.

Literally hundreds of studies have been done in recent years to determine the extent to which goal setting works in increasing performance levels. To date, four ingredients seem to be necessary for effective goal setting programs.[3]

1. Goals must be challenging.
2. Goals should be specific and expressed in quantitative terms; it is useless to say something like "Do your best."
3. Individuals must have the ability to attain or at least approach their goals.
4. Individuals should be given feedback about how close they are to performance targets.

Research studies show a high degree of consistency in results when all of these factors are present in a job situation. In one experiment, for example, a team of loggers was studied for twelve consecutive months.[4] The loggers' performance improved dramatically after they were assigned specific hard goals. In fact, company accountants calculated that in order to get the same increase in performance without goal setting, the company would have had to spend a quarter of a million dollars to buy new logging trucks. Other studies have also shown that workers are almost twice as productive when they are given a difficult goal.[5]

The practical implications of goal setting theory are quite clear. People need to be challenged by the setting of goals that are both difficult and specific. To further enhance motivation, the effective manager must provide feedback to employees to let them know whether they are achieving their performance targets.

USING MOTIVATION AS A MANAGER

There are probably as many different motivational programs as there are stars on a clear summer night. Each manager's personal view of the nature of motivation will determine to a large extent the type of programs that he or she will implement. A few of the more common programs are job enrichment, participative decision making, cafeteria incentive plans, flextime, and behavior modification. George Jenkins, founder of Publix Super Markets, offers a basic approach to employee motivation in the Managerial Dialogue on pages 104–105.

Job Enrichment

If Maslow's hierarchy of needs accurately reflects the desires of employees in an organizational setting, then one effective form of motivation would be to help employees reach their own self-actualization levels. Frederick Herzberg suggested that this could be done through job enrichment programs. Such programs are designed to change the nature of an employee's job to make it more challenging, with opportunity for achievement, recognition, responsibility, and advancement.

Herzberg distinguishes between horizontal and vertical job loading. *Horizontal loading* refers to giving an employee new tasks that are supposed to enrich his or her job but really just enlarge its meaninglessness. These include increasing the amount of production expected from the employee, adding another meaningless task to the original one, rotating existing assignments, and removing the most difficult parts of the worker's task to free him or her for less challenging assignments. Herzberg reports that all of these measures add up to zero.

Vertical loading concentrates instead on such factors as:

1. Increasing the accountability of employees for their own work. (A dramatic example of making employees accountable for their own work is discussed in the box on page 106.)
2. Giving a person a complete, natural unit of work.
3. Granting additional authority to an employee in his or her activity.
4. Assigning employees specific or specialized tasks, enabling them to become experts.

Through vertical loading, actual job enrichment occurs and increased productivity is measurable. But job enrichment is not a panacea. Some jobs defy attempts at enrichment. For example, telephone sales is an in-

Managerial Dialogue ///   *"There are many things that motivate employees other than a paycheck."*

George W. Jenkins, chairman of executive Committee and founder of Publix Super Markets, Inc.

Publix Super Markets is a 280-store chain with sales in excess of 3.2 billion dollars.

The well-dressed customer moved regally through the aisles of the elegant new Publix supermarket in Palm Beach, Florida. In the checkout lane, he complimented the cashier on her place of employment and asked her, "Who owns this store?" With a smile, the cashier said, "I do." Pointing to George Jenkins enthusiastically greeting customers, she added, "That man over there started the company, but I'm a stockholder, so I own it." This anecdote helps explain why the Publix Supermarket chain has had a high level of employee satisfaction for more than five decades. "When I started fifty-five years ago with our first store, I realized there were many things that motivate employees other than a paycheck," Jenkins says. "Things like vacations and sick pay and other benefits." Since Jenkins founded his first market in central Florida in 1930, Publix has become perhaps the best-run and most profitable supermarket chain in Florida's highly competitive retail climate. Publix now employs 37,000 workers, of whom 15,000 are stockholders. "That's one thing that makes Publix very different. The company is owned by the employees," Jenkins says.

Besides a high level of employee shareholders, Publix has done other basic things to promote job satisfaction and high morale:

Provide a clean working environment, making stores attractive to both customers and employees.

Hire more store staff members than usual, allowing employees to concentrate on doing one job well rather than trying to cover three jobs at once.

Emphasize courtesy toward customers, which rubs off on employees as well.

Promote from within. Nearly everyone on the retail side of the business got his or her start by bagging groceries.

By stressing these basics, Jenkins built a company in which employees, even those in high turnover spots like cashiers and baggers, know that they counted for something.

Has emphasis on employee satisfaction worked? The facts speak for themselves:

In 1984, Publix had sales of 3.2 billion dollars in one state alone. The company's market share in Florida is 30 percent.

Industry polls have consistently named Publix the best-run supermarket operation in the country.

Compliments come pouring in from customers, salespeople, and rivals.

"There has not been one single time in twenty years of dealing with Publix where I felt in any way, shape, or form mistreated in any fashion," asserts Tom Rice, president of a Tampa-based firm, in an interview in *Grocer's Spotlight.* "There's no other company in the United States that I have had dealings with that I can say that about." Publix is a company with traditions. Jenkins, now chairman of the executive committee, still pins on those five-year, ten-year, and twenty-five-year service buttons and hands out certificates honoring long-time Publix employees. One of those Publix traditions disappeared in the early 1980s. Publix had steadfastly refused to open on Sundays because of its founder's moral commitments and respect for the employee's traditional day off. A changing market, driven by the needs of younger, single customers, led Publix to open for Sunday business in 1983.

Yet the respect for tradition and for employee performance hasn't slowed Publix down. Quite the contrary. The 280-store chain was one of the first in the country to put optical scanners on all checkout lanes. Its new automated teller machines, which allow customers to withdraw money night and day from their banks or savings and loans, have made a big hit and reduced the labor-intensive demand for cashing checks.

Publix is now in the forefront of debit-card technology. Rather than write a check at the checkout lane, a customer can use a coded debit card and have the funds transferred immediately. It's convenient for the customer, and it speeds the cash flow into the store.

As the company's 1984 annual report states: "Today we have proved that old-fashioned values of courtesy, cleanliness, and pride in our work can be enhanced by the latest efficiencies of technology."

"There may be some negative consequences of job enrichment, in terms of level of productivity."

herently repetitive job, using few skills, allowing almost no autonomy, and having very little significance. The employee simply dials number after number and repeats the same sales script in order to sell do-it-yourself books one week and long-distance service the next. Such a job is virtually impervious to enrichment, and motivation comes primarily from the commissions earned through sales.

Additionally, sometimes cost or technological considerations prohibit the use of job enrichment. Tearing down an assembly line in the automotive industry and substituting a work group responsible for building a single car would be quite an expensive venture. Actually, Volvo attempted to do something like that in their Kalmar plant in Sweden.[6] The plant consists of several workshops in a star-shaped factory. At each point of the star, an autonomous team of employees works on a particu-

WE TRUST OUR EMPLOYEES

It is managerial hooky, known at Quad/Graphics Inc. as Spring Fling. Each May, for just one day, the entire management team of the Pewaukee Wis., printing company gets up and walks out—leaving the rank-and-file to run the plant. Workers take the controls of eleven presses, each of which is worth more than $3 million. They supervise the binding and the shipping. They handle the paperwork and deal with the customers—among them, *Newsweek, Harper's, U.S. News & World Report, Playboy,* the National Football League, and the Jacques Cousteau Society. For 24 hours, the employees have nobody to solve their problems for them; nobody to second-guess their decisions.

The tradition began in 1974, when founder and president Harry V. Quadracci was looking for a way to get his managers out of the plant for a day of strategizing and socializing. The plan was to shut down production for the day, he says, "but then some [printing] work came in, and rather than cancel Spring Fling, we decided to let the hourly employees run the presses." Just like that? "Just like that."

Quadracci enjoys comparing Spring Fling to what is known in some high schools as "senior-class sneak-out"—a day when the seniors are allowed to skip their classes in order to give the juniors a taste of life without upperclassmen. But this is much more than a sanctioned prank. Leaving 570 of his 700 employees unsupervised for a full day is, Quadracci concedes, nothing short of a high-stakes business risk. Ask him what could go wrong, and he hurriedly ticks off a list of potential glitches, as if dwelling on them would be a jinx.

In a state-of-the-art printing plant such as Quad/Graphics, where presses transform rolls of paper into magazine pages at a rate approaching 1,600 feet per minute, any slipup that goes undetected for long can ruin a considerable amount of the day's production and perhaps leave the printer with a six-digit loss. Just the "make-good" for an ad inadvertently run in the wrong edition of a magazine can cost up to $15,000. Then, of course, there is the immeasurable cost of the damage done to a printer's reputation if the blunder somehow embarrasses a customer. Quad/Graphics's mistakes have been relatively small ones, Quadracci says, but even the minor errors that no printer can escape are too expensive to shrug off. Something as simple as correcting a typographical error is often a $1,500 proposition.

Yet, year after year, Quadracci's gamble pays off. The managers meet, the presses run, and the problems are few. What is more, employee morale always seems to be better for the experience, because, although it wasn't planned that way, Spring Fling is something of a symbol for the kind of work environment Quadracci has fostered at Quad/Graphics.

"We operate on the concept of individual initiative and responsibility," Quadracci explains, "and Spring Fling gives many of our people their first chance to take the initiative—to get involved, and see what responsibility feels like. By putting the employees in charge, even for a day, we show them that we mean what we say—that we trust them and that we're willing to give them the freedom to make mistakes." Laughing, he adds, "Just so long as they're little mistakes."

Source: E. Wojajan, "Management by Walking Away," *Inc.* (October 1983), p. 68. Reprinted with permission from INC. Copyright © 1983 by INC. Publishing Company, 38 Commercial Wharf, Boston, MA 02110.

lar section of the Volvo and is responsible for their own quality control. There have been both positive and negative concepts associated with this enrichment program. Employees seem to like the concept, absenteeism has dropped significantly in the plant, and the factory produces high-quality cars. Output is much lower than typical automobile factories, however, and operating costs are much higher.

Participation

As a motivation tool, participation helps people achieve their higher-order needs. It helps workers realize the extent to which they rely on the business organization to fulfill their personal needs, and at the same time it gives them a sense of pride in the fact that the organization needs them. Worker participation is also a force for stability and orderly change. The most efficient manager cannot increase production or change employees' attitudes unless he or she has their support and cooperation.

To illustrate this point, consider an experiment carried out by a garment manufacturer, Harwood Manufacturing Company.[7] Circumstances made a job change necessary, and one group was allowed to participate in the decisions while the others were not. They were told why the change was necessary and given full information about the new requirements and price rates. The informed, more participatory employees produced at a dramatically higher rate than their uninvolved fellow workers. Turnover rates and the amount of hostility against management were inversely related to the degree of participation.

Cafeteria Incentive Plans

If we believe in the adage "different strokes for different folks," it makes good sense to design incentive programs to let employees choose their rewards for good performance. These are called *cafeteria incentive plans*. Like a diner deciding between fruit salad and cole slaw, an employee who performs well is able to choose among alternative incentives. This type of plan was tried in two retail stores that are part of a Florida chain.[8] Five steps were involved in the project's implementation:

1. *Generating lists of viable incentives.* Meetings were held between store managers and their department supervisors to develop lists of possible performance incentives for sales personnel. A final list of fourteen incentives was proposed.

2. *Developing performance targets.* Sales targets were established by analyzing past sales during a comparable time period. All target sales

TABLE 4.1   Three-Tiered Cafeteria Incentive Plan

Highest sales in a department
1. Selection of any merchandise
2. Dinner for two
3. Portable TV
4. $75 gift certificate

Midrange incentives
1. Day off with pay
2. Birthday off with pay
3. Ten gallons of gas or $15.00 worth of bus tokens
4. Two sets of movie tickets
5. Appointment as "Employee for a Day" (get picked up for work, taken out to lunch, and driven home)

Minimum-range incentives
1. Freedom to schedule own average weekly hours (for one week)
2. Coffee breaks free for one week (free coffee or tea)
3. Choice of day off
4. One-half hour extended dinner/lunch hour (for one day)
5. Assistant manager for a day

Source: Reprinted by permission of the publisher, from "EEO Alert: Watch Out for Discrimination in Discharge Decisions," by J. Klotchman and L. L. Neider, *Personnel*, January-February 1983, p. 62. © 1983 AMACOM Periodicals Division, American Management Associations, New York. All rights reserved.

figures were broken down by department, to ensure storewide equitability, and by ranges. The company decided to set three levels of accomplishment. The fourteen incentives were then arranged in a three-tiered hierarchy according to the three ranges of sales targets and their cost to the company (see Table 4.1). Employees who achieved the minimum-range sales targets over the eight-week program were able to choose one of five incentives. Similarly those employees achieving the midrange sales targets were able to choose one of five more costly incentives or two of the minimum-range incentives. Individuals who attained the highest sales level within a department could choose one of the four incentives in the top-level list or two incentives from either of the lower lists.

3. *Conducting a brief employee survey.*   Before the incentive program was actually launched, a survey was sent to sales employees in all the chain's stores. They were asked to rate the attractiveness of the various incentives and the realism of the sales goals. Table 4.2 shows how the top three incentives fared.

TABLE 4.2   Rankings of the Top Three Incentives

Rank	Marital Status		Sex		Age			
	Single	Married	Male	Female	18–21	22–30	31–50	50–Up
1	$75 gift certificate	Day off with pay	Portable TV	Merchandise at cost	Portable TV	Day off with pay	Day off with pay	Schedule own hours
2	Portable TV	Schedule own hours	Dinner for two	Schedule own hours	Day off with pay	Choice of day off	$75 gift certificate	Day off with pay
3	Dinner for two	Choice of day off	10 gallons of gas/bus tokens	$75 gift certificate	Two sets of movie tickets	Dinner for two	Merchandise at cost	"Employee for a day"

Source: Reprinted by permission of the publisher, from "EEO Alert: Watch Out for Discrimination in Discharge Decisions," by J. Klotchman and L. L. Neider, *Personnel*, January-February 1983, p. 62. © 1983 AMACOM Periodicals Division, American Management Associations, New York. All rights reserved.

4. *Launching the program.*   A meeting was held with employees to explain the program and to answer any questions they might have. Additionally, the sales targets were broken down by departments within the stores and posted, along with the incentives. It was stressed that the program was experimental, for a two-month period. Every two weeks, employees were told as usual how well they had done individually for the prior two-week period. At the end of the eight weeks, winners in the three sales categories were identified and asked to choose their incentives.

5. *Measuring performance.*   The performance of the sales employees within the incentive program stores was compared with that of employees not in the program. Average sales per employee were 5 percent higher in the incentive stores compared with prior years' sales during a comparable period.

In undertaking any type of incentive plan, managers must convey a sense of enthusiasm and commitment to the project. When the incentive system just described was launched, the owner of the chain was present along with store managers to answer questions. This meeting ensured that employees understood the key elements of the incentive project, and the president's presence indicated that he was committed to carrying out the plan. The importance of taking care in selecting rewards and performance targets should not be underestimated. If the rewards are not particularly appealing to the employees or the performance goals seem unreasonable, the plan will not provide the desired motivation.

Also keep in mind that there may be international differences in preferences for various incentives. Table 4.3 displays a comparison ranking of the importance of needs for employees representing four different countries. A ranking of 1 indicates that the benefit is viewed as most important.

The final determinant of the success of any type of incentive plan is the extent to which employees understand their jobs. Employees involved in the project just outlined had all gone through two weeks of on-the-job training in selling techniques. Thus, they knew how to achieve high performance in order to meet the sales targets set for them. In some job situations, however, employees are not certain how more effort on their parts will lead to higher levels of performance. High performance itself may not even be clearly defined. In such cases, regardless of how well they are developed and implemented, incentive plans are likely to fail.

Flextime

Think about some of the people you have worked with in recent years. Some of these people are parents of small children, some are taking

TABLE 4.3 Rankings of Various Benefits by Executives Representing Four Different Countries[a]

Benefits	Nigerians (N = 36)	Malaysians (N = 21)	Bahamians (N = 42)	U.S. (N = 53)
1. Flexible starting time	4	1.5	6	3
2. Service and/or seniority awards	3	7	3	10
3. Annual bonus	7	3	7	4
4. Career clothing	6	8	11	12
5. Merchandise purchasing plan	2	5	4	6
6. Educational opportunities and subsidies	1	4	1	7
7. Loan services	8	1.5	5	5
8. Health insurance	9	11	10	1
9. Life insurance	5	9	8	8
10. Day care services	12	10	9	9
11. Transportation and parking	11	12	12	11
12. One week extended vacation time	10	6	2	2

Source: L. L. Neider, "Cross-cultural Motivation Plans," *International Journal of Management* 11 (December 1984), pp. 5–10.
[a] A ranking of 1 indicates the benefit is most important.

classes to get a college degree, some like to sleep late, some are committed to a demanding exercise program, and so on. Flextime is one of the devices that can be used to help accommodate individual scheduling needs within the framework of the organization.

Flextime is structuring schedules so that people are able to choose their own starting and leaving times. The employee who likes to sleep late might start work at 10:00 A.M. and leave at 6:00 P.M. The individual who needs to pick up children after school might begin work at 7:00 A.M. and leave at 3:00 P.M. Usually the company specifies a core time, a period in which all employees must be present on the job, such as from 10:30 A.M. to 2:30 P.M.

One of the reasons why flextime has become so popular is that it tends to reduce absenteeism and tardiness. It helps people feel that they are involved in making decisions that affect them. It may also be associated with increases in employee performance, although the results are not clear-cut.[9] There may be some disadvantages associated with a flextime program. It requires considerable planning, which may become extremely tedious when the work group contains many people. Also, it sometimes makes coordination between colleagues difficult.

Behavior Modification

Behavior modification is an outgrowth of stimulus-response theories of motivation. In such a program, managers try to identify specific employee behaviors that they find desirable and then use rewards (or punishments) to ensure that such behaviors will recur in the future. Let's look at an example.

You are the new supervisor in a credit agency in charge of customer service calls. You have twenty subordinates working for you whose job entails answering the phones to handle credit card problems, incorrect billing, complaints, and so on. Although a job analysis has indicated that employees should be taking an average of twenty-seven calls per hour, performance has only averaged about nineteen calls per hour. Since you have been hired to increase performance, you must find a way to get the workers at least up to standard.

The first step in using behavior modification for this situation has already been taken: clearly specifying desirable behavior. We know that standard performance in this job is twenty-seven calls per hour. The next step is determining the types of rewards and how to use them in order to motivate employees to obtain this standard. A manager can use a variety of rewards to achieve the desired behavior, such as monetary incentives and contests. After you have chosen a reward or "positive reinforcer," you must then decide how to administer it.

Should praise, for example, be given every time a worker achieves standard performance in an hour? When a reward is linked to desirable behavior every time such behavior occurs, a manager is using a *continuous reinforcement schedule.* Unfortunately, employees probably would get tired of hourly praise after a few days, and it would no longer be a source of motivation. You also might forget to do it every hour, and your employees would miss the reinforcement and performance might immediately drop to a low level.

A more appropriate way to schedule reinforcement might be an intermittent schedule, in which desired behavior is rewarded only periodically. Since employees won't know when their supervisor is likely to come by and praise them for meeting standard performance, they should stay on their toes constantly. The principle of intermittent reinforcement is often used by professors who decide to give pop quizzes. Students do not know in advance when a quiz is coming, so they are likely to keep abreast of the material on a continuous basis.

Ideally, a reinforcer should be given as closely in time as possible to the desired behavior. This leads to the formation of a clear link in the minds of employees: certain types of behaviors are related to rewards or outcomes they want. Further, in some instances, it may be necessary to use a procedure called *shaping* in achieving the behavior levels wanted by a supervisor. *Shaping* is defined as the creation of new behaviors by successively reinforcing parts of the behavior until an individual can finally perform all aspects of the task. For example, when tennis instructors attempt to teach the game of tennis to a novice, they start by first praising the individual for holding the racket correctly. When the student has mastered the basic position, he or she then might be praised for successfully returning a shot. Ultimately, the individual will only receive praise when he or she learns to play a competitive game. By breaking up a complex behavior into parts and successively reinforcing these parts, individuals can learn to master such activities easily.

"All managers try to change the behavior of their employees; behavior modification simply gives them a tested tool to use."

Behavior modification strategies have been applied very successfully in a number of organizations. Implementation of such a program at Emery Air Freight Corporation, for example, saved the company hundreds of thousands of dollars per year. Other companies that have been extremely enthusiastic about the benefits of behavior modification include Michigan Bell, General Electric, and B. F. Goodrich.[10]

ON THE JOB
REVISITED . . .

Boys Club leader Leo Keaton wondered how to motivate his teenage boys so that they could accomplish the town's goal of cleaning up the beach, while having some fun in the process. When he woke up that morning, he made a phone call, then set off for the club. When he arrived, he told them, "Well, guys, today we've got to clean up the beach. Now don't make a fuss because I'm going to put in just as much work as each of you. Besides, we're going to do something different this time.

"Each of you will get a garbage can with your name printed on it. You can cover any area you choose, placing all the garbage in your own pail. Every two hours, I'm going to blow my whistle and when you hear it, come up with your pail to the beach shack. I'm going to weigh each pail on the scale, and whoever has collected the greatest amount of trash in weight will receive a reward—a pair of tickets to a Red Sox game. We'll be working for six hours, so there will be three winners. If anyone starts fighting over a piece of garbage, both will automatically be eliminated from the contest. Start when I blow my whistle!"

Ten days later the town supervisor came to the Boys Club meeting. In addition to handing out the tickets to the three winners, he complimented Leo Keaton and the boys for the excellent job they had done. He said the beach had never been cleaner.

SUMMARY

This chapter covered several different types of motivation theories and specific motivational programs. The theories were placed into two major categories—content views and process theories. Content theories are concerned with identifying the specific needs that employees are assumed to have. Maslow's hierarchy of needs and McClelland's achievement motivation theory are two examples. Process views of motivation tend to be more elaborate than content perspectives, since they try to explain the "how-tos" of motivation. Stimulus-response theory, expectancy theory, and Locke's goal setting theory are three different perspectives on the way supervisors can motivate their subordinates.

The theories are the basis of motivational programs. Job enrichment strategies attempt to change the job to make it more challenging. Participation in decision making can also be used as a motivator to increase an employee's interest in and commitment to an organization. Flextime and cafeteria incentive plans recognize the fact that individuals differ greatly in their needs and that motivational programs should be tailored with this point in mind. Finally, behavior modification approaches provide supervisors with a cookbook recipe for motivating employees. When used properly, each of these programs can be very effective. The effective manager understands how, when, and for whom motivational programs apply.

HUMAN RELATIONS APPLICATIONS

Conclusion 1: Employees are motivated by a variety of different needs.

Application: Before launching any motivational program, organizations must find out what types of motivators are appropriate for their workers. Then they can choose from a large selection of motivational programs, including flextime, incentive plans, behavior modification, and job enrichment.

Conclusion 2: Process theories of motivation attempt to suggest to a supervisor how he or she can motivate subordinates.

Application: Many of the process theories state that employees will be motivated when they understand what behaviors their supervisors want and feel certain that such behaviors will be rewarded.

DISCUSSION QUESTIONS

1. How do content theories of motivation differ from process theories?

2. Give an example of how managers could attempt to fulfill each of the needs in Maslows's hierarchy for their employees.

3. What is a projective technique, and how was it used in developing a specific motivation theory?

4. Describe how you would motivate an employee to produce at a higher level using the stimulus-response model.

5. How is the expectancy theory of motivation similar to the stimulus-response theory?

6. Using Locke's goal setting theory, explain how performance goals must be set in order to stimulate high levels of employee motivation.

7. Distinguish between horizontal and vertical job loading. Whose theory are such concepts related to?

8. Explain how you would develop a cafeteria incentive plan. What are the major conditions for the success of such plans?

NOTES

1. L. L. Neider, "Cross-cultural Motivation Plans," *International Journal of Management* 1 (2) (December 1984), pp. 5–10.

2. H. A. Wainer and I. M. Ruben, "Motivation of Research and Development Entrepreneurs: Determinants of Company Success, Part I," *Journal of Applied Psychology* (June 1969), pp. 178–184.

3. E. A. Locke, K. N. Shaw, L. M. Saari, and G. P. Latham, "Goal Setting and Task Performance: 1969–1980," *Psychological Bulletin* 90 (1981), pp. 125–152.

4. G. P. Latham and J. J. Baldes, "The Practical Significance of Locke's Theory of Goal Setting," *Journal of Applied Psychology* 60 (1975), pp. 122–124.

5. T. Matsui, A. Okada, and R. Mizuguchi, "Expectancy Theory Prediction of the Goal Theory Postulate," *Journal of Applied Psychology* 66 (1981), pp. 54–58.

6. P. G. Gyllenhammer, "How Volvo Adapts Work to People," *Harvard Business Review* (July/August 1977), pp. 102–113.

7. L. Coch and J. R. P. French, Jr., "Overcoming Resistance to Change," *Human Relations* 1 (1948), pp. 512–532.

8. L. L. Neider, "Cafeteria Incentive Plans: A New Way to Motivate," *Supervisory Management* (February 1983), pp. 31–35.

9. S. D. Nollen, "Does Flextime Improve Productivity?" *Harvard Business Review* (1979), pp. 16–18, 76, 80.

10. W. C. Hammer and F. P. Hammer, "Behavior Modification on the Bottom Line," *Organizational Dynamics* (Spring 1976), pp. 8–21.

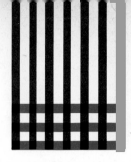

EMPLOYEE ATTITUDES AND JOB SATISFACTION

CHAPTER 5

ON THE JOB . . .

EVERYBODY HAS AN ATTITUDE

WHAT ARE ATTITUDES?

What Attitudes Do for the Individual
Opinions, Beliefs, and Values
Changing Attitudes
Three-Component Attitude Model

ATTITUDINAL EFFECTS ON BEHAVIOR

Consistency of Attitude
Attitudes and Job Satisfaction
Positive and Negative Attitudes
The Relationship Between Job Satisfaction and Performance

MEASURING ATTITUDES TOWARD THE JOB

Survey Design
Administration Issues
Survey Feedback

ON THE JOB REVISITED . . .

SUMMARY

HUMAN RELATIONS APPLICATIONS

DISCUSSION QUESTIONS

NOTES

MANAGERIAL DIALOGUE: M. Anthony Burns

ON THE JOB . . .

Stuart K. List, a steelworker for thirteen years at the Jones and Laughlin Steel Corporation, has experienced an attitude change in the past year. "I've been exposed to the company's problems, and I know if they're not solved, I won't have a job." List says. He works in a control room operating a machine that feeds coal into coke ovens. When Local 1272 of the United Steelworkers agreed to change work rules in List's department, reducing the work force from 470 to 405, List was given the added duty of greasing valves. He did not complain and said, "If I were a greaser who had been laid off, I'd have a different view."

Earlier in the year the steel industrywide labor agreement called for a wage reduction of $1.25 per hour. Just recently List received a 15 cent per hour raise, bringing his salary back up to slightly over $11.00 per hour. "I knew we had to take some cuts," List says. He is irritated by reports of employers who force wage cuts by threatening plant closings. List says, "To date J&L has not taken this position." More to come . . .

EVERYBODY HAS AN ATTITUDE

The case of this steelworker at Jones and Laughlin raises a number of interesting questions. How are employees' attitudes changed? Why is it, for example, that a worker who took a wage cut associated with doing more (not less) work seems so positive about his company? How are such positive attitudes developed?

Among other questions we will cover in this chapter are the following:

How are attitudes and behavior related?

How are attitudes about one's working environment formed?

Are job attitudes related to performance?

How can a manager change employee attitudes?

How are job attitudes measured?

WHAT ARE ATTITUDES?

Attitudes can be defined as an individual's feelings toward or against certain people, groups, situations, objects, and ideas. For example, some employees like supervisors who provide them with a good deal of direction in carrying out tasks, while others prefer working for individuals who give them much more autonomy. Such feelings—negative or positive—represent attitudes toward supervision.

Attitudes superimpose an order and structure on an individual's environment because, like perceptions, attitudes are highly selective. Our attitudes toward the dizzying array of people and situations that surround us prevent us from being inundated by feelings, many of them conflicting. We are attracted in some directions because our attitudes predispose us to like certain things, and we reject the rest because we are unfavorably disposed or just plain indifferent.

What Attitudes Do for the Individual

In a now classic article[1], Daniel Katz specified four basic functions that attitudes perform for individuals:

1. Adjustment
2. Ego defense
3. Value expression
4. Knowledge

Katz describes the *adjustment* function as the development of attitudes that will lead most efficiently in any situation toward perceived rewards and avoid most conveniently any punishments involved. If an employee with very liberal political views takes a job in a strongly conservative law office, she probably will adjust her political view somewhat to the right rather than argue frequently with colleagues and superiors. A secretary who has already learned that using a word processor makes his work much easier will quickly agree to invest his time in learning to use a spreadsheet computer program to make financial projections.

The *ego-defense* function of attitudes helps the individual maintain a desirable self-image. For example, a salesperson may ward off threats to his self-image by developing positive attitudes toward self-enhancing products such as fashionable clothes, grooming aids, an impressive car, and other visible indications that he is a competent, attractive person. In some cases, ego defense leads to projecting one's personal weaknesses onto others and thus developing an unfavorable attitude toward them, rather than toward one's own shortcomings. A salesperson whose paperwork is unusually sloppy and late may rail against the sales manager's vague memos and tardy instructions that make it impossible to know what must be done.

A third function of attitudes is to give positive expression to the external world of a person's own values. For example, attitudes of ecological concern may be expressed in choosing a job with a company that doesn't cause pollution, recycling old files as scratch paper, organizing car pools for company employees, and supporting proposals to install expensive pollution-prevention equipment.

The fourth function of attitudes is designated as *knowledge*. This may have both positive and negative effects on personal adjustment. It can lead to racial or national stereotyping because it is a shortcut to "knowing" just what the next member of some ethnic subculture one meets is going to be like. It can also serve as an information filter, making it easier to sort out what one will read and agree with and what one will reject from the abundance of news items about some controversial issue. Attitudes thus provide frames of reference for understanding the world. For example, an employee may "know" that she prefers working in a small, flexible company rather than a monolithic corporate giant. Thus, she is able to narrow down a job search to a manageable scope.

Opinions, Beliefs, and Values

Opinions, beliefs, and values are sometimes mistaken for attitudes. *Opinions* are commonly held to be the verbal expression of attitudes: "I think the district manager is doing a good job." *Beliefs* are what a person holds to be true about some object, without any particular response to the object indicated: "I believe the district manager is the first woman who has ever held that job." *Values* can be thought of as larger beliefs or ideas about what is good and correct: "I value honesty in a district manager above any other quality."

At the individual level, personal values tend to serve as an integrating structure for attitudes. An employee's global values—the generalized, enduring ideas that form a person's basic value system—will dictate predispositions toward or against certain types of bosses, co-workers, and organizations. They are also strongly held and resistant to change. For example, many women who grew up in the 1950s and early 1960s valued the traditional female roles as wives and mothers. Even though a great number of these women are now working, they feel a strong need to reconcile those traditional values with their working responsibilities. For example, they may ask for such fringe benefits as extensive maternity leave or company-sponsored day care programs, even if they don't expect to take advantage of them personally. They also dislike being treated like "one of the boys." A person who values a beautiful body highly may exhibit favorable attitudes toward exercise equipment; high-protein, low-fat foods; company recreational facilities; and revealing clothes. The more central an attitude is to a person's values, the more difficult it will be to change.

Changing Attitudes

"It can take a lot of persuasion to change someone's attitude."

Changing attitudes has become a business in itself. Long before *Madison Avenue* became a synonym for the advertising industry, salespeople, public relations officials, and even preachers and rabbis made livings from the desire of many organizations to change attitudes about their products and themselves.

A classic example of the desire to change public attitudes came in the early 1980s. After the gas crises of the 1970s, and the mammoth profits that accompanied the increase in prices, Exxon, Mobil, Shell, and other major oil companies began individual campaigns to change the public's attitude toward "big oil." Mobil scaled back its product advertising through a series of "advertorials" in major papers—advertising messages designed to look like news stories—that promoted the corporation's public record. Shell Oil began publishing consumer aid booklets that it gave away at its stations, and Phillips 66 broadcast a number of TV ads extolling its concern for the environment.

Of course, it is not always in a company's best interest to attempt to change public attitudes. American Telephone and Telegraph and the new, independent Bell companies struggled through the turbulent months of 1984 to 1985 after their long-time links were severed by court order. In their fight with new companies for the profitable telecommunications markets, however, they were undoubtedly aided by the public's attitudes toward "Ma Bell" as a reliable, technologically advanced provider of telephone service.

Three-Component Attitude Model

How do you and I form our attitudes toward life, liberty, and the pursuit of happiness . . . and the company for which we work? Any given attitude is the conclusion of a chain of thought with both logical and emotional components. The traditional approach to attitude structure identifies three components: cognitive, affective, and action tendency. Let's use the decision to go to work for Company X as an example of this structure:

First premise.   Company X offers the best benefits in this area.

Second premise.   Having good benefits makes me feel secure.

Conclusion.   I will apply for work at Company X.

The first premise is a matter of cognition. A person can obtain interviews at a number of companies to find out which ones have the best benefits. The second premise is affective; it concerns a matter of feeling or emotion. The conclusion contains a strongly implied action tendency. Since benefits are important to this person, he or she is likely to apply for work at Company X.

The cognitive component.   The cognitive components of an attitude consist of the way an individual evaluates a given object or class of objects. For example, attitudes toward an organization include cognitive beliefs about its pay structure, supervision, working conditions, and so on. These cognitive beliefs may also include certain evaluation aspects—whether the object is seen favorably or unfavorably—and prescriptions about what should be done if the object is viewed unfavorably.

For instance, an individual employee may hold a highly negative attitude toward bureaucracies, believing that they are degrading and that they undermine the intelligence of the American work force. A part of this cognitive component would be the employee's view of how to deal with bureaucratic organizations—outlawed, controlled by government regulations, or boycotted by potential employees.

The affective component.   The *affective* component of attitude refers to its emotional aspects, such as feelings of pleasure or displeasure, love or hate. The reasons a particular object, person, company, or nation may touch off positive or negative feelings in an individual are a complex blend of factors, many of which cannot be identified by the individual. Perhaps parents held similar beliefs, or teenage peers helped shape such attitudes; perhaps a book was a strong influence, or an often repeated television commercial.

The emotional aspect of attitudes is interrelated with the cognitive side. Our emotions often shape what we do or do not perceive. If we have an emotional predisposition against Japanese people, we may not be able to perceive the possible advantages of Japanese-style management, no matter how favorably they are discussed.

The action-tendency component.   The *action tendency* component refers to a person's readiness to respond to the attitude object. If an employee's attitude toward a supervisor is positive, he or she may be more willing to work overtime as a favor to the supervisor. On the other hand, if the employee's attitude is negative, he or she may consider sabotaging departmental work procedures to make the supervisor look bad. Because the action tendency component seems most closely related to employee behavior, the majority of studies probing attitude structure have focused on this aspect. But too many research efforts leap to the third component without a full understanding of the cognitive and affective aspects.

ATTITUDINAL EFFECTS ON BEHAVIOR

"In order to change behavior, you must change the attitudes that lie behind it."

Attitudinal effects on behavior are complex and require adequate knowledge of cognitive and emotional processes before sensible predictions can be made. In addition, not all behaviors are of the same complexity. A decision to take your coffee break with two friends may be easy to make, whereas a decision to switch jobs involves a great many more attitudes.

What is particularly helpful about viewing attitudes in terms of the three-component model just discussed is that it clarifies the attitudinal change process. A program designed to change only the emotional aspects (affective components) of an attitude will not necessarily alter the other two components. Similarly, one might be able to alter the action tendency component of an individual's attitude, but if the cognitive and affective components have not been changed, such a behavior change will be short lived.

Take the example of a group of employees who feel that the company is underpaying them for their services. They conclude that this is unfair. The result is that they take turns leaving early, at 4:00 P.M., while someone else punches their time cards out at 7:00 P.M. This deception allows them three hours of unearned pay and, in the minds of the employees, helps to compensate for the unfairness of their low pay. Management could try changing the behavioral aspect of this situation by closely monitoring the time clock to prevent employees from punching out for one another. The behavioral manifestations of the attitude would be changed, but would the affective and cognitive components? Obviously not. In all likelihood, the resentful employees would simply look for another way to get what they believe the company owes them. The only effective way to improve this situation is to alter all three components.

Consistency of Attitude

The three-component model suggests that there is a high degree of consistency both within the structure of a given attitude and among the various clusters of attitudes that exist in each individual. This is called *attitudinal consistency.*

It is logical to expect that the cognitive, affective, and action tendency components of each individual attitude will be consistent with one another. An employee who remains with the same company year after year (action tendency) probably believes that the company treats employees fairly (cognitive) and that there is a personal rapport between himself and management (affective.)

According to one theorist, M.J. Rosenberg, the affective and cognitive aspects must exist together in harmony for an attitude to be maintained, because no one can tolerate an inconsistency between these components. When the two are not in accord, a threshold is reached and the attitude crumbles. To reaffirm the original attitude, the cause of the inconsistency must be isolated and rejected as insignificant by the individual. For instance, if the employee we just cited should find that his boss has become surly and uncommunicative, he must either decide that a personal rapport with one's superior really is not needed for job satisfaction or else change his attitude toward his job and find a new one.

The clusters of attitudes within an individual's system also should be similar for interattitude consistency. It's unlikely that a person who drives a Subaru, resents paying a high price for gasoline, and is a member of Sierra Club would take a job with a wildcat oil-drilling corporation.

Suedfeld divides attitude consistency theories into three categories[2]:

1. Balance theory
2. Congruity theory
3. Cognitive dissonance theory

Balance theory states that an imbalance among the aspects of attitudes leads to change when the individual becomes aware of the imbalance and is motivated to reduce it. Different people may have different thresholds of tolerance for imbalance. To achieve balance in an unbalanced situation, we must adjust one or both of our conflicting attitudes. For example, if a bookkeeper hears of a good job in an area of the city she has always considered difficult for commuting, she faces an imbalance. She can make an adjustment by deciding that the job really isn't so good after all, or she can decide that it wouldn't be as difficult to commute to that area as she thought.

Congruity theory states that when two differently rated objects become related in the individual's mind, they achieve more similar ratings. For example, a previously disliked colleague may become more likeable when you discover that he shares your enthusiasm for Formula I racing or that he too thinks the new office building in Omaha is an eyesore.

Cognitive dissonance theory asserts that people perpetually strive for harmony among all their beliefs, values, attitudes, feelings, and actions. Whenever they perceive that one area is out of line with the others, or dissonant, they will modify all systems until harmony is achieved. A middle-aged accountant who wants to be thought of as a young swinger, but who cannot stand to listen to any music composed since 1975, must change either musical appetite or self-image.

Attitudes and Job Satisfaction

"Is the worker with the best attitude also the one with the best record of performance?"

Can you recall a friend who really did not like the job she held? How likely was she to call in sick? To look for another job? To waste time on the job? From a managerial perspective, the attitudes that employees hold toward their working life are particularly vital.

Attitudes involving satisfaction at work have been shown to be related to a wide variety of job behaviors. It is primarily for this reason that researchers and consultants have been interested in studying job satisfaction. In fact, one author noted that through the mid-1970s, more than 3,350 articles were published on this crucial topic.[3] Most interest focuses on how attitudes relate to job satisfaction and performance. One point of view is expressed by Anthony Burns, chief executive officer of Ryder System, in the Managerial Dialogue on pages 125–126.

Positive and Negative Attitudes

What causes low levels of job satisfaction? Is it low pay, poor working conditions, an overly nasty boss? The work of two theorists—Frederick Herzberg (whose theories of job enrichment were discussed in Chapter 4) and Stacy Adams—has been especially helpful in answering such concerns. Herzberg developed one of the more controversial theories of job attitudes and employee motivation. Studying a group of accountants and engineers, he asked them to describe situations in which they felt bad about their work. This type of research device, which asks participants to describe specific situations, is called the *critical incident technique*.

When Herzberg analyzed the results from these interviews, he found that the elements that made people feel good about their work were com-

Managerial Dialogue

"If you work hard, you get paid well."

M. Anthony Burns, president, chairman of the board, and chief executive officer of Ryder System, Inc.

Ryder System, Inc. is a nationwide truck leasing and rental company

There is a lot of talk in management circles about the importance of giving employees jobs that make them feel good about themselves. However, Anthony Burns, Chairman and CEO of Ryder System, believes that a good paycheck is still a vital ingredient in promoting job satisfaction. Burns, whose nationwide truck leasing and rental company has consistently been cited for excellence in management, believes employees who like their jobs are the foundation for corporate success.

"I think it's absolutely critical, particularly in the service industry, for employees to be satisfied with their jobs. They have to have the right attitude," Burns says. How do you create satisfied and motivated employees? An important part is good communication. "Give employees the common respect of communication," advises Burns. "Even bad news can make a stressful situation more calm. We take an attitude survey every two years— the last one found 95 percent of employees liked working for Ryder."

Burns believes that economics, advancement, and recognition are the three critical factors in motivating employees. "Job satisfaction is part of all three factors, but if one is a shade ahead, it's economics." At Ryder there is no lack of recognition of outstanding employees. Top leasing and rental agents receive yellow and blue blazers that become badges of distinction. They can win merchandise or tropical vacations. The ten best managers are recognized in annual reports and at the annual shareholders' meeting.

"That personal recognition is very important," claims Burns. "In most all communications I write, there's a thank you—and a recognition that we wouldn't be where we are without our employees."

To achieve all the honors and awards, Ryder managers and salespersons have to perform. The company has a slogan, "People plus principles equal performance," that emphasizes results.

"We have management principles that highlight pay for performance," Burns says. "First we show the objectives, then we give them incentives— and they *will* achieve them."

Ryder has a bonus system based generally on return on equity. "You know what the rules are. If you do make your goal, you get a bonus, and if not, you'll know why."

Good performers can motivate themselves, provided the company backs them up," Burns explains. "Money in our company is very important. We tailor our economic incentives to achieve goals. Fundamentally, we make a commitment as management to our employees, to our customers, and to our shareholders and lenders."

Ryder came through deregulation of the trucking industry and the recession of the early 1980s in good shape. "While the gross national product grew at 2 percent annually, our real growth has been better than 8 percent per year," says Burns. "Our employee count has gone up 2 percent a year. The difference is increased productivity." Ryder has prospered in an industry with a decidedly nonglamorous image. "A truck is a a truck—a computer is a computer. What counts is the corporate environment. It really gets down to attitude. For instance, we have clean trucks. We have new trucks. Our oldest truck is newer than our competitor's newest truck." Burns doesn't trust researchers who find that the modern American worker is disaffected and is not interested in working hard.

"I must not talk to the same people Yankelovich and Skelly talk to," Burns says, referring to the authors of an influential study about the changing nature of work in America. "I believe that may be the case in other companies, but it may also be an excuse for bad management. I believe your culture dictates what kind of employees you have. At Ryder, if you work hard, you get paid well." Burns believes a corporation is similar to a person: "It has to have self-esteem and dignity for itself or it won't accomplish its goals. IBM is the best example because it may be the best-managed company there is. I have never met an IBM employee who didn't think he was the best."

That means job satisfaction is essential to corporate success. As Burns says, "You provide quality to customers by providing quality employees."

pletely different from those associated with bad work feelings. When people felt good about their jobs, they discussed elements such as work itself, increased responsibility, a sense of achievement, recognition for accomplishments, and opportunities for personal growth. Herzberg called these dimensions related to positive job attitudes *motivator factors.* The elements that led to negative job attitudes had to do with the environment in which employees were working. These elements, which Herzberg called *hygiene factors,* included company policies and administration, relationships with co-workers and supervisors, working conditions, and money.

One of the more intriguing aspects of Herzberg's two-factor theory is his contention that hygienes and motivators are independent of one another and affect behavior in very different ways. For example, money is a hygiene factor. This means that when people are not paid well, they experience dissatisfaction. However, when employees feel they are receiving fair compensation, it does not necessarily mean they will be satisfied. According to Herzberg, money is not related to job satisfaction, only dissatisfaction. Figure 5.1 shows Herzberg's view of job satisfaction and dissatisfaction compared with the perspective of traditional attitude theorists. As you can see from these diagrams, the traditional view of job attitudes assumed that job satisfaction and dissatisfaction were simply opposite sides of the same coin. When employees are paid well, they have high satisfaction; when they are not, they have low levels of satisfaction. Herzberg's perspective is quite different.

Herzberg believes that most managers emphasize the wrong factors when they try to achieve high productivity levels from their employees. Changing company rules, increasing pay levels, and training managers to be more sensitive to employee needs may put an end to dissatisfaction, but they will not lead to positive job attitudes. Instead, companies must strive to enhance motivator elements in a worker's job. Jobs should be redesigned so that they are challenging, give workers a sense of achieve-

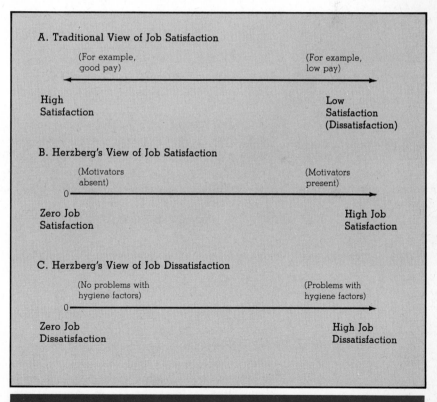

FIGURE 5.1   Traditional Theorists' View of Job Satisfaction Versus Herzberg's View

YOU SEE THE PACKAGE FROM BEGINNING TO END

Specialization has become just as boring, error-prone, and labor-intensive on a paper-assembly line in a bank as on a car-assembly line. At Continental Illinois National Bank & Trust Co. of Chicago, where there are no clerical unions, Christine Szczesniak worked for seventeen years on a check-processing line, performing one function over and over. Now she works at a computer terminal in a "modular" arrangement and performs nearly all the tasks necessary to handle checks sent in by companies that buy goods and services from some 3,000 corporate clients of Continental. "I think it's exciting and different," Szczesniak says. "It's cut down on error ratio, and that's very important for me."

Szczesniak now processes checks that arrive in the mail, deposits them in customer's accounts by computer, telephones customers with up-to-date information on their accounts, and mails the data to them. Under the automated system, each employee processes an average of fifty checks per hour, a 40 percent increase in productivity over the old approach. "I like it," Szczesniak says, "because you see the package from beginning to end. It's better to be part of the whole thing. Everyone should have change in their life."

Source: *Business Week* (May 16, 1983), p. 103. Reprinted from the May 16, 1983, issue of *Business Week* by special permission. © 1983 McGraw-Hill, Inc.

ment and responsibility, and provide opportunities for personal growth. One application of Herzberg's theory is job enrichment, a program discussed in Chapter 4. As you can see from reading the box on this page, job enrichment can sometimes have a major impact on the bottom line.

Although some studies lend support to Herzberg's two-factor theory, many others have shown inconsistent results.[4] For example, some studies have shown that salary is a motivator and thus related to positive job attitudes.

Another view of the formation of job attitudes is equity theory.[5] This theory is based on attitude balance theory and so-called social comparisons; that is, an employee compares what she puts into her job (inputs) and what she gets out of her job (outcomes) with the inputs and outcomes of an individual perceived as similar to herself (comparison person). Inputs include such things as effort, education, experience, and intelligence. Outcomes represent the reward that an employee receives for her services and may involve compensations, status, and promotion opportunities. When an employee feels that her outcome/input ratio is equivalent to her comparison person's, a state of equity or job satisfaction is said to exist. When the ratios are not equal, inequity or dissatisfaction occurs.

There are two possible types of inequity. One occurs when an employee finds that her ratio of outcomes to inputs is greater than her comparison person's. This type of inequity will make her feel guilty. In the other type of inequity, the employee finds that her outcome/input ratio is less than her comparison person's. This leads to anger and the feeling of getting a "raw deal." In both instances, a considerable amount of anxiety and pressure is created internally to reduce the inequity and put the individual into a state of attitude balance.

Take the example of Alexa and Daniel, both new M.B.A. graduates working as market researchers in the same large corporation. They have the same educational background and put a similar amount of effort into their work. Their offices are the same size, they earn the same salary, and they drive the same model company car. A state of equity is perceived by both Alexa and Daniel. Then Alexa receives a promotion that is linked to considerably higher pay and better benefits. Because Alexa's new outcome/input ratio is higher than Daniel's, a state of inequity arises. Alexa feels a bit guilty about her promotion, and Daniel is ready to explode with anger. What will happen?

According to equity theory, Alexa and Daniel need to relieve the tension of inequity. Their options might include one or more of the following:

1. Both could try to adjust their inputs and outcomes. For example, Daniel could significantly reduce his effort level while Alexa could increase hers, to adjust their respective inputs to the outcomes. Thus, each would perceive their differing status to be fair.

2. Alexa and Daniel could try to psychologically distort or rationalize their ratios. For example, they might try to convince themselves that Alexa really did work harder all the time, so that she deserves the promotion.

3. Daniel could reduce his perceived inequity and anger by leaving the company. His intentions would be to find a new job in which he would be "fairly treated" in contrast to what he believes happened currently.

4. Alexa might be able to relieve her guilt feelings by choosing another comparison person—someone who is now similar to herself.

Perceptions of inequity are seen most typically in organizations when individuals performing the same job receive different compensation levels. In such situations, inequity may be associated with high levels of absenteeism and turnover. Thus, managers need to be certain that they distribute rewards and punishments in accordance with the behaviors displayed by their subordinates.

"It is important that workers perceive the distribution of rewards as being fair."

The Relationship Between Job Satisfaction and Performance

Many managers are concerned about job attitudes because they believe there is a relationship between such feelings and performance. A happy worker will be a more productive one, or as the old adage goes, a contented cow gives more milk. This view is consistent with Herzberg's theory of job attitudes. According to Herzberg, if a manager increases the motivator factors in an individual's job, high levels of satisfaction will occur, along with high motivation and performance.

Research studies, however, have not demonstrated a consistent relationship between job satisfaction and performance. In fact, the work of Porter and Lawler indicates that the relationship between these two highly desirable outcomes may be quite different from what was originally thought. Their model is based on the expectancy theory of motivation (discussed in Chapter 4).[6] They contend that when high levels of performance are linked to rewards viewed by employees as equitable, high levels of satisfaction are likely to result. Rewards include both the types of elements Herzberg referred to as motivator factors and such things as monetary increases, better projects, and good working hours. According to Porter and Lawler, the relationship between performance and satisfaction is complex. High levels of performance may lead indirectly to high levels of job satisfaction, depending on the types and perceptions of rewards offered by the company. In return, job satisfaction indirectly affects the amount of effort an employee puts into the job. Thus, the relationship between satisfaction and performance is not direct, but rather is influenced by a number of other variables.

Although job satisfaction may not be directly related to performance, there has been consistent research showing that employees who are not satisfied with their working situations are more likely to be late for work, to be absent, and to leave their jobs for other employment opportunities when they occur.[7] However, such behavior naturally is affected by other factors as well. Job satisfaction is just one element in the personal decision an individual employee makes about taking the day off or changing jobs.

MEASURING ATTITUDES TOWARD THE JOB

Managers interested in measuring employees' attitudes toward their jobs can use a variety of techniques. Eavesdropping is an ancient method that is often quite effective, although American courts frown on wiretaps, tape recorders, and other such technologically sophisticated methods. Company informants have also been used since time immemorial to find out what employees are saying behind the boss's back.

On a more positive level, remotely placed suggestion boxes are a popular technique. If employees have a number of suggestions for improving work methods, it is reasonable to assume that they have positive attitudes. On the other hand, if there is no response to the suggestion box, that may mean any number of things, including the possibility that the suggestion box is in the wrong location.

Perhaps the most reliable means of assessing employees' attitudes is to ask them in one form or another. Attitude surveys may be conducted regularly or, perhaps, only when an employee decides to leave the organization. This is called an *exit survey.*

The more information managers have about employees and their attitudes, the better able they are to pinpoint key problems and develop action steps for dealing with them. Exit surveys may consistently indicate, for example, that certain supervisors are treating employees inconsiderately, showing a clear lack of human relation skills. Thus, managers know that it is time to consider developing supervisory selection procedures. Information about attitudes also provides a company with an opportunity to assess the affects of policy changes, the results of training programs, and the use of communication channels. For example, a firm that has recently instituted a human relations training program for supervisors will want to find out whether the training had a positive effect on employee attitudes.

The value of an attitude survey, however, depends on how well the survey is developed and conducted. Poorly thought-out surveys can cause more harm than good by yielding inaccurate or misleading information about employees and their needs. To prevent such problems, attention must be given to three key areas: survey design, administration, and feedback.

"A badly carried out survey of attitudes may actually create negative attitudes."

Survey Design

Perhaps the most crucial aspect of designing an attitude survey is to keep the questions or statements short and easily understandable. Use words that are familiar to the employees being surveyed. For example, asking employees to "indicate the extent to which management utilizes and fosters the upward communication network" probably is not the best way to ask a question about communication. A better approach would be to ask them the extent of their agreement to the statement, "My boss is always willing to listen to my ideas."

Although there are a variety of ways to format questions, the kind of scale developed by Rensis Likert seems to be among the easiest for employees to understand. A typical Likert format statement might be:

"My supervisor treats everyone the same."

1	2	3	4	5
Strongly disagree	Disagree	Neither agree nor disagree	Agree	Strongly agree

In this question, an employee selects the extent of his or her agreement with a number corresponding to five choices. The format of the questions should be varied occasionally to reduce response tendencies, the patterns that people fall into when answering questions. For example, some employees may go through the list of questions circling all 5's (strongly agree). To minimize this tendency, some of the questions should be reversed so that a 5 means "strongly disagree" and a 1 means "strongly agree." This should make survey respondents pay closer attention to the questions being asked.[8]

The questions should be tested on a handful of employees before being used for the entire group. This gives important feedback about the clarity of the questions and also provides the developer with a chance to incorporate any suggestions into the revised survey.

Because developing an attitude survey involves a considerable amount of time and expense, some firms opt to use standard attitude consultants. Two of the more popular of these are the Job Descriptive Index (JDI) and the Minnesota Satisfaction Questionnaire (MSQ). Table 5.1 shows some sample items from the Job Descriptive Index. Respondents are requested to put a *yes* in front of a word if it is descriptive of the category (work, co-workers, supervision), a *no* if it is not descriptive, and a question mark if they cannot decide. These responses are then scored to give a total job satisfaction estimate.

TABLE 5.1   Some Sample Items from the Job Descriptive Index

Work	Co-workers	Supervision
_____Routine	_____Lazy	_____Impolite
_____Satisfying	_____Slow	_____Tactful
_____Good	_____Ambitious	_____Up-to-date
_____Challenging	_____Stupid	_____Hard to please

Source: The complete forms, scoring information, and instructions can be obtained from Dr. Patricia C. Smith, Department of Psychology, Bowling Green State University, Bowling Green, OH 43403.

Administration Issues

There are two major concerns in administering an attitude survey. One is how to distribute the survey forms, and the other is how to keep the answers confidential. The following are some administration guidelines from one survey expert[9]:

1. Allow for voluntary rather than compulsory participation.

2. Let respondents fill out the surveys in large groups, preferably on company time, so that they feel more anonymous.

3. Have the survey sent directly to the group or individual performing the analysis, and make this clear to the respondents.

4. Be prepared to answer questions frankly concerning the use of the survey.

A company must also decide how to maximize the number of responses it receives from the survey. Some firms enclose questionnaires with employees' paychecks, specifying a certain return date. Although this ensures that all employees receive the survey, the actual return rate may be quite low. To prevent such a problem, many firms distribute and collect the surveys the same day, during working hours. Sears Roebuck, for example, schedules specific sessions for its employees in which they go to a survey site on company time to complete their questionnaires. This practice obviously indicates to employees that the company thinks their opinions and ideas are very important. Additionally, it maximizes the number of completed surveys that the company will have to pinpoint problem areas and concerns.

Regardless of how the survey is completed, respondents must be assured that their results will be kept confidential. Employees are sometimes very suspicious of a survey's motives and may not be honest in filling out the forms. In fact, they may respond in ways they believe the organization wants to hear. To prevent such response biases, no individual identification information should appear on the survey and voluntary participation should be stressed. Occasionally, surveys are coded with numbers so that the results can be summarized by units within the firm. However, employees may feel that such numbers identify them individually. When such coding schemes are used, the purpose should be made clear to the respondents. Indeed, a number of companies have found surveys returned with the coded numbers cut off the forms by employees who felt such codes jeopardized their anonymity.

Survey Feedback

"The worst thing the management can do is try to keep the results of an attitude survey a secret."

The last major consideration in using attitude surveys is interpreting and summarizing the results for employees. Although numerous techniques are available, one of the best ways to view survey results is to compare trends across different groups of employees or departments within an organization. For example, the marketing department's responses might be compared with those of the research and development team. Additionally, each department's averages on various questions could be compared with the overall company averages. If the survey is used regularly, it can also reveal changes in attitudes. A firm can compare current attitudes and concerns with those of a previous period.

Irrespective of the type of technique used to interpret survey results, it is essential to explain the findings to the respondents. Survey participants expect that their answers will be taken seriously by the organization. When a company decides to keep the results secret, or ignore them, it creates a tremendous amount of frustration on the part of the employees. They feel they have been manipulated, and their attitudes about the company will take a turn for the worse. Launching attitude surveys creates expectations in the participants, and these expectations, if unfulfilled, can have a negative effect on what the company is trying to gauge and improve—attitudes.

ON THE JOB REVISITED . . .

Wage cuts were not being used by the company to undermine morale, according to List. This attitude was fostered in large part because the company had invited List to join a labor-management participation team. He met once a week with eleven other employees to analyze production problems and suggest ways of improving efficiency. "We're not going to lie down. Look at the last fifty years in steel. We were up and down and up and down and sleeping together and fighting with each other. That's not going to work anymore. Hell, we're not even competing in America."[10]

How long do you think these positive attitudes will endure? What else can the company do?

SUMMARY

This chapter focused on the formation and importance of employee attitudes. The first topic was the structure of attitudes and the ways they satisfy an individual's psychological needs of adjustment, ego defense, value expressions, and knowledge. Attitudes differ in concrete ways from opinions, beliefs, and values.

Two important theories of job attitudes are Adams's equity theory and Herzberg's two-factor theory. The field of job attitudes has received considerable attention because of the assumed relationship to such behavioral outcomes as productivity, turnover, and absenteeism. The Porter and Lawler model illustrates contemporary thinking about the relationship between job satisfaction and performance. The most commonly used attitude assessment device is the attitude survey. To be effective, however, it must be well designed and carefully administered. The final step is providing the participants with feedback on the results.

HUMAN RELATIONS APPLICATIONS

Conclusion 1:   Attitudes consist of three major components: an affective component, cognition, and a strongly implied behavior pattern.

Application: Changing only one component of an attitude structure will not lead to permanent attitude change. The effective manager designs programs to alter all three components—affective, cognitive, and behavior.

Conclusion 2:   According to Herzberg, positive job attitudes are related to motivator factors and not to such elements as money, working conditions, or policies (hygiene factors).

Application: Improving job attitudes and, in some instances, motivation may require changing the nature of an employee's job to make it more challenging and to allow more responsibility and an opportunity for personal growth.

Conclusion 3:   Adams's equity theory suggests that job attitudes are formed on the basis of comparisons workers make between themselves and other similar workers in terms of what each puts into and gets out of the job.

Application: The effective manager must distribute rewards (such as compensation) in accordance with the effort and other inputs displayed by subordinates.

DISCUSSION QUESTIONS

1. Discuss how opinions, beliefs, and values are related to attitudes.
2. Describe the three elements involved in the three-component attitude model.

3. What is the critical incident technique, and how has it been used in attitude research?

4. Distinguish between motivator and hygiene factors. Which of these two factors is related to productivity?

5. How are work attitudes typically assessed? Why is it important to measure such attitudes?

6. According to equity theory, how are poor job attitudes developed? What can be done to improve them?

NOTES

1. Daniel Katz, "The Functional Approach to the Study of Attitudes," *Public Opinion Quarterly* 24 (1960), pp. 163–204.

2. P. Suedfeld (ed.), *Attitude Change: The Competing Views.* Chicago: Aldine Atherton, 1971, p. 1.

3. Robert A. Baron, *Behavior in Organizations: Understanding and Managing the Human Side of Work.* Boston: Allyn & Bacon, 1983, p. 205.

4. J. Schneider and E. Locke, "A Critique of Herzberg's Incident Classification System and a Suggested Revision," *Organizational Behavior and Human Performance* (1971), pp. 6, 441–457.

5. J. Stacy Adams, "Toward an Understanding of Inequity," in *Organizational Behavior: Classical and Contemporary Readings,* B. Armandi, J. Barbera, and H. Berkman (eds.). Dubuque, IA: Kendall/Hunt, 1982, pp. 92–104.

6. E.E. Lawler and L.W. Porter, "The Effect of Performance on Job Satisfaction," in *Organizational Behavior and Industrial Psychology,* K.N. Wexley and G.A. Yukl (eds.). New York: Oxford Press, 1975, pp. 32–39.

7. Robert A. Baron, *Behavior in Organizations*, pp. 217–220.

8. W.D. Todor, "Using Employee Surveys in Human Resource Management," in *Readings in Personnel and Human Resources Management,* 2nd ed., R.S. Schuler and S.A. Youngblood (eds.). New York: West Publishing Company. 1983, pp. 359–372.

9. Ibid., pp. 366–367.

10. This case was taken from "A Work Revolution in U.S. Industry," *BusinessWeek* (May 16, 1983), p. 102.

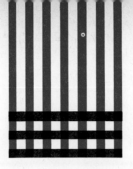

THE ORGANIZATIONAL ENVIRONMENT

P A R T 2

CHAPTER 6
Organizational Patterns and Views on Design

CHAPTER 7
Groups in the Organization

CHAPTER 8
Participation and Productivity

ORGANIZATIONAL PATTERNS AND VIEWS ON DESIGN

CHAPTER 6

ON THE JOB . . .

WHAT IS AN ORGANIZATION?

    An Organization Pursues Goals
    Defining Profits
    The Structure of the Organization
    Formal Structure
    Organizational Design

CLASSICAL ORGANIZATION THEORY

    Frederick W. Taylor
    Henri Fayol
    Max Weber
    Evaluating Classical Theory

HUMANISTIC ORGANIZATION THEORY

    Chester Barnard
    Chris Argyris
    Rensis Likert
    Evaluating Humanistic Theory

    ON THE JOB REVISITED . . .

SUMMARY

HUMAN RELATIONS APPLICATIONS

DISCUSSION QUESTIONS

NOTES

MANAGERIAL DIALOGUE: William Schaefer

ON THE JOB . . .

For years you have gotten dressed every morning, secure in the knowledge that your Super Spatula Company would be rolling along. You have been president of a company whose middle name might well be stability. For the past decade Super Spatula has produced one product—the popular kitchen utensil—at its Springfield, Massachusetts, plant and has about 50 percent of the spatula market in a three-state area (Massachusetts, Rhode Island, and Connecticut). Your organization is divided into two parts, production and sales (Figure 6.1).

But a funny thing happened on your way to a peaceful retirement: one of your stock clerks by the name of Bob Cratchit has invented a new self-scraping spatula that might become the hottest-selling kitchen tool since the spoon. Housewives, bachelors, even kids, have been clamoring for the convenience of the self-scraper ever since they read about Cratchit's invention in the newspapers. When the inventor was invited to appear on TV talk shows in New York City and Boston, the phone calls poured in even faster.

You've decided you have no choice—you're going to have to produce the self-scraper and retire a multimillionaire. You've already ordered the extra plastic you'll need, you've picked out a site for a second plant, and you're hiring salespeople as fast as you can interview them. But there's one important factor you have overlooked. What about the structure of your organization? Can you fit a second manufacturing division into your simple structure? Do you need to change your existing structure, or is that an unnecessary complication?

Better give it some thought . . .

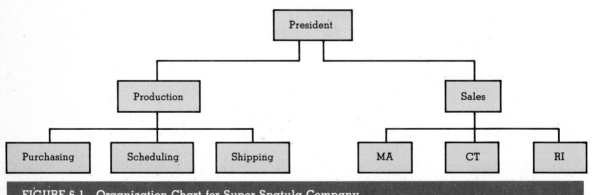

FIGURE 6.1   Organization Chart for Super Spatula Company

WHAT IS AN ORGANIZATION?

"Put any two human beings together and they'll form an organization."

Two people on a date form an organization; so do all the citizens of the United States. Almost any group of humans might be called an organization, once they develop a recognizable pattern of behavior toward each other. For example, the group of people inside a bus traveling from Los Angeles to Denver make up an organization. Each person knows his or her status—driver or passenger—and the accepted rules of behavior. If a male passenger gets drunk and starts making indecent advances to the woman across the aisle, other group members will take the responsibility for stopping his unacceptable behavior.

The urge to organize seems to be a basic part of human nature. Anthropologists who study primitive societies can trace highly complex patterns of organization far back into the past. From the evidence of burial customs, they deduce that as long as 100,000 years ago, humans had an organized system of religious beliefs and a hierarchy of religious authorities. By the Neolithic Age, about 10,000 years ago, there were signs of governmental and religious organizations. Some towns had virtual factories that produced stone tools in great quantities. There was an elaborate clan system, of which every person was a member, that determined the occupations one could follow and the person one was allowed to marry.

This chapter looks at the nature of the organization itself:

What does an organization *do?* What goals does it pursue?

How are organizations structured?

Is there a difference between the formal structure of an organization and its informal patterns of cooperation and conflict?

How have the classical theorists defined the organization? How has their work subsequently been revised by others?

Why are there so many conflicts between line and staff in most large organizations?

What difference does size make to organizational structure?

An Organization Pursues Goals

Although we can trace patterns of social structure in all human groups, the term *organization* is used to mean a specific category or group. An organization is a social group that has been deliberately formed to pursue certain definite goals.

Organizational goals vary widely. The goal of the Young Republicans is to promote the political ideology of the Republican Party. The goal of General Motors is to make automobiles at a profit. The goal of the Centertown Saturday Supper Circle is to give its members a pleasant evening of dinner and conversation once a week. The goal that is selected becomes the chief purpose of the organization and its members. Sometimes the goals are explicitly stated in a charter or other document, and sometimes they are expressed informally or tacitly understood by members.

The main factor that sets the organization apart from other types of groups is its goal-seeking activity. Those who study groups have found that their goals can be an important guide to both classifying and evaluating any organization. Peter M. Blau and W. Richard Scott have devised a useful system for classifying organizations according to the benefit to be derived from the fulfillment of the group's goals. They set up four different categories:

1. Mutual benefit association, such as a social club, in which the main benefit of group goals is the enjoyment the members of the organization receive.

2. Business concern, such as General Foods, in which the main benefit of group goals goes to the owners of the business.

3. Service organization, such as a hospital or a school, in which the main benefit of group goals goes to users or clients of the service.

4. Commonwealth organization, such as the U.S. government, in which the main benefit of group goals is enjoyed by the entire society.

In studying human relations within the context of the business world, we will deal primarily with organizations in the second of the Blau-Scott categories, that of the business concern. The main goal of such an organization is the production of some good or service that can be sold to earn a profit. Naturally, the main beneficiaries of this goal would be the owners of the company.

Defining Profits

When we say that the goal of the business concern is to earn a profit, we must be careful not to use too narrow a definition of the term. The concept of profit should not be limited to accounting profits or to the difference between costs of operation and sales revenues. Economist Joel Dean suggests that the definition of profit is now generally extended to refer to all kinds of economic benefit generated by the activities of the business firm. Dean says:

Economic theory makes a fundamental assumption that maximizing profits is the basic objective of every firm. But in recent years "profit maximization" has been extensively qualified by theorists to refer to the long run; to refer to management's rather than to owner's income; to include non-financial income such as increased leisure for high-strung executives and more congenial relations between executive levels within the firm.[1]

"The successful organization is the one that achieves its goals."

If we accept this extended definition of profits, then we must conclude that the goals of the business organization will benefit both owners and members of the firm, since increased income or more comfortable working conditions for employees may also be a form of profit that the group is seeking.

We can use our knowledge of the goals of the business organization to evaluate its effectiveness. If the group is achieving its goal of generating profits for owners and employees—if the accounting profits are good—regular dividends are paid to the owners, employees are earning relatively high salaries for their category of skills or experience, and workers are generally satisfied with the conditions under which they work, then we can say that the business firm is successful. If the firm does not generate adequate profits for owners and employees, then we can conclude that it is not functioning effectively in terms of the goals it is seeking.

The Structure of the Organization

Once the members of an organization choose their goal, they must decide what type of organization to create, what sort of structure to build. Some of the decisions include:

1. What are the goals of the organization?
2. How should the specific tasks be divided to best meet those goals?
3. How many managers are needed, and how many people should each manager supervise?
4. What is the best way to ensure that information important to doing the job gets passed on to the right person?
5. How closely should employees be monitored?
6. How should new employees be hired and unsatisfactory ones discharged?

Such questions have been studied extensively by researchers.

Formal Structure

The *formal* structure of an organization includes all the explicitly stated rules and regulations that direct the activities of members and define their relationships to one another. In a business organization, the formal structure would include the charter of the corporation, the organization chart that diagrams the chain of command and authority, and even the production schedules to which the firm has formally committed itself.

The formal structure of an organization divides labor and power among the members. For example, the organization chart tells employees that the responsibility for sales lies in one department while the responsibility for marketing lies in another. It also tells everyone that the heads of both departments will report directly to the president, who is the only person in the company with the formal authority to give orders to them.

The formal structure of an organization explains not only the obligations of each member, but also the penalties for not meeting these obligations and the rewards for meeting them well. Many large business firms have formal rules regarding the conditions under which members may be fired or demoted. They also have salary schedules to indicate the extent of possible raises for productive employees and job descriptions that indicate which employees are eligible for promotion to higher executive levels.

It is important, however, to realize that the formal structure of an organization is only a generalization. It's like a blueprint that tells members what kind of an organization they are trying to build. The way the organization really works depends on the people who occupy the slots in the organization chart. For example, an ambitious employee may act as if he has more authority than the organization has formally granted him. He may write memos that are actually policy decisions, or he may "forget" to refer important issues to his boss. If he is clever enough at executing this strategy, and no one challenges him successfully, he can change the structure of the organization, no matter what the chart designates as the formal organization.

Organizational Design

In the early 1900s, Frederick W. Taylor, Henri Fayol, Max Weber, and others published their ideas on organizational structure. Their individual theories, discussed later in this chapter, became the foundation of the classical view of organizational design. These theorists believed that there was a logical and ideal way to structure organizations. By following their lessons, a manager could build the most efficient and productive organization possible.

Unfortunately, the classical concepts did not always lead to efficiency or productivity in the real world. In the past few decades, other organizational researchers have studied the human concerns of the group's members and the outside environment faced by the organization. These factors, say modern theorists, must be taken into account in designing a successful organization.

"There is no one 'best' way to design an organization."

Modern organizational theory holds that there are no right or wrong answers to the question of how an organization should be designed. After all, a General Motors auto assembly plant is organized very differently from the submarine sandwich shop down the street.

Regardless of the size or nature of an organization, certain types of structural questions must be addressed. The following are some of the key design issues.

Division of labor. When primitive people began political, religious, and economic groups, they discovered a key principle of organization. All men and women are not created equal. Some men made better hunters, others seemed suited to be fishermen. Some women were experts in planting wheat, others in weaving baskets. The tribes whose members specialized in areas that best used their talents had an edge over the ones that did not, and gradually more and more of the world was taken over by specialists as they pushed out the less efficient generalists.

The principle of specialization and division of labor persists to this day. Imagine how inefficient it would be to have each Toyota worker build a car from scratch! Workers would be continually bumping into each other, ordering parts would be a nightmare, and production would drop to almost zero.

Specialization is a necessary step if an organization is to become economically efficient. *Horizontal specialization* refers to the division of labor typified by the various departments or bureaus of a large organization, in which each is responsible for a different phase of the organization's work. *Vertical specialization* is the division of power by which authority is distributed throughout the company.

Adam Smith, the father of modern economics, was one of the first theorists to describe the universal advantages of division of labor and specialization. In a book written in 1776, he cited the trade of the pinmaker:

In the way in which this business is now carried on, not only the whole work is a peculiar trade, but it is divided into a number of branches, of which the greater part are likewise peculiar trades. One man draws out the wire, another straightens it, a third cuts it, a fourth points it, a fifth grinds it at the top for receiving the head; to make the head requires two or three distinct operations! To put it on, is a peculiar business, to whiten the pins is another; it is even a trade by itself to put them on paper. I have seen a small manufactory of this kind where the men only were employed [who] could make among them upwards of 48,000 pins in a day. . . . If they had all wrought separately and independently, and without any of them having been educated to this peculiar business, they certainly could not each of them have made 20, perhaps not 1 pin in a day.[2]

Since the days of Adam Smith, founders of organizations have considered how to divide their members to best use their talents. Local clubs may form membership, publicity, and program committees. An oil-drilling firm may have workers who search for likely oil-producing sites, workers who do the actual drilling, and workers who know how to write off the costs of a dry hole.

Flat versus tall.   Certain members of the organization are given authority, either through a formal process, such as election and appointment, or by some informal recognition. They are intended to use their authority to help direct the group toward the achievement of its goal.

When an organization consists of a single leader and the rest of the group, it has a flat structure of only two levels. (See Figure 6.2.) As the group grows more complex and additional levels of status and authority are added, the organization becomes "taller." Generally, a flat organization can react more quickly to the needs of its members because commu-

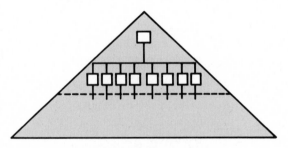

Decentralized Management
Broad Span of Supervision
General Supervision

FIGURE 6.2   Flat Organizational Structure

nication is simple and direct. In contrast, a tall organization takes time to react because messages must be passed up or down through several levels. (See Figure 6.3.) A large organization may be tall because it needs the additional structure. IBM could not function if its president had to manage every one of its employees directly.

Centralization versus decentralization. In a centralized organization, the president, owner, director, executive committee, or other authority has most of the power. Group members know who is in charge. Their roles are often clearly specified. An example of a centralized organization is the U.S. Army, with its clear hierarchy, from private to general, and detailed job descriptions for each position. Such centralized organizations generally follow the classical organizational principle of unity of command. The guiding rule is that each worker and each supervisor has only one boss. Orders flow smoothly down the chain of command.

In contrast, a decentralized organization contains several centers of authority and responsibility. Group members may be allowed more flexibility in their work, and the organization as a whole may respond more quickly to changing events. Many high-tech companies, for instance, try to decentralize their structure through special product task forces or committees so that they can react quickly to new needs in the marketplace.

Delegation. *Delegation* refers to the assignment of specifically stated duties, responsibilities, and authority from one group member to another. Delegation passes down the organizational chain of command. A vice president can delegate some of his or her duties and authority downward to a division head, but not to the president. The Managerial Dia-

"Highly centralized organizations are usually very rigidly structured."

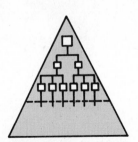

Centralized Management
Narrow Span of Supervision
Close Supervision

FIGURE 6.3 Tall Organizational Structure

Managerial Dialogue

"The best delegator in America . . ."

William Schaefer, mayor of Baltimore, Maryland

Baltimore is a sprawling city of 85 square miles located close to Washington, DC. The redevelopment of the inner city under Mayor Schaefer stands as a model to other problem-ridden urban areas.

Esquire magazine calls him the best mayor in America. He is a "genius mayor," according to Howard Cosell, and an ingenious delegator to boot. Baltimore's William Donald Schaefer has a not-so-subtle way of prodding his key staffers to clean up their acts. His mayor's action memos call their attention to litter in the park, abandoned cars along the highway, stray dogs, unmown grass, and broken curbs.

In his thirteen years in office, the former lawyer has penned more than 3,000 action memos, the end products of his rounds of the 85-square mile city and stints on his own weekly call-in radio show. Mayor Schaefer has also overseen the rejuvenation of Baltimore's showplace Inner Harbor, the refurbishing of its city hall, and the construction of five interstate highways. His administration has created a number of economic incentives to restore low-income and middle-income neighborhoods. He has the "bias for action" considered a primary trait of excellent companies.

"Years ago," says the mayor, "when I lived in a neighborhood, I noticed the city always took care of the big things. But it really bothered me when the light in front of my house burned out and wasn't replaced immediately. It's the little things that directly affect people in the community that I care about. When I became mayor, I had to find a way to call my people's attention to the things that weren't right."

What evolved is a quintuplicate form—legal size—containing a list of department heads, a space to describe the action required, and room for both the mayor's and the recipient's comments. A sample to the department of public works: "I just found an invisible car. It's invisible, that is, to everyone but me. We'll show you where it is so you can remove it." Another, scrawled in No. 2 pencil, stamped "rush," and dated March 26, 1984: "Washington Bld. and M. L. King Bld. NW corner. Bricks are displaced. In other words, the bricks are out." The typed reply: "Please be advised that the Bureau of Highways Maintenance Division . . . has scheduled the brick repair work at the northwest corner of Washington Boulevard & Martin Luther King Boulevard. It is anticipated that this project will be completed by Wednesday, April 11, 1984. [Signed,] Francis W. Kuchta." Kuchta has been public works director for ten years. "After the mayor's been out driving around or talking to people over a weekend," he says, "I usually get three or four action memos on Monday morning. The mayor, and rightly so, figures if he sees these things, why can't his staff? I don't take offense, but it might take new people a day or so to get used to them."

"It works," brags Schaefer. "I've got the best people working for me, and they take these things seriously. I don't have to check them so much now. But let me tell you what I just thought of today."

Annoyed to find trash accumulations in Harbor Place, he fired off a memo, then scribbled the date on a piece of garbage that he placed under a bush. Later, he would send someone to check for the dated garbage. "Maybe they can't see it," he says, "This way they'll remember."

Source: Reprinted with permission, INC. magazine, January 1985. Copyright © 1985 by INC. Publishing Company, 38 Commercial Wharf, Boston, MA 02110.

logue on pages 148–149 discusses the way in which Baltimore Mayor William Schaefer delegates his work to subordinates.

In theory, the president of a business firm has complete responsibility for the entire operation of the company. Clearly, one person does not have the time to hire every worker, write out all paychecks, place all orders for needed supplies, and make all the sales. Therefore, the president delegates a part of that responsibility and with it some degree of authority. The president hires a personnel manager to whom is delegated the task of screening and hiring new workers, as well as maintaining all necessary records of social security payments, pension plan contributions, and employment history. The president may tell the personnel manager exactly how he or she is to perform the day-to-day operations, perhaps even training him or her to follow specific procedures, or the president may choose the course of decentralization, allowing the manager to establish the method of working so long as certain performance goals are met.

There are several other advantages to delegation:

1. Lower-level employees may be closer to the action than their superiors. They can observe conditions in the marketplace at a closer range and react more swiftly.

2. Any sizeable organization is likely to employ experts who are highly qualified to make decisions in certain limited areas. It's unlikely for a corporate president, for instance, to be equally skilled in operations, finance, marketing, and personnel matters.

3. Delegation also satisfies the human need to control events. Children may feel secure knowing that their parents are making decisions for them, but an adult is likely to feel stifled. In a highly centralized organization, workers may feel they are treated like children and that their brain power is wasted.

In practice, delegation often turns out to be difficult for many managers to practice. An overworked executive may feel that she is admitting failure if she delegates the writing of reports or attendance at a meeting to a subordinate, or she may believe that the subordinate will not be able to achieve the level of performance she herself could turn in (if she had the time, which she doesn't), or she may fear that delegating important responsibilities to her subordinates will turn them into powerful rivals. What if the subordinate writes a brilliant report that makes even the president of the company sit up and take notice, or what if the subordinate sees the chance to attend meetings to take credit for all the department's successes?

These fears are not necessarily imaginary. Every experienced executive has probably seen at least one of these scenarios actually take place. Yet what many executives fail to grasp is that the alternative of not delegating work is likely to be even more dangerous. As the work load accumulates, tasks fail to be done. The manager doesn't have time or energy for the most important of tasks, and soon the combination of weariness and poor performance stops his or her career in its tracks.

Therefore, managers must learn to delegate. It frees them to perform the most significant aspects of their job thoughtfully and effectively, and it also helps develop their subordinates, so that they too become more competent, more involved, and more of an asset to the organization. In fact, outstanding organizations, such as IBM, evaluate their managers on how well they develop subordinates.

Line versus staff.   There are two types of workers in large organizations: line and staff. Line managers have the authority to give direct orders. They are in charge of a group of employees, and they are held responsible for accomplishing the basic goals of the organization. Staff managers, on the other hand, assist line managers. They give advice, but it is the line manager who decides whether or not to take it. Staff managers are usually specialists with useful knowledge in one particular area, such as designing computerized record keeping or publishing an in-house magazine and annual report or handling lawsuits by disgruntled ex-employees. Figure 6.4 diagrams the difference between line and staff employees.

An easy way to understand the difference is to think of an automobile assembly line. Each worker on the line is making decisions: how to attach a door handle or how to balance the tires. The foremen supervising them are also making decisions: how to keep the line running smoothly after two dozen workers call in sick or how to keep the conveyer belt from sticking. The plant manager is also making decisions: where to find an al-

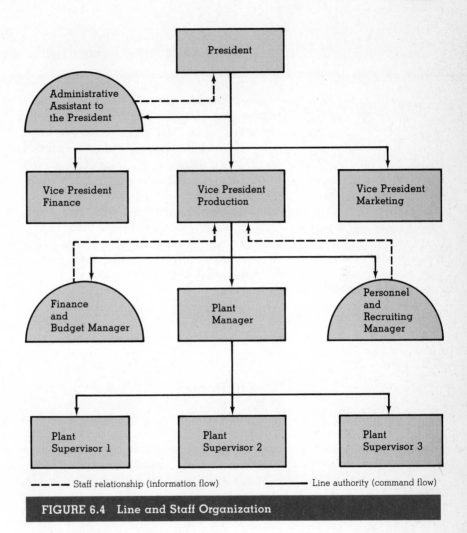

FIGURE 6.4 Line and Staff Organization

ternative supplier of machine tools or how to schedule auto production to match customer orders.

The worker, the foreman, and the plant manager all have line authority because they make decisions about corporate operations. Yet there are a number of other workers on the floor of the auto plant. There is the labor relations specialist, considering what type of pay package to offer the United Auto Workers union during the upcoming contract talks; the quality control specialist, monitoring the defects in the cars being produced; and the accountant, keeping track of the plant's costs. These specialists have staff positions. They may be experts, and their advice may always be heeded, but they do not have the authority to carry out their recommendations.

A central problem of management is the coordination of effort between these two groups, which often develop rivalries and jealousies that hamper communication and cooperation. For example, line managers often fear that staff managers are trying to make them look incompetent, usurping their power, and taking credit that belongs to the line manager. They criticize people on staff as being too wrapped up in their own little world, unable to understand the big picture, and without experience in handling bottom-line responsibility. Staff managers have their own set of complaints. They often regard their colleagues in line management as stubbornly unwilling to listen to new ideas. They also think line management underrates staff contributions to the organization's success. In many instances, staff employees are better educated and have experience in other fields; they may look down on most line managers as socially inferior.

"Line and staff employees often have very different personalities."

Although conflict between line and staff is probably inevitable, it can be minimized by making certain that organization goals are expressed clearly, by making the lines of authority clear, and by ensuring that staff managers are recognized for the value of their contributions.

Span of control. Managers can only supervise a limited number of people. The number of workers they oversee is considered their span of control. In practice, that number may vary greatly. The manager of a research and development team may only be able to supervise two or three other scientists because of the complicated work being done. In such a situation, each worker will need continual feedback from his or her supervisor in order to perform well. In contrast, a foreman in a foundry may be able to supervise several dozen workers because the nature of the work is simple. Each task is repetitive, and constant communication is not necessary. The workers don't need regular hand-holding sessions to know how they're doing; the nature of the work provides that feedback.

Regulation within the organization. A central problem of any large organization is the need to control or regulate the activities of members. Moreover, each member of the organization must somehow be motivated to participate fully in all the activities undertaken by the group. Therefore, the structure of the organization must reflect the group's specific needs for regulation and control.

Sociologist Amitai Etzioni suggests that complex organization can be classified on the basis of the way the group obtains members' cooperation and their compliance with goals and operating regulations. Etzioni distinguishes three major categories of regulatory activity. First, coercive control uses force to obtain compliance from members. Prisons and mental hospitals are coercive organizations, as is an army that drafts its members. Second, utilitarian controls lead to voluntary compliance because members see some benefits to themselves in such a course of action. A business firm is a utilitarian organization, in which employees submit to various regulations because they assume such regulations will help the organization produce more efficiently, thereby generating economic benefit for everyone. Third, in normative organizations, members cooperate because the group goals and values are identical to their own. An example of such a group might be an antinuclear organization, whose members are willing to write letters, circulate petitions, and stage demonstrations as a group activity because they would be doing exactly the same thing individually even if they were not group members.

Formal versus informal organization.   Formal structures usually lead to improved efficiency and therefore help the business organization to achieve its goals. However, certain problems are inherent in the formal structure:

1. It makes no allowance for the personal talents, abilities, and interests of the employees who fill the positions on the organization chart.
2. Formal structure may limit creativity and personal initiative in solving problems that arise. The existence of a rigid, formalized structure may also prevent a business organization from adapting to changing conditions and thus may endanger its very survival.
3. Perhaps the most serious problem is that the goal of maintaining the structure of the organization eventually may take precedence over the original goals of the organization.

An example of this problem was observed by Philip Selznick in his study of the Tennessee Valley Authority (TVA), the massive 1930s project that brought electricity to rural areas in several states by damming rivers. According to Selznick, it became apparent early in the project that many local residents were reluctant to cooperate with TVA objectives; the residents felt that they could approve such sweeping social changes only if their interests were represented in the decision-making process. The only way the TVA could accomplish its original goals was to alter its structure, so as to incorporate representatives of local residents. But the TVA's final choice was to alter its basic goals rather than its structure. The administrators thought that preserving the structure of the organization was more important than pursuing the original goals of the organization. Therefore, the TVA modified its goals, selecting only those that seemed acceptable to local residents without the need for further consultation.

More recently, Chris Argyris made an interesting study of the limitations of formal organization structure. Argyris did his research in a business corporation that seemed to have a satisfactory formal structure. Its profits were healthy, turnover and absenteeism were low, and few employees ever stated grievances, yet Argyris found that the employees' attitude was basically apathetic and indifferent to the success of the company. Argyris postulated that the formal organization, with its emphasis on specialization, can use only a limited range of its employees' skills and talents. This artificial limitation in turn creates needs in the worker—for attention, self-expression, and recognition—that may cause immature and inappropriate behavior on the job.

"Informal patterns of organization supplement formal organizational design and compensate for some of its weaknesses."

An organization can compensate for the limitations of its formal structure by establishing a complementary informal structure of organization. These are the personal relationships among workers. Formal rules and regulations are generalizations meant to apply to a broad variety of situations. The exact way in which the rule is applied to a specific situation usually is determined by the informal structure of the organization. Workers pool their experience and help each other discover ways to work faster or more efficiently. Informal structure also helps to adjust the demands of various positions in the organization to the capabilities of specific employees. For example, a plant foreman might be an excellent supervisor, capable of keeping production running at a high level, and yet have trouble writing the necessary reports that must be filed with superiors. Although writing the reports is a formal requirement of the job, an informal understanding between the foreman and his or her immediate supervisor might change the procedure so that the foreman makes oral reports, which the supervisor writes up and sends to top-level executives. Such an arrangement is actually much more efficient than requiring the foreman to spend hours of valuable working time struggling to find the proper word and discovering how to spell it correctly.

CLASSICAL ORGANIZATION THEORY

In the early 1900s, industries in the United States and Europe began questioning whether their traditional ways of operating were right for the new Industrial Age. Companies were looking for ways to streamline their operations. Their goal was to increase production while lowering costs. The ideas of three formidable men—an American, a Frenchman, and a German—were most influential during this phase of industrial history. The contributions of Frederick W. Taylor, Henri Fayol, and Max Weber are still with us today.

Frederick W. Taylor

Long before Sony built its mammoth computer-controlled TV appliance plants in Japan or Henry Ford thought about his famed Model T assembly line, there was Frederick W. Taylor. Often called the "father of scientific management," Taylor began his career in the late 1800s as a laborer at Midvale Steel Company. Through the years, he worked his way up to become chief engineer.

While at Midvale, Taylor began to experiment with time-and-motion studies to pinpoint just what constituted a fair day's work in an industry where performance standards were unknown. In 1898, Taylor went to work for Bethlehem Steel Company, where he conducted several of the more important experiments during that period. In one investigation, Taylor looked at one particular job at the steel company—carrying steel ingots ("pigs") up a ramp and dropping them into a railroad car. Each steel pig weighed about ninety-two pounds, and workers were loading an average of 304 a day.

"There is a right and a wrong way to do everything—even carrying steel ingots."

Taylor's scientific study of the job indicated that workers should be able to load 1,144 steel ingots a day. To prove this, Taylor began training one of the workers, named Schmidt. As Taylor wrote:

> *One of the first requirements for a man who is fit to handle pig iron as a regular occupation is that he more nearly resembles in his mental makeup the ox than any other type. . . . He must consequently be trained by a man more intelligent than himself into the habit of working in accordance with the laws of this science before he can be successful.*[3]

Such was the attitude of many of the classical theorists. Taylor's experiment, however, was quite a success. After being trained in the most efficient way to handle steel ingots, Schmidt was able to carry 1,157 pigs a day—more than even Taylor had thought possible.

This Bethlehem Steel experiment was outlined in Taylor's 1911 book, *Principles of Scientific Management* (New York: Harper). The book is most noted for the delineation of Taylor's major principles of successful management:

1. Study each part of an employee's work scientifically, rather than relying on tradition.

2. Scientifically select and then train the employee instead of allowing the worker to choose his own work and learn his job as best he could.

3. Cooperate heartily with the employees to insure that all the work is being done in accordance with the scientific principles that have been developed.

4. There is an almost equal division of the work and the responsibility between the management and the employees. Managers do the work for which they are better fitted than the employees. In the past, almost all the work and the greater part of the responsibility was thrown on the workers.

In addition to his famous principles, Taylor was noted for suggesting the differential piece rate system as a means for motivating workers to produce more. A worker in such a system is paid a set amount of money per item produced until he or she reaches the standard level of performance. If the worker can surpass that standard, then he or she receives a higher rate per piece. Such a system assumes, of course, that money is a prime motivator for production workers.

Henri Fayol

While Taylor looked mostly at low-level jobs requiring mechanical skills, Henri Fayol was concerned with developing general theories on how to manage. From his experience directing a large coal mining operation in France, Fayol developed his administrative principles. Fayol's principles were meant to provide guidelines on how to structure a firm. Although Fayol stressed the importance of adapting such principles to the diverse needs of different companies, this point was often overlooked by his readers, who often treated Fayol's principles as *the* guide for any organization.

Some of Fayol's most frequently cited principles are:

1. Division of labor.   Fayol believed that specialization was one of the most efficient ways to make use of workers. Ideally, work should be split into smaller subtasks so that employees could become experts in their areas. In a modern office, for instance, one worker might do nothing but type all day while another would simply work the copying machine so that both would become experts in those tasks.

2. Authority and responsibility.   Fayol wrote that there should be a clear-cut link between the authority and responsibility given to a

manager. If a manager is expected to direct subordinates, he or she should also be given the power to make them follow those orders. Fayol also made a distinction between statutory authority, based on the position that one holds, and personal authority, which comes from the individual. Effective managers possess both types of authority.

3. **Scalar chain of command.** Authority, responsibility, and communication should flow in an unbroken chain from the top to the bottom of any organization. Not everything in a company needs to go through channels; Fayol believed that individuals at the same level of the hierarchy should be allowed to talk with each other. Such horizontal communication, however, should only occur with the permission of each person's superior to preserve the authority of the hierarchy. Fayol called this concept of horizontal communications the *gangplank principle.*

4. **Unity of command.** Each worker should report to one and only one supervisor. Having more than one boss not only could confuse employees, but might also undermine the existing hierarchy.

Fayol outlined the key elements of administration: planning, organizing, commanding, coordinating, and controlling (see Table 6.1). College courses in management are still structured around Fayol's elements of administration, which have formed the basis for training at least a generation of top managers and supervisors.

Max Weber

Unlike Taylor and Fayol, Max Weber was not a practicing manager recording his ideas on "how to succeed in business." He was an academic, a

TABLE 6.1 Fayol's Functions of Management	
Planning	Forecasting of relevant future events to use as a basis for a strategic operating plan.
Organizing	The structuring of all activities and resources to accomplish and coordinate the operating plan.
Commanding	Using effective leadership to keep the organization on track.
Coordinating	Providing the glue necessary to pull the organization together to meet its goals.
Controlling	Monitoring processes within the organization to ensure meeting targeted goals.

German sociologist in the early 1900s who felt that the ideal form of organization was a bureaucracy.

For most of us, the word *bureaucracy* carries a lot of negative connotations. We think of managers who shuffle paper all day, snarling the rest of us in red tape. To Weber, however, bureaucracy meant something different: the ability to achieve maximum efficiency and predictability in company operations. Among the advantages of bureaucracy, as Weber saw it, were these features:

1. *Specialization.* Like Taylor and Fayol, Weber felt that jobs should be broken down into small tasks and workers given expert training to accomplish them.

2. *Impersonality in relationships.* Weber believed that on-the-job dealings between bosses, workers, and customers should be formal and impersonal to prevent emotions and personalities from getting in the way of a truly efficient organization.

3. *Personnel procedures.* Forget about race, creed, or religion in hiring workers, Weber wrote. Instead, select employees on the basis of objective qualifications. But promotions in such a system should be based primarily on seniority.

4. *Rules.* Each job should be done according to a system of abstract rules to ensure consistent procedures and coordination of activities.

5. *Centralization.* Control of an organization should be concentrated at the top of the hierarchy. Subordinates should have clear areas of responsibility laid out for them.

6. *Recordkeeping.* Effective organizations should keep a full set of files to summarize key company transactions. These files ensure that key managers can learn of everything that happens within the organization.

Weber believed that the ideal bureaucracy is a place where work is tightly controlled from the top according to a set of standards and rules. If problems occur, it is because individuals aren't going by the book.

The first Western bureaucracies grew up in governmental offices during the nineteenth century, and the form has spread rapidly so that today nearly every large organization is bureaucratic in form. Bureaucracy has numerous advantages. The system provides great continuity despite turnover of personnel because the office is more important than the person who fills it. The impersonality of such a system, which encourages employees to view each other in terms of their offices rather than their personalities, helps to neutralize many potential conflicts. The fact that

"Believe it or not, when the bureaucracy was first introduced, it was hailed as the efficient new organization of the future."

each official's work is reviewed by his or her immediate superior acts as a check on the accuracy of that person's work. The detailed job descriptions and list of qualifications ensure that new employees will be able to perform their jobs. Such a system is not very imaginative, but in most cases it yields better results than hiring someone on the basis of looks or because he or she is related to the boss.

Evaluating Classical Theory

Many of our major institutions—from Detroit to Washington, DC—are built on the framework put forth by Taylor, Fayol, and Weber, and we have them to thank for hundreds of management self-help books on the market. They made business aware that management is, at least in part, a science that can be taught rather than an inborn art. Since the 1960s, we have become aware of some of the other legacies of the classical thinkers. Critics have pointed out a number of things they overlooked, as well as some negative consequences of organizations structured strictly according to classical principles. For example, a number of recent studies show that rigid rules and extreme specialization on the job can have a dysfunctional effect on workers and on the company.[4] Individual creativity and initiative may be stifled.

The organization may fall prey to the bureaucratic syndrome, in which employees concentrate on narrowly following the rules rather than looking at the goals the rules were meant to achieve. Modern critics also point out that a manager who relies on Weber's impersonal system to accomplish goals may find it takes a long time. Getting things done in modern bureaucracies requires charisma as much as competence.[5] Other critics point out that the classical rules don't always work in all situations. If a company is in a constantly changing environment, it makes little sense to rely on formal procedures that may be obsolete by next week. Finally, other researchers have pointed out that Fayol's famous principles don't really describe the work that managers do today.[6]

Although the bureaucratic organization is certainly a prominent feature of the business world today, there is no reason to assume that it is irreplaceable. In a 1966 article, Warren Bennis remarked:

> *A short while ago, I predicted that we would in the next 20 to 50 years, participate in the end of bureaucracy as we now know it and in the rise of new social systems better suited to the twentieth-century demands of industrialization. This forecast was based on the evolutionary principle that every age develops an organizational form appropriate to its genius, and that the*

prevailing form, known by sociologists as bureaucracy and by most businessmen as "damn bureaucracy" was out of joint with contemporary realities. I realize now that my distant prophecy is already a distinct reality so that prediction is already foreshadowed by practice.[7]

Bennis listed four relevant threats to bureaucracy: rapid changes, growth in organizational size, complexity of modern technology, and a change in managerial behavior. He suggested that the trend would be toward project-oriented groups of workers who are placed together on the basis of necessary skills and training and whose work is coordinated by an executive. Once such temporary groups have completed their tasks, they would disassemble and be reassigned to other projects.

HUMANISTIC ORGANIZATION THEORY

"The humanists placed more emphasis on the needs of human beings than on those of the organization."

Recognition of the limitations of formal patterns of structure within an organization led to a changed emphasis in the study of organizational behavior. During the twentieth century, the classical theory of organization, with its emphasis on formal structure, gave way to more humanistic theories, which focused on the importance of integrating employee needs with organizational desires. Among the most important humanistic theorists were Chester Barnard, Chris Argyris, and Rensis Likert.

Chester Barnard

Chester Barnard, like Taylor and Fayol, was a practicing manager who felt that experience was the key to developing effective ideas on organization design. In his 1938 book, *The Functions of the Executive* (Cambridge, Mass.: Harvard University Press, 1938), Barnard stressed the importance of cooperation and communication between management and subordinates.

Barnard believed that incentives should be used to get employees to identify with the objectives of the company. He was one of the earliest writers to stress the importance of linking individual needs with organizational goals. Barnard also outlined a noteworthy theory of authority. A superior cannot count on authority alone to make an employee cooperative in every instance. Each individual has what Barnard called a "zone of indifference." Commands that fall within this zone are automatically accepted and followed through. Barnard felt that it was an executive's responsibility to widen this zone of indifference by making employees feel that the organization is giving them more than they are putting out. They will then be more likely to accept orders agreeably.

Barnard's work stimulated study on communication processes, motivation, and managerial leadership. It led the way for further exploration of the individual-organization link.

Chris Argyris

Chris Argyris primarily was concerned about the meshing of individual characteristics with organizational structure. He suggested that effective organizations are those that enable individuals to fulfill their normal developmental growth patterns. An individual moving from infancy to adulthood goes from being passive to active; from being dependent to independent; from having few interests to many; and from having a short time perspective to a much longer one. However, organizations can sometimes work against such personal growth patterns. Argyris believed that many classically oriented organizations force their employees to be passive and dependent and make use of only a few low-level abilities. In reaction, frustrated employees may become apathetic or have high rates of absenteeism. They may even deliberately sabotage the organization's attempts to reach its goals. Although these problems may be found in any organization, they are most typical in highly structured, bureaucratic firms.

Argyris recommended instituting flexible job roles as well as open communication among all levels in a firm. Team projects, sensitivity training, and other organizational development programs are among his other suggestions for ways that the organization can help individual employees meet their own needs. An example of a company that has taken these principles to their logical limit can be seen in the box on page 162.

Rensis Likert

A third humanistic theorist with a formidable impact on our thinking about organizational design is Rensis Likert, who launched a large-scale research project during the 1950s through the Survey Research Center at the University of Michigan. Likert's project was designed to study the relationship between a company's structure and its effectiveness. After assessing the results of a questionnaire, Likert classified organizations into four types.

Under Likert's spectrum, System 1 companies adhere strictly to classical design principles. Decision making is centralized, communication

A COMPANY WHERE EVERYBODY IS THE BOSS

Two things catch the eye of a visitor to a cable plant owned by W. L. Gore & Associates Inc. near Newark, DE. One is that the people work with great intensity, whether they operate machines that extrude brightly colored insulation for computer cables or inspect every inch of the finished cable. The second is that nobody seems to be in charge. Workers rely on their own initiative. That's largely why Gore remains as entrepreneurial as it was 27 years ago, when Chairman Wilbert L. Gore and his wife, Genevieve, now secretary-treasurer, started the business in the basement of their home.

A former chemist at Du Pont Co., Gore discovered a way to use Du Pont's Teflon polymer as an insulator for electrical cables. Today his company also uses Teflon in producing vascular grafts and the well-known Gore-tex fabrics for outdoor apparel and spacesuits. A closely held concern, Gore does not disclose revenue and earnings but says its business is growing at a 25% annual rate. Last year's sales probably approached $250 million, and the company now has 30 plants.

Some 3,000 U.S. employees—they're called "associates," in keeping with Wilbert Gore's dislike of the boss-employee relationship—own 10% of the company through an Associate Stock Ownership Plan. Gore contributes 15% of each person's annual pay to the plan and reinvests the rest of its earnings in the business. Some workers with 15 years of service have accumulated $100,000 worth of stock. Of the total $692 million in equity, 80% is owned by Gore family members and other veteran "associates" who work at Gore. Outsiders hold only 10%.

The atmosphere at Gore is informal, familylike. "You're free to learn as much as you want and assume responsibility and leadership," says Brian M. Linton, a group leader. Close supervision is rarely needed. "Area leaders," such as Linton's father-in-law, Ralph G. Bateman, solve problems rather than bark orders. "People work harder in this type of atmosphere than when somebody stands over you with a club," he says.

To keep a friendly workplace atmosphere and ensure that everybody is treated fairly, the company limits plant size to about 200 workers. "It takes more investment to build new plants [than to expand old ones]," Wilbert Gore says, "but this is offset by the overall performance of the firm."

It is hard to find someone at Gore who doesn't like the job. "I love it," says H. Edward Smith, 24, who took a $3-an-hour pay cut to come to Gore. Says Frances Hughart, an inspector with 22 years of service: "We manage ourselves here. If you waste time, you're only wasting your own money."

Source: *Business Week* (April 15, 1985). Reprinted from the April 15, 1985, issue of *Business Week* by special permission, © 1985 by McGraw-Hill, Inc.

flow is primarily downward, and employees are given little autonomy or opportunities for initiative. At the opposite end, System 4 companies were humanistic in their structure. Participation was encouraged. Goals were discussed. There was a free flow of communication, and employees had a favorable attitude toward the firm.

Likert found that the classical System 1 companies were not as effective as the System 4 firms. He suggested that a number of changes were occurring in the business world that were making System 1 organizations obsolete. Among the changes were increased competition from foreign countries, a societywide trend toward greater individual freedom and initiative, higher levels of education, an increasing concern for mental health and the full development of one's potential, and increasingly complex technologies requiring expertise beyond the capabilities of any one individual.

To create a System 4 organization, or help an existing organization evolve into that form, three major elements are required: supporting relationships, group decision making, and high performance goals. For supportive relationships to develop, Likert thought that management must be aware of employees' needs, taking them into consideration before making decisions that affect them, and that managers must give employees the opportunity to be creative and show initiative.

The key to extensive group decision making is the use of individuals who serve as "linking pins" between their department and another department or between levels in the organization. A vertical linking pin, for instance, might be a manager who is a liaison between subordinates and superiors. A horizontal linking pin, who works closely with two departments, would serve to improve lateral communications.

The final crucial element in System 4 firms is high performance goals. Likert believed that when an organization has supportive relationships and uses group decision making, high performance goals will automatically follow; Likert assumed that participation will increase employees' commitment to organizational goals. This commitment, in turn, will then lead to high levels of motivation.

Evaluating Humanistic Theory

The theories of the humanists are dramatically different from those of the classical theorists; however, both groups can be criticized for assuming that their ideas were universally applicable. Both perspectives are simplistic either/or choices. Neither gives much attention to the different external environments that firms face and how those environments create varying design requirements. As one modern critic summarized it: "A great many problems in organizational design stem from the assumption that organizations are all alike: mere collections of component parts to which elements of structure can be added and deleted at will, a sort of organizational bazaar."[8]

There have been two other major criticisms of the humanist's approach to design. Because they have concentrated primarily on human relations ideas and concepts, the specifics concerning how to set up a company have been neglected. For example, although participative decision making is widely advocated, the humanists do not tell us how much is appropriate or when to create participative groups. They also have provided little insight into the content of workers' jobs and other motivational methods.

"Like the classical theorists, the humanists made the mistake of thinking their theories would work for everyone."

Other critics have noted that one of the underlying assumptions behind the humanistic theories is that employee participation, job satisfaction, and performance are linked. Participation in decision making is assumed to lead to high levels of job satisfaction, which in turn creates high levels of productivity. Recent research, however, shows that neither assumption is correct. Participation does not lead directly to job satisfaction, and the relationship between satisfaction and performance is not at all clear-cut.

Today most theorists agree there is no "best" way to structure an organization. (This view is called the *contingency,* or *systems, approach* to organizational design.) Management must consider a number of different variables before picking a design that will suit their needs most effectively for a particular period. Variables include the size of the firm, the integration of its various branches, the way work flows from supplies through the firm to final customers, and the competitive environment in which the firm must function. Since business firms are organized not by computers but by humans, the beliefs and even personality traits of its members will also be important factors.

See Table 6.2 for a summary of management theory.

TABLE 6.2 Four Decades of Management Theory

The 1950s

Computerization. The first corporate mainframes were displayed as proud symbols of progress.

Theory Y. As propounded by MIT Professor Douglas McGregor, this philosophy held that people produce more if they have a say in their work.

Quantitative management. Trust the numbers. Running a business is a science, not an art.

Diversification. The strategy of countering cyclical ups and downs by buying other businesses.

Management by objectives. Peter Drucker popularized the process of setting an executive's goals through negotiation.

TABLE 6.2 *(continued)*

The 1960s

T-groups.   Encounter seminars for managers, designed to teach them interpersonal sensitivity.

Centralization/decentralization.   One school of thought says that headquarters should make decisions, while the other places the responsibility in the hands of line managers.

Matrix management.   A system by which a manager may report to different superiors according to the task.

Conglomeration.   Putting disparate businesses under a single corporate umbrella.

Managerial grid.   A method of determining whether a manager's chief concern is people or production.

The 1970s

Zero-based budgeting.   Throw out last year's numbers, and start from scratch when making up this year's budget.

Experience curve.   Generating profits by cutting prices, gaining market share, and boosting efficiency.

Portfolio management.   A ranking system that identifies some businesses as cash cows, some as stars, and some as dogs.

The 1980s

Theory Z.   Proponents of Japanese management methods argue that U.S. companies should adopt such techniques as quality circles and job enrichment.

Intrapreneuring.   Encouraging executives to create and control entrepreneurial projects within the corporation.

Demassing.   A popular euphemism for trimming the work force and demoting managers.

Restructuring.   Sweeping out businesses that don't measure up, often while taking on considerable debt. Wall Street usually applauds these moves.

Corporate culture.   The values, goals, heroes, and rituals that characterize a company's style.

One-minute managing.   Balancing praise and reproach in sixty seconds.

Management by walking around.   Leaving the office to visit the troops instead of relying on written reports.

Source: Adapted from *Business Week* (January 20, 1986), pp. 52–55. Adapted from the January 20, 1986, issue of *Business Week* by special permission, © 1986 by McGraw-Hill, Inc.

ON THE JOB
REVISITED . . .

With the popularity of its new product, the Super Spatula Company needs to rearrange its organizational structure. Taking the perspective of a contingency design theorist, what type of structure would you recommend for Super Spatula? Take into account the company's environment, its prospects for growth, and the new problems it will face.

SUMMARY

An organization is a social group that has been deliberately formed to pursue certain definite group goals. There are four different kinds of organizations: mutual benefit associations, such as social clubs; business concerns; service organizations, such as hospitals; and commonwealths, such as the U.S. government.

Organizational goals for business concerns revolve around the need to produce a product or service that can be sold to earn a profit, and these organizations are structured accordingly. One type of structure is known as formal; through formal structure, power and labor are divided among the members. Included in the formal structure are elements such as division of labor, delegation of power, line versus staff positions, and the "height" of the organization.

The informal structure of an organization comes about as members interact with one another in the performance of their duties. Problems that are not dealt with in the formal structure may be handled through informal structuring.

The theorists who have dealt with the formal structure generally fall into three camps: classical, humanistic, and contingency. Classical theorists, including Taylor, Fayol, and Weber, stress the importance of maximizing efficiency in the company's operations. The humanistic writers, including Barnard, Argyris, and Likert, advocate high levels of worker autonomy and participation in decision making.

Although their positions were frequently poles apart, both classical and humanistic theorists assumed that their prescriptions were appropriate for all settings. However, recent theory clearly shows the importance of environment, as well as other factors, to a firm's organization.

HUMAN RELATIONS APPLICATIONS

Conclusion 1: An organization can compensate for the limitations of its formal structure by establishing a complementary informal structure of personal relationships among workers.

Application: Informal structures and relationships among workers can help to clarify unclear or ambiguous communications passed through the formal structures of an organization.

Conclusion 2: Recent research and theory in organization design indicate that there is no one best way to design all organizations.

Application: Managers must consider a variety of factors in choosing an appropriate organizational structure. The type of environment the firm faces, the type of technology being used by competitors, and the type(s) of strategy being employed by the top executives of the firm will all have an impact in deciding on the appropriate organization design.

DISCUSSION QUESTIONS

1. Describe and give an example of horizontal and vertical specialization.
2. What are the major advantages of delegation?
3. What are the similarities between Taylor's scientific management ideas and Fayol's management principles?
4. What is an ideal bureaucracy according to Weber, and what advantages would such an organization have?
5. According to Likert, what three elements are necessary for an organization to be effective?
6. Overall, what are the major weaknesses associated with both the classical and humanistic ideas on organizational design?

NOTES

1. Joel Dean, *Managerial Economics.* Englewood Cliffs, NJ: Prentice-Hall, 1951, p. 28.
2. Adam Smith, *The Wealth of Nations.* New York: Vintage Books, 1937, pp. 4–5.
3. Frederick W. Taylor, *The Principles of Scientific Management.* New York: Harper, 1911, p. 59.
4. K.N. Wexley and G.A. Yukl, *Organizational Behavior and Personnel Psychology.* Homewood, IL: Irwin, 1977, pp. 38–39.
5. R.K. Hancock, "The Social Life of the Modern Corporation: Changing Resources and Forms," *Journal of Applied Behavioral Science* 16;3 (1980), p. 295.
6. D. Robey, *Designing Organizations: A Macro Perspective.* Homewood, IL: Irwin, 1982.
7. Warren G. Bennis, "The Coming Death of Bureaucracy," *Think* (November–December 1966), p. 30.
8. R. Likert, *New Patterns of Management.* New York: McGraw-Hill, 1961.

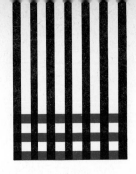

GROUPS IN THE ORGANIZATION

CHAPTER 7

ON THE JOB . . .

WORKING TOGETHER MEANS FORMING GROUPS

THE INFORMAL GROUP

The Peer Group
The Task-Oriented Peer Group

HOW DO GROUPS HELP?

How the Work Group Helps the Individual
How the Work Group Helps the Larger Organization

UNDERSTANDING BEHAVIOR IN THE GROUP

Norms
Sanctions
Learning the Norms

DEVIANCE

Causes of Deviance
Deviance Within the Organization
Controlling Deviance on the Job

THE MANAGER'S ROLE IN SMALL WORK GROUPS

THE SMALL GROUP AND ORGANIZATIONAL CONFLICT

ON THE JOB REVISITED . . .

SUMMARY

HUMAN RELATIONS APPLICATIONS

DISCUSSION QUESTIONS

NOTES

MANAGERIAL DIALOGUE: Janet Chusmir

ON THE JOB . . .

The Funger Swimming Pool Corporation has been constructing and installing swimming pools for the home for twenty-six years. When an order for a pool comes in, three crew members and a foreman are sent out. They generally take four or five days to finish the work.

One July, the foreman of one installation team became ill and Alan Shapiro, a 20-year-old go-getter eager to prove himself, was promoted. Shapiro was excited about the opportunity to show the boss how well he could handle one of the teams and didn't even consider the possibility of resentment from the older workers.

On his first job as foreman, Shapiro couldn't wait to get under way. But when he and the other three workers—Alexander, Croft, and Daniels—arrived at the customer's house, the workers said they needed a cold drink before starting. Shapiro was irritated, but he joined them in a round of beers before beginning installation.

Then, as Shapiro measured the yard, the others stood around and watched. Once it was time to begin the actual digging, Croft and Daniels suggested another break. When Shapiro objected, Daniels burst out: "We've been here a lot longer than you, kid. Don't think just because Mr. Funger calls you a foreman that you can tell us what to do. If you want to hang around and watch, that's OK—just don't start sticking your nose into our business."

Alan Shapiro was faced with a "work slowdown" by the three pool installers he supervised. This small group was headed in the wrong direction, from Shapiro's perspective.

The first afternoon, Shapiro tried unsuccessfully to reason with them. That night, he reassured himself that the workers were just feeling him out and would be back to normal tomorrow. But Tuesday and Wednesday were merely repeats of the first day. By Thursday, when the work should have been entering the final stages, the crew had completed less than half the job.

More to come . . .

WORKING TOGETHER MEANS FORMING GROUPS

If we could eavesdrop on a group of construction workers sitting against a fence and eating their lunches, we probably would hear a lot of talk unrelated to work. Out of earshot of management, they may also criticize their supervisor, laugh at the mistakes they think the architect has made, jeer at the ineptitude of a fellow worker, and speculate about the rumor that the builder is bribing city inspectors to ignore certain building code violations. If their boss overheard any of this, he or she probably would be furious; the boss might even try to separate the members of the group to keep them from spreading rumors and developing negative attitudes. Many managers instinctively feel threatened by the power of worker groups, but a wise manager knows that small groups, like the one formed by the hardhats, exist in all organizations and serve a number of useful functions. This chapter investigates their positive features, as well as some complications they present to management:

How does a task-oriented group improve communication within an organization?

What happens when the small group sees a difference between its own goals and those of the organization?

How does the small group protect its members?

How does the informal work group deal with an incompetent supervisor?

THE INFORMAL GROUP

Too many managers attempt to combat or to ignore the small group influence. The successful manager discovers how to use it to benefit both the organization and the people in it.

The corporation is itself a group, of course, but it is formally organized. It has a corporate charter, an organization chart that defines reporting relationships, and possibly, thick manuals that explain the way work is to be done. Within the context of the formally organized corporation, small informal groups inevitably arise. They may consist largely of workers at the same level, or more democratically, they may cut across formal levels of organization. They may be primarily oriented toward the

"Small groups lead to intimate personal relationships."

work itself, or they may be based on some other shared interest, such as playing softball or investing in the stock market.

The small group has historically served as an important form of social organization. Its earliest form was the family, and group membership was based on kinship or traditional alliances. Most small groups involve people who have intimate, personal relationships. The group tends to be small and closely knit and to involve a great deal of face-to-face contact. In fact, these elements of the small group were stressed by sociologist C. H. Cooley, seventy-five years ago:

> *We mean by the group a number of people who communicate with one another often over a span of time, and who are few enough so that each person is able to communicate with all the others, not as secondhand, through other people, but face-to-face.*[1]

As the definition suggests, small groups are emotionally significant to their members. Even groups that are primarily work related permit the individual members to express many different aspects of their personalities. Sociologists call the kind of small group formed by employees at about the same organization level an example of a peer group.

The Peer Group

Peer group membership requires the involvement of the individual's whole personality. In the course of time, each member interacts closely with other members of the group and thus reveals the many sides of his or her personality. The peer group member is in constant contact with fellow members, and communication takes place about a wide range of topics. Homans asserts that such groups are characterized by:

1. Close interactions
2. Sentiment
3. Mutual dependence
4. Social ranking[2]

As teenagers, we relied on peer groups for advice, comfort, and understanding. Our peer group influenced our opinion of school and colored our relationships with teachers and other students. If our peers generally looked favorably on education, then it is likely that we did, too. On the other hand, if education was not a priority for "our crowd," then those attitudes rubbed off on us. The peer group reflected its members' belief about their status and self-image compared with other students. We knew that our close friends approved of relationships with some people, but not with others. Before making a date, we probably checked to see if the potential partner was "in" or "out."

When we mature and enter the working world, we break away from our adolescent peer groups and waste little time in finding new ones. The company bowling or softball team, the "thank-God-it's-Friday" group unwinding at the neighborhood bar, the group shopping together on their lunch hour: these are the peer groups formed on the job. Interestingly, work-related peer groups are one of the most popular subjects for television shows, such as the gang at the television station on the *Mary Tyler Moore Show,* the medical personnel on *M*A*S*H,* the cops on *Hill Street Blues,* and the staff at the Mel's Diner on *Alice.* In an example of life imitating art, the actors still with *M*A*S*H* when it went off the air expressed sadness at the coming separation from the members of *their* work group, just as their characters did in the final episode.

The Task-Oriented Peer Group

The task-oriented peer group is a close-knit work group whose members have specific work-related goals and aspirations. Although members may discuss who's dating whom, the Redskins' chances to go to the Superbowl, the best new car to buy, or other personal and social matters, their primary focus is on their work and the work environment they share five days a week.

The task-oriented peer group is not a formally designated unit. It comes into being spontaneously, through social interaction among workers who are thrown together for eight hours or more each day. Since employees generally are hired for certain jobs because of their education and previous experience, people with similar backgrounds frequently find themselves in similar work environments. Workers with similar backgrounds tend also to have similar interests. These interests form a basis for conversation on a job and serve to give employees a feeling of belonging.

The task-oriented peer group cannot be controlled directly by managers. It is the consensus of the group itself that gives or withholds approval, rewards or punishes its members through social interaction. Even the manager who is part of the work group is at best only equal in power to the other members when it comes to making decisions.

One of the main reasons that the informal task-oriented group exerts so much influence is that it offers members a chance to fulfill personal needs in ways the organization cannot. A member of a task-oriented peer group can often resolve conflicts without going through the official chain of command in the formal organization. For example, suppose that a dishwasher in a hotel dining room wants to take Saturday night off to meet his girlfriend at the airport. He is afraid the manager will turn down his request, since Saturday is the busiest night of the week. He discusses the problem with the peer group of kitchen employees, and they come up with a solution. The chef will make the request, since she knows the manager well and has the most job seniority. The manager is more likely to say yes to her; moreover, the fact that she was the one to make the request indicates that the entire kitchen staff supports it. If that doesn't work, the group may suggest other solutions. A waitress can ask a friend who has worked in the hotel before to take over the job for the night, or another dishwasher might be willing to trade shifts. Through informal means such as these, the group can accomplish what the dishwasher acting on his own cannot.

"The work group can help individuals meet their personal needs, while still supporting the goals of the organization."

The task-oriented peer group functions as an intermediary, or buffer, between the individual and the larger organization. As an informal group, the small task-oriented group is able to adapt to fit the situation or the personalities of its membership. These informal groups generally operate by group consensus. In this group setting, authority is decentralized, and courses of action are adopted only after a democratic type of discussion has taken place. Members act together to decide whether or not to support organizational work rules, proposed changes, or new job assignments. If the group has an informal leader, he or she functions more as a spokesperson than as the ultimate decisionmaker. See the box on page 174, which presents traits of the task-oriented group in a high-performing system (HPS).

A stronger leader may arise within the task-oriented peer group when an important issue is raised within the organization. The group may then band more closely together and formalize the decision making and authority processes. Among clerical workers and low-level managerial personnel, a vital issue may cause group members to form a more formal, authority-oriented body, which eventually may evolve into a formal union.

Who are the leaders of a work group? How much authority or influence do they have? Some answers came from J. L. Moreno, a social scientist and pioneer in the field of group psychotherapy. He was one of the leading exponents of "psychodrama," a technique that utilizes role playing for both diagnostic and therapeutic purposes. Moreno developed a measuring device called a *sociogram,* which measures individuals' perceptions of one another in a group. By individual testing, Moreno was able to determine the feelings of attraction, repulsion, or indifference each person had for fellow group members. Persons who were rated highly by others in the group became "stars" or leaders, since they apparently possessed a variety of personal or objective qualities that others admired (see Figure 7.1 on page 175).

TEAMS THAT EXCEL

Task-oriented peer groups come in all shapes and sizes. Every so often, a diamond occurs—a work group that excels in performance. Such superstar work teams have propelled many small companies into the big time and allowed industry giants to remain on top.

Patrick J. Sweeney and Douglas M. Allen have identified the traits of a research group that excels, what they call a "high-performing system (HPS)":

1. *Language.* A private language develops that is full of jargon to outsiders but conveys the complexity of the problem being addressed.
2. *Task maintenance.* Completing tasks and feeling good are accomplished together.
3. *Leadership.* Leaders of the work group are viewed by the members as experts. They are the pacesetters and role models to the rest of the group.
4. *Experimentation.* Group members experiment with different roles and try new ways of operating the system.
5. *Execution.* Each HPS performs its tasks well and exactly. Accuracy of timing is important. Members may seem to be taking the job too seriously.

6. *Process awareness.* Members examine not only what they're doing, but how they're doing it. They consistently try to improve the process.
7. *Fragility.* HPSs are fragile and require some protection from the outside world. Things have to be just right.
8. *Evaluation.* Members develop their own rules for their performance, which may be very different from those of outsiders.
9. *Intense commitment.* Members don't choose to leave an HPS. They remain intensely committed to it, even when there are supposedly more attractive opportunities elsewhere.
10. *Varieties of motivation.* Simplistic theories of motivation don't explain the group's performance. Perhaps the thrill of the chase, the seeking of beauty in the operation of the system, or the satisfaction of accomplishment play a part.

Source: Patrick J. Sweeney and Douglas M. Allen, "Teams Which Excel," *Research Management* 27 (January–February 1984), pp. 19–22.
Photo courtesy of the University of Miami Athletic Department; photographers Richard and Micki Lewis.

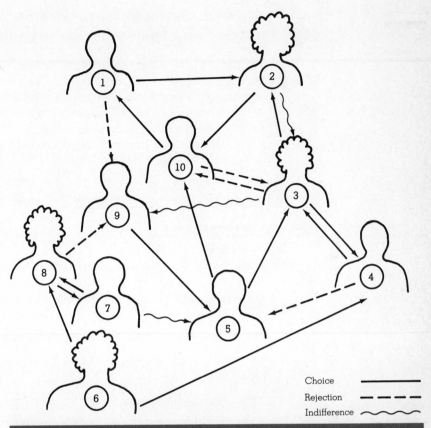

FIGURE 7.1 A Sociogram Measuring Individuals' Perceptions Within a Group

Choice ——————
Rejection – – – – –
Indifference ~~~~~~

The leader of such a group may be chosen by some sort of elective process, but it is more likely that he or she will simply evolve into a position of power. Even in work-oriented peer groups where no pressing issue is at hand, there are generally one or more recognized leaders. In times of crisis, these individuals tend to assume more and more responsibility.

Qualifications for work group leadership are similar to those for formal organizational leaders. The major difference between the formal and informal group leader is one of goals rather than of personal attributes. Both individuals are committed to furthering the goals and support of work group peers. In pursuing these sometimes divergent goals, there is often a clash of interest between formal and informal leaders.

George Homans's study indicated that positive social organization within a work group could be traced in part to the positioning of desks and the physical closeness of workers to one another. Homans also noted that one of the principal motivating factors in job satisfaction and performance was the friendships formed on the job.

For office workers, physical characteristics such as density of desks, lack of walls, and even the darkness of the walls affect employee job satisfaction.[3] An office that is open, densely packed, and relatively dark, with shared working places, increases the amount of contact people have with each other. Thus, it can be assumed, that management may exert some degree of control over the strength of small work groups by the way it physically organizes the work place.

HOW DO GROUPS HELP?

As we have seen, informal groups within the organization serve many different purposes. Some of these benefit the individual members, some the work group, some the organization as a whole, and sometimes the benefit to one conflicts with the welfare of the others.

How the Work Group Helps the Individual

The informal work group provides six different types of benefits for its individual members.

1. It provides opportunities for friendship and social belonging.
2. It provides a sense of identification and support for the individual's self-image.
3. It provides protection from impersonal policies that benefit the large formal organization but may in some instances work to the individual's disadvantage.
4. It provides informal training in job skills, as well as attitudes toward the formal organization and its goals.
5. It provides an opportunity to seek status.
6. It provides a source of information about the rest of the organization.

"Friendships within the work group evoke strong feelings of loyalty to co-workers and perhaps also the organization."

From a personal standpoint, the work group offers its members an avenue for making friendships. A person who spends each day working closely with other employees will almost inevitably make agreeable contacts with some of them. The task-oriented peer group certainly satisfies that need to belong and to interact with others. Moreover, members of the work group will listen to personal problems and perhaps even offer advice and assistance.

Friendships fostered within the work group in many instances give members a strong and direct feeling of loyalty to the group. If the group is positively oriented toward the company, employees have a better outlook toward their work situation. A person who enjoys interaction with fellow workers and is accepted as an equal by them is likely to show a lower absenteeism and turnover rate. Of course, the opposite can also be true. An employee who feels rejected by a work group may not be motivated to perform adequately on the job.

In an age when impersonal structures of large corporations dominate, the task-oriented peer group gives its members a sense of personalized belonging or identification. In the work group each person is able to establish and reflect a self-image to his or her immediate peers. The president of General Motors surely does not know who installs door handles on the second shift at the Olds plant in Detroit, nor does he have any special knowledge about that specific worker's hopes, dreams, needs, or motives. However, the door-handle installer is well known to the other members of the department in which he works. His work group personally accepts or rejects the many facets of his personality. They also lend support to his self-image. To General Motors, Detroit, and the nation he may be just another blue-collar assembly line worker who performs a certain task and is paid so many dollars, but to the immediate work group, he is a real person.

The work group also provides the individual worker with protection. From a historical standpoint, we might contend that the work-oriented peer group is nothing more than a reflection of individuals' desires to protect themselves. Traditionally, groups of people have banded together under the assumption that there is strength in unity and numbers. Present-day formalized organizations such as labor unions, farm co-ops, and even fraternal organizations can trace their informal beginnings to this basic assumption.

Workers often feel, rightly or wrongly, that there is a clear-cut difference between the work group's best interests and the goals of the organization. A common complaint from many workers is that the organization is not responsive to its employees' needs. A work group may shield its members against some of the demands of the formal organization.

Like the adolescent peer group, the work group also functions to teach members both the skills they need on the job and the prevailing attitudes toward work, the company, and its goals. This is especially helpful for new or recently promoted employees. The work group provides informal on-the-job training that can help its members work more efficiently; however, some of the practices taught by the group may be in direct conflict with the formal work rules.

Membership in an informal work group also gives the individual a chance to earn a certain social position, or status. It is safe to assume that

GROUP MEMBERSHIP MAKES MANAGERS PREFER WORKING IN THE OFFICE

There will be no stampede of workers from central offices to work at home, even if technological obstacles are cleared away soon. That is the message from a survey of managers and professionals whose job is to process information.

When Honeywell, Inc., researchers asked 700 of these "knowledge workers" if they would continue to go to the office if telecommunications technologies are improved enough for them to work at home, 56 percent said they would continue to go to the office every day, 36 percent said they would spend half their time at the office and half at home, and 7 percent said they would work at home, going to the office only when necessary. The remaining 1 percent were undecided.

The heavy preference for doing business as usual surprises Eugene Manno, the group vice president for Honeywell's small computer and office systems group, headquartered in Billerica, Mass. Manno thought that technical problems, not attitude, stood in the way of a migration to home offices.

By contrast, Jack Nilles of the University of Southern California Center for Future Research says the results indicate a better awareness of the possibilities of telecommunications than he would have expected. Even when the technical advantages become obvious, he says, no more than 10 percent at the outside will ever want to work full time at home. He does expect the percentage of people preferring to split time between home and office to increase.

The biggest reason for wanting to work in the office, the survey shows, is the need to be around other people to share ideas and camaraderie. "What we find is the people who can work alone are more interested in working at home," Manno says.

Professionals who spend much of their time writing or developing information tend to prefer a mix of home and office time. The higher the job in a company's chain of command, the greater the dependence on face-to-face meetings and the greater the corresponding need to work in the office.

The survey found some differences among job functions: 46 percent of marketers would prefer the office, and the same percentage would prefer splitting their time; 72 percent of lawyers prefer the office, compared with only 24 percent who prefer splitting their time.

Some of the influences on where someone wants to work have nothing to do with the nature of the position, Manno says. "The less secure the person," he says, "the more likely he is to want to work in the office" to get what Manno calls "the audience reaction" of supervisors and colleagues to his actions.

Because telecommuting, at least on a part-time basis, is particularly attractive to the disabled and women, Manno says, it could help businesses attract or retain skilled people whose services might otherwise be unavailable.

But "I've got to keep my eye on the office as the place" where business will continue to be conducted, Manno says. Honeywell will continue, he says, to think of the office—not the home—as the center of the business universe.

The survey's respondents make clear an important point about planning for automation: it is the needs of people—not new technology—that will determine the future. The survey's message is significant to those in the office automation business, because it shows technology even at its best will not bring revolutionary change to the way people work in an office.

Source: *Nation's Business* (March 1985), p. 40. Reprinted by permission. Copyright U.S. Chamber of Commerce.

each of us yearns for status within some group of people, and the work group provides an opportunity for this search. Status-seeking takes place in the executive boardroom and on the foundry floor. Take, for example, a factory that employs both skilled and unskilled labor. A group of trained workers, such as tool and diemakers, usually consider themselves in a higher work category than unskilled assembly line workers. They reflect this feeling by demanding higher wages and maintaining a general aloofness from the work groups who do not share their skills. However, status is not just a matter of skills. Within the group, status is achieved according to what the majority considers proper behavior. In one group it may be seniority, in another output, and in still another, non-work-related personality characteristics.

The work group functions as an information center in regard to the rest of the organization and the outside world. For example, an employee can learn of future organizational plans from the work group before they are announced officially. Work groups often swap news, rumors, and gossip. This information can sometimes be valuable to members in helping them understand unspoken expectations on the job or hidden emotional currents in the work environment.

The importance of the work group to its members is discussed in additional detail in the box on page 178.

How the Work Group Helps the Larger Organization

Perhaps the first step a formal organization (or its leaders) should take is to accept the inevitability of work-oriented groups. No corporation can possibly hope to supplement or replace the advantages offered by personal, small-group supportive activity. One executive who is keenly aware of the value of small groups in helping the organization achieve its goals is Janet Chusmir, profiled in the Managerial Dialogue on pages 180–181.

From a historical viewpoint, organizational attempts to regulate or disband the work group have resulted in decreased job satisfaction and increased dissent between labor and management. The labor conflicts of the late nineteenth and early twentieth centuries were based primarily on opposing economic outlooks, but underlying philosophical differences were also important. Corporate heads felt that if a worker was given a living wage for a hard day's work, both parties were fulfilling their moral, social, and economic contract. Worker opposition arose because the wages were, in many cases, less than adequate. Moreover, workers felt that unfair economic incentives and negative sanctions were used to coerce the employee.

Managerial Dialogue

"Group identity helps everyone work together."

Janet Chusmir, publisher and president of the Daily Camera

The Daily Camera *is a daily paper in the college town of Boulder, Colorado.*

Few organizations have as many competing internal groups as a daily newspaper. Few newspapers have developed as many ways of dealing with those internal tensions as the *Daily Camera* in Boulder, Colorado, under the leadership of publisher Janet Chusmir. "We have so many different kinds of operations—news gathering, manufacturing, distribution, and sales. We're an extremely diversified company," Chusmir says.

In a newspaper setting, it's considered natural and healthy for different departments to perceive themselves as subgroups of the organization. "You want the newsroom and advertising to have a certain amount of separation, for instance," explains Chusmir. "You want editors to make news judgments independently of advertising considerations. The circulation department wants the paper off the press on time, but the editors may have to accommodate a late story. Every group has to have its own identity, but for the good of the newspaper everyone has to work together."

At the morning paper (circulation, 30,000 +) in the college town of Boulder, a number of formal and informal methods have been developed to bring a spirit of cooperation into a company whose subgroups have differing goals. "We do a lot of team work. The department heads participate in strategy, planning, and decision-making. When we have problems that involve several departments—and that always happens at a newspaper—we set up action committees." For instance, if the problem is not meeting deadlines, an action committee might be formed to determine if the problem stems from late ads (advertising), late news stories (editorial), or inadequate staffing in the composing room (production). In each department, other committees might spin off from the action committee, which would disband when the problem is solved."

Running an organization consisting of a wide range of personalities and backgrounds requires a level of basic fairness. "You have to be careful to treat everyone equally, from arranging leaves of absences to sending out congratulatory notes," Chusmir stresses.

Making a point with educated, articulate reporters and editors is relatively easy for a publisher, but it takes a special effort to talk with skilled tradespeople who run the presses at night and the drivers who deliver the newspaper. "When I came here, I worked in every department, including putting on jeans and going into the pressroom at night, so they would all get to know me," Chusmir says.

The *Daily Camera,* owned by Knight-Ridder Newspapers, ran an opinion and attitude survey after Chusmir arrived in 1983. She met with each department and discussed the results. "We tried to find out what our internal problems were and what was at the root of them."

One strategy adopted by the publisher was to begin cross-training, a technique whereby senior members of each department spend time working with or observing one another. "That lets us understand each other's problems and we gain mutual respect for each other." Now the circulation manager sits in on newsroom meetings and may even suggest ideas for news stories, and when the publisher gets letters of complaint, she passes them on to the editor to answer personally. "We've made some real moves to overcome the natural isolation," Chusmir says. The process of building an "organization-wide" feeling continues at the *Daily Camera,* with informal interdepartmental coffee breaks. There are companywide newsletters circulated regularly. Middle managers from various departments attend quarterly meetings as well as hold their own meetings to explain procedures to each other. The result is better-informed employees, group leaders who are sympathetic to the problems of others, and a company whose separate parts are striving toward the same goals. As Chusmir puts it, "When one employee gets a good circulation service award or when one department consistently makes its deadlines, the whole paper knows."

"The wise manager accepts the existence of work groups and tries to enlist their help in meeting the company's goals."

Through often bitter struggles, as well as political and judicial processes, workers were granted the right to band together formally for collective bargaining. Corporate leaders had to accept the reality of labor unions.

Although supervisors have become used to dealing with unions, many still fail to comprehend the less obvious, but still powerful, influence of the informal work-oriented peer group. Work groups are found at every level of labor and management; they are more pervasive than unions. They are a powerful force within the organization, and they have the power to disrupt the organization or to encourage goals and values that differ from those of the larger organization. The wise manager recognizes that such groups will always exist and concentrates on the positive means by which the organization can work with informal work groups.

Among the benefits of the work group for the organization are:

1. Creating a more flexible organization
2. Supplementing the weak manager's work
3. Training new workers
4. Acting as an informal channel of communication

A positively motivated work group can be a help rather than a hindrance to the organization's goals. The group may interweave itself into the formal organizational structure, creating a more positive, flexible organization. According to Robert Dubin:

> *Informal relations in the organization serve to preserve the organization from the self-destruction that would result from literal obedience to the formal policies, rules, regulations, and procedures.*[4]

In fact, a common form of work slowdown takes place when workers observe all the formal rules. Without the mediation of the work group to teach its members which formal rules must be followed and which should be ignored, both morale and productivity drop.

The Swedish automaker Volvo demonstrated this point when it rearranged its assembly line into small teams.[5] Each team is provided with a private lounge for meetings, lunch, and coffee breaks. Groups can divide tasks among members themselves to take best advantage of individual skills and motivation. Within certain corporate guidelines, they also set productivity goals and quality standards and enforce them through the informal control mechanism of the group. The result has been high worker satisfaction, low turnover rates in the labor force, and a very high standard of quality in the Volvo.

The work group can and often does supplement a weak manager. Even in matters of specific planning procedures or coordination, a manager may find that the informal group's aid is essential in achieving the organization's goals.

The work group can also be helpful in the training of new workers. A supervisor with the responsibility for a large number of workers with varied work assignments can hardly be expected to know each job in detail. Members of the work group can provide a valuable service to the organization by giving new workers the benefit of their day-to-day experience on the job.

The small group's effective communication process can also serve organizational needs, especially when the company wishes to pass on information unofficially to employees. This is sometimes the most effective means of communication with employees, since matters of a controversial or sensitive nature are often better discussed person-to-person rather than through official channels. The organization may wish to correct a circulating rumor or to suggest an alternative interpretation of that rumor. For example, if workers hear through the grapevine that work cutbacks are imminent, the organization may feel the rumor should be dispelled by casual conversations in work groups rather than by issuing official statements. Official denials may accidentally give a rumor more legitimacy than it deserves.

Successful organizations use both direct and indirect means of communication. Unions or formal work groups can relay to management their members' views on the matter of wages, working conditions, and seniority, but the work-oriented peer group may serve as a vehicle for the more subtle attitudes and feelings of employees. Suppose a group of clerical workers hears that a manager is retiring, creating a vacancy that will soon be filled. They may have strong preferences among the obvious candidates; they may even believe a member of the work group should get the job. Since morale, motivation, and productivity may well depend on the selection of the new manager, some sort of unofficial link between management and the work group may be mutually advantageous.

UNDERSTANDING BEHAVIOR IN THE GROUP

"Members of an organization are often unaware of the rules and values that govern their behavior."

Although the work group may have a powerful effect on its members, most of the attitudes and behaviors of workers on the job are formed long before they join the organization. The way we view work reflects the influence of our culture.

A culture integrates the beliefs, prejudices, knowledge, and moral principles of a society. It therefore exerts an influence on each member's attitudes and behavior. The organization usually has goals and values that reflect those of the wider social culture, yet it also strives for production, efficiency, and profit. In pursuit of these goals, the organization may adopt values and rules of its own, some of which may conflict with the values and rules of society at large. An important objective of organizational management is to minimize the strain of such a conflict.

Anthropologists and sociologists study society to find the hidden assumptions and rules that govern behavior. The members of the society are often quite unaware of the existence of these culture elements, just as a fish might be unaware of the water in which it lives.

Norms

Norms are the rules, both stated and unstated, that specify what a person should and should not do within a given culture. The norm is the general rule against which each specific instance of behavior is to be measured.

If you look at an organization's formal rules as an iceberg floating on an ocean of conformity, the norms represent the nine-tenths that are out of sight. The norms usually are not discussed nor even thought about, but they are ever present as an influence on each employee's behavior.

Like any type of rule, norms call for enforcement. Since norms may be either formally or informally stated, their enforcement may also vary both in intensity and compliance.

Some of the norms of a group or organization may conflict with those of society as a whole or may even be against the law. For instance, it is against the law to discriminate against blacks in regard to public transportation, housing, jobs, or education, yet in some areas such discrimination is still clearly happening. In situations such as this, formal laws barring discrimination may sometimes be superseded by local cultural mores.

The implicit assumption is that norms are ideals to strive for. Realistically, no mortal can possibly adhere to all of the norms of his or her culture all the time. The system of norms, and the sanctions that support them, might be thought of as our continued striving for perfection and social acceptance. We all know that such a goal is impossible, but we keep trying.

Sanctions

Sanctions are the means society uses to enforce its norms. Positive sanctions encourage individuals to repeat approved behavior; negative sanctions discourage individuals from repeating behavior that breaks or disregards social rules. Sanctions are a system of punishments and rewards that induces people to behave in socially accepted ways. For example, a mother's smile when she sees little Susan playing quietly with her toys is a positive sanction. The frown on her face when Susan comes home from the playground with ripped and dirty clothes is a negative sanction.

Sanctions can be formal or informal. Even informal sanctions affect an individual's personal, social, or business life to such an extent that certain conduct is effectively discouraged. For example, in most companies there is no formal regulation against two employees having an affair, but even if they do not face the risk of being fired, informal sanctions may be applied. Their friendships with fellow employees could be damaged, or their chances of promotion diminished.

Formal sanctions are laws. An example of a law aimed at enforcing cultural norms is one prohibiting fraud. It is believed that people should be honest in their personal and business dealings. All laws don't carry the same weight. If we learn that Larry down on the fifth floor has been arrested for murdering his mother to get his hands on her financial assets, we are shocked and deeply disapproving, but if we learn he is being prosecuted for tax evasion, we might just shrug our shoulders.

A less binding form of enforcement is called a *regulation*. Regulations are similar to laws except that they apply to situations in which the norm is not quite so important to society as a whole. For example, a company's dress code is a regulation that requires office workers to wear suits and ties on the job. If an employee shows up for work in a T-shirt, he certainly won't be arrested, but pressure will be put on him to comply with the dress regulations of the company. His boss could tell him bluntly to return to acceptable attire if he wants to keep his job, or his fellow employees might look at him with raised eyebrows. In any event, he will soon get the message that he is breaking the dress regulation.

Even when there is no formal dress code, there is still an informal understanding of what constitutes appropriate office attire. In a broker's office on Wall Street, that might be a three-piece suit from Brooks Brothers—even for female employees. A branch office of the same firm in Marin County, north of San Francisco, might find such a suit too formal, too pompous, even ridiculous; there, the appropriate office outfit might be designer jeans, a silk shirt, and a leather jacket. Sociologists call this kind of social rule a *folkway*. Folkways define expected behavior, but failure to observe a folkway generally is considered to have only small moral or emotional significance. Those social rules that have greater moral force are called *mores*. An example might be prohibitions against murder, rape, or incest. Individuals who depart from mores that the culture considers vital to its continued existence are subject to strict penalties.

Learning the Norms

Members of a culture must be taught its norms so that they can engage in activities that society deems important and behave in ways that the majority finds acceptable. Norms are taught in the family, at school, in church, and on the job.

Public institutions, such as schools, necessarily teach generalized patterns of normative behavior, since they serve all groups within the society. Small group norms usually are excluded. For example, a high school teacher who belongs to a fundamentalist church may personally disapprove of dancing, sex education, and miniskirts, but if the school board, principal, and parents approve of these customs, then she will be discouraged from applying her personal norms to the conduct of her students. However, she may impart these norms to her own children and expect them to act in accordance with her set of rules.

By the time we reach maturity, we have a generalized understanding of the rules of our culture and of society's expectations about our behavior. Even so, throughout the rest of our lives, we must adjust to new situations in which varied behavior and responses are required.

Business organizations use a number of means to teach their norms and pass along company values. Many use on-the-job training to teach a new employee not only the specific skills the job requires, but also the behavior appropriate to it. The primary advantage of an on-the-job program is that the trainee learns in a real work environment. Experience and training occur in the situations in which he or she will have to function. This firsthand knowledge of the job is imparted by a supervisor who has direct, personal contact with the new trainee.

Classroom training is another way to learn the theories, concepts, and policies of an organization. People are not expected to work and learn simultaneously, so that they have time to sit back and take an objective look at the way the organization operates. Many organizations feel that classroom training allows a new employee to become thoroughly oriented and socialized to the expectations, rules, and values of the group. Classroom training is not without disadvantages: some of the new material may not be retained in memory. Without real work experience to use for reference, the new employee may view the organization correctly from a theoretical standpoint, yet fail to understand fully the realistic applications of his or her studies. Only when the knowledge is applied on the job will it take on meaning.

In some organizations, an apprenticeship program of training can provide an almost ideal combination of experience and objectivity. An apprentice works at the new job under close supervision and attends classes at the same time. Apprenticeship programs are widely used in teaching skilled trades, such as metal working or plumbing. Such learning programs are less useful at the managerial level. The necessary skills are too complex to teach on a part-time, on-the-job basis.

DEVIANCE

Deviance occurs when a person's behavior does not conform to the norms of society. We may think of a deviant as a hardened criminal or a bum who sleeps on a park bench, but in fact, all of us are sometimes deviant in certain respects. A person who fails to pay a parking ticket or exceeds the speed limit is deviating from formally stated laws, which presumably reflect social norms. The view held by many people is that a deviant is a person who, for any number of reasons, has "gone bad." But in his study of deviance, Howard Becker stresses that deviance is as much a matter of point of view as it is the actions involved. Social groups actually create deviance by creating rules whose infraction constitutes deviance.

In other words, the labeling of a person as a deviant is a result of social rules. An example might be seen in the Prohibition era in the United States. A sizeable group of Americans deviated from the formal sanctions against drinking, yet they were deviant only because of the law itself. In 1910, drinkers were not considered deviant, since no formal social rule had defined them as such. When the law was changed in 1920, the customary behavior of millions of Americans became deviant overnight. In this case, the law did not actually reflect social norms, so that drinkers were never socially looked on as deviants. Eventually, the law had to be changed.

Causes of Deviance

Deviance may occur for a variety of reasons. One is simple ignorance. There are so many formal and informal norms and values that even a well-socialized person may not learn them all. Consider an individual who goes to his first formal dinner. If he has never been taught the more sophisticated social graces, then he probably will be at a loss as to which fork or knife to use. He is deviant in the sense that his table manners don't conform to Emily Post's rules.

A second cause of deviance may stem from the fact that the formal or informal sanctions are ineffective. In our example of Prohibition, we noted that the formal negative sanction in the form of laws didn't stop many people from drinking. Speakeasies flourished, and the local bootlegger was often a popular person in the neighborhood. Formal laws alone were not effective, especially since there were still positive informal sanctions. The drinker was generally viewed as a convivial person, perhaps even an admirably daring one. Fear of legal prosecution alone will not deter people from actions that are informally approved by the social group of which they are members.

Psychologists say deviance may be a form of aggression caused by frustration. Aggressive workers who refuse to obey work or social rules may be attempting to vent their frustration against their supervisors. Deviance becomes their weapon.

"One group's deviance may be another group's conformity."

Many sociologists contend that deviance is a type of conformity to the norms and values of a certain group that differs from society as a whole. For example, schools expect students to strive for high grades, and students who make poor or failing grades are considered deviant by their teachers. However, these same students may be condemned by their peers as deviant if they spend their evenings studying instead of hanging out at the shopping mall.

Deviance Within the Organization

Within the business organization, a similar situation may develop. A study conducted in a Western Electric plant by Elton Mayo, often referred to as the "father of human relations," found that perceptions of, and reasons for, deviance were often quite different from the traditional view. Mayo discovered that workers refused to be more productive, even though there were economic rewards for productivity, because the work group disapproved of "rate-busters." Management considered the workers deviant for not producing at a higher rate, but working faster would label a worker deviant by fellow employees.

Becker, a noted sociologist, considers this aspect of deviance and refers to it as a form of value conflict. He points out that:

> *We must see deviance . . . as a consequence of a process of interaction between people, some of whom in the service of their own interests make and enforce rules which catch others who, in the service of their own interest, have committed acts which are labelled deviant.*[6]

Management generally feels that employees should work up to their capabilities, produce as much as possible, and seek the maximum economic rewards for their labors. If a worker refuses to behave in this manner, then supervisory personnel assume that he or she is deviating not only from organizational goals but also from cultural goals of making money and getting ahead. Yet the worker may feel that being labeled deviant by management is less of a threat to self-image and happiness than is being treated like an outsider by fellow employees. A worker may prefer acceptance by his or her peer group at the expense of the organization's production goals or own personal economic gain. In such a case, deviance may in fact represent the rational choice.

If a deviant is highly visible, identifiable with the group, or likely to cause the group as a whole to receive negative sanctions, then his or her deviant activities may be covered up by the work group. In a factory where each department is given an overall rating, other workers may produce a little extra in order to make up for lack of production by one of the department's members. Such protective measures do not necessarily mean that the group approves of the deviant behavior, but they may fear outside interference as a threat to the group's solidarity or strength.

Organizations usually have formal sanctions as well as informal ones. Rules or regulations make it clear to the individual exactly what is considered correct behavior on the job. For example, factory workers may know that they are expected to be on time, take specified rest and lunch breaks, wear safety goggles, and perform their tasks in a certain manner. These rules may be impersonal, but they are generally rational. Most workers can see the reasoning behind them. Safety goggles prevent accidents, regulated arrival times make the organization run more smoothly, and uniform use of machines maintains a standard quality of production. The rules also serve as a means of labeling and punishing deviating members. A worker who doesn't wear goggles or who shows up late for work is easily identifiable. Other formal negative sanctions, such as pay loss or suspension, may follow.

Executives too are controlled by the organization's formal rules and regulations. They are required to do certain paperwork, prohibited from accepting gifts of great value from suppliers, limited in the amount of money they can spend entertaining clients, and required to spend a certain percentage of time in the field. Executive deviance is not as visible as deviance among factory workers and therefore may more often go unpunished, either by formal or informal sanctions. Thus, many observers speculate that the rate of deviance is much higher at the executive level than it is among low-level workers.

Controlling Deviance on the Job

Formal controls cannot reach the varied motives that cause deviant behavior. They promote conformity only out of fear on the part of the individual that some undesirable consequence will follow. As such, formal controls are only a stopgap measure. A person may conform out of fear, but the motives of deviance will still exist.

Many sociologists and psychologists agree that formal controls are not the final solution to deviance. Strict management rules against deviant behavior seldom cause it to disappear. Instead, deviants find new ways to circumvent the rules. Mayo found that forbidding rest breaks did not stop workers from sneaking off to take them, nor did it help production. He suggested that management allow work breaks and introduce other positive measures—better lighting, refreshments—and the subsequent production figures improved.

"It's easy to make rules; the important question is whether or not they will be obeyed."

Implicit in Mayo's recommendations is the assumption that deviance may be dealt with more effectively by attempting to reintegrate the deviant rather then by isolating and labeling him or her. If an individual is made to feel that he or she has lost the esteem and approval of other group members, then that person loses much of the motivation to conform to group standards.

Of course, theories are easier to state than to put into actual practice, but finding and correcting the causes of deviance is a major function of enlightened managerial personnel. Anyone with a position can make rules; whether or not they are obeyed is in part dependent on whether the workers find them consistent with individual or group values and goals. In a combat situation, strict formal controls often save lives and ensure the success of the military objective. A lenient interpretation of rules and leadership could very easily result in disastrous consequences. On the other hand, rigid enforcement of rules at a laid-back Silicon Valley software company could lead to a rapid exit of a talent vitally needed by the firm.

If workers feel a company's rules are unfair or do not serve their best interests, then they lose their desire to conform. For instance, a plant that has a twenty-minute lunch break will find many instances of deviance. If the workers are forced to abide by this rule, they may find ways to grab an extra few minutes before or after lunch. More seriously, their attitudes toward breaking the rules may spill over in other ways. Thus, management must walk a thin line between enforceable rules that promote the organization's goals and too-strict rules that may actually promote deviance.

The following are a few of the positive results of the correct choice of rules and sanctions:

1. *Clarifying unstated or general rules.* A new worker may not realize that using a certain tool is frowned upon until he or she sees someone else punished or reprimanded for doing so.

2. *Increasing group solidarity as workers unite against the deviant.* A slow-paced worker who is not "pulling her weight" may be ostracized by the group.

3. *Effecting changes within the system.* For instance, if the twenty-minute lunch break was found to be promoting an "antirule" attitude among employees, it could be changed.

4. *Making conforming behavior seem more desirable.* When a worker sees or hears of a fellow employee being given a three-day suspension for continued tardiness, it usually reinforces his or her own commitment to arrive at work on time. The employer does not need to be given the punishment personally for it to act as a deterrent.

THE MANAGER'S ROLE IN SMALL WORK GROUPS

Wise managers seek to promote and protect their employees. After all, without their trust and cooperation neither the manager nor the organization will achieve sought-after goals. To be effective, managers must first study the forces and drives within the particular work groups formed by employees. This study, in turn, can lead to a structuring of peer relationships in small groups that can significantly reduce the demands on a manager to intervene in crisis situations. Tjosvold outlines a practical and powerful method of doing this, an approach he calls *goal-linkage.*[7] With the goal-linkage approach, managers "influence subordinate relationships by structuring their beliefs about how their goals relate to one another's goals."

Tjosvold says there are three kinds of linkages:

1. *Positive linkage, also called "cooperation."*   Workers believe that everyone can attain their goals together. For instance, an office manager might ask a group of typists to plan their new work space as a group.

2. *Negative linkage, called "competition."*   If one worker achieves his or her goal, then others are not likely to reach theirs. For example, a manager might have three salespersons write up a marketing proposal, explaining that only the best proposal will be used.

3. *Independent linkage, or individualization.*   Employees believe their goals are unrelated and their work neither helps nor hinders others. On an assembly line, the work of the door installers is essentially independent of the spray painters.

THE SMALL GROUP AND ORGANIZATIONAL CONFLICT

The sources of conflict within an organization can often be traced to the actions of work groups within the organization. Even within a single department, distrust and dislike can arise between employees belonging to different groups. For example, by oversight or deliberate actions, the workers on one shift may get the impression that workers on another shift are failing to be productive. This may ignite a vicious circle whereby each shift leaves faulty production, a sloppy work area, or undesirable shift runs to the following work group. The obvious result is an ever-increasing deterioration of morale, productivity, and quality. This situation will not improve without intervention by a manager. To ignore it or to try selective punitive measures is futile, and dealing with the informal leaders of the groups is not as simple as it may sound. They may have sound reasons, such as personal prestige or the desire to protect their group, for failing to cooperate.

One possible course of action is the one frequently used by President Reagan when he faces an uncooperative Congress. He bypasses the Washington power structure to appeal directly to voters. In the same manner, a skillful manager may achieve results by persuading the informal group to act against the advice of its intransigent leadership. However, this form of interaction is not without pitfalls. A manager may discover that his or her influence or appeal will not persuade workers in every situation. The manager also runs the added risk of alienating the informal group leader or leaders or damaging the effective functioning of the work group. Any attempt at intervention must respect the value of the work group to both its individual members and the organization as a whole.

ON THE JOB REVISITED . . .

Shapiro knew his chances of permanently becoming a foreman was on the line; therefore, when the men prepared for their first break at 9 A.M., he changed his strategy.

"I don't know what the hell you guys think you're doing," Shapiro said, "but you're not going to get away with it. Unless you shape up now, I'm going to report you all to Mr. Funger. I may be young, but I'm no dummy. So either you get off your rear ends and do some work, or Funger gets a list of complaints from me in the morning."

The rest of the work on the pool was finished within two days.

Do you agree with the action Shapiro took? If you had been the foreman, what would you have done? Could his action have any negative long-run consequences?

SUMMARY

The small group has traditionally been regarded as an important form of social organization. Members of large organizations tend to become involved in task-oriented peer groups to provide friendships, lend identity and acceptance, promote loyalty, and obtain assistance. The small groups also teach members the rules of the organization, both formal and informal. Task-oriented peer groups provide informal structures for communication and leadership.

Norms are the stated and unstated rules of a culture, enforced through a system of positive and negative sanctions. Mores are those social rules thought to have great moral force, while folkways are customs, rather like habits, that have less moral force attached to their observance.

Organizations are goal-seeking groups with their own norms and values that members must learn. Although the goals of the organization may not coincide exactly with those of individual employees, most employees manage to accommodate both individual and organizational goal demands. Through on-the-job training, classroom programs, and apprenticeship plans, organizations can teach skills and values to new members.

When an employee's behavior does not conform to the norms of an organization, it is called deviance. Much deviance is subject to internal control; in other words, an individual can learn to accept the norms and integrate them into his or her own set of values and attitudes. Sometimes deviance must be handled through external control—a complex and visible set of social sanctions that may be formal or informal.

Managers have the capability, through goal-linkages, of structuring the relationships of small groups in the work place. A group's cooperation or competitiveness often depends on how members perceive their goals in relation to others.

Conflict within an organization often may be traced to informal group leaders or their followers. These tensions might be overcome by appealing directly to the followers while circumventing the leader, or vice versa.

HUMAN RELATIONS APPLICATIONS

Conclusion 1: To be effective, a supervisor must understand and study the influential forces and drives within the work group.

Application: A supervisor can sometimes structure the types of interactions that will occur in work groups, making cooperative, competitive, or independent linkages as the need arises. Additionally, the adept manager pinpoints a group's informal leaders and uses them to assist in motivating employees to accomplish organizational goals.

Conclusion 2: Informal work groups can be used to help rather than hinder organizational goals.

Application: Groups can be helpful in training new workers to understand both work assignments and company rules. Further, informal groups serve as effective communication links when managers wish to pass "unofficial" information on to employees. They may also free supervisors from having to cope with the emotional crises and needs of individual workers since employees often use their peer groups to fulfill this function.

DISCUSSION QUESTIONS

1. What are the major characteristics of peer groups? How does a peer group differ from a task-oriented peer group?

2. What are the major types of benefits that informal work groups provide to their *members?*

3. What are the major benefits that such groups provide for the *organization?*

4. Describe the types of norms that might exist in groups that are merged to fulfill course project requirements.

5. Describe the major causes of deviance in organizations. What are some of the ways that supervisors can handle problematic deviance on the part of their employees?

6. What is goal-linkage, and how can a manager use this process?

NOTES

1. C.H. Cooley, *Social Organizations.* New York: Charles Scribner's Sons, 1950.

2. George Homans, *The Human Group.* New York: Harcourt Brace, 1950.

3. Greg Oldham and Nancy Rotchford, "Relationships Between Office Characteristics and Employee Reactions: A Study of the Physical Environment," *Administrative Science Quarterly* 28 (December 1983), p. 543.

4. Robert Dubin, *Human Relations in Administration.* Englewood Cliffs, NJ: Prentice-Hall, 1951, p. 68.

5. Frank Shipper, "Quality Circles Using Small Group Formation," *Training and Development Journal* 37 (May 1983), p. 80.

6. Howard S. Becker, *Outsiders: Studies in the Sociology of Deviance.* New York: Free Press, 1963, p. 9.

7. Dean Tjosvold, "Managing Peer Relationships Among Subordinates," *Supervisory Management* 60 (1983), p. 13.

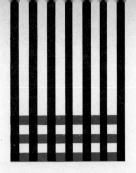

PARTICIPATION AND PRODUCTIVITY

CHAPTER 8

ON THE JOB . . .

PARTICIPATION IS THE KEY TO PRODUCTIVITY

ECONOMIC PRODUCTIVITY

THE CONCEPT OF PARTICIPATION

PARTICIPATION SHOULD BE LINKED TO PRODUCTIVITY

USING CONTROLS FOR INCREASED PRODUCTIVITY

Traditional Approaches
Modern Theory
Workers' Reactions

SUPPORTIVE MANAGEMENT

The Role of the Organization
The Role of the Labor Union

DELEGATING CONTROL

Consultive Management
Suggestion Programs
Democratic Management
Economic Participation and Democratic Management
Multiple Management

STAGES OF PARTICIPATION AND DELEGATION

HOW MUCH PARTICIPATION IS APPROPRIATE?

QUALITY CONTROL CIRCLES
  Japanese Methods
  Quality Control Circles in American Businesses
  ON THE JOB REVISITED . . .

SUMMARY

HUMAN RELATIONS APPLICATIONS

DISCUSSION QUESTIONS

NOTES

MANAGERIAL DIALOGUE: Frank Perdue

ON THE JOB . . .

It is the early 1970s, and you are the president of a major American manufacturer of televisions, radios, and digital clocks. Your company is in trouble because a Japanese industrial conglomerate that used to build fishing boats has gone into the electronics business. Not only are their products cheaper than yours, but they seem to be better made. *Consumer Reports* rated their sets as excellent and yours as only average. To top it off, 3,000 unionized workers at your main assembly plant have threatened to walk out unless their demands are met—a share in the company's profits, more variety in boring assembly line jobs, and an end to the practice of rotating shifts (where a worker starts at 8 A.M. one week, 4 P.M. the next week, and midnight the third week).

Your plant manager, who has studied Japanese management practices, advises agreeing to your workers' demands. They'll work harder, she asserts, if we let them have their own way; then we can make products that are both cheaper and better. Your controller, on the other hand, says that such an agreement is the road to financial ruin. He believes that you should make the union understand that because of the stiff competition, workers should actually take pay cuts so that your prices will be competitive. This is no time to start worrying about whether workers enjoy their jobs.

What would you do?

PARTICIPATION IS THE KEY
TO PRODUCTIVITY

For most of us, a paycheck is the most compelling reason for working. Yet once we're actually on the job, other factors begin to influence us as well. Money becomes a less important motivating force, and we need other "carrots" to induce us to work hard and well.

Traditionally, U.S. corporations have been run with an authoritative hand, largely because of the owners' conviction that employees' needs do not necessarily coincide with the company's profit goals. In recent years, however, some companies have changed their thinking. With tougher economic conditions and an influx of new participative management theories from Japan, some new attitudes have developed. Today, meeting the needs of employees may be viewed as a necessity rather than a luxury.

This chapter deals with these management theories and their success in achieving the ultimate goals of employee satisfaction and increased productivity. Some considerations include:

When is it useful to be democratic with employees?

When does it pay to be antidemocratic?

What is supportive management, and how does it affect employee productivity?

Why would labor unions fight attempts to give employees increased participation in decision making?

How much control should managers delegate to their subordinates?

Why might employees resent company suggestion programs, even when their suggestions may be rewarded with money?

What happens when employees "own" the company they work for?

Why may middle managers feel alienated, and what can be done about it?

ECONOMIC PRODUCTIVITY

In theory, employee participation goes hand in hand with higher productivity. It is assumed that workers who participate to a high degree—whether in manual labor, management, or upper-level planning—will be more productive. However, an economist is likely to question this assumption. In economics, production serves simply as a monetary measure of what each worker produces of value to the company. For example, the output of a dozen workers who produce an expensive Rolls-Royce is greater than a dozen who put together a Volkswagen that can be sold for only one-twentieth of the price. Therefore, the economist would say that the Rolls-Royce workers are more productive, even though they don't work longer or harder. Consider a factory that can turn out 100 corsets a day with one worker. With two workers to operate the machinery, they can turn out 500 per day. If the corsets sell for $10 each, then the first worker's output was worth $1,000 whereas the second worker has added $4,000 to the daily production of the factory. But it does not mean that the second worker is personally more capable or more efficient, it simply means that the factory's resources are more efficiently employed, so that production soars.

"From the strictly economic point of view, more participation may not always yield more productivity."

The economic view of workers as one of the firm's resources can help a manager with some decision making. As resources, workers should be employed to the fullest. Employers should match each worker's intelligence, talents, and abilities with the job being performed. Jobs that allow employees to use all of their abilities will often result in more productivity. For example, a salesperson for a publishing company who has only an average record of success may be much more valuable to the company as an editor because of a real flair for dealing with the written word.

The economic concept of productivity can also be very useful in helping a manager decide how many workers to hire. If there are too few, the manager is wasting resources of land and capital; if there are too many workers, they may be underemployed. But the economic concept of productivity cannot be applied to measure a single individual's contribution, nor can it determine a fair wage for a specific individual in the labor pool.

THE CONCEPT OF PARTICIPATION

Immediately after World War II, productivity generally was considered as the direct output of workers who actually made the new cars, homes, and refrigerators. As competition stiffened in the 1960s and 1970s, management became more concerned about higher worker efficiency. In the 1980s, management has been striving to increase effectiveness—doing the right things the right way—in order to be truly productive. One of the key factors is participation, a concept that was introduced in Chapter 4.[1]

Participation may be defined as the involvement—both mental and emotional—of workers that encourages them to help achieve the organization's goals. With full participation, workers are willing to take responsibility for achieving these goals. As one management specialist writes, "Productivity results when an employee can unleash all the skills, ideas and knowledge accumulated in his or her life experience."[2]

Participation may be an answer to the problems caused by efficiency-oriented, oversimplified jobs. The ideal is well stated by Sid Scott, the director of organizational development at a medium-size Midwest newspaper:

> *"If the employees have a part in the problem-solving of the organization, then they will help it prosper. Motivated employees who are allowed to participate will help the "bottom line" more than unmotivated, non-participating ones. It's as simple as that."*[3]

PARTICIPATION SHOULD BE LINKED TO PRODUCTIVITY

"It is up to the manager to create the proper link between participation and productivity."

It seems wise to add a few words of caution. A policy that gives employees more control of work goals is likely to increase participation, but it will not automatically result in higher productivity. If workers pursue personal goals that are opposed to organizational goals, then increased participation could lead to decreased productivity.

The following guidelines can help create a link between participation and productivity:

1. Managers must allow employees to participate on a full-time basis. During an emergency, workers may be given a greater chance to participate; examples are Chrysler and Eastern Airlines during recent periods of financial distress. But if that participatory spirit disappears along with the crisis, then it's unlikely that a feeling of mutual trust will develop between supervisors and workers. Quite the contrary; the workers may feel that the advantages of participating are one-sided and thus show little cooperative spirit. Pseudo-participation is then the result.

2. The area of participation must be relevant to the workers. The specifics depend on the job situation, organizational goals, and personalities of the people involved. In general, workers desire a voice in the way their personal work environment is organized. Therefore, the machine setup, the shift schedule, and the timing of breaks or other seemingly minor decisions may be very important to an employee. A manager's perceptions of important areas of worker participation may be far different from those of the workers themselves.

3. Managers should bear in mind that workers develop specialized skills or experience. For example, an assembly line worker can often figure out a way to increase productivity by altering the machinery, or a secretary may know how to eliminate the bottleneck that slows down the end-of-the-month reports. Wise supervisors make use of the close, day-to-day knowledge every employee acquires on the job.

4. Supervisors and their subordinates must be able to communicate. Supervisors may assume erroneously that they speak the same language. One example is the use of slang names. A worker may refer to the drive shafts as "jeep drives," while the supervisor calls them Order Number 11389, American Motors Product. Both terms are correct, but if the manager doesn't understand the production slang and the worker fails to recognize the correct title, then a satisfactory conversation about production procedures is unlikely to occur.

Communication also carries more subtle nuances. For any significant participation to occur, each party must feel that his or her position is secure. A supervisor who asks for increased participation should do so without using coercion. Pressure techniques seldom result in long-run involvement.

USING CONTROLS FOR INCREASED PRODUCTIVITY

Controls, like sanctions, may be either positive or negative. Suppose that the head of personnel notices that one of the clerks in her department consistently handles less work than others. She might decide to punish him by demoting him to the position of assistant to one of his former peers, or she might try another negative control and reduce his salary. More positively, the clerk could be offered monetary or emotional incentives to become more involved and more productive. Both approaches employ controls, but by opposite means.

Traditional Approaches

Taylor's scientific management, McGregor's Theory X, and the traditional U.S. management view lead to the same conclusion: the goal of increased productivity often conflicts with the goal of increased participation, and when it does, production should have a higher priority. The traditional managerial methods did indeed raise productivity, but as Mayo's studies (described in Chapter 7) showed, worker apathy and resentment also increased. The only control over participatory behavior seemed to be the small work group.

Modern Theory

A new outlook began to appear in the postwar period: contemporary studies seemed to show that positive controls were effective ways of increasing productivity. There was a new focus on the individual worker's needs and motivations. One of the best known of these studies was conducted by Rensis Likert. Likert noted that the degree of supervision was inversely related to productivity. Managers who employed indirect supervision had a significantly higher productivity quota than did the leaders who relied on close supervision for control. Through several other indicators, Likert arrived at a conclusion: the people-oriented managers were better able to increase participation and thus indirectly increase productivity than were the more traditional managers who made productivity their primary goals.

Even though he found that traditional management methods can increase productivity, Likert stressed that workers also frequently developed accompanying negative attitudes. These tended to result in high scrappage rates, lowered safety, higher absence and turnover, and more grievances.

Workers' Reactions

Because workers have a variety of motives for performing their jobs, their reaction to types of control can vary similarly. For example, Tannenbaum found that, although most employees reacted favorably to more participatory work organization, a few preferred to be submissive. They were, however, the exception. Most felt they had too little control over their own work. Tannenbaum found that a need for power is usually the motive behind a desire for more control.[4]

"A common complaint of all workers is the feeling that they lack power."

On the positive side, this urge for power can prompt the individual to take on a larger work load and to identify more with his or her work and the organization. But greater involvement may lead to greater frustration. Because the involved individual feels more personally responsible for the work within the department, failures can produce a great deal of anxiety.

SUPPORTIVE MANAGEMENT

The concept of supportive management, which we will also discuss in Chapter 10, is closely linked to positive motivation. Increased positive controls and incentives for workers also tend to allow an employee to display initiative and creativity. By extension, this theory of control can also be related to the goals of participation and productivity by organization members. Supportive managers are concerned about the morale of employees, as discussed in the box on page 203.

According to Likert, supportive managers should:

1. Make subordinates feel they are being dealt with in a supportive rather than a threatening manner.

2. Turn each individual into a member of a well-knit and effectively functioning work group with high interaction skills and performance goals.

3. See themselves as members of the informal work group, in addition to their formal role of leader.

For a supportive management relationship to function properly, communication and control should go both ways—up and down the hierarchy. Dowling and Sayles note that since work occupies such a large proportion of a person's life, each worker needs a reasonable balance of inputs and outputs. To achieve this balance for themselves and their employees, supportive managers should ask questions, elicit complaints, and give suggestions rather than direct orders. Managers must be both physically and emotionally available to workers.[5]

Managers may notice that many of the responses they receive from workers are not exactly related to the work situation. For example, on Wednesday an employee may give terse replies to questions because he and his wife had a spat the previous evening. By Friday this same worker may be responsive and friendly because his home situation has become more relaxed. Since so many factors can influence workers' responses, managers must gauge the mood and feelings of their employees before initiating controls. Supportive managers will attempt to use positive incentives to increase productivity—encouragement, a show of concern,

WAKE UP AND BE HAPPY

Morale is something of an obsession at Physio-Control Corp. The $100-million maker of medical electronic instruments goes out of its way to generate goodwill among the troops. It even holds quarterly kickoff meetings for its 800 employees at company headquarters in Redmond, Wash.

At the meetings, which feature refreshments, Physio-Control's president announces news about the company and its performance, hands out recognition awards, and leads a lively question-and-answer period. The company keeps secret the exact date of each meeting, and has been known to announce the surprise start of festivities with a band marching through the halls and offices at 7:15 A.M. It has chosen marching bands from the University of Washington and a local high school, but sometimes it opts for a little variety, such as bagpipers blaring away in full regalia.

If early-morning martial music seems like a rather strident way for a company to whip up esprit de corps, you won't hear much complaining from the people at Physio-Control. In fact, rallies and other morale-boosting efforts are among the factors that earned the company a berth in *The 100 Best Companies to Work for in America* (Addison-Wesley Publishing Co., Reading, Mass.; $17.95), a recently published bestselling book written by Robert Levering, Milton Moskowitz, and Michael Katz. According to Levering and his colleagues, disaffected employees are pretty hard to find at Physio-Control.

"We take great pains to make everyone feel like they're part of a team," says company spokesperson Craig Yamamoto. "In all of our printed material, and in conversation, every employee here is called a 'team member.' If someone refers to a team member as an 'employee,' other team members will get on his case. New people sometimes think it's kind of cornball, but after a while they see that it's genuine, and very much for real."

The collegiality at Physio-Control goes beyond both semantics and showmanship. The company uses four flexible work schedules to accommodate different lifestyles. It has created a generous cash profit sharing plan and savings plan, has a merit pay philosophy, and adheres to a strict policy of promotion within the ranks. It has also consistently maintained full employment. "In the 25-year history of the company, no one has ever been laid off for lack of work," boasts Robert Lowy, Physio-Control's director of human resources. "We're very proud of that track record, and we get a great amount of loyalty in return. If there's a crunch, we transfer people around to balance the workload, or we stop hiring from outside."

In other words, the only time an employee at Physio-Control is likely to get marching orders is at 7:15 in the morning.

Source: *Inc.* (September 1984), p. 138. Reprinted with permission, INC. magazine, September 1984. Copyright © 1984 by INC. Publishing Company, 38 Commercial Wharf, Boston, MA 02110.

or interest—but the most important factor is that controls should match the employees' needs and attitudes.

Supportive managers must be adaptable. Suppose a supervisor is faced with a situation in which one department's productivity has fallen off sharply. The Theory X manager probably would call for a time-and-motion study to try to find the physical problems that are limiting production. In addition, the manager might point out the monetary advantages of increasing participation. If these efforts failed, the traditional manager would be inclined to punish the workers who have the lowest production ratings, firing some and giving pay cuts to others.

In contrast, the supportive, Theory Y manager would concentrate on the social and psychological dynamics of the work group. He or she might check to see if there is any physical misallocation of resources, but most of this manager's effort will go into finding out if the workers have legitimate grievances or frustrations that should be corrected. In doing this, the Theory Y manager will break through the traditional hierarchical communication system in which information and motivation flow only from the top to the bottom of the hierarchy. Supervisors who interact closely with their employees don't just set goals, issue control systems, and then wait for the production figures, they attempt to learn the personal, direct reactions of the staff to the organization's goals and controls. Work patterns, production methods, and even certain short-term goals of the organization may be changed in response to the needs and desires of members. The effect of such changes will be to increase motivation and therefore the performance and productivity of workers, which will help the organization to achieve its long-run goal of profitable production.

The Role of the Organization

The structure of the business organization often plays a large part in determining the manager's choice of controls. A loosely structured or constantly changing organization may allow managers to be supportive. Rigid, production-oriented organizations often disapprove of a focus on employees' needs and reactions. Like every other member of the organization, a superior rates the managers on their performance. Thus, the accepted pattern of proper procedures influences the managers' decision. They have their own career goals to protect. Sometimes managers may be caught in the conflict between their boss's view of the best way to increase productivity and their own.

"The structure of the organization sets limits on a manager's choice of controls."

If top company management believes in purely objective indicators of performance and output, that attitude will trickle down to all managers. Yet higher echelon officials often are not as concerned with the subjective elements of participation as they are with the objective measures of productivity. More simply put, officials' message to subordinates is "I don't care about how you get more productivity; that's your department. But I do care about the results." It is not that upper-level managers have no feelings for their employees, but their main concerns are general, strategic problems and policies rather than specific personal problems of other employees. Therefore, supervisors frequently have the opportunity to handle that area as they see fit. Few organizations, no matter how traditional, can lay down guidelines for every situation that might arise. In the Managerial Dialogue on pages 205–206, Frank Perdue presents some thoughts on productivity and quality.

This degree of independence can produce two related, agreeable results for supportive managers. With skill, managers may be able to motivate their employees to produce at a higher level. Higher productivity, in turn, makes the managers and their methods a valuable asset to the organization. Their career opportunities will be heightened, and at the same time, their methods of encouraging productivity may be given more credence.

It remains quite possible that some organizations will frown on supportive management, even if it produces higher work yields over the long run. Even the most objective, well-organized corporations are staffed by people with personal and differing views of what constitutes good management. Moreover, in many instances, technology and work requirements are so complex that the manager's supportive role is almost

Managerial Dialogue

". . . The secret to productivity is quality, quality, and more quality."

Frank Perdue, chairman of the board of Perdue Farms

Saying that Frank Perdue sells chicken is like saying that A. J. Foyt drives cars for a living. Perdue has taken the mundane business of selling wings, legs, thighs, and all the rest of the bird and elevated it to a science.

Don't talk to Perdue about Japanese productivity—his Maryland chicken farm has perhaps the best reputation in the industry. For Perdue, productivity stems from quality, quality, and more quality, and all the emphasis on quality has an impressive result. Perdue has a much higher profit margin on his chickens than the industry average, and his market share runs close to 60 percent in major Eastern seaboard cities. "I have an unwavering commitment to the quality of my product," Perdue says. "This means sticking to clear, well-defined objectives. I am more interested in being the best rather than the biggest. I simply refuse to do anything that detracts from product quality."

Perdue's father started selling eggs in 1920 in Salisbury, Maryland, and five years later began hatching broilers. Frank Perdue got started in the business at the age of 10 when he was given responsibility for the care of fifty chickens. He operated his own egg business for several years, earning

*Perdue Farms is the
nation's fifth largest
chicken producer.*

$10 and $20 a month. After high school and two years of college, he went into the family business full time. The company had three employees including himself and his father.

Perdue Farms began a special cross-breeding program to improve the quality of their chickens, and the business began to expand. By 1950, when Frank Perdue became president, Perdue Farms had forty employees and was one of the largest chicken growers on Maryland's Eastern Shore. In 1968, Perdue Farms, 400 employees strong, purchased its own processing plant in Salisbury and Perdue-brand chickens went to market for the first time. Today the company employs more than 9,000 people, operates six processing plants, and markets nearly 6,000,000 chickens a week. It is the fifth largest poultry processor in the country.

Soon after the company began marketing Perdue-brand chickens, an ad agency decided Frank Perdue would make the best salesman in his commercials. "We had just completed a four-day tour of the company's facilities," said Stan Pesky, president of Scali, McCabe, Sloves International ad agency. "What impressed us most was Frank's personal concern for product quality. If a problem cropped up at the plant, at the hatchery, or in the distribution system, he would excuse himself and personally make sure it was solved. That's what spurred the idea, 'It takes a tough man to make a tender chicken.'"

Perdue attributes his thoroughness to his father, whom he says had to know everything that was going on. "Our business was much smaller then, and staying on top of things was easier. But I won't let size get in the way of staying involved in every aspect of our operation."

Perdue's style forces his top managers to be equally productive and concerned about quality. Vice chairman Donald Mabe said, "Frank pays particular attention to personality and drive. He is smart and has impeccable work habits. Because he's so organized, he forces everyone else to be. It's the only way he knows how to run the business." Perdue's brand of participation carries over to all aspects of his business. Tom Peters, author of *A Passion for Excellence* (New York: Random House, 1985), reports that during the course of a day Perdue delivers half a dozen minisermons about quality of the product to his employees. He has also purchased a giant blow-dryer powered by a 727 jet engine to reduce the number of hairs adhering to his packaged chicken wings from an average of eight to just two.

Perdue would be the first to admit it takes hard work to achieve the productivity—and the profits—that Perdue Farms prides itself on. That belief in the old-fashioned work ethic is reflected in his advice to young entrepreneurs. "Believe strongly in what you do. Make the objectives clear and realistic and then commit to them 100 percent. Be willing to make sacrifices to achieve your ultimate goal. A half-hearted approach will never get you there."

hidden. Think of the worker who wires a circuit board for a main-frame computer company. His work skills require manual dexterity, yet he need not know how his product is related to the whole computer to do a competent job. If a manager felt that this worker could be more productive by learning more about the overall operation, then the manager would have to convince both the employees and the organization that this man was capable of greater responsibilities. It might be difficult to prove that the benefits of additional training would far outweigh its costs.

The Role of the Labor Union

A manager's job is to delegate work roles and responsibilities to other organization members. In making these decisions, the manager must take into account not only his or her own judgment and the company's policy, but also the rules—formal and informal—of the labor unions to which many workers belong.

The history of labor unions indicates some limits to supportive management. From their start in the mid-1800s, unions have been faced with unremitting hostility from businesses. The classical theory of economics viewed workers merely as tools of production, and most managers were happy to accept this view. The militant attitudes that grew out of this conflict remain.

Unions, by their very nature, foster an "us against them" attitude. Union leaders often guard their present positions of power as jealously as did the business leaders in the past. In their eyes, a supportive manager usurps a labor union's power. By welcoming the grievances and fostering the goals of the union membership, he or she is asking them to join forces with the "enemy." It is not surprising that supervisory personnel are sometimes stymied in their attempts to be supportive, especially if their ideas run counter to the union's standards.

Suppose for example, that one computer worker busily assembling circuit boards is a union member. The supportive manager in this instance would be unable to offer incentives in the form of promotions if they violated previously agreed-on management-labor contracts. In most labor-related areas, the unions and management have agreed on the procedures by which a worker can receive a modified or new job assignment and the wages he or she will receive. Therefore, few supervisors are in a position to offer unrestricted rewards for participation or productivity.

Even if union officials are asked to participate in the decision-making process, unions may remain wary. Participation weakens their ability to challenge procedures. And it may put the union official in the weaker position in regard to his membership. Cooperation between management and labor leaders sometimes leads union workers to the conclusion that their union representatives have sold out to the company.

Some types of participation are acceptable to unions, while others are not. For example, a union may support a plantwide safety program because it benefits the membership, but oppose an incentive program that threatens the future contract bargaining power of the workers. There are no hard-and-fast rules for management-union cooperation. The supportive manager must realize that in many instances both sides are concerned with their positions of power and influence. For the organization as a whole to prosper, both sides must approach one another in a spirit of good faith. It is not usually necessary for management to exert control systems at the expense of unions, or vice versa.

DELEGATING CONTROL

"It's easier to order people around than to get them to cooperate, but it is usually much less effective."

Granting subordinates some degree of freedom or asking their advice occasionally is harder for a manager than simply ordering people around. It takes more skill and effort. Although some managers worry about losing their authority, delegation has numerous advantages.

The basic premise behind delegating control to employees is that involved workers will produce more. Along with higher productivity often comes a lower rate of absenteeism, turnover, and apathy. Far from jeopardizing the managers' control and power, this increase in production can boost their status within the organization, which in turn enhances their odds for advancement.

Delegating control as a means of gaining more control may seem contradictory. Let us examine the process. Systems of formal delegation are already institutionalized in most organizations. Policies and decisions are made by the management. At each level, a manager has formal policies to implement, but also some margin for personal choice and judgment. The manager who elects to delegate some control may soon carry some weight with both superiors and subordinates. Superiors will recognize outstanding success in fulfilling organizational goals and thus possibly allocate the manager more power, prestige, or wealth. At the same time, involved subordinates may be more responsible and loyal to a manager who includes them in the decision-making processes.

Among the popular forms of delegating control are consultive management, democratic management, and multiple management.

Consultive Management

As the name implies, a *consultive manager* confers with employees before making a decision. In a case that involves changes in job definitions, a manager might meet each employee separately, might convene an ad hoc committee, or talk to union representatives about the changes. In these ways, the manager can explain the reasons the changes are being sought and listen to employees' reactions, opinions, and suggestions.

After consultation, the manager might choose to revise the changes or even present an entirely new program to his or her superiors. With this type of management, the consultive supervisor is under no obligation to heed the advice of subordinates. The employees advise, but the manager decides. These consultive management practices require no changes in the formal company structure and policies or in the supervisor/subordinate relationships. They can exist merely at the option of the supervisor.

If the manager takes employees' advice seriously, then their informal authority is strengthened. Increased personal interaction also may help the supervisor settle grievances within the department. However, the manager who is arrogant about considering opposing views may diminish rather than increase participation. If workers gain the impression that they are merely being asked to approve a program already decided on, they may react with apathetic behavior at best and antagonistic attitudes at worst.

Suggestion Programs

The suggestion program serves as a form of consultive management. It encourages workers to participate by recommending new ways of increasing productivity. In some corporations, this plan takes the form of suggestion boxes placed throughout the buildings. Workers whose ideas are used often receive checks, bonds, corporate shares, or some other monetary reward. In addition, these employees are given companywide publicity for their contribution.

At first glance, this type of program might seem ideal. It caters to both the monetary needs of employees and their more personal desires for self-esteem and peer prestige. The organization demonstrates that it will give credit and reward to workers who participate. But there are at least two negative aspects of such a program:

1. Not all workers will react positively to suggestion programs. Many feel that suggestions are only a shallow way for the organization to share control.

Suggestion programs may fail to offer face-to-face communication between workers and management.

"In a business setting, democracy too often leads to chaos."

2. The company's rewards do not always match the value of the suggestion. The employee who is given $500 for an idea that he or she knows will save the organization $250,000 per year feels cheated.

A suggestion program offers no face-to-face communication between supervisor and subordinates. Therefore, it does not encourage personal interaction within supportive management. In addition, the very nature of the program limits the worker to an advisory position. He or she has no real control or means of forcefully advocating ideas.

Democratic Management

Although the vast majority of supervisors think democracy is an ideal form of government, only a small number would consider running a company that way. Ours is an age of transition. Many young managers have heard that democratic supervision is preferable to the more traditional, autocratic form of decision making. In an actual job situation, however, pressures from superiors and work peer groups discourage democratic interaction between managers and subordinates.

The main advantage of a democratic style of management is that it meets the needs and desires of many employees to become involved. Unfortunately, the needs of employees do not necessarily coincide with the organization's goals. One study of a nationally organized delivery company found that the units with democratic supervision did not have high performance records in comparison to the more traditional units. The author of this study concluded:

> *While this pattern of control may lead to high rank-and-file morale, it does not appear to promote basic identification with organizational objectives and practices or motivate actions leading to high performances. It appears that in this organization high rank-and-file control relative to the leaders may have the effect of members' acting simply in terms of their own self-interests and not accepting the contributions of the leader.*[6]

The implications of this study are clear. A democratic form of supervision may very well result in higher participation, yet yield less productivity. In addition, once such a program is initiated, attempts to diminish employees' control will cause hostility.

From the supervisor's standpoint, democratic management is always risky. The leader is in danger of losing control of subordinates. Democratic control mechanisms simply do not lend themselves to a segmented, formalized decision-making organization.

Economic Participation and Democratic Management

In spite of these problems, the democratic management style can be successful in some organizations. Voluntary organizations, such as the Red Cross or the Boy Scouts, in which members share similar interests often function with a great deal of harmony and productivity under democratic group controls. So might the organization that is owned by its employees. Each member, whether supervisor or subordinate, owns a share of the corporation. Each employee also receives proportional dividends from the profits of increased productivity. How much actual control the workers have over company policy is a matter of debate, but the idea is appealing to both employees and consumers.

To a lesser extent, an increasing number of organizations are using economic incentives in the form of stocks or shares as a form of indirect employee control. Buying company shares through a payroll plan is a way for employees to become more involved in the company's success, while the control remains in the hands of top management.

Multiple Management

The multiple management system was developed in the 1930s by McCormick and Company, in response to middle managers' desire for a larger role in decision making. It is designed to give junior executives a chance to formulate policy through a formal advisory committee. This committee brainstorms, screens, and develops ideas. Membership on the committee rotates to allow a large number of people to take part in planning. By having more managers participate, executives' decision-making skills are likely to increase and the organization should benefit from the wealth of new ideas. Because middle managers feel that they too have the chance to participate in making policy, they will become more involved, and therefore more productive, managers.

STAGES OF PARTICIPATION AND DELEGATION

The degree of participation in any company must depend on the orientation of the organization, managers, and workers. This combined orientation will determine the best way to delegate controls. As an illustration, let's look at an organization that each of us should be quite familiar with: the school system. A typical education hierarchy consists of school boards, a superintendent of schools, principals, subject area supervisors, teachers, and students. The business organization has a similar hierarchy, which includes a board of directors, president of the corporation, department heads, supervisors (in the form of junior executives to foremen), and workers.

Like business organizations, school systems set general policy guidelines and goals at the top. The board of directors and the school board both influence the tone of their respective organizations. The person picked to oversee the operations of the organization (either a corporation president or superintendent of schools) usually reflects the views of those who make the appointment. Likewise, the department in a business and principals in a school are expected to agree with the organization's goals and means of achieving them. Finally, the immediate supervisors in a business and teachers in a school are charged with motivating their subordinates toward participation and productivity. In other words, each manager, executive, or teacher is under pressure from superiors to perform in a prescribed manner.

"The choice of formal controls reflects the norms of an organization."

In a business organization, the incentives, sanctions, and amount of control given to employees are easily discerned, and they can give one an idea of the corporation's philosophy. Within a matter of weeks, a perceptive new employee would know whether the organization leans toward a supportive form of management or the more traditional one. Schools also reflect the system's orientation. For instance, it is a safe assumption that in schools where corporal punishment, strict seating arrangements, monitored hallways, and limited teacher-pupil interaction exist, a traditional view of both education and the nature of the student prevails.

In formal delegation, control is implicitly laid down to members of the education system by way of the general superior-to-subordinate relationship between teachers and their students. However, the less formalized, more autonomous social delegation of controls is more or less left in the hands of each teacher. Therefore, it is not uncommon to find some teachers in every school who choose to interact with students in a way that differs from the prescribed method. Teachers and work supervisors alike can deviate somewhat in the social controls they employ within the formal organization. In addition, authority figures in either system vary their behavior in order to facilitate participation and productivity.

In the course of the work day, the flexible teacher is likely to play the role of autocrat, benevolent dictator, and laissez-faire supervisor. Similarly, the manager exerts social controls according to the situation. Strict discipline may be necessary with one worker, while many workers will respond better to the supportive form of interaction. In making some decisions, such as the selection of a group spokesperson, the manager may be entirely democratic. In other areas, the manager might try to make the final choice personally, as when the decision is directly related to company goals or policy. Any system of controls and incentives must be applied with attention given to the attitudes, backgrounds, and goals of every individual or group involved.

HOW MUCH PARTICIPATION IS APPROPRIATE?

One of the issues managers continually face is how much input should subordinates have in decision making. To help this concern, Vroom and Yetton have developed a model to assist managers in choosing an appropriate decision style.[7] There are a total of five different styles that one might use, ranging from the manager making the decision with no input from subordinates to having a group of subordinates work with the manager in reaching a "consensus" for solving a particular problem. Each of these styles is displayed in Table 8.1.

According to this approach, the choice of a decision style depends on the nature of the problem facing a manager and his or her answer to seven questions about the situation. These seven questions are placed on a decision tree flow chart, as shown in Figure 8.1. If the answer to the first question—"Is there a quality requirement such that one solution is likely to be more rational than others?"—is no, the next question deals with whether or not acceptance of the decision by subordinates is critical. If the manager answers no to this question, then he or she should use A1, or the autocratic style, of decision making. The manager should make the decision alone, with no input from subordinates.

To further illustrate the working of this model, put yourself in the following situation. You are the manager of a two-year-old company that specializes in the delivery of small packages to customers. You employ a staff of fifteen delivery people, each of whom has a delivery vehicle provided by the company. All of these vehicles were purchased used, and each is five years old. The company has just purchased four new delivery trucks, and now you have to decide which of your employees will receive a new truck. Since all employees were hired at the same time, you cannot use seniority as a basis for the decision. Moreover, each person puts in approximately the same mileage each week. If you use the Vroom

---

TABLE 8.1 Types of Management Decision Styles

1. You solve the problem or make the decision yourself, using information available to you at that time.

2. You obtain the necessary information from your subordinate(s), then decide on the solution to the problem yourself. You may or may not tell your subordinates what the problem is in getting the information from them. The role played by your subordinates in making the decision is clearly one of providing the necessary information to you, rather than generating or evaluating alternative solutions.

3. You share the problem with relevant subordinates individually, getting their ideas and suggestions without bringing them together as a group. Then *you* make the decision, which may or may not reflect your subordinates' influence.

4. You share the problem with your subordinates as a group, collectively obtaining their ideas and suggestions. Then *you* make the decision, which may or may not reflect your subordinates' influence.

5. You share a problem with your subordinates as a group. Together you generate and evaluate alternatives and attempt to reach agreement (consensus) on a solution. Your role is much like that of chairman. You do not try to influence the group to adopt "your" solution, and you are willing to accept and implement any solution that has the support of the entire group.

Source: Reprinted by permission of the publisher from "A New Look at Managerial Decision Making," Victor H. Vroom, *Organizational Dynamics,* Spring 1973, © 1973 by AMACON, a division of American Management Associations, page 67. All rights reserved.

---

and Yetton model to choose your decision-making style (whether or not there is a quality requirement), the next question would be question D, "Is acceptance of decision by subordinates critical to implementation?" In this case, you probably answered yes. After all, if the employees did not feel that your choice was fair, you could have eleven angry delivery employees on your hands (missed delivery dates, resignations, absenteeisms, and so on). Having said yes to question D, you would move on to question E. "If you were to make the decision by yourself, is it reasonably certain that it would be accepted by your subordinates?" This is a real judgment call. If you said yes to this question, your style would be A1, an autocratic, no input from subordinates approach. If you answered no, the appropriate decision style would be C11; that is, you would share the problem with your group of employees and reach a consensus as a group.

The main advantage to using the Vroom and Yetton model is that it helps managers think about the issues that may be important in making good decisions—acceptance by subordinates and decision quality.

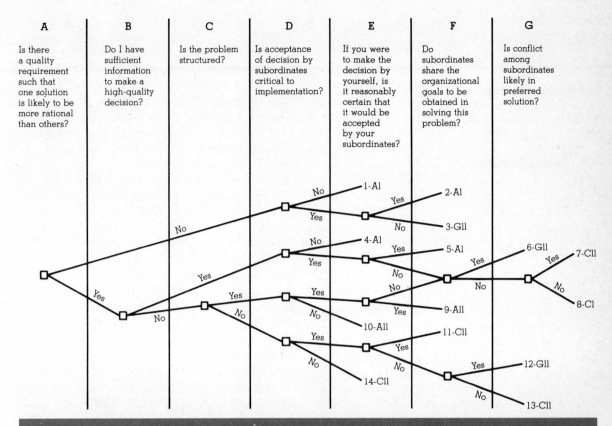

A	B	C	D	E	F	G
Is there a quality requirement such that one solution is likely to be more rational than others?	Do I have sufficient information to make a high-quality decision?	Is the problem structured?	Is acceptance of decision by subordinates critical to implementation?	If you were to make the decision by yourself, is it reasonably certain that it would be accepted by your subordinates?	Do subordinates share the organizational goals to be obtained in solving this problem?	Is conflict among subordinates likely in preferred solution?

FIGURE 8.1   Decision Process Flow Chart

Source: Reprinted, by permission of the publisher, from "A New Look at Managerial Decision Making," Victor H. Vroom, Orga-nizational Dynamics, Spring 1973, © 1973, by AMACON, a division of American Management Associations, page 70. All rights reserved.

QUALITY CONTROL CIRCLES

The use of quality control (Q-C) circles was one of the most popular methods of trying to increase participation, and therefore productivity, among American firms in the early 1980s. It had been borrowed from Japan.

Japanese Methods

In Japan, a Q-C circle usually consists of a small number of employees (no more than ten) taken from a larger group, such as a department or an assembly line. The task of each Q-C circle is to study problems of production or service that fall within the scope of the work group. For instance, a Q-C circle of eight workers who assemble the front doors of refrigerators might consider how they could reduce the time it takes to put on the doors. A Q-C circle of six engineers might examine how the work stations on the entire assembly line could be better organized.[8]

In Japan, Q-C circle members often receive extensive training in statistical methods to help them spot problems of quality control. Even low-ranking workers are expected to be familiar with statistical concepts such as the range or average and standard deviation, which lead to the discovery of quality control problems.

Each Q-C circle meets for one or two hours a week, not always on company time. If Q-C circle members have identified a problem, they will try to find ways to solve it—even to the extent of sending recommendations to the company's top management. If a problem appears to be industrywide, a Q-C circle might even be formed among rival companies so that all may take advantage of solutions.

Each company rewards and honors its successful Q-C circles, as does each major industry and the nation itself. November is "Quality Circle Month" in Japan. Many observers believe Q-C circles succeed in Japan because the culture as a whole rewards group participation, company loyalty, and high productivity.

In his best-seller, *Theory Z* (Reading, MA: Addison-Wesley), William Ouchi outlined some of the characteristics of the Japanese corporation that have been more successful than those seen in U.S. firms in raising productivity and improving the quality of products:

1. *Lifetime employment.*   About 35 percent of the Japanese work force need not fear losing their jobs, even in recessions.

2. *Nonspecialized careers.*   In the United States, a bright college marketing major might stay in marketing/sales through his or her whole working career. Not so in Japan, where job rotation is valued.

3. *Hefty bonuses.*   Many Japanese companies pay out bonuses equivalent to a third or more of an annual salary. This provides a cushion against poor economic years, since a smaller bonus may be paid if profits drop.

4. *Decisions by consensus.*   Unlike U.S. companies, which reward individual executives who say "the buck stops here," Japanese firms strive to make decisions by consensus. A new product might not be

introduced, for instance, until the sales force was convinced there was a market, the plant manager was sure it could be produced, the corporate treasurer knew there was a line of credit available, and the corporate president felt the product would fit in with the company's values. It might take the Japanese firm longer to make such a decision than an American firm, but once the decision was made, the Japanese company could implement it much more quickly. A summary of characteristics of Theory Z firms can be seen in Table 8.2.

Japanese management techniques grow out of Japanese culture. In Japan, the group is placed before the individual, whereas in the United States, a very high value is placed on individualism. The Japanese prize stability and try to avoid change. They respect loyalty, and they prefer strong and centralized leadership. Because they are very demanding consumers, expecting high quality and aesthetic value, as workers they are accepting of very high standards for finished products.[9]

Many observers believe a key element in the success of Japanese firms is their concern for human resources. Says one scholar:

> *Employees . . . perceive a close relationship between their own welfare and the company's financial welfare. Accordingly, behavior for the company's benefit that may appear self-sacrificing is not at all so.*[10]

Of course, there is a darker side to Japanese management. The heavily paternalistic style of Japanese companies, which offers "cradle to grave" employment, may lead to sexist and racist hiring and promotion practices. It may be tough for outsiders to penetrate higher management, even when fresh blood is needed. Rewarding managers, engineers, and scientists for their general knowledge risks destroying that sense of professionalism needed in many specialties.

TABLE 8.2 Characteristics of Theory Z Corporations

1. Long-term employment
2. Slow evaluation and promotion
3. Moderately specialized careers
4. Consensual decision making
5. Individual responsibility
6. Implicit, informal control (but with explicit measures)
7. Wholistic concern for the employee

Source: Nina Hatvany and Vladimire Pucik, "Japanese Management Practices and Productivity," *Organizational Dynamics* 9 (Spring 1981), page 20.

Quality Control Circles in American Businesses

What happens when Japanese management techniques are used in the United States? Will they work despite the enormous cultural differences between the two countries?

A handful of American companies—Hewlett-Packard, IBM, Eastman Kodak, and Procter & Gamble among them—have taken the Japanese approach of using Q-C circles to increase participation and productivity. Unfortunately, many other American firms have tried to add the Q-C circle without changing their corporate climate, which encourages competition and individuality rather than team effort. Using Q-C circles as a quick fix for productivity problems is likely to fail without a true commitment from top management to the concept of employee participation. It takes time, training, rewards, and a real delegation of authority for the Q-C circle to succeed.

"Q-C circles are not a quick-fix solution."

Researchers who have evaluated the American approach to Q-C circles say the major reason for failure lies in the managers' unrealistic expectations.[11] They look for immediate results, measurable leaps in output from week to week. In fact, Q-C circles are a long-term solution, and it may take many months of support for the program before results are noticeable. Some Q-C circles have succeeded in the United States. At Ford Motor Company, for instance, statistical quality control methods get at least partial credit for a 48 percent improvement in quality since the 1980 model year.[12]

The verdict is still out on Q-C circles in the United States. They may be just another management fad, or they may become a valuable new tool for improving productivity. In the long run, it may be the commitment of management to the Q-C circle concept that makes the difference.

ON THE JOB REVISITED . . .

As the president of our hypothetical company beset by internal and external problems, you might choose to adopt some Japanese management practices, such as quality control circles. But you should recognize that these are long-term changes that will do little to solve your immediate crisis. If you decide to give in to the workers' demand for greater freedom, you may be able to hand them greater responsibility as well. Faced with the possible loss of their jobs, the workers might be very receptive to improving productivity, particularly if they can feel a greater sense of participation.

What are the long-term implications of your action?

SUMMARY

Because the concept of equality is deeply rooted in our social system, participation in decision making is generally accepted as a social ideal. In theory, participation, economic productivity, and benefits are positively correlated. *Participation* in this sense may be defined as a person's involvement, both mental and emotional, that encourages him or her to work actively toward group goals. Participation is encouraged when it is established on a full-time basis, when the area of participation is relevant to workers, when specialized skills are considered, and when communication is standardized for all concerned. Productivity may be increased through the use of control mechanisms, which may be both positive and negative.

In Likert's view, widely adopted by modern management, people-oriented managers are more likely to increase productivity than are production-oriented managers. This is the theory of supportive management, which requires managers to be insightful, solicitous of employee opinions, and adaptable. Yet the style of participation adopted also depends on the size and character of the organization. Also, worker participation may not be totally approved by labor unions involved.

Delegation of control represents another method through which employees may achieve a modified form of supportive management, in which the superior consults with subordinates before making decisions. Suggestion programs offer another participatory device. Democratic management is desirable in theory, but workers' needs are not necessarily consistent with profit goals. In multiple management, the often neglected ranks of middle management are called on to make innovative decisions.

A number of American companies have adopted participative management practices from Japan, among them the idea of Q-C circles. These Q-C circles, whether part of an all-embracing cultural and corporate system in Japan or just another management technique for a U.S. company, are aimed at improving corporate productivity directly by increasing worker involvement.

HUMAN RELATIONS APPLICATIONS

Conclusion 1:   Participation by employees in work-related decisions that affect them can sometimes be used as a motivational device.

Application: In deciding whether or not to involve employees in decisions, a manager must take into consideration several factors. Participation should be relevant to workers; supervisor and employee must be able to communicate effectively with each other; employees must have the expertise necessary to contribute to the participation process; and a feeling of mutual trust must exist between supervisors and their workers.

Conclusion 2:   Supportive management practices are closely linked to positive work motivation on the part of employees.

Application: The supportive manager asks questions, tries to solicit employee feedback, and gives suggestions instead of direct orders. Managers who use positive incentives to encourage high productivity are more likely to build high morale levels within their sections and in turn promote motivation.

DISCUSSION QUESTIONS

1. Describe the economic view of workers. What are the strengths and weaknesses of this perspective?

2. What are the major guidelines for creating a link between participation and productivity?

3. How can a manager become more supportive in dealing with his or her workers?

4. Describe the differences between consultive, democratic, and multiple management.

5. What are the elements that determine the amount of participation a subordinate should have in the decision-making process?

6. What is a quality control circle? Do you think that such a concept is a fad? Why or why not?

NOTES

1. Kenneth F. Misa and Timothy Stein, "Strategic HRM and the Bottom Line," *Personnel Administration* 29 (October 1983), p. 27.

2. Doris Savage, "Trust as a Productivity Management Tool," *Training and Development Journal* 26 (February 1982), p. 57.

3. Sid Scott, "The Design Group in Action," *Training and Development Journal* 35 (April 1982), p. 72.

4. A.S. Tannenbaum, "Control in Organizations: Individual Adjustment and Organizational Performance," in *Seminar on Basic Research in Management Controls.* Stanford, CA: Stanford University, 1963, p. 6.

5. W.F. Dowling, Jr., and L.R. Sayles, *How Managers Motivate: The Imperatives of Supervision.* New York: McGraw-Hill, 1971, p. 274.

6. Clagert G. Smith and Ogus N. Ari, "Organizational Control Structure and Member Consensus," *American Journal of Sociology* (May 1964), p. 638.

7. V. Vroom and P. Yetton, *Leadership and Decision Making.* Pittsburgh: University of Pittsburgh, 1973.

8. William Ouchi, *Theory Z.* Reading, MA: Addison-Wesley, 1981, pp. 262-263.

9. Ken Moroi, "A New Style for Japanese Management," *Economic Eye* 6 (September 1985), pp. 14–15.

10. Nina Hatvany and Vladimir Pucik, "Japanese Management Practices and Productivity," *Operational Dynamics* (Spring 1981), p. 18.

11. Robert Wood, Frank Hull, and Koya Azumi, "Evaluating Quality Circles: The American Application," *California Management Review* 26 (Fall 1983), p. 48.

12. Ernesto Poza, "A Do-It-Yourself Guide to Group Problem Solving," *Personnel* 60 (March–April 1983), p. 76.

ORGANIZATIONAL PROCESSES

PART 3

CHAPTER 9

The Role of the Manager
in the Organization

CHAPTER 10

Leadership

CHAPTER 11

Evaluating Subordinates: Performance
Appraisal and Discipline

CHAPTER 12

Managing Conflict

CHAPTER 13

Improving the Quality of Working Life

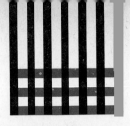

THE ROLE OF THE MANAGER IN THE ORGANIZATION

CHAPTER 9

ON THE JOB . . .

A GOOD MANAGER PLAYS THE ROLE

WHAT IS A ROLE?

Are Role Players Born or Made?
Never Underestimate the Power of the Individual

DEFINING THE MANAGERIAL ROLE

Leader
Executive
Negotiator
Developer
Innovator
Human Being
The Mintzberg Model

ROLE STRAIN AND ROLE CONFLICT

A Manager Faces Conflicting Demands
A Manager Must Satisfy Many People
Resolving Role Conflict

THE SPECIAL ROLE OF THE WOMAN MANAGER

The Stereotypes and the Realities
Overcoming the Barriers
The Managerial Woman

DEMANDS OF THE OUTSIDE ENVIRONMENT

ON THE JOB REVISITED . . .

SUMMARY

HUMAN RELATIONS APPLICATIONS

DISCUSSION QUESTIONS

NOTES

MANAGERIAL DIALOGUE: Harold Geneen

ON THE JOB . . .

With his fifth anniversary rapidly approaching, Amos Marsh began thinking about getting a special present for his wife, Laurie. Marsh decided to get her a piece of jewelry because he noticed that she had none. He purchased a striking sterling silver necklace at Hanson's Jewelry Store and returned home to give his wife her anniversary surprise.

But when Laurie unwrapped her present, it was Marsh who was surprised. Laurie's face dropped as she explained, "Even though this is a very beautiful piece of silver, I just couldn't wear it. I can't even wear a watch. Any piece of jewelry just feels uncomfortable on me. I hope you understand, Amos."

The next day, Marsh returned to Hanson's, told the sales clerk what had happened, and asked for a refund. The clerk, Lois Whittner, explained that it was the store's policy not to give cash refunds. They would gladly accept the silver necklace and give Marsh credit toward another purchase, but they would not give him his money back.

Marsh: This is incredible. You people are supposed to be running a reputable organization. You can plainly see that there's no damage to the necklace. Why can't you just take it back, put it in the display case, give me my money back, and tear up yesterday's receipt?

Wittner: I'm sorry, Mr. Marsh, but store policy is store policy. I only work here. There's nothing I can say or do to change the existing rules.

Marsh: You only work here? What the hell does that mean? This is not such a tremendous business that you can't afford to use a little human understanding. If you were the size of the electric company or something big, I could understand it. But this is ridiculous!

Wittner: There's nothing else I can say, Mr. Marsh. You can either keep the necklace or return it for credit.

Marsh: Let me speak to the owner, Mr. Hanson. I'm sure he'll understand. (Mrs. Wittner leaves the room and returns with Mr. Hanson, a tall gray-haired man dressed in a dark suit.)

Hanson: I understand you're having some difficulty with a piece of merchandise you purchased yesterday. Is there anything I can do to help?

Marsh: There sure is! This sales clerk of yours claims that she is not allowed to give me a refund for a silver necklace I bought here yesterday. It was an anniversary present for my wife, but she can't use it. Therefore, I need a refund so that I can get something else for her.

Hanson: I'm sorry sir, but Mrs. Wittner was correct in what she told you. It is the policy of this store not to give any cash refunds on returned merchandise. I'm sure Mrs. Wittner explained that you can, of course, receive a credit voucher for the full amount you spent.

Marsh: But I don't want credit—my wife refuses to wear jewelry of any sort. It would be nothing short of idiotic for me to have credit at a jewelry store under those circumstances.

Hanson: I'm sorry, but our policy on returns is clearly posted on the cash register, so it was your own responsibility to read it before you made a purchase. I'm sorry for the inconvenience, but store policy is store policy.

Marsh: You can keep store policy! And I'll tell you one more thing. Several of my friends are regular customers here. But you can bet your life that you won't see them in here again!

Marsh stormed out of the store. Watching him leave, Hanson remarked to his sales clerk, "Carry on, Mrs. Wittner. You've done the right thing. Some people are just too self-absorbed to understand that we've got a business to run here and that a business just can't be run without good, strong rules."

If you were the owner of the jewelry store, how would you have handled the situation? Would you have supported your employee or bent the company rule?

A GOOD MANAGER PLAYS THE ROLE

Roles are assumed by virtually everyone at one time or another—student, friend, consumer, worker, and citizen. The role of manager brings additional responsibilities that must be carried out to the satisfaction of both employers and employees. At the same time, a manager must find personal satisfaction in the role and integrate it into the demands of the other roles he or she has also assumed.

Consider just one implication of role playing. The role of student allows considerable personal freedom. A student works on his own schedule and can even cut classes when some other attraction seems irresistible. He can wear his hair any way he wants to and dress in the style that makes him feel most comfortable. But when he leaves school and takes on a management role in a big organization, a different set of rules applies. Managers are asked to keep a fairly tight schedule of attendance. They must conform to general standards of dress and behavior, and they are obligated to assume responsibility for others' activities as well as their own. The transition from the role of student to the role of manager can be very stressful.

In this chapter we will consider the manager as role player, including such topics as:

Where do people learn the roles they will play throughout their lives and careers?

How does a manager reconcile personal roles, such as husband or wife, mother or father, with the requirements of the organization?

What roles must a manager play in a supervisory position—roles that he or she would not be called on to play outside the organization?

Can an executive avoid role conflict in dealing with superiors and subordinates?

What are some of the barriers that women managers face, and how do the effective ones surmount them?

WHAT IS A ROLE?

A *role* is defined as a set of behavioral expectations associated with a specific position in a social system. Roles are taught to us by the process of *socialization,* or the passing on of a group's culture, morals, values, and rules of behavior. Parents, schools, the Cub Scouts, the 4-H club, and the Saturday morning reading group at the library are all agents of socialization. The values and goals of society are taught to us over and over throughout childhood as we pass from infant dependency into adulthood. We learn how to play our social roles through socialization, so that when we are adults, we know what is expected of us.

"Throughout our entire lives, we are being socialized to fit into the demands of society."

Are Role Players Born or Made?

Other animals are also taught how to behave by their elders. For example, birds reared in isolation are unable to sing correctly the songs by which their species identifies and courts other members. Baby tigers must be taught by their mothers how to hunt successfully. Baby baboons are taught by all the older members of the group to recognize their place in the hierarchy. All such learning, passed from one generation to the next, is a form of socialization. Human socialization is unique because it takes such a long time. Most people spend at least the first sixteen years of their lives dependent on the care of adults. This allows the transmission of very complicated social behavior. The use of highly developed language also helps convey highly complex concepts, such as patriotism or altruism, which compose an important part of human culture.

Is all human behavior the result of socialization? Many scientists feel that biological forces must also be taken into account. Starting with infancy, biological needs such as milk, warmth, and comfort are directly linked to emotional needs, like security and love. In fact, several psychological studies have concluded that human contact and affection is the most important basis for a healthy infant's development. One such study observed infants in orphanages who received adequate health care, but little human contact, and found that these infants had a much higher death rate than infants raised in orphanages with more emotional and physical human contact.[1]

Several psychological theories stress the importance of the biological or inherent forces in determining an individual's socialization. One example is Freud's theory of personality (see Chapter 2). Freud stressed the id as the root of all biological and emotional drives, with the superego and ego controlling and mediating the basic urges of the id. In Freud's view, socialization consisted of mediating basic biological drives to conform to the expectations of society.

Sociologists, on the other hand, stress cultural surroundings rather than biological drives as elements of socialization. As sociologist Charles Cooley summed it up many years ago, each individual is a product of society. Cooley said that we define ourselves and our roles in society primarily by looking at the way others view us. This "looking glass self" has three main components: our perception of how our behavior appears to others, our perception of their judgments of this behavior, and our feelings about these judgments.

The junior executive might serve as an apt example of the concept of the looking glass self. Fred, a young, entry-level executive, must decide what to call his boss. Should it be "Ms. Carmichael" or "Alice"? Fred's worry about this question is due in part to his worry about how his boss, as well as his fellow workers, will view his decision. If he chooses "Alice," will the boss think he is being friendly or impertinent? Will co-workers disapprove of this seeming intimacy, or will they be impressed by it? Once Fred answers these questions about how others judge his behavior, he must then decide how he feels about their judgments. Some people might be quite willing to risk the hostility of co-workers to gain approval from the boss. Others would be unable to accept disapproval from those they work with every day. Each individual's final choice is partly guided by the reactions of the group, and his or her feelings about the group will be based on these reactions. If they approve of his or her choice, then the individual will approve of them.

All the forces or drives that motivate human behavior contribute to the way we act and react within an organization. They may be biological, emotional, or cultural. The important point is that they serve to socialize our behavior.

Never Underestimate the Power of the Individual

The varied forces that socialize us as members of a certain group, organization, or culture also produce our individual personalities. As discussed in Chapter 2, personality is an individually organized system of behaviors, attitudes, beliefs, and values. Personality is a product of both positive and negative reactions to an individual's behavior. Influential reactions come from a variety of sources—family, peer group, school, church, and place of employment. From the reactions of people around

"Despite the strong forces of socialization, individuals still turn out to have unique personalities."

her, one woman may learn that hard work and honesty are rewarded with approval. If these ideals are reinforced by the other agencies of socialization to which she is exposed, then she probably will incorporate them into her personality. Another woman, who was reared in an atmosphere in which getting ahead by any means was seen as a desirable behavior, may make that particular outlook part of her personality.

Biological determinants may play a part in the development of personality traits and thus the social roles that follow. Men predominate in social roles as hunter, fisher, soldier, and protector, presumably because of their superior muscular strength. It is sometimes assumed that other traits such as aggressiveness and bravery are also inherently masculine, but cultural anthropologist Margaret Mead denied that many of the traditional sex roles in our society are biologically determined. Her studies in primitive New Guinea reported that in one tribe both men and women were passive and unaggressive, while in another both sexes were quite aggressive and even violent. A third tribe possessed definite sex roles, but they were in sharp contrast to those of traditional Western societies. In this tribe, the men were passive and subordinate while the women were aggressive and dominant. Although questions recently have been raised about the validity of Mead's methodology, her studies do suggest that cultural influences may be at least as important as biological determinants.

What are the social determinants of personality? A number of institutions such as school, church, and even the news media exert pressure on the individual so that his or her personality reflects their views. Yet the individual should not be viewed as totally at the mercy of these socialization agencies. Influence will be felt in both directions. Agencies of socialization can be changed by those who are being socialized.

The college campus serves as a ready illustration. Twenty-five years ago, college students exerted almost no pressure or influence on the administrative leadership. Their courses of study, required curriculum, living quarters, and social activities were, for the most part, regulated by the school officials. Today, there is a striking difference on the campus, because students and faculty have collectively changed the goals and values of the institution. The physical trappings like dress codes, dormitory hours, visitation bans, and compulsory ROTC are practically nonexistent on most campuses. Moreover, students have also influenced the curriculum so that there are fewer required courses and more individual flexibility. From this example we can see that socialization and personality development are a two-way interaction. Students change the character of college campuses, yet at the same time their own values, beliefs, and goals are being modified by the socialization that takes place there.

Although no one can escape all socializing agencies, it is often possible to resist socialization by nonparticipation. You probably know some fellow students who seem untouched by their surroundings. Students who live at home and commute to college are often involuntarily placed in this situation. After they attend classes they return to a nonacademic environment. Thus, they find it difficult to become involved in campus activities or issues. The intangible influences on personality are also missing. The student who lives off campus is unlikely to be influenced by the values and beliefs of his or her peers except in the classroom. The informal social interactions that occur in both academic and nonacademic areas are simply no part of the commuter's daily life.

In some situations, people may feel that there is no social role available that fits their personality. If so, they may attempt to create an entirely different role for themselves. In the 1950s a number of individuals carved out a new role for themselves by growing beards or long hair and calling themselves "beatniks." In the 1960s, the "hippies" grew long hair and advocated drugs, peace, and love. In the early 1980s, the "punk" look repeated the appearance of an antiestablishment role. The first beatniks, hippies, or punks to express themselves in this manner were undoubtedly considered deviant. If, however, a number of people in the social group followed suit within a short period, then the original few might be considered the leaders of a social revolution.

"While the organization shapes us, we are also shaping the organization."

Social changes like this are not uncommon even in rather rigid organizations. For example, the Roman Catholic church has made some rather dramatic changes in the past twenty years—embracing ecumenism, saying mass in English, abolishing the limited fasting formerly practiced on Fridays. The church, like any institution, has been changed by the influence of its participants. Each individual within an organization is a potentially influential member, able to shape the organization just as much as it influences the personality of the individual.

DEFINING THE MANAGERIAL ROLE

The role of manager is actually very complex. Even successful executives may take years to learn to play it correctly on all occasions. A manager behaves differently with superiors than with subordinates, and an effective manager varies behavior to adapt to individual personalities within the organization as well. There is no simple book of rules that can tell a manager how to play the role. The former head of ITT, Harold Geneen, gives his ideas on the subject of the managerial role in the Managerial Dialogue on pages 233–234. For additional insight into Geneen's ideas about management, see his book *Managing,* published in 1984 by Doubleday.

When a manager wants to gain trust and good feelings, one type of role behavior is employed. But if she wishes to dispense criticism or disapproval, she will use different role behavior. In both instances, the manager's role behavior is designed to accomplish a specific goal.

Another important aspect of role development is the reciprocal role of the person or persons with whom the individual is interacting. When a supervisor speaks to a subordinate, she reveals through her use of explicit words, actions, gestures, facial expressions, or tone of voice the role she assumes the other person should adopt. When this same supervisor meets higher managerial personnel, she may have a very different expectation of their role behavior, which in turn will be conveyed by her own behavior. For example, the manager will address her boss formally as "Mr. Jones," and she will ask him what time would be convenient to hold a meeting. In contrast, she will address her subordinate informally as "Mike" or perhaps simply as "Robinson," and she will tell him what time she expects a meeting to take place.

Managerial Dialogue

"Managers must manage. Managers must manage. Managers must manage."

Harold Geneen, retired board chairman emeritus of ITT

The quote at the top of the page is the business credo of Harold Geneen, the man who ruled International Telephone and Telegraph Corporation (ITT) for fifteen years and took the worldwide conglomerate from annual sales of $766 million up to a staggering $22 billion.

For Geneen, it is not enough for a manager to aim for certain results—he or she must achieve those results to qualify as a successful manager. Forget the personal excuses, forget the "bad economy," forget the strike last quarter, Geneen says. Find the reason for those bad results and change your product, your company, or your environment to achieve success. "What you don't do is go on accepting inadequate results and explaining them," Geneen said.

Geneen developed a hard-nosed management style during the 1960s as he demanded continual 10 percent annual growth from each of the 250 companies that formed the ITT multinational corporation. Corporate managers assembled every month in New York or Brussels (headquarters of the European arm of ITT), where problems were identified and solutions sought in marathon discussion sessions. Not all ITT managers thrived in

International Telephone and Telegraph Corporation is a multinational company that employed over 350,000 workers at its peak.

that pressure-cooker atmosphere, but those who did were able to achieve the results that Geneen expected. For Geneen, the goal of the manager in any organization is simple: achieve results.

For a business, that means making profits for the owner or owners. For a nonprofit organization it might be the achievement of a certain level of service or care. Thus, the first role a manager will play is that of goal setter, both personally and for others.

A manager must play many roles in achieving those goals, according to Geneen. He or she must be a leader, for one thing. Leadership is an intangible quality, but it is one of the roles a successful manager must master. Leadership may be an innate skill, but it can also be developed with training. Geneen defines *leadership* as the ability to inspire others to work together as a team, following your lead, to reach the common objective. It is leadership that is most responsible for getting results.

Being a leader, however, is only one of the many roles a manager must play every day in an organization. In fact, the roles of a manager may only be limited by the number of employees, their needs, and the manager's skills. In broad terms, a manager must be a good recruiter so that the right people are hired, a shrewd evaluator of personnel so that the right people are promoted, and a concerned boss who is able to motivate the right people to do the right jobs.

"The relationship with people is what is important," Geneen says. "Good management is creating high morale—a successful team where everyone shares." The morale that a manager inspires helps an organization achieve results, as does concern for individual employees. "If you help this guy grow and become competent, he works for you because he wants to—not because he has to," asserts Geneen. A manager must understand the internal processes of the business, whether the organization makes cars, provides haircuts, or writes software. Such an understanding is essential to a manager hunting down the facts he or she needs to make decisions. All facts are not created equal, Geneen emphasizes. By digging for the right facts, a manager learns about problems and perhaps finds a means of solving them. The numbers are only warning signals—a manager has to find out what's happening behind them. By playing the role of fact finder, a manager can avoid some surprises in life. "Surprises are mostly negative," Geneen says. When a manager can't avoid the surprises, he becomes a problem solver. "The desire to improve as a driving force *will always* find a better solution, and so you will receive a sure satisfaction and, probably, profits, but the latter only if you think it *all* the way through."

It's a simple message, but the ITT mastermind believes the principles of good management are timeless. "There are no trick answers."

A manager is a person who achieves organizational goals by arranging for other people to perform necessary tasks. To achieve results, the manager carefully selects his or her precise role and the way he or she will play it with others. For example, with some employees, a warm, personal friendship is an effective way of goal-directed interacting, while with others, a more formal approach works best. The manager, like everyone else, must choose a role that he or she feels is proper for the particular person or situation. If the manager is talking to an old classmate at a party, the roles played may take on a chummy, nostalgic flavor. A week later, as business associates, these same two people will act out pragmatic, no-nonsense roles together.

These different roles may arise in response to a complex set of needs. The two aforementioned executives probably played the role of pals in order to satisfy the needs for security, affection, and approval. Their subsequent work-oriented roles might be attributable to the needs for esteem, prestige, or even self-realization.

Among the most important roles a manager must play in the course of a career are:

1. Leader
2. Executive
3. Negotiator
4. Developer
5. Innovator
6. Human being

Leader

"You don't become a manager unless you truly want to play the role."

If one word could describe the manager's role, it might be *leadership*. Of course, management and the roles associated with it require more than leadership alone, but management is a voluntary commitment and with it go a number of roles and needs. Leadership is a conscious choice.

Leadership implies that a person has a high need to achieve. A leader must shape and direct the policies of the group, helping the group and its members achieve their desired goals. Managers are deemed successful if they achieve the goals of the organization, and in the process of furthering organizational aims, they hope also to meet and satisfy their own personal needs.

A leader must also possess self-assurance. Psychologists label this attribute as a positive self-image. In everyday language, we might simply say that it is an asset for managers to like themselves. They must feel that they are capable of providing able leadership and then effectively implementing procedures.

Self-assurance generally stems from one's social environment. People who aspire to the status of manager do so, in part, because they have been socialized to believe that they possess the capabilities to perform well in such a role. Even in childhood, bright, outgoing people are encouraged by their superiors or peers to assert themselves as leaders. Given this support, they learn to test their abilities as an organizational leader and, with success, they gain self-confidence.

Another aspect of socialization for a position of leadership is the desire for upward mobility. In part, upward mobility is a culturally learned goal that is especially prevalent in competitive societies such as the United States. Few if any employees expect to enter a business organization and remain in the same position for a prolonged period. The implicit assumption of almost every management-related area is that capable, conscientious, aggressive people can move upward in job status, prestige, and power.

In fact, American workers, supervisory or otherwise, move from one job to another and one company to another at a much higher rate than those in other advanced technological societies. Unlike the Japanese, who often want to stay in one company for life, the American worker will readily switch jobs to gain a better position. Managerial and professional people are particularly prone to moving around, perhaps because the very nature of their work leads them toward higher-level needs and goals. Their needs transcend security and gravitate more toward satisfying higher needs such as esteem, prestige, and self-realization.

Executive

The executive is the traditional role of a manager. The executive is a decision maker in the business organization. In this role, an executive is expected to be fair, firm, and above all, prudent. The role is learned either through courses or from observing other executives on the job. The executive may be a specialist in one discipline, such as marketing, finance, or production, or a generalist.

The focus of the executive's role is on subordinates—how to motivate them, how to communicate with them, and how to achieve the organization's goals through their efforts. It is primarily an other-directed role.

The most obvious demand of the executive role is the need to assume authority. An executive who supervises the line production is expected to be decisive and firm about sticking to established organizational procedures. Part of the supervisory task might include interacting with foremen, telling them what parts need to be produced, reducing waste, and promoting efficiency.

As a specialist, the executive must be well informed about the type and level of production in his or her area of supervision. He or she should know the techniques of producing specific parts, plus the time, expense, or waste involved in completing them. In addition, the executive is expected to act as a combination of leader, spokesperson, and "defender" of his or her supervision area.

No matter how well the executive knows and manages one special area, overall plant production procedures force him or her to play a generalist role as well. For the organization to function smoothly and achieve its goals, each operating unit must work toward the goals set by the overall organization and follow its policy. An area supervisor will not be informed about every decision, its background, and the probable consequences. He or she will simply be expected to coordinate his or her particular area of responsibility as instructed. Therefore, if the executive is told that the division will stop producing door handles, his or her area of expertise, and start making antennas, about which he or she knows nothing, the executive follows the same game plan.

Negotiator

In recent years, the role of manager as negotiator has increased dramatically. As one writer puts it:

> *There are matters to be worked out with governing bodies, with other organizations that share an interest in the problem, with clients, with suppliers, with associations (supporters as well as opponents), with unions, with the media, and even with the courts.*[2]

Negotiating situations are no longer solely the province of top management. Supervisors at every level are becoming involved in the process. In addition, managers must now know how to negotiate with their peers—how to "trade off" favors with other departments or functional areas so as to increase their own unit's productivity. In large bureaucracies, this is frequently the only way to quickly obtain necessary signatures on routing documents, essential supplies, and even personnel.

Developer

Recruiting, training, and developing employees is another role that a modern manager plays. Regardless of the type of employee sought by the organization—blue collar, white collar, or technical specialist—there is always a limited pool of talent. To paraphrase the words of St. Peter, a good manager must become a good "fisher of men." Once hired, the new employee will need immediate training in job techniques, as well as socialization into the organization's culture and goals.

When the new employee identifies with the organization and begins contributing fully, the manager must then attempt to assist the employee in meeting personal goals (without, of course, creating conflict with the organization's needs and goals). By furthering the development of their staff, effective managers gain an improved work force, which in turn will help their career in the organization. In pursuit of their goal of staff development, managers may play the role of coach, sponsor, or mentor.

As a coach, the manager helps employees meet specific job needs. He or she may give them challenging tasks, counsel them on their projects, and give positive feedback. The sex of the coach and team members may affect this role. There are well-established models for a male-male coaching relationship, but if the boss is a man and the employee is a woman, the situation may strike both participants and observers as unusual, thus limiting its effectiveness. Since women are still a rarity in management, there are few examples of female-male coaching.

Whereas coaches prepare their workers for specific assignments, sponsors attempt to push employees to higher-level jobs. Sponsors get the names of specific individuals onto promotion lists, tout their employees' potential abilities, advise their protégés, and actively seek promotions for them. This type of help may backfire if the protégé fails, but a sponsor with a good track record will find that his or her influence and power in the organization grow commensurately. A manager who can find good personnel and match them with the right job will always be in demand.

A third and more subtle method of personnel development is becoming a mentor. This type of relationship, in which a more experienced manager becomes a valued role model, ally, and counselor to a younger or newer employee, exists outside normal channels of authority. The relationship is often a long-term one, enduring through many years and job changes. It is marked by caring, compassion, and mutual respect. When successful, a mentoring relationship can be productive and satisfying for both parties. The risk for the mentor is that his or her reputation may be harmed; the risk for the protégé is that he or she may be suffocated or experience only secondhand learning.

A number of management writers believe that one of the reasons women have been slow to ascend to the ranks of top management is that they lack mentors. The intimacy of the mentoring relationship may discourage a man from mentoring a young woman and having his motives questioned by his co-workers.

Innovator

A manager's role also includes being an agent of change. Close personal knowledge of the work area gives the manager the chance to introduce and implement new work systems and techniques. In the course of these activities, the individual's need to be innovative and creative can be satisfied.

It would be naive to assume that even the most progressive, individualistically oriented business organizations would allow managers to make all the changes they wanted. Even so, thanks to an intimate knowledge of the work and employees, the manager is in an excellent position to effect many changes. If the changes are a success and result in lower costs, better productivity, and higher quality, then the manager's own career is enhanced along with those of subordinates.

Human Being

Much as they sometimes might wish they were robots capable of making difficult personnel decisions without emotion, managers must face the fact that they are human beings just like the people they are supervising.

As a management professor puts it:

In a world that is increasingly emphasizing the importance—and rights—of the individual, the manager needs to be seen as someone who feels for others, who shares their hopes and expectations, who understands—or at least tries to understand—their problems. This does not relieve one of making difficult and often painful decisions, or of deciding, as one so often must, for the group rather than for the individual. It is merely a reminder that, in doing so, one must not overlook the human implications of what is done. [3]

"The successful manager never forgets to be a human being."

All employees know that at times they are the victims of events beyond their control. When that happens, they should be treated with dignity and respect, whatever the circumstances.

The Mintzberg Model

In the early 1970s, Mintzberg developed a useful model for the roles a manager plays. He studied managers of all levels, from factory foreman to chief executive officer (and a few street gang leaders for good mea-

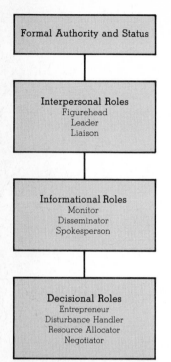

FIGURE 9.1 The Mintzberg Model: The Manager's Role

Source: John Hayes and Tony Dunn, "Is Training Really the Answer? A Diagnostic Approach to Improving Operational Effectiveness," Journal of European Industrial Training 7; 1 (1983), p. 11.

sure!), and found that whatever their level, managers show very similar behavior. He divided the manager's roles into three categories—interpersonal, informational, and decisional. The model is shown in Figure 9.1.

In the interpersonal category, Mintzberg included the role of figurehead, the duty of representing the organizational unit in formal matters. For example, one manager might write an article on the company for a management journal, greet distinguished guests at corporate headquarters, serve as a company representative on a government commission, or simply attend an after-hours birthday party for an employee. The second role is that of leader, which includes hiring, motivating, guiding, and developing subordinates. The third role is that of liaison, the linking of the organizational unit with the outside world. In the role, the manager may entertain clients, meet with lawyers or accountants, and participate in companywide meetings.

The informational roles of the manager are played in both the internal and external environments of the organization, and Mintzberg suggests that they are the most important aspects of a manager's responsibility. As monitor, the manager receives and collects useful information from colleagues, subordinates, and contacts. As disseminator, the manager transmits this information otherwise inaccessible to his or her organization. As spokesperson, the manager sends information into the outside environment, both to his or her bosses and to the public.

The third category of Mintzberg's roles involves decision making. When managers act as innovators within the organization, for example, to launch a development program, they play the role of entrepreneur. When managers are thrust into problems that arise outside their control, such as a supplier's bankruptcy or a currency devaluation, they act as disturbance handlers. When they consider how best to apply their organizational unit's manpower, machinery, or supplies, they become resource allocators. That role includes scheduling their time and that of their subordinates. Managers' final decisional role is that of negotiator, a role enhanced by their formal authority and informal abilities.

In the decade since Mintzberg published his model, other researchers have used its categories to improve their understanding of the manager's role. The model can also help an organization improve its training program. A more recent study suggests that Mintzberg's ten categories can be grouped into two sets of roles—those that deal with the generation and processing of information and those that deal with decisions.[4]

ROLE STRAIN AND ROLE CONFLICT

■■■■■■■■■■■■■■■■■■■■■■

"You can't please everybody all the time."

Being an innovator, motivator, or investigator requires a complex, interrelated set of decision responses on the part of the manager. Identifying the manager's separate roles is helpful in analyzing a manager's work, but in most real life situations, a manager must combine several roles or behaviors.

Of course, many management decisions can be beneficial to everyone involved; no conflict or strain is created. More frequently, however, manager's decisions are made from choices that conflict. In his role of innovator, for example, a manager might come up with an idea that he would have to disapprove in his role as developer of personnel. Conversely, a step that he must take as executive—shutting down an unprofitable division, for example—may impair his effectiveness as a negotiator on other matters with the union. This kind of problem is called *role conflict,* or *role strain.*

A Manager Faces Conflicting Demands

The role or roles a manager plays in work-related areas can correctly be defined as direct roles. These roles refer to modes of behavior the manager adopts as his or her general life-style. Both direct and secondary roles are subject to strain or conflict, depending on the situation and the roles challenged.

On the job, a role strain is always a potential source of frustration. The manager plays a multitude of roles, and sometimes, the attempt to play them all leads to behavior that seems contradictory. A supervisor placed in a position of authority must often be firm, make criticisms, take disciplinary action, and in some cases, even personally fire employees. On the other hand, managerial personnel are expected to be open to suggestions and to try to foster a feeling of cooperation and teamwork among their subordinates. The roles strain here is clear. How can a manager criticize an employee for frequent tardiness and then moments later attempt to ask for her suggestions on handling a difficult problem in her area? An effective manager assumes many subroles while playing major supervisory roles, yet the emotions associated with each of them cannot just be switched off by any of the parties concerned.

Role strain affects a manager's relationship to the organization as a whole. For example, managers are expected to be creative, innovative employees full of suggestions for improving operations under their control. Yet they may also be expected to be loyal to the organization and to follow directives from top management. In such a situation, the conflict in roles is evident. A recent study of one company's sales personnel—men and women who were expected to be independent while simultaneously following company policy—found that the sales representatives experienced more role conflict when their supervisor had a larger span of control. In other words, the fewer salespeople such supervisors had to direct, the better the salespeople liked it.[5]

A manager may encounter role conflict in work and social interactions. Most managers have been taught to view a manager's role in terms of acting forceful, aggressive, and sometimes even a bit ruthless. Yet other, less competitive roles are expected in the outside environment. When he arrives home from work, a manager must switch from more aggressive work roles and take on the gentler roles associated with being a father, husband, or community member. Later, if he spends a few hours with friends, they expect him to interact as a friend. Behavior learned on the job would be received with bewilderment or downright hostility. On the other hand, using behavior practiced at home would be equally inappropriate at the worksite. Role strain may be even more severe for women executives. The stereotyped roles of wife and mother they may assume outside the office require a passive, often subordinate attitude that is in direct conflict with the forcefulness they must display on the job.

A Manager Must Satisfy Many People

Role conflict arises because it is impossible for a manager always to satisfy every constituency—employees, employer, and self. For example, a manager may pride himself on being an outgoing, friendly person, and his employees may appreciate this attribute and respond with cooperation and a high level of participation. What happens when a company directive instructs him to cut back personnel and distribute the additional work load among the remaining employees?

It may cause the manager a great deal of inner conflict to fire someone with whom he had been very friendly only a few days before. The manager is caught between the role he must play as an organizational decision maker and the role he has played as friend to subordinates. This conflict may weaken the manager's ability to play both roles in the future. The employees, having been reminded that the manager has the power to fire them, may be reluctant to view him as a friend. Their resentment over the firings may undermine the manager's ability to play the role of supervisor in the friendly way he had done in the past. Moreover, his own self-image suffers since he is no longer certain he can be either a good friend or a good supervisor.

The role conflict reduces the manager's power, prestige, and esteem. He might respond by wondering, "Why my department?" and then conclude that the organization made a mistake or that his influence within the organization was dwindling. Either conclusion presents the manager with further conflict because his views about his role as a policymaker or as a shaper of company policy are shaken. What he sees as his failure may cause him to be apprehensive about his job security, and insecurity is a behavioral trait incompatible with successful performance of many aspects of the managerial role.

The causes of role conflict or role strain are both personal and situational. Roles that the organization, subordinates, or the outside environment expect a manager to play are often diverse. Managers must attempt to satisfy the role expectations of others while remaining consistent with their personal view of their role.

Resolving Role Conflict

It may seem that many role expectations thrust on a manager would leave him or her in a perpetual state of inner turmoil over the conflict, but research suggests that several remedial measures are available. A manager should carefully choose his or her employer. An individual with strong inclinations to be aggressive, upwardly mobile, and innovative may find more job satisfaction in a new, expanding corporation than in a staid, well-established firm. A company with a clearly defined hierarchy and formal channels of communication might strike one manager as well-organized and another as appallingly rigid. Because each person's personality and goals enter into his or her perceptions of the ideal work situation, certain types of organizations appeal to certain people. A manager should understand his or her own preferences and look for an organization that provides a favorable climate for them.

"If you work for an organization whose goals and values you believe in, you have already eliminated alot of role strain."

A manager should be willing to adopt personal definitions of role behavior in order to conform to organizational expectations. Managers carry with them from job to job a general set of role perceptions about the superior-to-subordinate or the employee-to-organization relationship. They have developed certain expectations of the way business roles should be played, based on their previous experience as well as on conversations with colleagues, friends, and even family. Unfortunately, managers sometimes stick tenaciously to their personal definitions of role behavior even in the face of clear signals that the organization does not agree with those definitions.

A female publishing executive defined her role of editor-in-chief as being primarily an executive. Because she prided herself on a department that ran on budget, met schedules consistently, and generated continually increasing sales, she was upset that her boss, the president, kept harping on the high turnover rate in her department and the fact that all the senior editors, candidates for eventual promotion to top administrative posts, had quit. "I can't understand that man," she would fume to her husband over dinner. "Here I've acquired and published books that have brought in a record sales volume, and all he can do is criticize because some of the editors quit in the process." In other words, she ignored the obvious fact that her boss considered personnel development an important part of a manager's role. She expected to win promotion, prestige, and an increase in salary based on her performance in the role *she* thought was important. Needless to say, she was stunned when she was demoted to just plain editor.

As her story makes clear, a manager should check personal role definitions against those of the organization and make adjustments where necessary. Excelling at the wrong role is not likely to bring positive rewards.

THE SPECIAL ROLE OF THE WOMAN MANAGER

■—■—■—■—■—■—■—■—■—■—■—■—■—■—

"Women in management often face severe conflicts between the role of manager and the other roles society expects them to play."

One of the organizational roles that has received increased attention in recent years is that of the woman manager. Part of this concern is due to the fact that female labor participation rates have risen dramatically over the last few decades from 37 percent in 1960 to 52.1 percent in 1981. (See the box on page 245 and Figure 9.2 on page 246 for further details on women in the work force.) As the educational levels of females have increased (50.2 percent of the college enrollment in 1981), women have become more interested in holding higher-level managerial and professional positions. The fact that only about one percent of top management positions are held by women is just one indicator of the many barriers that women must bypass in securing the recognition they deserve.[6]

The Stereotypes and the Realities

How many times have you heard the following comments?

Women are too emotional—they get irrational at certain times of the month.

ARE TODAY'S WOMEN BETTER OFF? A SURPRISING ANSWER

There is no denying that women have made massive progress in U.S. labor markets and have recently begun to close the gap between male and female earnings. But are they ultimately better off relative to men than they were 25 years ago? The question is probably unanswerable, since it obviously depends in part on women's subjective valuations of their new roles in society, but economists believe a partial answer may be gleaned by examining changes in their "full income"—a concept that includes both money wages and the imputed value of leisure and nonmarket production activities such as housework.

That is exactly what Stanford University economist Victor R. Fuchs is attempting to do in an ongoing research project. And his startling initial finding is that in the period from 1959 to 1979, the full income of women relative to men—that is, their access to goods, services, and leisure—actually declined somewhat. The reason: While women's earnings relative to men's showed little change, the shift in their living arrangements had a depressing effect on their full incomes. Because more women are unmarried and live alone, for example, they do not benefit from income-sharing with their spouses or from the economies of scale that accrue from larger households.

Black women are a case in point. While they improved their labor market positions tremendously in recent decades, by 1979 an astonishing 55% between 25 and 64 years of age were not married. Moreover, the ratio of children per adult is almost 50% higher for single black women than for their married counterparts, and children reduce the amount of income available to their parents. Similar though less pronounced trends prevail among white women.

Fuchs is now assessing the extent to which the dramatic increase in women's wages relative to men's since 1979 may have altered the male-female equation. His preliminary finding is that in "full-income" terms women's relative position is probably no longer below the levels they enjoyed a quarter of a century ago. But it also is probably not much better because changes in living conditions continue to offset relative earnings gains. As to whether women are ultimately better off, Fuchs says this depends on many factors, "including the value they assign to their newfound independence."

Source: Reprinted from January 28, 1985, issue of *Business Week* by special permission, © 1985 by McGraw-Hill, Inc., pp. 20–22.

By the time you've trained a woman to handle a job, she'll get married, have kids, and leave the company.

Women don't need to be compensated as well as men, since men have to support their families.

Women can't handle heavy weights and physical labor.

Hiring women managers disrupts their family life and gives their children a bad deal.

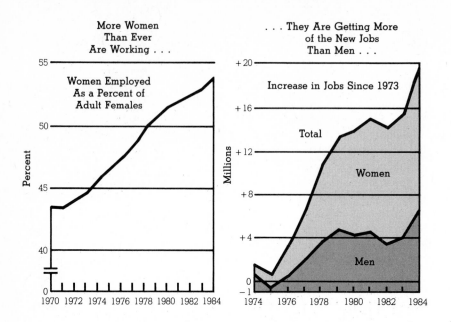

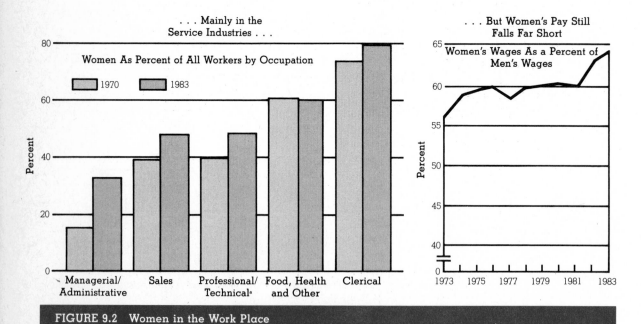

FIGURE 9.2   Women in the Work Place

a Includes accountants, doctors, engineers, lawyers, and teachers.

Source: Reprinted from the January 28, 1985, issue of BusinessWeek by special permission, © 1985 by McGraw-Hill, Inc., p. 81.

These statements are just a few of the stereotypes sometimes expressed about a professional or managerial woman. Although prejudice against women managers is often considered a male characteristic, this is inaccurate. Some men may be extremely supportive of women managers. In some cases it is female co-workers who are not.

When people hold such distorted attitudes about women, it can influence their judgment about selecting, promoting, training, and compensating women fairly. For example, one of the most prominent theorists in management, Douglas McGregor, describes the managerial role as follows:

> *The good manager is aggressive, competitive, firm, and just. He is not feminine, he is not yielding or dependent or intuitive in the womanly sense. The very expression of emotion is widely viewed as a feminine weakness that would interfere with effective business processes.*[7]

If a personnel director or president of a corporation held such views of effective management, he would not be likely to put a woman in a top level position.

Is there any evidence that women are less effective than men as managers? A large-scale investigation of 2,000 male and female managers was designed to answer this question. Out of forty-three different behavioral comparisons between the sexes, they found that in forty-one of the instances there was no difference. One of the differences was that female managers tended to have higher achievement motivation needs than male managers. The other significant difference was that the male managers were more open and candid with their colleagues than were female managers. One explanation might be due to the fact that most of their colleagues were men.[8]

Role conflict may undermine the effectiveness of women managers. Although attitudes are changing, the traditional female role has been making a home and raising children. The woman manager whose husband and children are not supportive of her career is placed in a highly stressful situation. The managerial role asks her to be aggressive and organization minded, but as her family interprets her other roles, she is expected to be nurturing and giving. Typically, the success of the woman manager in handling such roles is dependent on having a supportive mate and children.

Overcoming the Barriers

In recent years, attention has been focused on removing prejudicial biases and other forms of barriers for women who want to move up the corporate ladder. Legislation has been passed by the federal government to prohibit discrimination based on sex in all personnel decisions. The impact of such legislation, however, has not been totally positive. In some companies that have made special attempts to promote and hire women as managers through affirmative action programs, women can be viewed as "tokens." They are perceived, sometimes even by themselves, as being in management only because of their sex and not by virtue of their abilities. Such perceptions can undermine morale and hurt interpersonal relationships.

Another problem with governmental intervention is that measurable results from legislation have been slow in coming. Although the Equal Pay Act, which prohibits sexual discrimination in pay, was passed in the early 1960s, statistics compiled in 1981 show high levels of discrepancies between men's and women's earnings in management positions (see Table 9.1). Even when the figures are adjusted for differences in education and job experience, there are still large earning differences between men and women.[9] Obviously, pay discrimination still exists. Further, despite the fact that the Civil Rights Act and the Equal Employment Opportunity Act prohibit discrimination in hiring decisions, women are still employed predominately in the lowest paying industries (see Table 9.2).

Although federal intervention has not been particularly effective in eliminating the barriers women managers face, there are other options. Some organizations, for example, are changing their personnel policies to accommodate the special needs of their professional women. Flex-

TABLE 9.1 Median Weekly Earnings of Wage and Salary Workers Employed Full Time in Occupations by Sex[a]

Occupations	Men	Women
Accountants	$507	$356
Computer systems analyst and scientists	599	504
Personnel and labor relations managers	700	407
Executive managers and administrators	568	358
Financial managers[b]	612	407
Managers, medicine and health	563	417
Purchasing agents and buyers	472	324
Sales representatives, other business services[c]	408	279
Insurance sales	457	343

[a]1984 annual average.

[b]Includes other financial institutions besides banks, no separate category for bank managers anymore.

[c]Closest we could find to retail sales managers. They are now lumped in with all salesworkers, which brings the earnings down a lot. The sales representative category seems to be more at the managerial level, at least in terms of wages.

Source: Bureau of Labor Statistics, *Employment and Earnings,* January 1985.

TABLE 9.2 Percentage of Women in the Lowest and Highest Paying Industries[a]

Highest Paying Industries	Percentage of Women Employees
Petroleum and coal products	17
Mining	17
Railroad transportation	9
Aircraft and parts manufacture	21
Motor vehicle and equipment manufacture	18
Lowest Paying Industries	Percentage of Women Employees
Private households	86
Apparel manufacture	81
Eating and drinking places	58
Leather and leather products	60
Personal services	67
Agriculture	20

[a]1984 annual average.
Source: Bureau of Labor Statistics, *Employment and Earnings*, January, 1985.

time, in which employees are allowed to choose their starting times, and company day care centers are two programs designed to assist working mothers. Additionally, many companies are educating their personnel to understand the causes of sexual discrimination and to avoid it.

In recent years, organizations have been especially concerned about preventing another illegal form of discrimination: sexual harassment or repeated and unwanted sexual advances. Much of this concern has taken the form of publicizing the types of behaviors that can be construed as harassment and the types of negative sanctions that will be taken against employees who engage in such behaviors.

Another way in which women are currently surmounting work place barriers is by developing mentor relationships. There are very clear career development advantages to such mentor relationships. But when the mentor is a man and the protégé a woman, some people believe there must be a sexual connotation in their relationship. The woman who desires upward mobility must choose her mentors carefully.

The Managerial Woman

Perhaps the best advice for the aspiring woman manager comes from Margaret Hennig and Ann Jardin, authors of an article in *Psychology To-*

day. They contend that if women want to be in top organizational positions, they should adopt the following guidelines[10]:

1. Decide on clear-cut career objectives and whether or not you really want a managerial career.

2. Make a specific list of every job you have ever held, including how well you did at each, and the skills, knowledge, and experience you gained.

3. Develop a five-year career plan.

4. Try to find ways to increase your experience in planning, problem solving, and group leadership—all crucial skills for a successful career in management.

5. Study the informal system of personal relationships that exists in your company.

6. Try to establish an informal system of relationships with other women in the company.

7. When dealing with male colleagues, don't try to engage in their male joking and bantering. You really don't have to know who won the World Series last year.

8. Learn to control your emotions and the way you express them at work.

9. Ask yourself why you are so vulnerable to criticism.

10. Stop trying to separate the worlds of work and home.

11. Stop waiting to be chosen and start letting people at work know what you want.

Women managers who are determined to make it to the top still confront many barriers. The optimistic sign of the times, however, is that a number of women have accomplished it. They now serve as role models for others aspiring to such positions. Three such women are profiled in the box on pages 251–252.

DEMANDS OF THE OUTSIDE ENVIRONMENT

To many men and women, conflicting role demands from outside the work environment prove to be the most difficult to resolve. After all, a manager experiencing role strain on the job can balance the problem with the rewards of security, prestige, and economic benefits. The real

Three Who Made It to the Top

Long before women started crowding into the nation's business schools, there were a few who made it to the top. All faced obstacles unknown to their male peers, and most found that success forced some painful personal trade-offs. The following is a look at three women who made it.

When Betty McFadden got married in the mid-1940s, she decided that she wanted to devote full time to raising a family. But while she was waiting for the babies to arrive, she took a job at Jewel Companies, Inc., in Barrington, Ill., because, she says, "it looked like an interesting building." At first she worked in the accounting office for $35 a week, but by the late 1950s she had worked her way up to fashion coordinator for the big retailer, and in 1967, at the age of 45, she became the company's first woman officer. One year later, McFadden finally got pregnant.

"I had been at Jewel 23 years, so I thought I would retire and have a new life," she recalls. But after a few weeks at home, McFadden realized that she had to return: "I knew I'd drive myself and the child crazy." Before long she was back at her old job, at a much higher salary, and in 1976 she was named president of Jewel's direct-marketing division. Three months ago, when Jewel spun off the division to form a separate corporation, IHSS Inc., McFadden became its chairman and chief executive officer.

It had been lonely at the top. In the course of her career, McFadden made few personal friends and developed few outside interests. Eventually her marriage disintegrated. Although she thinks the new generation of women executives is better prepared and better qualified than she was, she thinks all two-career marriages are vulnerable. "I'm sure there are successful relationships, but not too many," she says. "Somebody suffers." But even so, says McFadden, if she had it to do over again, she would not give up her serendipitous success.

Paula Hughes never went to college, but it seems to have made little difference. Today she is a first vice president, director and top producer at Thomson McKinnon Securities, Inc., managing nearly $600 million in customer accounts—and last year she grossed more than $1 million in broker commissions. Under the Carter Administration, Hughes was named the first woman governor of the U.S. Postal Service. She was the first woman member of Pittsburgh's blue-chip Duquesne Club, and, despite her lack of a college degree, she now sits on the board of trustees at Carnegie-Mellon University.

Hughes, 49, became a broker after eight years in advertising, when the breakup of her first marriage left her with a daughter to support. In her first job as a broker, she was paid $200 a week less than her male peers. Frozen out of the professional organizations patronized by men, Hughes turned to The Women's Forum, a group organized to give women the same kind of contacts provided by the "old boys' network," for what she sees as essential support. "The higher up you go, male or female, the lonelier you get," she explains. "You tend to think your problems are unique, and you find you have to reach out to others." Success also took a toll on her personal life. Her second marriage broke up after twenty years, and she says candidly that it is difficult to find "eligible men who can preserve their self-esteem and still tolerate" a women earning about $1 million a year.

A decade ago physicist Betsy Ancker-Johnson shocked her bosses at Boeing Co. by asking for a change of career: she wanted to drop her highly successful work in electronics research in favor of a management job. "I was just getting restless," explains Ancker-Johnson, now 52. "I guess I wanted a bigger playpen."

She got it. After surviving three tough years in Boeing management during the company's massive retrenchment, Ancker-Johnson served four years as the first female Assistant Secretary of Commerce, then moved on to become an associate lab director at Argonne National Laboratory. Today she heads the environmental-activities staff at mighty General Motors—the first woman vice president in GM history.

Looking back, Ancker-Johnson says her Boeing years were the most difficult. Unlike most of her male colleagues, she never had a top-management mentor to guide her. On the contrary, her employers viewed her ground-breaking success with passive astonishment. "Ye

gods, this woman is handling this thing!" she mimics.

Ancker-Johnson and her husband, Harold, chairman of the mathematics department at Trinity College near Chicago, have kept their marriage intact through what she calls a "weird arrangement." When she was first hired by GM, she commuted from Chicago. Now Harold and their four children, 17 to 21, have moved to suburban Detroit—and Harold commutes. "We're both doing exactly what we want to do," says Ancker-Johnson. And, she adds, she hopes the majority of other women will soon be able to say the same. "I can hardly wait until the day when this article you're doing would just be utterly boring," she says with a smile.

trouble occurs when a manager realizes that secondary role expectations, whether directly connected to the organization or not, do not coincide with personal self-image.

An executive may discover that the organization has implicit rules about social conduct. Some corporations apply positive or negative sanctions to matters of dress, choice of residential neighborhood, political party affiliation, church attendance, and even membership to social clubs. The individual who cannot reconcile his or her self-image with the social demands of the company experiences role conflict. Socially related role expectations are less frequent now than in the past. Organizations of today exert far less influence over their employees than did the paternalistic corporations of the nineteenth century. Still, subtle indicators of role expectations do exist. The young CPA who takes a job with a conservative firm of public accountants will quickly learn that flashy clothes, raucous laughter, and rock music on the radio in his office are frowned on as "unsuitable" for an accountant. On the other hand, if he took a job as a salesperson for a line of trendy but inexpensive women's shoes, he might feel pressured into displaying those very same personal traits that got him in trouble at the public accounting firm.

"The demands of a manager's role may spill over into off-the-job situations."

The individual's work-related roles may also create conflict with other chosen roles. Consider the manager with a position that requires a great deal of traveling. Perhaps her work roles satisfy needs for power, esteem, wealth, or autonomy and partially fulfill the highest need of self-realization. Even so, the extended absences from her family and friends are a likely source of secondary role conflict. In this situation a less demanding work assignment, different personal roles, or restructured social commitments might be helpful.

Our society has taught us that a coherent sense of identity is normal and healthy, but too much emphasis may be placed on role consistency. This emphasis may lead a person to feel that playing a diverse number of roles is inappropriate, hypocritical, or deviant, even though these roles achieve desired goals and satisfy needs. One proponent of diverse roles, Kenneth J. Gergen, refers to roles as "masks" and contends that seemingly conflicting roles are really more consistent with human responses than is generally assumed. To clarify this concept, he says:

The individual has many potential selves. He carries with him the capacity to define himself as warm or cold, dominant or submissive, sexy or plain. The social conditions around him determine which of these options are evoked.[11]

Gergen argues that our social structure encourages one dimensionality, and as a result, people are taught to behave in a prescribed, universally accepted manner. He concludes that inappropriate role behavior is sometimes more honest and healthy than the roles prescribed by society.

ON THE JOB
REVISITED . . .

As the owner of Hanson's Jewelry Store, you were faced with two choices: supporting your clerk and maintaining the "no return" policy or bending the rules and returning Marsh's money.

Hanson followed the first course and maintained his role as owner, leader, and rule maker for the store. The price he paid was in the loss of a customer and the possible loss of others.

If you had chosen to bend the rules for Marsh, you would have eased the immediate situation and put yourself in the role of a flexible decision maker. However, this could create long-term problems for you. In the future, Mrs. Wittner may come to you on every disputed return, seeking your advice and occupying your time. How often should you bend the rules for a customer?

This is a clear case of role conflict for the store owner. See if you can resolve the conflict by applying Mintzberg's model of ten different managerial roles. For instance, as a disturbance handler, you might choose to treat each situation individually, while as a disseminator you might choose to keep the "no return except for credit" sign above the cash register.

SUMMARY

A manager must integrate personal roles, norms, and values with those expected by the organization. Biological determinants account for some behaviors, while social determinants—school, church, media—influence role adoption, as do psychological and cultural factors.

Within the organization, some of a manager's roles correspond to those he or she plays off the job, such as friend or rival, while others are unique to the management process, including those of manager, leader, negotiator, developer, and innovator. In these roles, the manager is expected to possess self-assurance and the desire for upward mobility.

There are a number of ways to examine the variety of roles played by a typical manager. Among the most frequently discussed is a model by Mintzberg, who categorizes managers as playing ten roles grouped into interpersonal, informational, and decisional categories. In real life, many of these roles occur simultaneously.

As a decision maker, a manager may suffer from role strain and role conflict. In that event, it may be difficult to reconcile two different roles required on the job. The roles a manager plays in work-related areas are referred to as direct roles. They affect personal, social, and economic status.

Women in management often suffer from a conflict in roles. Male colleagues may perceive them as lacking in the "masculine," aggressive qualities they associate with running an organization. However, research indicates that women in management act as men do. Despite this, women are not yet found in great numbers in higher management, making it difficult for upwardly mobile women to find suitable mentors to assist their career growth.

Both men and women suffer from role conflict because it is impossible for an executive to satisfy everyone—employees, employer, and self. Resolving role conflicts requires that the manager weigh personal inclinations, the character of the organization, and the demands of the outside environment in decision making.

HUMAN RELATIONS APPLICATIONS

Conclusion 1: Managers must learn to play several different types of roles during their career progression.

Application: The effective manager is adaptable and able to successfully take on the roles of leader, executive, negotiator, developer, innovator, and human being.

Conclusion 2: Role conflict is an inevitable part of every manager's life since it is impossible to simultaneously satisfy every different constituency (e.g., superiors, employees, colleagues, friends).

Application: To help ease the stress involved in role conflict, the effective manager tries to work for an organization that matches personal needs and expectations.

Conclusion 3: Women who take on managerial roles still face a number of barriers because of unfounded stereotypes and discriminations.

Application: Government legislation and innovative organizational programs, such as new personnel policies and training efforts aimed at discouraging sexual discrimination, have helped to alleviate some of the barriers faced by women managers.

DISCUSSION QUESTIONS

1. What is the looking glass self, and what are its three major components?

2. Describe four of the major roles that managers must play in the course of their career. Which of these do you feel would be the most difficult? Why?

3. Distinguish between direct and secondary roles.

4. How have organizations attempted to eliminate biases against women who take on managerial roles?

NOTES

1. John Bowlby, *Child Care and the Growth of Love.* Baltimore: Penguin Books, 1964.

2. David Brown, "The Changing Role of the Manager," *Supervisory Management* 27 (July 1982), p. 17.

3. *Ibid.*, p. 20.

4. Zur Shapira and Roger Dunbar, "Testing Mintzberg's Managerial Roles Classification Using an In-Basket Simulation," *Journal of Applied Psychology* 65 (February 1980), p. 87.

5. Lawrence Chonko, "The Relationship of Span of Control to Sales Representatives' Experienced Role Conflict and Role Ambiguity," *Academy of Management Journal* 25 (June 1982), p. 445.

6. S. M. Natala, "Women in the 'Old Boy Network' Thrust," *Journal for Employment and Training Professionals* 4 (Winter–Spring 1982), pp. 25–33.

7. D. McGregor, *The Professional Manager.* New York: McGraw-Hill, 1967, p. 23.

8. S. M. Donnel and J. Hall, "Men and Women as Managers: A Significant Case of no Significant Differences," *Organizational Dynamics* (Spring 1980), pp. 60–77.

9. N. F. Rytina, "Earnings of Males and Females: A Look at Specific Occupations," *Monthly Labor Review* (April 1982), pp. 25–31.

10. M. Hennig and A. Jardin, "Women in the Old Boy Network," *Psychology Today* (January 1977), p. 78.

11. Kenneth J. Gergen, "The Healthy, Happy Human Being Wears Many Masks," *Psychology Today* (May 1972), p. 64.

LEADERSHIP

CHAPTER 10

ON THE JOB . . .

LEADERSHIP

LEADERS ARE MADE, NOT BORN

    Managers Versus Leaders
    Can Leadership Be Developed?

WHAT DOES A LEADER DO?

    The Executive Function
    Other Leadership Functions
    How Should a Leader Behave?

HOW DOES A MEMBER BECOME A LEADER?

    Personal Qualifications
    Situational Factors
    Formal Versus Informal Leadership

HOW DOES A LEADER EXERCISE CONTROL?

    Power and Authority
    Other Means of Control

NEW VIEWS OF LEADERSHIP

    Blake and Mouton's Managerial Grid
    Hersey and Blanchard's Situational Leadership Model
    House's Path-Goal Theory

ON THE JOB REVISITED . . .

SUMMARY

HUMAN RELATIONS APPLICATIONS

DISCUSSION QUESTIONS

NOTES

MANAGERIAL DIALOGUE: George E. Johnson

ON THE JOB . . .

People in Collegetown, a small university city near Atlanta, sometimes joked that Martin Rudge's epitaph would read: "Don't argue with me, I know what I'm doing." Rudge has been the owner and general manager of University Book Store since it was founded forty-seven years ago. In that time, the shop has gone through very few changes.

Rudge has always believed that a college book store had one function and one function alone: to provide students with the books they needed for their courses. He felt that students are busy enough with their required reading and therefore have no time for light reading. In fact, it was only a few years ago that his daughter Janna convinced him to stock a few books of outside interest to students. Rudge grudgingly gave in, and now the store carries about two dozen paperback best-sellers.

For forty years, University Book Store monopolized the textbook business in Collegetown. Every now and then, a competitor would open, but Rudge's reputation of carrying everything a student needs quickly drove the newcomers out of town.

Recently, however, another bookstore, called "Read As You Please," opened in town. The manager of the store, Alberta Holmes, stocks most of the required texts for the university and also carries a deep and well-balanced line of other books, newspapers, and magazines. While the majority of students still patronize Rudge's store, others are now giving their business to Holmes.

The reason for this is simple: the students enjoy browsing around the store, leafing through the nonrequired books. Once they're in the store, they are likely to buy their textbooks in the same trip. Rudge believes his decline in business is due to natural curiosity about something new and that with time, his business will return.

On Janna's 25th birthday, her father decided to turn the managership of University Book Store over to her, while he would remain president and owner. Janna was thrilled with the prospect and immediately began thinking of new ideas to improve business. She spoke to all the store employees about what they thought was needed. The employees all agreed that University Book Store needed a wider range of books to sell. Janna, who had suspected this was the case, now brought the matter up with her father:

Janna: Dad, I've spoken with our employees, and I've formulated a few of my own ideas to help perk up business. It seems that the most urgent thing we have to do is get more books, books from a greater variety of fields. Students don't want to read only textbooks. They've got free time, and they want to spend it enjoying themselves. We can help them and ourselves by stocking more than standard textbooks. Holmes is doing it, and if we don't do something to compete, she might drive us right out of business.

Rudge: Now you know Janna, no one is ever going to drive us out of business. All the students know where to shop for texts: University Book Store. That's the way it's always been, and that's the way it's always going to be.

Janna: But Dad, listen. I've been looking over the books and it's obvious that since Holmes went into business, our gross has gone down consistently month by month. We've got to stock a wider range. . . .

Rudge: So you're looking through the books, huh? You're really turning into quite a businesswoman, Janna. But just remember one thing: you may be the manager now, but I'm still the boss. And that means that what I say goes. I can take the job away from you just as easily I gave it to you in the first place. So don't get too cocky and sure of yourself. I know what's right for this store. I've been here a lot longer than you have."

More to come. . . .

LEADERSHIP

Whether the leader is Joan of Arc, George Washington, or the Godfather, a fundamental question applies. Does a leader emerge through the power and brilliance of his or her own personality, or are there simple circumstances in the course of human relationships that determine who will lead and who will follow?

Traditionally, folk wisdom and expert opinion have agreed that leadership is a personal phenomenon. Psychologists point to exhaustive studies on the "leadership personality," an individual favored with traits such as aggressiveness, proficiency in communications, and high motivation to take charge of a situation. But a growing number of sociologists are reluctant to accept this personal model of leadership. They offer an alternative model of the leader-follower relationship as an outcome of group dynamics. Through group interactions, one person emerges who is capable of making his or her intentions the one the groups accepts. When the relationship is mutually rewarding, the leader and follower roles become institutionalized. In this context, personal attributes (while still important) are seen in the larger process of group interaction.

This chapter considers some fundamental questions of leadership:

What circumstances turn a group member into a group leader?

What is the most important function a leader can perform?

Are there any personal qualifications a group member should exhibit if he or she expects to become leader?

How can an informal leader emerge when formal leadership of an organization is ineffectual?

What is the ultimate source of a leader's authority?

How can a leader use (or abuse) power in controlling the activities of the group?

How do different types of leadership style affect the group's efficiency?

LEADERS ARE MADE, NOT BORN

"Leadership is more than a matter of mere charisma."

Leadership has been a popular subject for discussions. Many papers, articles, and books have been written about the elusive subject. In most of these works, leadership is considered to be a purely personal attribute.

In the popular imagination, a great public figure such as Abraham Lincoln or Indira Gandhi is thought of as a "born leader." Leadership thus becomes the result of the individual's innate charisma. But some researchers and theorists would deny that there is such a thing as a person who is destined to take over the leadership role. In their view, a leader is a person who, in the course of personal interaction within a given group, is able to impose his or her conscious intentions on the majority of the other members of the group. In other words, leadership arises out of group dynamics. Once someone is in a position of leadership, he or she takes on the characteristics of a leader.

Thus, leadership could be said to be a relational rather than a personal attribute. It is the result of a given set of circumstances within a group. This is not to deny that certain personal qualities are necessary for the man or woman who wants to become a leader. But, as we shall see in this chapter, those qualifications are much less rigorous than has been supposed in the past. In fact, many leaders acquire the attributes of leadership only after circumstances put them there.

This distinction is important because it means that leadership can be taught. Many critics of modern American business cry out for better leadership among the nation's top companies. If leadership was simply an inherited trait, like freckles or curly hair, we as a nation could do nothing to encourage the development of more and better leaders. But since it is learned, we may, with proper teaching, continually improve our leadership.

One thing is clear: a leader does not function in a vacuum but in a group. There cannot be a leader without at least one follower. Therefore, to understand leadership, we must study it in terms of group dynamics.

Perhaps we should begin our study by defining the term *leader*. A leader might be one who:

Holds a particular office designated as one of leadership.

Is the major focus of interpersonal behavior in the group.

Is the person who is best liked by the other members of the group.

Exercises a strong influence over the actions taken by the group.

Has the highest status of any group member.

In the Managerial Dialogue on pages 262–263, George E. Johnson of Johnson Products offers his own definitions of a leader. In this text, we will define leadership in relation to the dynamics of the group. A leader is a person who is able to communicate his or her conscious intentions to one or more persons in such a way as to influence the others to act in accordance with those intentions.

Managerial Dialogue

"My style is leadership by example. I try to get people to do things because they want to"

**George E. Johnson,
president and chairman of
the board of Johnson
Products Company, Inc.**

**Johnson Products is a
recognized innovator in the
beauty care industry.**

George Johnson has been demonstrating his leadership in the business world for more than thirty years. In 1954, he and his wife, Joan, took out a $250 loan and began manufacturing a hair straightener for black men. In the following years, Johnson's Chicago-based company became a leader in the ethnic beauty care industry, producing and marketing such grooming products as hair dressings, hair relaxers, conditioners, shampoos, and cosmetics under the brand names of Ultra Sheen, Afro Sheen, Ultra Style, Gentle Treatment, Classy Curl, Ultra Curl, Ultra Sheen Cosmetics, and Moisture Formula Cosmetics. Almost since its inception, Johnson Products Company Inc., has been a leader in a turbulent industry with a 12 percent growth rate that now approaches $1 billion a year. How did Johnson lead his company past the pitfalls of growth and the changing hair and cosmetics styles of black men and women?

"I'm an entrepreneur," Johnson says. "We operate a little differently here than those managers who come from B-schools."

Johnson learned his early lessons in leadership working for the Fuller Products Co., a black-owned cosmetics manufacturer whose proprietor, S. B. Fuller, was a legendary entrepreneur. When Johnson and his wife founded their company, the small size dictated a certain style of leadership. Decisions could be made swiftly by Johnson as he experimented with various formulas for hair straighteners and other products. With his wife and brothers taking part in the company, Johnson became a family leader as well. One brother became director of distribution; another became vice president of sales and general manager.

But with his organization's continued growth—more than 500 people now work for the company at manufacturing and sales offices around the nation and in Nigeria—Johnson is taking a different approach to leadership. "My style is leadership by example," he explains, "I try to get people to do things because they want to." For Johnson that does not mean "management by wandering around," as some writers have advocated. "I do talk with people, but I deal through channels. There are nine people who work directly under me. I've learned I can't deal directly with their subordinates or the organization becomes confused." Johnson's company itself has taken a leadership role in many areas. In December 1969, for example, Johnson Products became the first black-owned company to become publicly held. Two years later, the stock was traded on the American Stock Exchange. During the 1970s, Johnson Products was a prime sponsor of "Soul Train," the first black advertiser of the nationally syndicated dance program. In 1975, the company launched Debbie's Beauty college to provide a "beauty culture education," and by the mid-1980s it had opened schools in eleven cities. As corporate leader, Johnson believes his employees contribute more to the company when they feel good about working. "You can get people to do things better if people feel like they're part of *our* organization," Johnson says. "Success means a lot to our employees, to everyone."

To implement that philosophy, Johnson long ago instituted a profit-sharing plan that helps give his 500-plus employees an additional incentive for achievement.

Besides sharing company profits with his employees, Johnson has become a leader in philanthropy as well. He founded the George E. Johnson Foundation in the 1960s to serve as a source for funding worthy causes. Over the years, the foundation has aided studies of black-owned businesses and contributed regularly to the United Negro College Fund. For the company's 25th anniversary, Johnson commissioned a series of portraits of famous black women; the exhibition has been shown nationwide. Johnson has demonstrated that leadership by example works, both in his company and in the community.

Leadership in a group is thus defined as an interaction involving two kinds of behavior: that of the leader and that of the follower. Many members of the group may at times assume the role of a leader in relationship to some of the other members. Expertise, previous experience, acquaintance with a particular person or place—any of these factors may allow a person to act as the leader of the group in given situations. In most groups, however, it will soon be observed that certain people assume a leadership role more frequently than do other members of the group. These people thus become identified as group leaders.

A leader's freedom of action is therefore always limited by the nature of his or her relationship to the group. Contrary to popular belief, the leader is the member most totally obligated to the group. Although he or she may be the most powerful group member, the leader is also the member most closely bound to and by the group. Because of his or her obligation to uphold the group norms, the leader is the member most subject to those norms; deviance is the one sure way to lose a leadership role. A leader is similarly limited by the group's own definition of its images and its goals, and he or she can act only within that frame of reference.

Managers Versus Leaders

In our organizations, management and leadership may exist in the same person, or they may not. Many institutions are managed well, but led poorly. "Management is the science of getting things done through people, while leadership is the art of getting people to do things," writes Samuel Feinberg. "Election or appointment of a man or woman as a manager does not automatically carry with it the privileges and responsibilities of a leader about whom others rally."[1]

Managers are concerned with keeping control of an organization in a rational manner. According to Theodore Levitt:

> *Management consists of the rational assessment of a situation and the systematic selection of goals and purposes (what is to be done?); the systematic development of strategies to achieve these goals; the marshalling of the required resources; the rational design, organization, direction and control of the activities required to attain the selected purposes; and finally, the motivating and reward of people to do the work.*[2]

In many organizations, managers tend to adopt goals out of necessity rather than emotional desires. When your job consists of sending paperwork from one department to another, it's unlikely you'll feel deep emotional attachment to your goals. Leaders, on the other hand, are likely to have a strong emotional attachment to the group and its goals.

The chairman of General Motors from 1958 to 1967, Frederic Donner, typified the manager's approach when he talked about new car developments:

> *To meet the challenge of the marketplace, we must recognize changes in customer needs and desires far enough ahead to have the right products in the right places at the right time and in the right quantity. We must balance trends in preference against the many compromises that are necessary to make a final product that is both reliable and good-looking, that performs well and that sells at a competitive price in the necessary volume. We must design, not just the cars we would like to build, but more importantly, the cars that our customers want to buy.*[3]

Contrast Donner's managerial attitude with the stirring call to action by President John F. Kennedy in his inaugural address:

> *Let every nation know, whether it wishes us well or ill, that we shall pay any price, bear any burden, meet any hardship, support any friend, oppose any foe, in order to assure the survival and the success of liberty.*

That emotional quality of leadership is exactly what is missing in many managers. Managers like to calculate the odds and minimize the risks.

Leaders often enjoy risks and show great bravery in the face of dangerous situations. According to one study, effective leaders in fire-fighting situations were judged to show more personal bravery than ineffective leaders. The same was found to be true of effective wartime military leaders in combat.[4]

Leaders, in fact, may be temperamentally disposed to seek out high-risk situations, particularly when there is the chance for a correspondingly big reward. "From my observations, why one individual seeks risks while another approaches problems conservatively depends more on his or her personality and less on conscious choice," writes Abraham Zaleznik. "For some, especially those who become managers, the instinct for survival dominates their need for risk and their ability to tolerate mundane, practical work assists their survival. The same cannot be said for leaders who sometimes react to mundane work as an affliction."[5]

Some analysts point out that there has been a change in the last decade or so in the personal characteristics of top business managers. In the postwar period, managers were expected to be conservative traditionalists. They tried to stay within the bureaucratic structure. Their leadership consisted primarily of making rational business decisions. Today, top management has become more attuned to personal leadership. Managers, even in large corporations, are expected to take risks, even to express some rebellion against the traditional way of doing things. They are encouraged to be real leaders, even at the cost of mistakes, and they are allowed to display their own personalities, even indulge their eccentricities.

Can Leadership Be Developed?

If one assumes that leadership is primarily a personal phenomenon, then social institutions would be unable to produce leaders. An organization could only wait passively for some individual to show that spark of in-born personal leadership. Fortunately for our governments, schools, churches, and business organizations (and managerial consultants!), leadership skills can be taught. The ability to persuade, to delegate authority, to concentrate on particular goals, to set an example for the group, are all skills that can be developed in individuals.

"Since leadership skills can be taught, organizations can develop future leaders."

That's not to say the job of developing leaders is easy. One recent study of the American presidency highlights the difficulty in developing leaders. One might expect that the greatest presidents would have had the most prior experience and success in the U.S. political system. Yet a close examination of family background, personal characteristics, education, occupation, and political experiences provided few predictors of presidential performance. Outside events—particularly wars—appeared to determine which presidents were rated the greatest.[6]

WHAT DOES A LEADER DO?

One very important connection between the group that provides the leadership role and the individual who assumes it should be discussed here as a background to the question of the leader's role in the group: the way in which the group looks at leadership. Much of the group philosophy of leadership can be inferred from group norms; some of it may be explicit in written documents such as the rules of procedure, which define the obligations and limitations the group places on its leader.

The Executive Function

The first question the group must answer when defining its philosophy of leadership is: What does the group want its leader to do? The obvious answer is that it wants the leader to lead. Although that is usually true, the leader may perform other functions that are even more important than actually leading the group.

One of the primary responsibilities of a leader is influencing group behavior to conform to his or her conscious intentions. This is called the *executive function.* It is the leader's job to:

Perceive the group as a totality.

Consider individual aptitudes and capabilities and balance them against the group goals.

Determine both the group's course of action and the entity that the group is going to become.

Decide on tactics by which the group can carry out this course.

Persuade the members to accept this evaluation and to work for the goals the leader has set.

In carrying out this executive function, the leader must be capable of performing four different processes: (1) observing group behavior, (2) interpreting group behavior, (3) formulating ideas about the group, and (4) convincing the group to accept the leader's analysis and decisions. The ability to perform these tasks successfully is one of the chief requisites for leadership.

The first of the processes is observation of group behavior. The leader must be able to watch and listen to the group and to remember what was observed. Since many indicators of group interaction are extremely subtle—a glance exchanged between members, a momentarily extended silence, an uncharacteristic remark—a leader must be capable of close observation.

The second process that the leader must undertake in his function as executive is that of interpreting the observed behavior. In this the leader is aided by a knowledge of the individual personalities of the members; a familiarity with group norms, both explicit and tacitly understood; and an understanding of the cultural context in which the group is operating. The leader, as executive, must try to determine the causes of the events he or she observes, and their meaning to the various members, so that he or she can infer their significance and the group meaning. This aspect of leadership helps to develop group consciousness. One person is assigned the task of becoming aware of the system that operates within the entire group.

The third process in the executive function is the formulation of ideas about the group. With the aid of the inferences the leader has made from observations, he or she establishes a conception of the structure and identity of the group, its needs and desires, capabilities and goals. As the leader gradually adds evidence from his or her observations, the clarity of this conception of the group increases, until at last the leader is sure enough of both its accuracy and definition to be willing to expose it to the members.

The fourth process of the executive function is convincing the group to accept the validity of the leader's concept of the group and to concur in his or her analysis of its needs direction. This aspect of leadership is the most observable indication of leadership function. Just because it is the most visible, however, does not mean it is the only, or even the most important, part of executive leadership. All four phases must be carried out to ensure effective leadership. Convincing the members of the accuracy of the leader's concept of the group and motivating them to behave in the way he or she thinks will most benefit the group are merely the last steps in a series of events.

Assuming the executive function can expose a leader to several psychological difficulties that may threaten his or her effectiveness. One of these problems arises from the ambiguity of the leader's position in regard to the group. As the leader, and the center of the group consciousness, he or she is totally identified with the group. He or she is also morally obligated to the group, which is sharing the same goals and norms. Like all the members, the leader is dependent on the group for individual satisfactions, perhaps even more so than other members, since his or her rewards are greater. Yet in the executive role, the leader must try to view the group through the eyes of a stranger. The leader must ask questions about the group and act as a sort of spy on its inner workings.

Other problems come from the difficulty the leader's task. As sociologist Theodore Mills comments, "Consciousness of the human group, by its very nature, cannot be fully realized."[7] Therefore, the leader's fulfillment of his or her task will be only partial at best. No leader will ever be able to observe and understand everything that happens in the group. Knowledge of this destined failure is an emotional burden that the leader must carry, and carry alone.

Other Leadership Functions

"A leader's function as symbol of the group helps keep members loyal and committed to group goals."

The group often assigns certain other functions to the leader that are not directly related to the executive role. The leader may serve as a symbol of the group's identity. In this way, he or she strengthens group identity and often increases the dedication of the members to the group.

The leader may serve as a sort of model for the other members, demonstrating to them an ideal of behavior, the perfect conformity to group norms, a complete expression of group values. It is this function of the leader as symbol or model that explains, for example, how a person famous for his career as movie actor can become a successful politician. President Ronald Reagan, who starred in Hollywood films of the 1940s and 1950s, was elected governor of California in the mid-1960s, not because voters knew of his executive capabilities but because, through his movie roles and public relations image in Hollywood, he had come to symbolize and personify a valued ideal. It is an interesting sidelight that one of his early Democratic opponents in the 1984 presidential campaign was John Glenn, the first American astronaut to orbit the earth. Glenn, too, was able to turn the symbolic nature of such leadership into a successful political career in Ohio.

A third function that the leadership role may perform for the group is to give it status. Thus, a fund-raising drive will pick a foreign princess or a former first lady to head its committee. Whether or not she has any executive ability, she will lend the whole group desirable prestige in the eyes of the rest of the community. As social status is often an individual goal that motivates a person to join a group, it is a perfectly legitimate leadership function to assist the group members in this goal. If the leader can do it by the mere sound of his or her name, so much the better for the group.

How Should a Leader Behave?

This question is closely related to the preceding one, and the way in which the group answers the first question will influence the answer to the second one. The kind of leadership one exercises will determine the way one behaves. Ideas governing leadership behavior will be found primarily in the group norms, and perhaps secondarily in the group goals and group identity.

According to Mills, five principal types of relationships may exist between a leader and the followers in a group:

1. The dependent-nurturant relationship
2. The insurgent-coercive relationship
3. The bureaucratic relationship
4. The idealistic relationship
5. The democratic relationship

The dependent-nurturant relationship.   In the dependent-nurturant relationship, the members see the leader as kind, understanding, beneficient, and able to solve problems (both personal and group) and answer questions. In short, they depend on the leader for a variety of gratifications, a dependence similar in kind if not extent to that of a child on its parents. The leader sees the other members as requiring care and attentions, being weak without his or her support, and depending on him or her for protection as well as reassurance. In this kind of leader-follower relationship, the leader may never be permitted to display any uncertainty before other members, nor should he or she consult them about group executive decisions. The leader must be careful to provide a more or less impartial treatment of all members, for the problem of jealousy among the members competing within the group for the single source of support and gratification will be severe and could easily damage the group's cohesion.

The insurgent-coercive relationship.   In the insurgent-coercive relationship, each side sees the other as a dangerous aggressor. The group members see the leader as powerful but hostile to them, trying to block their desires and gratifications, putting a limit on their growth and capability. The leader sees the group as trying to undermine his or her authority, to remove him or her from power, to destroy the group cohesion. In a group with voluntary membership, such as a business organization, this type can remain a viable relationship only as long as both sides tacitly agree that their aggressive impulses need to be restrained by the balance of the relationship. The leader who is involved in this kind of situation will naturally exhibit a very aggressive and highly authoritarian kind of behavior. He or she will keep the group under strict surveillance and tight controls; he or she may initiate a complex system of sanctions, with much greater emphasis on punishment than reward. This coercive-insurgent relationship is rarely found in a highly goal-oriented group for the simple reason that maintaining the balance of aggression will take up most of the group's time and energy.

The bureaucratic relationship.   In a bureaucratic relationship, the leader and the group are bound together by a common need to avoid the unhappiness of making mistakes. To avoid the guilt of doing the wrong thing, they all follow an elaborate set of rules. The group sees the leader as a support in their efforts to achieve the group goal and as a source of information about the "right" way to do things. The leader personifies both the rules, or group norms, of which they are fearful and the safety found in conformity. Therefore, their attitude toward him or her is ambiguous. The leader has similarly mixed feelings about his or her followers. They are necessary tools for carrying out the group activities and thus represent allies in this project, yet they are also a potential source of disruption of the program and must therefore be regarded as enemies. The behavior of a bureaucratic leader toward his or her followers is apt to be an odd and idiosyncratic blend of friendliness and stringency. This kind of leader-follower relationship is particularly useful for goal-oriented groups and is in fact held together principally by the shared desire to achieve the goal.

The idealistic relationship.   In an idealistic relationship, the group sees the leader as the personification of some ideal that the group seeks to achieve or promote; as a model, guide, or teacher; as an object of love and admiration. The leader sees the other group members as apprentices or students, those whom he or she must teach to understand and cherish the ideal in the same way that he or she has done. The group is bound together by the intensity of its belief in the ideal—and by its agreement that the leader is the best possible expression of that ideal. In his or her interpersonal group behavior, the leader may challenge or test the other members and will surely lecture to them at times. The leader will always preserve a certain unapproachable distance from the rest of the group, no matter how kindly and generously he or she may treat them. This pattern of behavior encourages group collaboration in pursuit of goals and does not lead to the rivalry among members that is characteristic of the dependent-nurturant relationship, since the leader as ideal is equally accessible to all members. Its chief drawback is that the group will be extremely inflexible in its attitude toward its goals and incapable of altering them in any way, as long as it has a leader whose main purpose is to express them.

The democratic relationship. In a democratic relationship, the group members see the leader as the embodiment of its collective will, the tool of its goal-seeking activities. The leader sees the other members as parts of the entity with which he or she identifies and, in some measure as his or her bosses. It is characteristic of this kind of relationship (and the bureaucratic one as well) that the leader and follower can exchange roles, for leadership becomes just that—a role rather than a personal attribute. It is impossible to imagine a coercive or idealistic or nurturant leader trading places with a follower, for they must either lead or be totally discredited. In this democratic situation, the leader's behavior typically will be friendly and unassuming and there will be a clearly egalitarian atmosphere about the group. The main drawback to this form of relationship is that the leader may lack the authority to persuade the other members in his or her executive role, and goals will then be hard to achieve. It can also lead to crippling battles over the leadership role, as various members contend for it.

HOW DOES A MEMBER BECOME A LEADER?

If we accept the idea that a leader is simply a person who has assumed that role within the context of a particular group, then we must look carefully at the way the leadership position is assumed.

Personal Qualifications

"The most important personal qualification for becoming a leader is simply wanting to be one."

Are there any qualifications that are prerequisites for leadership? Most sociologists say that the answer is no. Since leadership is defined primarily as a relationship attribute rather than a personal one, the situation matters more than the individual personalities involved. In a group whose leadership pattern is democratic, it is axiomatic that any member may become a leader. In other patterns of leader relationships, it has often been demonstrated that there is a great variety in the personal qualifications of the leaders.

Nevertheless, there are certain kinds of people who are more likely to become leaders than others and certain personal qualities that give an individual a push toward leadership if the group situation is favorable. Some examples of these personal attributes are:

An ability to verbalize feelings and concepts.

Intelligence above the level of average but below the level of genius.

Empathy with other group members.

A degree of insight into the group situation.

A high level of proficiency at the kind of task that the group will be undertaking in its goal-seeking activities.

Flexibility in formulating new concepts and accepting new ideas.

A keen interest in the group goal.

A fairly aggressive type of interactional behavior.

Although not one of these personal attributes is absolutely necessary, they all predispose the individual toward leadership.

The single most important personal attribute for those who assume the leadership roles is motivation to be a leader. Even this is not always necessary, as for example, in a democratic leadership pattern with some chance-dependent method of selecting those who take leadership roles. In this case the lot might fall on someone who has no desire to be a leader and undertakes the job only because the group says he or she must, in performance of membership obligations. It is much more customary for leadership to be on a voluntary basis, however, and in this case degree of motivation to attempt leadership can be a very important factor in determining which member is to become a leader. In general, the stronger the motivation of the individual, the more likely it is that he or she will achieve a leadership position. There are many reasons why an individual might desire to become a group leader. Among them are a desire for measurable achievement, a sizeable fund of self-confidence and self-esteem, an urge to dominate the other members of the group, a devotion to the group, a conviction that the individual possesses specialized knowledge that is crucial to the leadership, a keen interest in a particular challenge facing the group at that time, and a need for signs of prestige and status.

Situational Factors

Although all of the personal attributes just mentioned may influence the group's choice of a leader, the most important determining factors are situational rather than personal. A member of the group becomes a leader because he or she is the one in the right position to do so. For example, the leader may have a specific knowledge or ability that directly fits into the requirements of the leadership role at the time it falls vacant, or he or she may have the greatest seniority of any group member, or the most experience. He or she may be the person in the group structure who has the easiest access to information important to the group. He or she may control the means of communication between members. He or she may be a protégé, disciple, or relative of the previous leader. He or she may be a person who has ably handled an earlier leadership responsibility or one who has received the necessary training for the processes of leadership. Finally, he or she may be the member who can best afford the price, in time, energy, and money, that leadership will cost.

Leadership may be based on mere happenstance, such as being the first member of a group to arrive or the first to be selected at random by some bureaucratic system. An interesting study of the results of picking leaders at random was made in 1951 by R. L. French. Studying a naval training station where arriving recruits were given positions of minor authority in what was virtually a random fashion, he found that those so selected also tended to be selected later by the other recruits as their preferred leaders and viewed by the group as possessing of significant leadership ability. Thus, we might say that one way to become qualified to be a leader is to be chosen as one.

Every group has some formal means of selecting its leaders. The means will differ with the pattern of leadership chosen by the group. In some groups the leaders will be appointed or chosen by the existing leaders; this is true of both the bureaucratic and the idealistic leadership patterns. Other groups may hold elections to determine who will be the leaders, with those who desire the position putting forth their candidacy; this is always true of the democratic leadership pattern. Some democratic groups may institute a policy selecting officers and leaders by lot or by a fixed rotation of leadership among all members. Occasionally, as in juvenile gangs, there may be some kind of fitness test, in which the winner is ratified by the group as its leader. In the dependent-nurturant and the insurgent-coercive patterns, there may be a variety of means of leadership selection. Often the coercive leader is appointed by some outsider with authority over the whole group, or he or she may have exerted informal control of the group to force his or her election.

Formal Versus Informal Leadership

Formal leadership includes the apparatus of offices, such as group president, vice president, treasurer, chairman of the committee, head of the task force, and so on. These offices are the group's way of institutionalizing its choice of a leader.

Sometimes the person with the title of leader has only weak powers; his or her authority may be shared with, or even appropriated by, some of the group members. This informal mechanism of leadership may act in a way that is complementary to the formal selection of a leader or, in some cases, in opposition to it.

"Informal leaders may actually have more influence on the group than the leaders who are formally designated."

A common pattern is for a new leader to arise in the group by informal means and then gain ratification from the group through a formal mechanism of leadership selection, replacing a leader whose influence is on the wane. This is especially likely to occur in a democratic leadership pattern, in which it is understood that leadership is subject to frequent change. Informal mechanisms of leadership are also found in a bureaucratic leader-follower relationship, in which an informal leader may usurp the functions of a formally appointed leader.

How does one get to be a leader through informal means? This kind of leadership is more apt to rely on personal attributes, for informal leadership generally must be won in opposition to an entrenched formal leader who does not to want to delegate his or her authority.

Informal leadership occurs spontaneously when some member of the group displays conspicuous abilities lacking, or only partially present, in the leader. Perhaps in group discussions the member shows a deeper observation and understanding of other members' behavior, or when working on some task, he or she displays a technical knowledge superior to that of the official leader. The result is that other group members will recognize and respond to this ability, and the leader will therefore be able to influence their behavior in the direction of his or her conscious intentions.

The extent to which informal leadership presents a threat to the informally selected leader of the group varies with the situation. In some cases, the informal leader is obviously limited to the one area of his or her competence; this would probably be true of the member with great technological expertise. He or she could lead the group in the working situation but would lack qualifications for effective leadership in other interrelational situations. Sometimes an informal leader is limited by his or her own lack of motivation. When there is a clear limitation on an informal leader, the titular leader is likely to accept the informal leadership for the duration of its effectiveness, because he or she does not pose a serious threat.

Other instances may be more threatening. In this case, the formally recognized leader has two possible courses of action. He or she may acknowledge the informal leadership and try to turn it to his or her advantage by incorporating it into the executive structure. He or she might appoint the informal leader as an assistant or to some important group office. In other words, the leader will share the leadership role with the informal leader. The group gains and benefits from the additional leadership ability being exercised, and the ambition of the informal leader may be appeased by the extent of this recognition. Thus, the formal leader is able to maintain his or her position.

The other course he might follow is to try to suppress the informal leadership. He can use his executive authority to try to separate an informal leader from the leadership situation. He can attempt to discredit the informal leader in the eyes of the other members. If this strategy is successful, he eliminates the threat to his leadership and maintains his exclusive grasp on the role. However, there is always the risk that in choosing to oppose an informal leader, he will precipitate a bitter struggle over the leadership position. He may lose his standing in the group, either because he is defeated by the informal leaders, or because the group later rejects him when they come to realize the cost of the leadership battle to the group in terms of loss of cohesion and attractiveness. Generally, a leader who tries to suppress informal leadership is motivated by a desire to further his own individual goals rather than those of the group, which could best be served by encouraging any effective leadership.

Fred E. Fiedler, of the University of Illinois, has advanced a model of leadership, the *contingency model,* that has greatly influenced current attitudes toward leadership. In Fiedler's model, the nature of leadership style is based on the situation that confronts the leader. (See Figure 10.1.) Fiedler's model shows that people who are task-oriented perform best in situations that are either very favorable or very unfavorable. A favorable situation is one in which the task confronting a manager is very structured, the amount of authority he or she has is great, and the level of support from subordinates is high. An example might be a well-liked plant manager in a profitable, well-established business who is asked by the boss to rearrange work schedules. An unfavorable situation might be that of an advertising manager who is not sure whether his idea for an ad will be effective or whether anyone else in management will support this concept. In either case, task-oriented management will be most effective. Only in situations of intermediate favorableness are relationship-oriented managers more effective.

Fiedler later went one step beyond his contingency theory to assess whether certain personality traits characterize successful leaders. By giving psychological tests to a number of leaders and nonleaders, he arrived

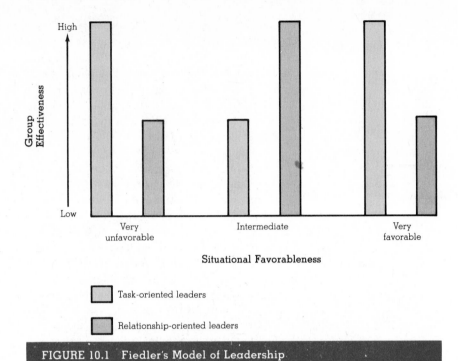

FIGURE 10.1   Fiedler's Model of Leadership

Source: Harold W. Berkman and Linda L. Neider, "An Analysis of Leadership Effectiveness: A Pilot Study" (February 1986), unpublished study.

at the conclusion that successful leaders have a particularly high degree of perceptual discrimination, a special ability to tell the difference between effective and ineffective co-workers. Carefully performed research eliminated the possibility that this discrimination was the result of prior experience with those co-workers, but it does leave open the interesting question of whether this ability is innate or a skill that has been learned in previous leadership experiences.

HOW DOES A LEADER EXERCISE CONTROL?

Apparently it takes a combination of personality traits and the right situation to become a leader, but what does it take to exercise control over the group?

Power and Authority

Authority means having the capability to perform an action. A general, for instance, has authority over lower-ranking officers in an army and can issue orders to them. Power in a group setting means the ability to bend others to your will. A foreman, for instance, might have authority over an employee but lack the power to change her shift, move her to another machine, give her a raise, or otherwise motivate her. A manager might have the authority to give orders without having the power to exact obedience to them.

"To be fully effective, a leader must possess both power and authority."

Any group leader possesses, by virtue of his or her role in the group, a certain degree of power and authority. Two factors influence the exact extent of his or her possession of these adjuncts of leadership: personal abilities and the group's values.

The ultimate source of a leader's authority must always be the group itself, and this is true no matter how the leader is chosen or what kind of leadership pattern he or she is working within. No leader can exercise any authority without the consent of the group. Even a coercive leader has the group's tacit consent to his or her authority. If they ever become totally convinced that his or her authority is really against their collective interests, they will force the leader to leave, either voluntarily or involuntarily. They accept his or her authority, even when they fear and hate it, because they are afraid of the destructive effects of their unleashed aggressions, and because they are afraid of the consequences of unsuccessful rebellion. They desire to accomplish something either as individuals or as a group, and they realize that the balancing force of the leader's authority assists them in their goals. Likewise, the idealistic leader would have no authority if the group members ceased to believe in him or her and replaced him or her with what they thought was a truer embodiment of their ideal. Of course, in the democratic pattern of leadership, the leader obviously derives all of his or her authority from the group, but it is only a more open recognition of a basic rule of group interaction. Every kind of group is governed by the same rule.

An elected leader's source of authority is obviously the group, which can replace him or her at will in the next election. The same is also true of the appointed leader, for the authority to appoint him or her also arises from the group. Even the authority of the Dalai Lama over his followers rests on the group's belief in the deity. If the group for some reason ceased to honor its religion, the fact that the Dalai Lama was God incarnate would not be enough to preserve his authority.

The extent of the leader's authority is also dependent on the group. It will be determined at the same time as is the group's philosophy of leadership. The group may delegate vast authority to its leader, including perhaps even the right to decide between life and death for individual members. The more strongly hierarchical the group organization, the greater is the authority with which the group will invest its leaders. Conversely, egalitarian groups, or any group with a loose organization, probably will be sparing in the amount of authority they bestow on their leaders.

A leader's power is more dependent on personal attributes, in contrast to authority, which comes from relational ones. In Renaissance Italy, Machiavelli wrote *The Prince,* which advises would-be leaders how to acquire power. As you may recall from Chapter 2, Machiavelli advocated the use of deception, coercion, and fear—not to mention poisoning, stabbing, or drowning a foe—to achieve power. In a more modern context, the leader of a juvenile gang may be given the authority and the normative right to beat up any member of the group whose behavior appears to be deviant. But if the leader were a ninety-pound weakling, no amount of authority could give him or her the power to beat a larger and stronger member. (On the other hand, of course, a leader who was very strong might have the power to beat up any other group member, but if he or she did it without having been given the authority by the group, the leader would soon lose his or her leadership.)

> *"The most able leaders are usually the ones who are granted the most power."*

Personal abilities and limitations largely determine the extent of the leader's power to exercise his or her authority. As a corollary to this rule, we might say that the greater the powers of the leader, the more likelihood that the group will grant him or her extensive authority.

Other Means of Control

The leader has certain other means through which he or she can exercise control. Chief among these is the group system of sanctions. In most groups, the job of dispensing the punishments and rewards falls to the leader. Thus, he or she is in control of, and identified by the members with, the whole normative system. This gives the leader a concrete means of forcing the group to behave in accordance with his or her intentions and is used by the leader to fortify his or her authority. It also gives the leader a psychological advantage, because refusing to follow his or her leadership is accordingly emotionally equated with deviating from the group norms.

Another help to the leader in his or her effort to exercise control of the group may come from the extent of his or her identification with the group. In a group with a leadership pattern that exalts and idealizes the leader, or clearly singles the leader out as an embodiment of the group identity, there is a built-in psychological resistance on the part of the group to defying or unseating the leader. It is tantamount to attacking the group itself, an act of great disloyalty. It is also self-destructive, since the group also represents an extension of the individual ego. Each member has invested a significant amount of emotion in such a leader, and his or her instinct will be to protect his or her investment rather than to threaten it.

We have seen that a leader influences the group in certain specified ways; this is the aspect of the phenomenon of leadership that is most familiar to everyone. But, with the help of the sociologist's eye, we have also seen that influence does not flow one way only. The group simultaneously exerts a strong influence on the leader. It is the group that determines a leader's behavior, the limits of his or her role, and who shall be leaders, something that successful leaders must always bear in mind. No group can function viably without some sort of leader, and no leader can function outside the context of his or her group.

NEW VIEWS OF LEADERSHIP

In recent years a number of theories have been developed to explain the leadership process. Three of the more widely discussed contemporary theories are those of Blake and Mouton (the Managerial Grid®), Hersey and Blanchard (situational leadership model), and House (path-goal theory). The first two approaches are used in training managers to become more effective in leadership roles, while the third theory, developed by House, is based on expectancy theory of motivation, which was covered in Chapter 4. We will discuss each of these approaches.

Blake and Mouton's Managerial Grid

The Managerial Grid, developed by Blake and Mouton, emphasizes two major types of concerns or attitudes that a manager might have. One concern is task accomplishment, and the other is a consideration for the needs of employees. These two dimensions—concern for production and concern for people—are arranged in the Grid displayed in Figure 10.2. As can be seen from this diagram, five major styles of leadership are illustrated.

The Managerial Grid is used primarily as a training for managers. A manager's leadership style can be assessed through a questionnaire that scores each dimension on a scale from one to nine. After assessing a man-

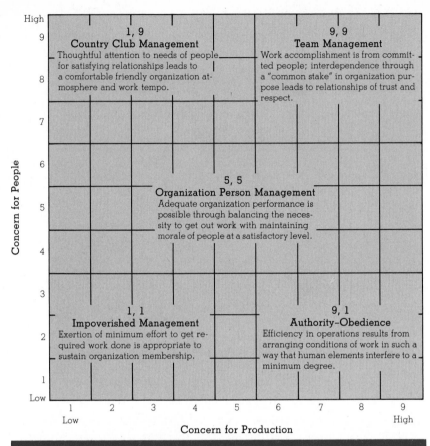

FIGURE 10.2 The Blake and Mouton Managerial Grid

Source: The Managerial Grid figure adapted from The Managerial Grid III, by Robert R. Blake and Jane Srygley Mouton. Houston: Gulf Publishing Company. Copyright © 1985, p. 12. Reproduced by permission.

"Whenever experts come up with the best way to do something, there is sure to be a reaction against it."

ager's score, Blake and Mouton then spend time coaching participants in the techniques necessary to become "9–9," the team-style manager who looks for work accomplishment from committed people. It is their contention that such a style is the most desirable one in most situations.

Although the Managerial Grid concept is very popular, the idea that there is one best leadership style has received a great deal of criticism. Fiedler's work, mentioned earlier, pointed out that different situations require different leadership approaches or, as the old adage goes, "different strokes for different folks."

Hersey and Blanchard's Situational Leadership Model

The Hersey and Blanchard approach to leadership is based on three major elements:

1. The amount of direction structure that a manager gives (task behavior).
2. The amount of emotional support the manager provides (relationship behavior).
3. The ability and willingness of subordinates to perform specific tasks (maturity).

Hersey and Blanchard contend that there is no one best way to influence the behavior of subordinates. Instead, the effective manager must assess the maturity level of individual subordinates and use the style of leadership that best matches this assessment. Figure 10.3 shows a schematic representation of the theory. As you can see from this diagram (somewhat similar to the Blake and Mouton Managerial Grid), four styles of leadership are displayed: telling, selling, participating, and delegating.

The telling style of leadership (high task behavior, high relationship behavior) is appropriate for subordinates who are low in maturity and skills. This style of leadership involves telling employees exactly how, where, and what needs to be done. The selling style is used for employees who do not have all the skills necessary to perform a particular task but are willing to take on the responsibilities (low to moderate maturity level). This selling approach provides directive behavior but simultaneously gives support to subordinates to reinforce their willingness and enthusiasm. When subordinates have the ability necessary to perform tasks but are unwilling to do so (moderate to high maturity), the appropriate leadership style is participating. A leader allows subordinates to share in the decision-making process to build confidence and improve motivation. Perhaps the ideal position for a leader is to have subordinates who are both able and willing to take responsibility (high maturity). With such individuals, a manager can use a delegating style of leadership. Self-motivated subordinates are permitted to decide how, when, and where to carry out particular activities.

A manager must correctly assess subordinates' maturity level. If a manager were to assume that a high maturity employee was at a low to moderate level, more directiveness than necessary would be provided. These mature employees would clearly rebel against being told how to perform a job that they felt they quite knew well. Providing that a manager can be taught to make proper maturity assessments, the situational

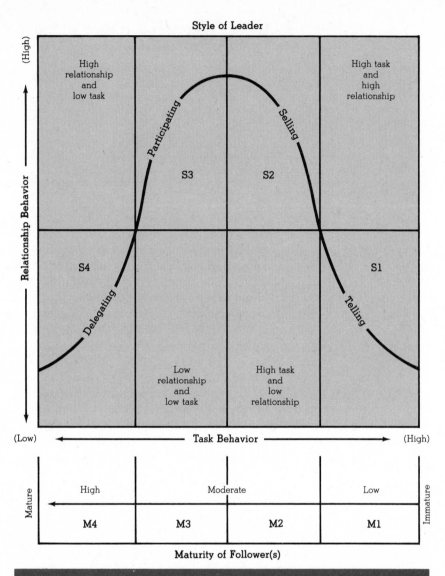

FIGURE 10.3 Hersey and Blanchard's Situational Leadership Model

Source: Adapted from P. Hersey and K. Blanchard, Management of Organizational Behavior: Utilizing Human Resources, *© 1982, p. 248. Reprinted by permission of Prentice-Hall, Englewood Cliffs, New Jersey.*

leadership model is an intuitively useful approach to influencing subordinate behavior.

House's Path-Goal Theory

Whereas the previous two approaches to leadership have evolved primarily as training devices for managers, the path-goal theory of leadership is based on the expectancy theory of motivation. Like the model of Hersey and Blanchard, this view also stresses the need for flexibility in leadership styles. Specifically, four different styles of leadership may be used, depending on the characteristics of subordinates (their abilities, needs, and so on) and characteristics of the work environment (types of tasks, authority systems, and so on). The four styles are:

1. *Instrumental behavior.* With this approach a manager concentrates on planning, organizing, controlling, and coordinating subordinate activities. It is very similar to the telling style in the model of Hersey and Blanchard.

2. *Supportive behavior.* This leadership style involves displaying a concern for the welfare of subordinates and creating a friendly environment.

3. *Participative behavior.* This approach is characterized by consulting with employees and using their input in making decisions that affect them.

4. *Achievement-oriented behavior.* This approach is concerned with setting challenging goals for subordinates and continually encouraging them to improve their performance.

In addition to discussing the need for effective managers to be fluent in the use of all four styles, the path-goal theory also elaborates on the motivational functions of a leader, as interpreted by Vroom's expectancy theory of motivation.

The term *path-goal* refers to the idea that managers must clarify for subordinates the paths leading to high performance and rewards in the company. In House's words:

> *The motivational function of the leader consists of increasing personal payoffs to subordinates for work-goal attainment, and making the path to these payoffs easier to travel by clarifying it, reducing road blocks and pitfalls, and increasing the opportunities for personal satisfaction en route.*[8]

When Janna heard her father, Martin Rudge, speak with such authority about University Book Store, she felt frustrated about making any real improvements. Just a few months later, Janna left to become a manager trainee at a large regional chain of bookstores. Her father resumed active management of University Book Store, which continued to lose business to its competitor.

How do you think this unhappy ending could have been prevented? Armed with more knowledge of personality and leadership traits, do you think there was any way for Janna to have convinced her father that he should let her carry out her plan? How would you have handled the father-daughter controversy?

SUMMARY

Leadership in a group is defined as an interaction involving two kinds of behavior, that of leaders and that of followers. This leadership is a relational rather than a personal attribute.

There are often differences between managers and leaders. Managers are oriented toward the status quo, while leaders are risk takers and actively seek changes. Despite folklore that says leaders are born, not bred, it is possible to develop leadership skills in many ways.

A group leader performs four functions: to observe and interpret group behavior, then to formulate ideas about the group and persuade others to accept his or her ideas. A group leader's behavior is determined by the type of relationship he or she maintains with his or her followers. There are five distinct types: (1) dependent-nurturant, (2) insurgent-coercive, (3) bureaucratic, (4) idealistic, and (5) democratic.

A group member may become leader of the group through a number of processes. While personal characteristics are now considered less important than situational factors, motivation to become leader does count. However, more often than not, a person assumes a leadership role because he or she is simply in the right place and position to do so.

Every group has formal means of selecting its leaders, but informal leaders may arise when the formal leadership is weak. An informal leader is most likely to take over in the democratic form of leadership. Any group leader needs authority to maintain leadership, and this authority comes from the group itself. This holds true for all types of leader-follower relationships. Much modern research into leadership has been aimed at improving the skills of managers. Among the approaches that have been developed are those of Blake and Mouton, the developers of the Managerial Grid, and of Hersey and Blanchard, who devised the situational leadership model. Along with Hersey and Blanchard, the House path-goal theory stresses the need for a leader to be flexible in using various styles. The concept of an effective manager as adaptable and flexible characterizes most modern-day training approaches and theorizing in the leadership area.

HUMAN RELATIONS APPLICATIONS

Conclusion 1:   Leadership should be thought of as a combination of relational characteristics and personal attributes.

Application: The adept manager becomes a leader when he or she is able to use his or her own personal competencies to understand, influence, and fulfill the needs of the organization and subordinates.

Conclusion 2:   Current thinking in the leadership area contends that effective leaders use a contingency approach—different styles for different situations and employees.

Application: Managers need to assess the maturity level of their employees, their personality characteristics, and the amount of guidance needed in particular situations before choosing a particular leadership style. A directive approach is needed for new or insecure employees, while more participative or delegative styles can be used for employees who can be counted on to perform effectively.

DISCUSSION QUESTIONS

1. Describe the difference between management and leadership.
2. What is the executive function of leadership? What processes are involved in fulfilling this function?
3. What are the major ways that a leader exerts control over his or her group members?
4. According to Hersey and Blanchard, how should a manager treat an employee who is low in maturity? What about an employee who has a high maturity level?
5. What are the major styles of leadership discussed in House's path-goal theory?

NOTES

1. Samuel Feinberg, "Measuring Your Executive Leadership Quotient," *Creative Living* (Spring 1980), pp. 2–6.

2. Theodore Levitt, "Management and the Post Industrial Society," *The Public Interest* (Summer 1976), p. 73.

3. Alfred P. Sloan, Jr., *My Years with General Motors*. New York: Doubleday & Co., 1964, p. 429.

4. Dean E. Frost, Fred E. Fiedler, and Jeff W. Anderson, "The Role of Personal Risk-taking in Effective Leadership," *Human Relations* 36 (February 1983), p. 185.

5. Abraham Zaleznik, "Managers and Leaders: Are They Different?" *Harvard Business Review* (May–June 1977), p. 51.

6. Dean Keith Simonton, "Presidential Greatness and Performance: Can We Predict Leadership in the White House?" *Journal of Personality* 49 (September 1981), p. 306.

7. Theodore M. Mills, *The Sociology of Small Groups*. New York: Prentice-Hall, 1967, p. 97.

8. Robert J. House, "A Path-Goal Theory of Leader Effectiveness," *Administrative Science Quarterly* 16 (September 1971), p. 323.

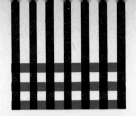

EVALUATING SUBORDINATES: PERFORMANCE APPRAISAL AND DISCIPLINE

CHAPTER 11

ON THE JOB . . .

EVALUATING WORKERS IS TOUGH

THE EVALUATION PROCESS
    Evaluations Are Necessary
    Legal Aspects of Performance Appraisals

EVALUATION TOOLS
    Three Ways of Measuring Individual Employee Performance
    Evaluations by Comparison with Other Employees
    Errors and Problems with Evaluation Tools
    Minimizing Appraisal Errors and Problems

CONDUCTING APPRAISAL SESSIONS
    Giving Performance Feedback
    Structuring the Appraisal Interview
    Dealing with the Problem Employee

    ON THE JOB REVISITED . . .

SUMMARY

HUMAN RELATIONS APPLICATIONS

DISCUSSION QUESTIONS

NOTES

MANAGERIAL DIALOGUE: Judith Berger

ON THE JOB . . .   Sam Davidson has worked for the Jenson Company for fifteen years. He started out as a maintenance worker but showed so much potential that he was transferred to the Sales Department, where he has worked for the past ten years. Two years ago, Sam was the top salesperson in the company and was being considered for a possible promotion to district sales head. Over the past year, however, Sam's sales have been leveling off and there have been a few customer complaints about his attitude. What would you, as Sam's boss, do?

EVALUATING WORKERS IS TOUGH

One of the most important duties of any manager is finding out how well subordinates are performing. Such a task is not always easy, particularly when the job involves more than washing dishes or digging ditches. Many experienced managers say they've struggled with performance appraisals more than with any other process in their organization.[1]

All employees want to know what is expected of them in their jobs and how well they are doing. Therefore, all managers must struggle to answer such questions and develop their skills of performance appraisal.

The first section of this chapter provides an overview of the evaluation process. The next section delves into the actual tools of performance appraisal and the problems they raise. The final section covers giving the positive feedback they seek as well as taking appropriate action against the problem employee.

Some of the specific concerns that will be described are:

Why should managers conduct performance evaluations with their employees?

Will criticizing an employee hurt performance levels?

When a manager has to talk to an employee about a performance problem, what's the best way to begin?

THE EVALUATION PROCESS

We are always watching other people's behavior and making judgments about them based on our experiences, attitudes, and values. Sometimes we even tell our friends or co-workers what we think. The performance

"Informally, we are constantly evaluating the behavior and intentions of our colleagues"

appraisal process in organizations is simply a more formal way of handling this everyday behavior. Large organizations are more likely to handle employee evaluations in this formal way.

To find out how well an employee is doing, managers must ask themselves the following questions:

1. What do I expect my employees to accomplish?
2. By what standards can I measure their performance?
3. How well has each employee measured up to my goals and standards?

To answer the first question, a manager must carefully analyze the nature of the employee's job. One way to do this is to break the job down into its separate tasks: coordinating orders so they know what to prepare, actually preparing the food, and putting it in appropriate containers on the counter where employees working the register can pick it up.

The second question—by what standards do you measure performance—is also easy to answer. You would keep records on the number of burgers produced at peak hours and the length of time a customer had to wait for an order. These statistics would provide the standard that each employee would be expected to meet.

The answer to the final question—how well has each employee measured up—could be answered through observation and recordkeeping. By counting the number of burgers produced (and subtracting the ones that were burned, or dropped or otherwise made inedible), you'd have a solid performance record. Your job as supervisor would be easy. Just look at the numbers.

Most jobs, though, are not quite as simple to assess. An employee may be doing a number of different tasks, each with a different standard. With higher-level managerial jobs, in which a successful boss motivates others to do their work well, measuring performance is as much an art as a science. For example, if you were company president, how would you evaluate the performance of your personnel manager?

Evaluations Are Necessary

Over the past decade, management has become increasingly concerned about performance evaluation techniques. Aside from letting employees know where they stand, well-developed performance appraisal systems help the company by motivating employees to work harder and to produce more. One expert in the field, Judith Berger, says flatly, "If you don't do it, your company is going to fail." See the Managerial Dialogue on pages 290–291 for more of Berger's views.

Managerial Dialogue

"You can counter a negative with a positive."

Judith Berger, president of MD Resources, Inc.

MD Resources, Inc., specializes in recruiting physicians and health care professionals.

In elementary school, you took home a report card. In college you saw your final exam grades posted on a classroom door. The performance evaluation process doesn't stop when you enter the working world—it intensifies—and, in the opinion of Judith Berger, the appraisal process is essential for any organization. "If you don't do it, your company is going to fail," Berger says flatly. Berger is the president of MD Resources, Inc., a rapidly growing company that recruits physicians and other health care professionals. The company is in the personnel business, and it prides itself on taking the same care with internal performance evaluation and appraisal as it does with external clients.

"Historically, the purpose of evaluation is for management to rate employees," Berger says. "That's a one-way function which ignores the possibility that management may not have trained someone to do a certain job or supported them in their efforts to do so." MD Resources has about thirty personnel professionals who are evaluated twice a year. In the first year on the job, a new worker may get a pay raise each time; after that the raise comes just once a year. "We do a formal written evaluation," Berger explains, "and they evaluate us—our management team." On the written form are fifteen areas of job responsibility. "I rate them, and they rate themselves. They also rate management's ability to help them." The process of formal performance appraisal starts six months earlier, at the previous evaluation session. At that time, each employee fills out:

1. Work-related objectives.
2. Personal development goals.
3. Action plans, with specifics on achieving these goals.
4. Measures of performance. Six months later, the employee adds an appraisal of performance in achieving those goals and objectives through the action plan.

The evaluation process at MD Resources does not begin or end with the formal appraisal. There are weekly meetings and plenty of individual contacts. Could the process work as well in a larger company with hundreds of employees? "Yes," Berger says, "but you might only be able to do it once a year." Perhaps the most important part of the performance appraisal, however, is not what goes down on paper, it's how the whole process is handled. "People always go into a review as a total wreck and come out feeling wonderful," says Berger. "It helps motivate people tremendously." Putting goals and objectives down on paper gives the supervisor and employee an opportunity for discussion. "The developing dialogue is very important. Sometimes you really have to force communication."

The appraisal process goes on throughout the year. Supervisors are encouraged to keep records of critical incidents during the year—both good and bad. If an employee does something well, the supervisor may praise him or her on the spot. The company also keeps a personnel mailbox, where employees are encouraged to drop memos to Berger about their peers. Berger says the response rate has been overwhelmingly positive. Berger believes that this "positive power and influence" permeates the whole evaluation structure. "We train our managers to use personal power rather than position power and to be communicators. In any type of situation, you can counter a negative with a positive."

That positive thinking helps reduce the stress on both managers and employees during the evaluation process. It also allows both parties to concentrate on the most important questions: Where is the company going and where is the employee going?

A review of current research on the practice of job evaluation indicates that telling an employee how he or she is doing can produce three benefits[2]:

1. It may lead an employee who does not have a job-related goal to adopt one.

2. It may help an employee who has achieved his or her goals to set new ones based on higher performance.

3. It may tell a marginal employee that more effort is needed to reach the job's standards.

"Performance evaluations help employees achieve more rewards for their work and make organizations more productive."

Performance appraisals also help the company in broader ways. They assist in pinpointing individuals who need remedial training to do their jobs correctly, and they identify the high achievers who have potential to go into management.

When managers consider giving pay raises, making promotions, or scheduling work, performance evaluations play a major role. Performance appraisals also help a company determine how well its selection process is doing. If a job applicant is given a skills test, the company hopes that the test will show whether the applicant will perform well on the job. If that test is to be of value to the company, there must be a connection between such predictors and actual job performance. Thus, performance evaluation information provides a way to check the validity of hiring policies.

Legal Aspects of Performance Appraisals

Since job evaluation measures significantly affect the welfare of employees, the government has been particularly concerned that they truly reflect performance and are not biased by prejudice and discrimination. Since the mid-1960s Congress has passed a number of bills aimed at preventing discrimination based on race, color, religion, national origin, age, and sex. The most important of these are the *Equal Opportunity Employment Act of 1972,* the *Equal Pay Act of 1963,* and the *Age Discrimination Act of 1967.* These bills prohibit unfair treatment in hiring, firing, promoting, and compensating employees. Performance appraisals may be discriminatory in the following ways:

1. If the performance rating has not been shown to be job related.
2. If the content of the performance rating method has not been developed through job analysis.
3. If the evaluators have not been able to observe employees consistently.
4. If the ratings are based on subjective, vague factors.
5. If racial, sexual, or other biases may have influenced an employee's score.
6. If the ratings have not been collected and scored under standardized conditions.

The *Federal Register,* a guide to government policies, occasionally publishes guidelines for performance evaluation systems. It recommends the use of job analyses, clear-cut instructions for evaluators, and follow-up checks for possible biases.

People who believe they are the victims of discrimination are filing more lawsuits every year against their employers. A recent analysis of court cases in which companies *successfully* defended their performance appraisal systems showed that evaluators were given specific written instructions on how to complete appraisals. Job analyses were used in developing the performance appraisal forms. Results of performance evaluation measurements were thoroughly reviewed with the employees whose performance had been evaluated.

The implications of these governmental policies and court cases are clear. Organizations must be committed to developing and using valid job evaluation tools. This involves analyzing the content of jobs, developing performance standards and evaluation tools, training managers in evaluation techniques, and assessing performance evaluations to detect any possible biases.

EVALUATION TOOLS

There are a number of different ways to measure employee performance. Before choosing any method, however, two questions need to be answered:

1. Is the evaluation tool reliable and valid?
2. Who should be responsible for conducting the evaluation?

Reliability deals with the stability and consistency of the measurement device. For example, if we developed a checklist to evaluate a bank teller's friendliness to customers, we would expect the rating to be the same three days in a row, as long as the teller's behavior itself hadn't changed. That would demonstrate that our checklist was stable over time. Consistency is achieved when two techniques for obtaining the same performance information produce identical results. For example, if the rating of "friendliness to clients" were a consistent measure of performance for a bank teller, two supervisors evaluating the same employee should arrive at identical ratings.

Graves suggested the following guidelines to judge the reliability of a performance appraisal system[3]:

1. Would you expect the performance ratings to be the same whether they were going to be used in face-to-face feedback sessions between a manager and his or her subordinates or kept confidential in personnel files?
2. Would you expect the evaluation to turn out the same whether performed by a task-oriented "Theory X" rater or a human relations–oriented "Theory Y" manager?
3. Would you expect the ratings to look the same whether performed by a manager trained in evaluations or untrained?
4. Would you expect your performance ratings to be the same whether appraisal was on a Monday morning or a Wednesday afternoon?

The second criterion that an appraisal tool must meet is *validity.* That means the evaluation technique must be related to the specific job being appraised. For example, a rating device that measures "leadership ability" probably is not a valid measure of performance for a typist who rarely gets the opportunity to leave the word processor. Instead, measures of speed and accuracy of typing, as well as co-operation with co-workers, are more valid measures of job performance.

After selecting a measurement tool that is both reliable and valid, the company must decide who should perform the actual evaluation. There are several logical options. The evaluation might be done by an immediate supervisor, by co-workers, by subordinates, or by the employee. Most frequently, the employee's supervisor evaluates job performance. Sometimes when a team is working on a particular project, appraisals by co-workers are used, although their value depends on the appraisal skills of co-workers and their willingness to provide an honest evaluation. Evaluation by one's subordinates or by types of clients is most helpful for improving an employee's skills. Generally, such appraisals as well as self-evaluations are used to complement other methods.

When making a decision about who should evaluate an employee, the two key considerations are the purpose of the evaluation and the familiarity with the job being evaluated.

"Choosing the right person to carry out a performance evaluation is critical to its effectiveness."

Three Ways of Measuring Individual Employee Performance

There are three major types of individual performance evaluation tools, each with its own advantages and disadvantages. We will discuss each of these methods.

Objective, direct measures. In certain types of jobs, productivity and performance are easily measured. For example, a salesperson's performance can be measured directly by noting the number of sales or leads produced over a given period. Two main types of direct measures are available:

1. Those dealing with production, such as sales, units produced, quality of work, amount of wastage, and so on.

2. Those concerning personal information, such as absenteeism, tardiness, tenure, number of on-the-job accidents, and so on.

Generally, a company will use two or more direct measures for each employee to provide a more complete picture of his or her contributions to an organization. There are, of course, some problems with using direct measures of performance to evaluate an employee. For instance, simply measuring sales or output isn't enough for a company that wants to encourage other positive behaviors. Maintenance of company equipment, cooperation with fellow employees, and a concern for company image are just a few examples of other important organization goals. The overly aggressive salesperson who tops the year-end sales chart may do so at the expense of fostering long-term relationships with major clients. Thus, while the company may gain in the short run, rewarding such actions may hurt the organization's future prospects.

Management by objectives. For over two decades, the management by objectives (MBO) evaluation technique has been popular in many organizations. Its success is due primarily to the efforts of two men, Peter Drucker and George Odiorne. The MBO process is best defined by Odiorne, who wrote:

> *The system of management by objectives can be described as a process whereby superior and subordinate managers of an organization jointly identify its common goals, define each individual's major area of responsibility in terms of results expected of him, and use these measures as guides for operating the unit and assessing the contribution of its members.*[4]

Basically, the MBO procedure involves four steps. First, each subordinate works with his or her boss to establish acceptable monthly or annual goals. Ideally, the goals should be specific, measurable, and reasonably attainable. Second, the subordinate meets with his or her supervisor at points throughout the evaluation period to monitor and discuss any changes that may have taken place to affect the agreed-on goals. In some instances, performance targets are modified. Third, at the end of the period, the subordinate and his or her boss determine how many of the objectives were met. Together, they pinpoint the barriers to meeting the objectives and generate ideas for improving future performance. Fourth, the last stage involves having the subordinate and boss set new goals for the following performance period.

Management by objectives has four significant advantages as an approach to measuring employee performance:

1. It allows for participation by employees, giving them a voice in how they will be evaluated.

2. It helps develop problem-solving skills in subordinates.

3. It can lead to better relationships between subordinates and their superiors.

4. It provides a good way to evaluate managers whose work does not lend itself to objective rating scales. For instance, an information specialist whose job can't be measured in "units produced" can be evaluated on an MBO yardstick.

Like other evaluation tools, MBO is not perfect. A number of companies that have tried to improve their evaluation practices by adopting

MBO plans have failed dismally. According to Odiorne, an analysis of such unsuccessful MBO programs shows four main reasons for the failure. One was haste; companies looking for quick solutions set up MBO systems. Another was ignorance; companies didn't explain to their employees how the MBO system worked. A third problem was lack of commitment; top management failed to follow through with an MBO program. Finally, many companies got bogged down in paperwork. Too often these companies overemphasized filling out MBO forms.

Subjective procedures.   Unlike the first two methods discussed, a subjective evaluation procedure relies on the judgment of an evaluator to assess good performance. Subjective procedures are undoubtedly the most common evaluation techniques found in the working world. Two different approaches involve evaluating employees either on the basis of absolute standards or by comparative methods. Some of the more widely used absolute standards are:

1. Rating scales

2. Critical incident technique

3. Behaviorally anchored rating scales (BARS)

4. Essay evaluations

5. Checklists

6. Forced choice

"The most common way to evaluate employees is to rely on the subjective judgments of others in the organization."

The *rating scale* is the most commonly used method of measuring an employee's ability. Usually, several different qualities assumed to be indicators of performance, such as "encourages participation by subordinates" or "follows directions," are listed. The evaluator checks off the numbers rating or circles a label that best fits the employee. (Table 11.1 shows a typical rating scale format). Rating scales are popular because they are simple to use; an evaluator can rate a large number of employees in a relatively short time. Unfortunately, rating scales have many problems. Perhaps the most serious is that an evaluator's biases can greatly influence the results. A supervisor can give high ratings to a favored employee and low ratings to one who is in disfavor. Another major limitation of rating scales is that the qualities being rated are unclear. For example, what does "initiative" or "motivation" really mean? Not everyone will say the same thing. A third difficulty is that each rated characteristic is assumed to be equally important. But in some jobs "ability to get along with others" may be much more important than "creativity."

TABLE 11.1   Examples of Typical Rating Scales

A. Initiative			
Unsatisfactory 1	Questionable 2	Satisfactory 3	Outstanding 4

B. Motivation

Poor	Below average	Average	Above average	Excellent

C. Relations with others

Poor			Exceptionally good

The *critical incident technique* is an evaluation method that involves having a supervisor record on-the-job situations that the employee handled either well or poorly. Each situation is called a *critical incident.* Usually, the incidents are recorded daily by a supervisor and placed into a diary or log for each employee. The diary is then used to evaluate the worker at the end of a period. The critical incidents may be sorted into categories showing different aspects of performance. For each category, incidents showing good, bad, and average performance are illustrated. An evaluator then indicates which of the incidents in each category is most descriptive of that worker.

The major advantage of critical incident technique is that it provides concrete information to be used in an evaluation interview. Rather than saying vaguely to an employee, "You've been having a lot of problems acting like a team player," the evaluator can describe specific facts that demonstrate the problem. The incidents also provide valuable insights into areas where the employee may need training.

There are at least three major problems with the critical incident technique. One is that negative incidents tend to be far more noticeable than positive ones. An evaluator may concentrate on problem areas, rather than looking for a well-rounded picture or performance. A second difficulty with critical incidents is that they may lead to overly close supervision. Since workers know that their bosses are recording their behavior, they begin to feel that "big brother" is always watching. This can lead to anxiety and friction. Finally, some supervisors tend to regard the diary as a chore and put off doing it as long as possible. This undermines the technique, since important situations may be forgotten before they've been written down. It may also lead lazy supervisors to ignore 360 days of the year and just take notes the week before the evaluation interview.

Another evaluation technique that uses absolute standards is the *behaviorally anchored rating scale (BARS),* also known as the *behavioral expectation scale (BES).* The BARS combines the critical incident technique with a rating scale and usually is designed by personnel experts. Table 11.2 shows an example of a typical BARS.

There are a number of advantages to the use of a BARS. Well-designed rating scales based on job analyses are far more valid than rating scales based on job traits or attitudes. Many researchers contend that BARS hold a great deal of promise for improving performance evaluations.[5] Like the critical incident technique, they provide concrete feedback for employee development purposes. Training programs can be developed to improve specific behavioral weaknesses as indicated in the critical incidents listed on the scales.

The major drawback to using the BARS is that a great deal of time and expense goes into developing the forms. This disadvantage may rule out the technique for smaller firms, which cannot afford to develop their own BARS.

A fourth absolute standard evaluation method is the *essay approach.* In this procedure, an evaluator usually is asked to write an open-ended

"Ideally, evaluation tools can also assist employees in their own development."

TABLE 11.2   Example of a Behaviorally Anchored Rating Scale for College Instructors

Dimension: Accessibility to students

Definition: How available an instructor is to meet with students regarding course difficulties or questions.

Extremely good performance	5	This instrtuctor could be expected to have an "open door" office policy and also give out his or her home phone number to students.
Good performance	4	This instructor could be expected to keep assigned office hours and also meet with students, by appointment, outside of office hours.
Average performance	3	This instructor could be expected to be in his or her office during scheduled office hours.
Poor performance	2	This instructor could be expected to show up for assigned office hours about 50 percent of the time.
Extremely poor performance	1	This instructor could be expected not to show up for posted office hours and to run out the door at the end of class to avoid meeting students.

essay about the employee's weak and strong points. In most cases, there are guidelines concerning the job areas that should be covered. The advantage to using this particular approach is that an employee is provided with a good deal of specific information about his or her perceived performance. However, a major weakness is that such a technique depends a great deal on the evaluator's writing skill and effort. It is also difficult to make comparisons among employees when the essay method is used.

Checklists are a fifth individual evaluation method. Like report cards, the checklist typically describes different kinds of behavior that reflect on-the-job performance. Sometimes these behaviors are given different weights to show that some are more important to good performance. Other behaviors are ignored if they do not apply to performance in a specific job. Like the BARS, the checklist is an excellent tool for employee development, since specific descriptions of behavior can be reviewed with an employee during feedback sessions. Also like the BARS, a great deal of time and energy must be invested to obtain a checklist that is linked clearly to performance.

A final type of subjective assessment procedure is the *forced choice method*. The evaluator typically is presented with sets of two phrases concerning job behavior and forced to choose the one that best describes a particular employee. Usually, both phrases will appear positive or both will appear negative to an evaluator. However, only one may truly be related to top performance in a job. (Table 11.3 is a typical choice assessment.) The forced-choice method was developed because other subjective methods were leading to inflated ratings, making personnel decisions difficult. This forced-choice technique requires comment on both good and bad aspects of performance. But the forced-choice technique is often irritating to the supervisors, who are not told which statements bear the greatest relationship to performance. They may feel that they aren't being trusted to make accurate evaluations.

TABLE 11.3 Sample Forced-Choice Statements

Directions: For each pair of statements, check the one description that best describes your subordinate.

_____ Is always cooperative and friendly to co-workers.
       or
_____ Always meets scheduled work deadlines.
_____ Can be counted on to support company policies.
       or
_____ Is cool and collected at all times.

Evaluations by Comparison with Other Employees

Some organizations prefer to rate their employees by comparative evaluation tools. Is Cindy a better switchboard operator than Joe? Is Jack a better regional sales manager than Janet? This type of evaluation is especially useful when companies have to cut back their personnel.

There are three major types of comparative evaluation tools: ranking, paired comparisons, and forced distribution. The simplest type of comparative technique is probably the ranking procedure. A supervisor is required to rank employees in his or her work group from the lowest performer to the highest. This technique can be improved somewhat by using alternative picking—choosing the top and bottom employees first, then the next highest and lowest, and so on. Although the ranking procedure is relatively easy to understand and use, it fails to recognize that performance is related to many things both on and off the job. It also becomes tedious when a supervisor has to rank more than twenty employees.

In the paired comparison procedure, each employee in a work group is compared with all other employees being evaluated. For each pair of employees, the rater must decide which of the two is the superior performer. Then the rater calculates the total number of times each employee is preferred over others.

For example, let's assume a manager has four subordinates: Thompson, Mathieson, Elsman, and Bauer. That means there are six pairs to be compared:

Thompson versus Mathieson

Thompson versus Elsman

Thompson versus Bauer

Mathieson versus Elsman

Mathieson versus Bauer

Elsman versus Bauer

After raters have picked the better individual in each pair, a matrix (shown in Table 11.4) can be constructed. As you can see from the table, Mathieson is the "superstar," followed by Elsman and Bauer.

A problem with the paired comparison technique is the large number of judgments a manager must make. Consider how many comparisons a McDonald's restaurant manager with thirty-five employees must make! Another difficulty is that paired comparison does not provide any clue as to how much better one employee is compared with another. Thus, such a ranking has limited value in making pay decisions.

"Comparing employees with one another can be very difficult for a manager."

TABLE 11.4 Matrix Summarizing Choices Made with the Paired Comparison Method				
	Thompson	Mathieson	Elsman	Bauer
Thompson	X	1	1	1
Mathieson	0	X	0	0
Elsman	0	1	X	0
Bauer	0	1	1	X
Total number of times preferred	0	3	2	1

A final comparative method is the forced distribution method. In this method, a rater is asked to rank employees in percentiles. For instance, 10 percent are slotted as the lowest performers, 20 percent are in the low average range, 40 percent are average, 20 percent are high average, and the remaining 10 percent are the highest performers. This approach is similar to the professor who grades students on a normal distribution curve. Obviously, a major problem with such a technique is that not all employee work groups fit into such nice and neat patterns. Most work groups consist of employees who are average performers or higher. Also, some managers resent being forced to place employees in fixed categories. It may be difficult to discuss these evaluations face-to-face. After all, 70 percent of employees must be rated average or below. Imagine having to hold a round of performance sessions with 70 percent of your employees rated average or below.

Errors and Problems with Evaluation Tools

Any evaluation system is bound to have occasional problems. This section will discuss three major types that can arise: system difficulties, evaluation biases, and employee resistance. In designing any appraisal procedure, these problems must be understood and minimized.

Difficulties can arise if the organization is not totally committed to the use of performance evaluation procedures. One personnel expert notes:

Some programs fail to reach their potential because top management did not get involved or organizational goals were undefined. Systems will also fail if performance standards are installed as a crash program or the system is not adequately taught to the user.[6]

Appraisal systems are often initiated by the personnel department but lack the support of other executives. Thus, managers may go through the motions of filling out the paperwork, but they don't take the process seriously. If evaluation forms are lengthy or require a lot of writing, some managers may not even bother to go through the motions.

When the system is accepted by most managers, there can be another set of problems—evaluator errors and biases. These errors may occur because some managers are not comfortable about assessing someone else's performance level. For instance, supervisors may hesitate to make accurate performance assessments for fear they might lead to problems such as employee resentment, group conflict, and poor relations with subordinates in the future.

Such difficulties occur most frequently when evaluators have not been trained properly in the use of an evaluation tool. When this happens, six different types of errors can result: the halo effect bias, leniency bias, strictness bias, recency error, central tendency bias, and other personal biases.

The halo effect occurs when the rater's impression of one particular characteristic of a person ends up coloring all other aspects of the individual's performance. For example, as head of a team developing new computer software, you are rating a programmer who is always cheerful and willing to do any task. You might be influenced by the halo effect to give her higher ratings for her programming skills than are justified by the quality of her work. The halo effect can be a particular problem with rating scales, although training has been found to reduce such errors.

The leniency and strictness biases are opposite sides of the same coin. Evaluators subject to the leniency bias give inflated performance assessments, while those with a strictness bias give evaluations that are depressed (and that may depress employees). College instructors who are "easy A's" are probably making leniency errors, while an instructor who never gives an A is probably too strict. There are other managers who feel that all employees (or students) are, at best, average performers. When an assessor gives average scores (or C's) to everyone, he or she is making a central tendency error.

The recency error occurs when only the most recent behavior displayed by an employee is used in making a performance assessment. If the supervisor is a procrastinator who puts off making performance evaluations until two days before they are due in the personnel department, he or she is likely to commit a recency error.

Another type of evaluator error results from personal biases. Job appraisals have been found to be affected by an employee's physical appearance, sex-role stereotypes, kinship, religious affiliations, race, and ethnic group.[7] These biases may be obvious, or they may be so subtle they are hard to detect. For example, if a male supervisor believes that an effective salesperson is aggressive and independent and further believes that women do not have these qualities, his evaluations of female subordinates may be seriously biased. Such a bias creates problems at all levels—for the individual, for the performance appraisal system in general, and for the company's position in the law courts.

A third category of appraisal problems are those that deal with employee resistance to the performance appraisal methods. All employees are likely to be anxious about their appraisal, but as long as they believe the method is fair, they will probably cooperate. That is not the case, however, when they believe the performance standards are unfair or that the work cannot be measured accurately.

Most employees believe they are at least average performers. A study at General Electric, for instance, found that only two out of ninety-two supervisors estimated their performance as below average.[8] You can imagine their resentment when some of them were told that their superiors rated them much less highly.

Resistance also results when employees feel that the standards they are being measured against are too high or that important parts of their jobs are not found on the evaluation forms. One chain of retail stores ran into serious morale and turnover problems when they set up an evaluation system designed solely to measure hourly sales figures for its sales personnel. Because at this company, the sales personnel were also responsible for restocking the shelves, running cash registers, and monitoring the fitting rooms, employees resented being evaluated on just one aspect of their jobs.

Much employee resistance can be eased by getting employees to help design the appraisal tool. If this is not possible, clearly explaining the rationale behind certain job measures may help.

Minimizing Appraisal Errors and Problems

There are a number of ways organizations can make their job performance tools more accurate and effective. The following are six suggestions for improving them:

1. *Familiarity.* The appraiser should be thoroughly familiar with the behavior being assessed and with the person being rated. Ideally, the rater should observe the employee on a daily basis.

2. *Training.* Evaluators should be trained to recognize various sources of errors and biases. They should also be trained how to use the evaluation method and how to explain the system and results to employees.

3. *Clarity.* The instructions in the appraisal tool should be clear and easy to follow. Ambiguous terms such as *average* or *initiative* should be avoided. Behavior should be linked to specific definitions.

4. *Documentation.* Performance appraisals should be documented and filed throughout the appraisal period. Appraisals themselves are most effective when conducted more frequently than once a year.

5. *Relevance.* The dimensions of job performance should be derived from thorough job analysis. In addition, the behaviors being assessed should be only those over which an individual employee has control.

6. *Interrater reliability.* Whenever possible, two or more raters should evaluate the same individual. This allows for a more reliable assessment.

CONDUCTING APPRAISAL SESSIONS

The most important aspect of the performance appraisal process is giving employees accurate and useful feedback about their performance.

Giving Performance Feedback

When employees get feedback about their performance on the job, a number of good things happen. Feedback provides employees with a clear understanding of how well the boss thinks they're doing. It clears up any misunderstandings about what is expected from the employee. It provides an employee with a chance to ask questions and to give their own views. It helps to generate ideas for improving future performance. Some studies have even presented evidence that it is the feedback process itself, rather than the evaluation method used, that most influences the employees' willingness to work harder in the future.[9] Other experts say these favorable results are more likely to happen when employees have the chance to state their views during the review session and when the session includes talk about their future plans and opportunities.[10] In some companies, the chance for employees to criticize the performance of their managers becomes a separate evaluation process. See the box on page 305 for more details.

TELLING OFF THE BOSS

At Photocircuits Glen Cove, a division of Kollmorgen Corp., employees tell their supervisors exactly what is wrong with them—as honestly and bluntly as their hearts desire. Each year, the 750-employee manufacturer of printed circuit boards, located in Glen Cove, N.Y., hands out a three-page questionnaire to every manager, supervisor, and foreman—some 200 in all. Two pages consist of such questions as: Does your immediate supervisor show interest in you? Does this supervisor take criticism well? Is he or she a good listener? The third page is reserved for the employee to write a synopsis of his or her opinion. The questionnaire must be signed by the employee.

"When we first started this two years ago, I expected people to sugarcoat their answers," says Frank Fuggini, vice-president of human resources and one of the originators of the questionnaire. "I was surprised at how honest and open the answers were. Sometimes, the opinions are brutally honest, but with a few exceptions, very fair. The practice has definitely improved communication and morale."

The company recently completed this year's round of questionnaires, and among the people Fuggini critiqued was Photocircuits president John Endee. His opinion of the big boss? "Sometimes the guy doesn't listen."

Source: *INC.* (July 1984), p. 104. Reprinted with permission, INC. magazine (July 1984). Copyright © 1984 by INC. Publishing Company, 38 Commercial Wharf, Boston, MA 02110.

If feedback sessions are handled improperly, future employee job performance may be even worse. When General Electric conducted a long-term study on the effects of performance appraisals, they found that criticism had a negative effect on achieving future goals. The average subordinate reacted defensively to criticism during the appraisal interview, and defensiveness led to poorer job performance.

To avoid such problems, managers must be trained thoroughly in giving employees constructive feedback. The following are some of the major ground rules for giving constructive feedback:

1. Give examples of specific incidents—what was said or done.
2. Make the example recent.
3. Describe the incidents without evaluating them by using terms like *bad* or *good.*
4. Convey your concern for the employee and your intention to be helpful.
5. Aim feedback only at behavior over which the employee has control.
6. Give criticism at a time when the employee appears to be able to accept it. Avoid giving too much criticism at one time.

7. Make sure that the employee understands what has been said. Check this by asking questions or by giving the employee the chance to rephrase the comments.

Structuring the Appraisal Interview

Typically, the evaluator dreads the appraisal interview as much as does the employee. Such anxiety can be minimized by training evaluators in the feedback techniques just discussed and by carefully structuring the interview.

In preparing for an evaluation session, a physical setting should be chosen for privacy to minimize outside interruptions. Answering phone calls every five minutes during an appraisal interview tells the subordinate that his or her boss doesn't really care that much about the whole subject. The evaluator should be thoroughly prepared for the meeting. He or she should review the employee's past record and highlight specific incidents for discussion.

The employee should be told immediately how the meeting will be structured, and both positive and negative aspects of performance should be included. The evaluator should strive to put the employee at ease by stressing that the interview is not a disciplinary action but a chance to review past work and generate ideas for future performance. Ideally, employees should leave the session with clear objectives and an understanding of how to reach them.

Dr. R. F. Maier describes three major approaches to handling evaluation interviews: tell and sell, tell and listen, and problem solving.[11]

The objective of the tell and sell method is to get an employee to accept the evaluator's findings and convince him or her to change any problem areas. In order to sell his or her performance assessments to employees, a manager usually requires incentives or "carrots." This technique does not work well if employee resistance is encountered. If the employee doesn't appreciate the boss's advice, the boss is put on the defensive. The session can then easily turn into an argument rather than a shared evaluation.

The tell and listen method starts our similarly. During the first part of the interview, an evaluator communicates strong and weak aspects of the employee's performance. Instead of trying to sell the employee on the evaluation, however, the boss spends the second half of the interview letting the employee express his or her feelings. The assumption behind this approach is that when employees have the opportunity to release and express feelings, it reduces or removes defensiveness. Psychologists call this a *cathartic process*. The evaluator must have certain skills to use this technique. He or she must be a good listener, know how to reflect the employee's feelings, and understand that some defensiveness is a natural reaction. The advantage of the tell and listen approach is that it can improve supervisor-worker relationships. It also gives the evaluator more information about the employee's responses. One of the major problems that can occur with this approach, however, is that when an evaluator acts in an accepting manner, the employee may feel no need to change poor behavior.

The problem-solving approach is designed primarily to stimulate growth and development of problem-solving skills in the subordinate. It encourages a high level of participation and places primary attention on improving future performance rather than past difficulties. The skills needed for conducting this type of session are the same as those in the tell and listen procedure. In addition, the supervisor asks a series of exploratory questions aimed at helping an employee generate new ideas for future performance. To encourage a problem-solving session, supervisors need to share feelings openly and honestly with the employee. They begin by asking the employee what they as a boss may be doing that contributes to performance barriers for a subordinate. Then they ask the employee to conduct a self-appraisal and to define any key problem areas or issues. Together they identify objectives for the future. The final step is to discuss ways the supervisor can assist the employee in improving performance and achieving future objectives.

Dealing with the Problem Employee

There are always a few employees whose performance records are consistently poor. After trying to find out the causes behind such performance problems and giving appropriate training, it may be necessary to institute disciplinary action: assigning a difficult task, withholding a promotion or raise, sending the employee home on a disciplinary layoff, or ordering a period of retraining. There will be negative effects of any disciplinary action, but these can be minimized by providing a clear warning well in advance, by administering the discipline as quickly as possible, and by applying discipline fairly, consistently, and impersonally.

"Sometimes appraisal must end in disciplinary action."

Effective managers take careful steps to document poor behavior and provide employees with clear-cut information on how certain actions will be handled. For example, in some organizations, an employee will be given an oral reprimand first, followed by a written reprimand the second time the behavior occurs. If things don't improve, a third step might be probation. The fourth offense may lead to firing.

Once the decision to fire an employee is made, the possibility of discrimination must be carefully ruled out. To prevent the fired employee from winning a discrimination lawsuit in court, companies must:

1. Provide clear documentation of unsatisfactory work records.
2. Keep employees routinely informed about the quality of their performance and give them time to improve.
3. Inform all employees about the contents of their own job description and company rules and policies.

The need for documentation is of prime importance. This requirement is fulfilled by conducting regular performance evaluations and keeping the results in employee files. Following standard disciplinary steps satisfies the need for documentation.

ON THE JOB REVISITED . . .

As Sam Davidson's boss, you want to know the reasons behind his apparent change in attitude and you want to make sure that Sam knows you're looking at him in a different light than before, when he was one of the company stars. Among the questions you should ask are:

What type of evaluation interview would be most appropriate in this situation?

How would you structure the interview?

How, specifically, will you give Sam feedback about his performance?

Now it's time for you to talk with Sam. What will you say?

SUMMARY

Appraising employee performance is one of the most crucial human relations activities in an organization. This chapter discussed the various purposes of performance evaluations and the legal constraints facing managers who evaluate employee abilities. We also looked at the importance of reliability and validity in constructing evaluation tools. These tools fall into three main categories: objective measures of performance, management by objectives, and subjective measures of performance (individual and comparative techniques). Some of the elements that can strengthen an evaluation system were pointed out, as were a number of potential key problems. The last section of the chapter discussed the appraisal interview itself, providing hints on structuring the interview. Three different methods of conducting appraisal sessions were described. Finally, disciplinary action was mentioned as a last resort for dealing with the problem employee.

HUMAN RELATIONS APPLICATIONS

Conclusion 1:   It is illegal to use a performance evaluation instrument that discriminates on the basis of race, religion, national origin, age, sex, or physical handicaps.

Application: The content of any appraisal device must be based on a factual job analysis and should not include vague or subjective factors.

Conclusion 2:   Criticism of an employee during an appraisal interview may have negative effects in achieving future goals.

Application: An effective manager must learn how to discuss problem areas within the context of a constructive interview that motivates the employee to try to correct the problem.

Conclusion 3:   There are negative side effects associated with disciplining employees, but with care, these can be minimized.

Application: Discipline should always be applied consistently and fairly. Disciplinary action should be taken as quickly as possible after the undesirable behavior has occurred.

DISCUSSION QUESTIONS

1. What are the legal considerations associated with performance evaluations? What can be done to prevent discrimination in evaluation?

2. What is meant by reliability? Validity? How can one ensure that an evaluation tool is both reliable and valid?

3. How would you go about developing a BARS to evaluate an instructor's teaching ability?

4. What are the major strengths and weaknesses associated with the critical incident technique?

5. What are the major errors or problems associated with performance appraisal? How can these be minimized?

6. What type of appraisal interview would be most appropriate for dealing with hostile employees? Why?

7. How can a company prevent charges of discrimination in termination decisions?

NOTES

1. "Appraising The Performance Appraisal," *BusinessWeek* (May 19, 1980), p. 156.

2. G. P. Latham and G. Ukly, "A Review of Research on the Application of Goal Setting in Organizations," *Academy of Management Journal* 18 (1975), pp. 18, 824–845.

3. J. P. Graves, "Let's Put Appraisal Back in Performance Appraisal," *Personnel Journal* (November 1982), pp. 844–849.

4. G. Odiorne, *Management by Objectives.* New York: Pitman Publishing Corp., 1965, p. 55.

5. R. Atkin and E. Conlon, "BARS: Some Theoretical Issues," *Academy of Management Review* 3 (1978), pp. 119–128.

6. T. G. Alewine, "Performance Appraisals and Performance Standards," *Personnel Journal* (March 1982), p. 213.

7. J. S. Kane and E. E. Lawler, "Performance Appraisal Effectiveness: It's Assessment and Determinants," in *Research in Organizational Behavior*, B. M. Staw (ed.). Greenwich, CT: JAI Press, 1979, p. 454.

8. R. S. Schuler, *Personnel and Human Resource Management.* New York: West Publishing Co., 1981, pp. 230–238.

9. F. J. Landy, J. Barnes-Farrell, and J. H. Cleveland, "Perceived Fairness and Accuracy in Performance Evaluation: A Follow Up," *Journal of Applied Psychology* 65 (1980), pp. 355–356.

10. L. Dipboye and R. de Ponbriand, "Correlates of Employee Reactions to Performance Appraisal Systems," *Journal of Applied Psychology* 66 (1981), pp. 248–251.

11. R. F. Maier, *The Appraisal Interview: Three Basic Approaches.* La Jolla, CA: University Associates, 1976.

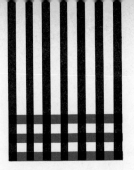

MANAGING CONFLICT

C H A P T E R 12

ON THE JOB . . .

CONFLICT IS INEVITABLE

WHAT IS CONFLICT?

WHY CONFLICTS ARISE

GOALS AND CONFLICT

    Conflicting Expectations
    Job Assignments Create Conflicts

THE PERSONAL NATURE OF CONFLICT

    Satisfying Needs
    Frustration

PSYCHOLOGICAL REACTIONS TO CONFLICT

    Defense Mechanisms
    Aggression
    Substitution Reactions
    Avoidance Mechanisms
    Personal Styles of Handling Conflict

CONSEQUENCES OF CONFLICT

    Negative Effects
    Positive Effects for the Individual
    Positive Effects for the Organization

ON THE JOB REVISITED . . .

SUMMARY

HUMAN RELATIONS APPLICATIONS

DISCUSSION QUESTIONS

NOTES

MANAGERIAL DIALOGUE: Norman R. Weldon

ON THE JOB . . .

Last year, 22-year-old Peter Richter found a job at Al's Gas Station in downtown Buffalo. The only position available was the night shift, from 4:00 P.M. to midnight. Richter signed on at a base wage of $3.50 per hour and an overtime rate of $4.60 per hour for occasional work on Saturdays and Sundays. After eight months on the job, Richter asked Hank Crowley, the night shift manager, why he had not yet received a pay increase. Richter complained that he had been led to believe by Al, the owner, that he could expect a salary increase about every six months.

Crowley: I'll tell you, Pete, Al is sometimes real funny about increases. He'll tell you one thing, then he'll do another.

Richter: Do you think I should ask him about it? I mean, he did give me the impression that I would get periodic raises. But so far no one has mentioned a word to me about it.

Crowley: I wouldn't ask him for it, if I were you. He sometimes gets real upset when one of the kids gets "brash," as he calls it.

Richter: Well this is ridiculous! I deserve the raise, and I'm going to get it somehow.

Crowley: I'll tell you what. It seems to me like you've been doing pretty good since you started here. I'll go speak to Al and see what I can work out. (He winked at Richter.) Know what I mean? I sometimes have a way with him.

Two weeks passed, and nothing more was said about the subject. Finally, one afternoon when Richter arrived at work, he saw a message that Al wanted to speak with him in his office.

Al: Pete, good to see you. Hank has just spoken to me. I guess nobody explained the raise process around here. Basically, no one gets a pay hike until their shift manager tells me they're doing good work. Well, today Hank came in and told me that he thought you were ready for a raise. Congratulations! You'll be getting $3.75 an hour now and $4.90 for overtime.

Richter: You mean you were waiting for Hank Crowley to give you the OK for my raise?

Al: Yep. I know you work hard, but we have a policy around here that says I wait for the shift manager to recommend any and all raises.

Richter: I just don't get it. He seemed to be on my side from the beginning.

When Crowley showed up at the station around 6:00 P.M., Richter cornered him and asked just what was going on. Crowley admitted he had been stalling because he wanted to make sure that Richter wasn't just another fly-by-nighter who would quickly leave. Richter began yelling at Crowley and said "even a moron" could see he was a hard worker. "If you can't see that I work just as hard as anyone else around here, you're blind!"

The next day, Richter went into Al's office to tell the boss that he would either have to be transferred off Crowley's shift or he would quit his job. He said he couldn't work with Crowley any longer.

How would you handle this conflict?

CONFLICT IS INEVITABLE

Conflict in organizations arises out of the differences within and among people and groups in terms of their goals, their needs, their experiences, their outlooks on life. Conflict may be expressed in hundreds of ways in the organization, from an angry silence to outright fistfights. Such conflicts may also be managed in any number of ways, leading to either positive or negative results for the individual or the organization. Robert Townsend, the former boss of Avis Rent A Car, calls conflict a sign of a healthy organization:

A good manager doesn't try to eliminate conflict; he tries to keep it from wasting the energies of his people. If you're the boss and your people fight openly when they think you're wrong—that's healthy. If your men fight each other openly in your presence for what they believe—that's healthy. But keep all the conflict eyeball to eyeball.[1]

It's not always easy to regard conflict as healthy. After all, when you're trying to finish your monthly budget report at 4:00 P.M. on the 31st, the last thing you want to do is spend an hour listening to one of your colleagues rant and rave about the unfairness of the boss. Dealing with conflict as a member of the organization is time consuming and energy-draining and often yields unpredictable results. Conflict is inherent in social groups, thus, every group member—especially managers—must learn to cope with conflict successfully.

This chapter addresses considerations such as:

How does the organization create conflict for its employees?

What ethical conflicts do executives face most often in making corporate policy?

Which psychological mechanisms do people use to resolve personal conflict?

What psychological mechanism underlies organizational "power plays" that attempt to upset existing authority?

What are the positive effects of conflict in an organization?

How can conflict be effectively managed?

WHAT IS CONFLICT?

In the 1700s, Adam Smith wrote that the mechanism of the marketplace mediated conflicts of individual interests. Each person made choices on the basis of self-interest. Through the "invisible hand" of the market, the total of each person's interest added up to the common good. But in recent years, as attention has been focused on the wide variety of personal needs and motivations (in addition to financial security) that influence individual behavior within the business organization, it has become clear that the market mechanism cannot prevent many kinds of individual conflicts. Moreover, market forces may actually create some kinds of conflicts. An example can be seen in the recent trend to two-tier wage systems in the box on pages 315–317. It is the task of the modern manager to supplement the invisible hand, managing conflicting interests so that they do not interfere with the joint goals of the business organization and its members.

THE DOUBLE STANDARD THAT'S SETTING WORKER AGAINST WORKER

"It makes me mad," declares Chris Boschert, who sorts packages 18 hours a week at United Parcel Service Inc.'s hub in St. Louis. Boschert complains that because his union, the International Brotherhood of Teamsters, accepted a so-called two-tier wage system at UPS in 1982, "I get $9.68 an hour, and the guy working next to me makes $13.99 doing exactly the same job."

Even more unhappy is Dennis W. Morgan, who has worked for 16 years as a produce clerk at Fazio's supermarket in Cleveland, owned by Fisher Foods Inc. "I saw my husband cry for the first time," says his wife, June, after the United Food & Commercial Workers agreed last year to let Fazio's hire new employees at $4 an hour, compared with Morgan's $10.30.

Least Despised

Soon after, Morgan was put on a part-time schedule, and the company, whose profits are faltering, told him that he will be laid off in June. The Morgans are all the angrier because in agreeing to new contract provisions, the UFCW may have weakened the seniority rights of veteran employees so that they can lose their jobs even while Fazio's hires new low-paid help. "They want to get rid of everybody who makes $10.30 and bring in 18-year-olds," complains Mrs. Morgan, who has led picketing at both Fazio's and at UFCW Local 880, Morgan's union.

As unionized companies negotiated two-tier wage systems over the past five years, they brushed aside the idea that these would inevitably cause friction on the job. But they seem to have been wrong. Although problems are just now showing up, evidence is growing that the new systems—which employers insist are indispensable to combat nonunion or foreign competi-

tion—are pitting workers against their companies, their unions, and one another. Much of the conflict so far is confined to the retail food industry, which began negotiating multilevel wages in the late 1970s. But what's happening there may be a harbinger for other major industries as the number of second-tier workers catches up with the number of workers in higher pay scales.

There are two basic versions of multi-tier scales. The one least despised by workers is a so-called hiring-in-rate. In some supplements to the Teamsters' national trucking contract, for instance, companies can hire at 70% of the going rate of $13.30 an hour. But they must raise pay for these employees, in steps, to the full rate after three years.

A second type leaves new workers permanently trailing top-tier employees. At American Airlines, Inc., pilots hired after November, 1983, earn half the pay of pilots hired before then—theoretically until all of the old pilots are gone and only the lower-paid ones are left. Retail food companies took up this approach before most other industries, and they have carried it to unpopular extremes. At some stores, Kroger Co. has clerks doing the same work at five different wage levels ranging from $6.34 an hour to $10.02, depending on when they were hired. "This is the only way we've been able to stay alive in an industry where there is strong, unorganized competition," says Don A. Hirsch, Kroger's vice-president for corporate labor relations.

Hirsch says that multilevel wages are not a problem at Kroger. "It's a constant communication thing to show employees that it's in their best interest" to allow lower-paid jobs, or there will be none at all, he says. This argument convinced many unions to accept two-tier scales. But elsewhere, workers are deciding that what sounded acceptable when unemployment was 10.8% sounds unfair now that the rate is down to 7.3%.

Top Complaint

In some cases, the friction over two-tier wages stems from the difficulty workers have living on low starting pay. At age 29, with a 16-month-old child, UPS's Boschert has had to take second jobs—such as working at a moving company—to make ends meet. The obvious inequity, especially of permanent multilevel pay rates, also rankles employees. "It creates two groups and causes divisiveness between them," says Robert Potter, president of UFCW Local 951 in Grand Rapids. Ironically, there is often little solace in being at the top of the wage scale. These workers, says Potter, think there is "an incentive for management to get rid of them, though we haven't seen this happen."

These concerns are starting to cause problems for unions and, consequently, for management. Meijer Inc.'s supermarkets in Grand Rapids had few problems with a two-tier deal it won from Local 951 in 1978. But by late last year more than half of Potter's 11,000 members were in the second tier. "When it became clear that the wage gap was one of their top complaints, we started trying to get rid of it," he says.

"Serious Issue"

A new pact ratified last December cut the gap in half, to 20¢ less than the top-tier wage of $11.15 an hour—although senior workers took a smaller increase to help pay for this. The union also raised the fringe benefits of second-level workers to top-tier levels. Other food retailers will soon face such demands. "We're going to equalize wage rates," says UFCW President William H. Wynn, who has been under increasing pressure from his locals to eliminate permanent two-tier scales. Wynn does say he is willing to accept hiring-in rates.

Other unions are fighting back before their percentage of second-tier workers reaches the high level at Meijer's. The Air Line Pilots Assn. has resisted a two-tier system for months in bargaining at United Air Lines Inc. Future conflicts are likely at the U.S. Postal Service, which since January has hired 13,243 employees at up to 25% below regular pay scales. The International Association of Machinists will try to get rid of a two-tier system its Seattle local accepted, to the dismay of the international union, for 26,000 workers at Boeing Co. in 1983.

And two-tier wages "could be a serious issue when our contract is up in 1987," says Ronald F. Gamache, secretary-treasurer of Teamsters Local 688, which represents UPS workers in St. Louis. About half of the company's 40,000 part-time employees work for second-tier pay, according to Teamsters for a Democratic Union, a dissident group.

Potential Battlefields in the War Over Two-Tier Wage Systems

Union	Industry	Workers Covered by Two-Tiered Contracts
Postal workers	U.S. Postal Service	720,000
Food and commercial workers	Food wholesaling and retailing	133,000
Teamsters	Trucking, warehousing	100,000
Machinists	Aerospace, airlines	75,000
Pilots, flight attendants	Airlines	35,000
Auto workers	Auto industry, aerospace	30,000

Source: DATA BUREAU OF NATIONAL AFFAIRS INC. BW

Drawbacks

Two-tier wage systems can have drawbacks outside of bargaining, especially in a tight labor market. As demand for pilots has grown since 1983, some of American Airlines Inc.'s second-tier pilots have jumped to carriers that pay full rates. The UFCW's Potter argues that two-tier systems "hurt [worker] productivity and loyalty." This is especially true, critics argue, once workers have been with a company for several years.

By then, the distinctions that first separated them from higher-paid workers have blurred.

Employers counter these arguments with an observation that is no doubt correct. Second-tier employees, says a UPS spokesman, "knew what the job paid when they took it." But if the economy stays healthy, it is an argument that workers may not buy much longer.

Source: Reprinted from the April 8, 1985, issue of *Business Week* by special permission, © 1985 by McGraw-Hill, Inc., pp. 70–71.

> *"You don't need two people to create a conflict; one person can face conflicting choices."*

The term *conflict* refers to any situation in which two mutually exclusive goals are sought and cannot be obtained at the same time. Sometimes the conflict arises from two or more choices facing a single individual. For example, suppose a marketing manager has a chance for a good promotion, but it requires relocating to another area of the country. The increase in pay, power, and prestige is undoubtedly desirable, but so is remaining in the community where she has friends, a lover, a dream house. The conflict in this instance is between two things she finds desirable: a promotion and a home environment.

Such conflicts can be very complex. The much-desired promotion carries with it not only the need to move to a new city, but also the necessity of adjusting to a new group of co-workers and, perhaps, the increased risk of being fired in case of poor performance. Staying in a familiar community carries the risk of getting into a rut and the loss of an opportunity to find an even better house or more congenial group of friends. Psychological makeup, combined with the social environment, creates conflicts that may not be apparent to the casual observer.

Faced with a conflict such as this choice, perhaps the hardest part of the individual's effort is to identify the alternatives and gain enough self-awareness to choose the most satisfying course of action.

WHY CONFLICTS ARISE

The individual's relationship to the organization is frequently the cause of conflict. A person may sometimes be at odds with organizational goals and the methods used to reach these goals. For example, the economic goal of a business concern is to earn a profit for the owners (possibly by keeping wages and salaries at the lowest reasonable level), while the economic goal of the employee is the fattest paycheck and best benefits possible. That puts the individual in conflict with the organization right from the start.

To achieve its goals, the organization sets down relatively inflexible rules, regulations, and policies. Even the most concerned, humanistic organization cannot help but encounter resistance because it is unable to change policies to meet the desire of every individual. Part of an organization's inflexibility can be attributed to size. The largest organizations often have the greatest or the most visible conflicts. That's certainly the case in our gigantic "commonwealth" organization, the United States, where conflict makes up the greatest part of the evening news shows. Fortunately, the founders of the nation recognized that conflict was an inevitable part of society and planned the democratic government so that conflict would contribute to the nation's well-being. The representative electoral system is intended to ensure that disagreements are discussed openly and publicly, with decisions made on the basis of majority will.

Governments of any type generally are set up with humanistic motives. The United States Constitution makes provisions for basic personal and social freedoms. Many business organizations are founded on principles of social responsibility, but the primary emphasis is usually on profit. To survive in a competitive market, a business organization must engage in careful, rational planning and rule making. Thus, the subjective, emotional elements within the overall organization scheme generally are subordinated to the organizational profit goals. Consider a hospital that employs workers on three shifts. A majority of the workers want to work the 6:00 A.M. to 2:00 P.M. shift since it is the one that can be combined most conveniently with a normal family life. Hospital managers realize that working the second or third shift creates conflicts between employees and the organization because of the physical strain of night work and the problems that such a schedule creates for personal life. Yet, to make the best profits, the hospital must put its own goals first. It might, however, make the evening and night shifts more attractive by offering a higher rate of pay to compensate for the disadvantages.

GOALS AND CONFLICT

Most organizations base their goals on the assumption that employees will behave rationally and in accordance with the organization's planned objectives. It is further assumed that they will cooperate with the organization to achieve mutually advantageous results for everyone. To the board, it means higher dividends; to the managers, a chance for promotions and raises; to the workers, a good wage and decent working conditions. A second, closely linked assumption is that employees will perceive the wisdom of the organization's plans, reap a part of the benefit, and thus be loyal to the organization. An organization composed of rational, loyal, efficient employees is a circular, self-perpetuating group of ideal workers. Unfortunately, there is no guarantee that employees' personal goals can be met through cooperation with organizational goals and policies. What may seem to be the best objective, long-run policy in the eyes of top management can run counter to the needs, aspirations, and goals of most employees. Therefore, the workers' most reasonable course of action sometimes conflicts with formal policy.

"However sensitive or supportive the management might be, there will be times when a worker's needs conflict with the goals and policies of the organization."

For an apt example, we might refer back to Mayo's Hawthorne studies, in which an informal group at the Western Electric plant ostracized the hard workers who might make less productive workers appear lazy. This behavior might seem irrational; after all, if all the employees worked harder, they would earn additional wages. Yet to line workers at Western Electric, limited production and mistrust of management was a sensible choice. They believed that any additional output on their part would simply prompt management to change the pay scale and expect more work for the same money. Therefore, there was no economic justification for working harder, and since the work offered no intrinsic challenge, it was not a fulfilling choice in any way to exert more energy on a mindless task. Mayo's Hawthorne studies point to a clear lesson: pragmatism and productivity at the expense of personal needs cause conflicts that can harm the organization.

Conflicting Expectations

Certain kinds of conflicts may be built into the very structure of a business organization. Marvin Dunnette and John Campbell describe just such a case.

> *A serious problem grew out of ambiguous and often conflicting role expectations surrounding one of the organizational units. In the eyes of some company officials, the unit was formed for the sole purpose of servicing present and potential company customers—a kind of consulting service to develop equipment and machinery enabling customers to make optimal use of the company's products. However, in the eyes of an increasing number of other*

officials (among them, the unit manager's boss), the unit was to be regarded as another profit center in the company—billings for services and equipment should be sufficient to avoid the necessity for subsidies from other company divisions.

The manager of this organizational unit was caught in the middle of these sharply conflicting expectations. Unfortunately, he transmitted the same ambiguous and conflicting expectations to key people in his unit. Most of his subordinates had difficulty understanding either his verbal or written communications, and he seemed entirely unaware of both his impact on other people and what they were trying to tell him. Because of these problems of perceptual impermeability and distortion, the manager seemed constantly embroiled in destructively belligerent interpersonal exchanges—with key officials throughout the company, with customers, and with his own subordinates. [2]

In this instance the conflict was caused by two differing definitions of a unit's goals. Being a service branch and showing profit were mutually exclusive goals, so that the manager was unable to meet both of them. This institutional conflict rapidly widened, bringing with it a variety of personal conflicts. Although better management by the unit leader might have minimized the problem, the basic conflict of goals was part of the organization's structure and was therefore beyond the manager's influence.

Another potential source of conflict is the clash between certain elements of human personality and the procedures of successful corporations. Argyris noted that people in our culture tend to develop from a passive state as infants toward increasing activity and independence. This activity may continue within the organization, but in many instances employees are forced to revert to a more passive state. Because business organizations have rules, regulations, and a hierarchy of commands that limit the autonomy and independence of employees, the potential for conflict is always present.

For instance, suppose a healthy, active young man is hired as a clerk. His duties include filing, simple tabulations, light typing, and some interoffice contact. A rigid organizational structure may block this employee's desire to be more active if it fails to allow him an opportunity for expanded duties and more responsibility. Of course, the young man may have built-in personal or social limitations, such as lack of training, education, or confidence, which preclude advancement. Even so, if he feels his activities are limited, then a conflict is present between personal and organizational goals.

Conflicts are related to both the organizational structure and the individual's psychological makeup. Some organizations allow a great deal of freedom and independence, while others expect employees to perform within rather narrowly defined limits. A person who likes freedom of action might find this latter type of organization confining and experience both personal and social conflicts. But another individual could have a sense of disorder and helplessness in an organization in which formalized duties were not clearly defined. In either case, the amount of independence granted by the organization or desired by the employee can lead to conflicts.

Job Assignments Create Conflicts

Job assignments also vary in their demands on the individual, and some are more likely to create conflict than others. For example, most high-level executive positions require playing many different roles, some of which may conflict (a subject discussed in Chapter 9). Conflicts arise when an employee capable of interpreting and playing many roles is limited to just one or two. Junior executives are often resentful that they are not allowed to function as entrepreneurs, spokespersons, and figureheads. Even their roles as leader and executive may be severely limited by organizational policy, which creates conflict for the young, ambitious executive. If a manager's desire to come up with innovative solutions to organizational problems is consistently stifled, he or she will either leave the company or attempt to undermine its structures and policies—and in either case, both employee and organization lose.

"When an employee believes he or she can handle more responsibililty than he or she has been given, it creates a source of conflict."

In other words, conflicts occur when an employee's perception of his or her duties and responsibilities is not shared by the organization. A restaurant manager may assume that he is qualified to judge the best way to increase productivity and quality in his own restaurant, yet executives at the chain may ignore or veto his suggestions. Managers often enter their job confident that they are able to make effective decisions only to find that the overall organizational structure limits their decision-making ability. Decisions to change structure, procedures, or goals are often made over their heads, without their participation.

The following is one argument in favor of limiting employee participation in decision-making processes. The success or failure of any organization depends on long-range planning. Therefore, those who have the highest stakes in the organization should be allowed to make the major decisions and set policy. Business leaders contend that lower-level employees are likely to be both transient and uninformed about the organization's needs and goals. Their immediate interests may be detrimental to the long-term well-being of the organization. Yet there are indications that workers at all levels are concerned with the long-term goals of their organization. Unions have learned to link productivity increases to pay raises they seek, and in many industries, union leaders work along with top management to introduce automation that will improve the company's long-term financial position, even though it will also eliminate some union jobs. Union officials are able to recognize that a company that stays financially healthy is best for their own long-run interests.

Lower-level managers also are quite capable of putting long-run organizational goals above short-term personal benefit. The manager of home furnishings in a department store may work nights and weekends planning special displays, arranging media coverage of some promotional theme, working out the best schedules for full-time and part-time employees, and reading about new developments in the field. Even when she expects no immediate benefit, such as a bonus or promotion, she will work to increase sales. One reason may be the recognition that it will be to her long-run benefit; it will increase the possibility of an eventual promotion, raise, or chance at a better job at another store, to have a good track record. Another reason may be personal pride in doing a good job. A third reason may be the socialization process that takes place when an employee joins a business organization. Many employees will externalize to some extent the organization's roles and continue to seek them even without the reward of immediate personal benefit. Yet when pursuing organizational goals begins to demand a great deal of personal sacrifice, the resulting conflict may lead the employee first to abandon the organizational goals and then to abandon his or her belief in those goals.

THE PERSONAL NATURE OF CONFLICT

Although it might be tempting to blame the organization for producing all on-the-job conflict, that is too simple an explanation. All of us have weaknesses and limitations that impede and frustrate our striving for personal as well as organizational goals. The background and expectations of the individual may introduce many independent sources of conflict that are acted out within the context of the business organization.

A common example of the personal nature of conflict can be observed in the case of a line employee promoted to foreman. Suddenly, the new foreman finds he is on the side of his traditional enemy, management. Placed in the role of supervisor, the foreman may feel a sense of conflict because his old views about fellow workers are altered. As a worker, he probably condoned certain rule-breaking practices, such as leaving work early and having a buddy punch you out at 5:00 P.M. But as foreman, he now sees such activities in a different light. He worries that they may decrease production or lead to even more flaunting of the rules—outcomes that will jeopardize his own job. The conflict centers around the foreman's perceptions of where his loyalty is due.

Does he consider his friendship with former co-workers to be paramount, or is he more interested in the status and esteem he derives from his new position? There is no "correct" answer to such a question; it depends on his values, self-image, and psychological needs.

Satisfying Needs

"When one need is satisfied, another arises."

We are never completely satisfied with our position or acquisitions. Satisfying one need only leads to the desire of another. As soon as an executive achieves the desired raise, the longed-for promotion, he or she begins to want something else. It may be increased autonomy or more free time or another promotion to the next rung on the corporate ladder.

Continuous need satisfaction probably is related to humankind's highest achievements. The poet Robert Browning put it in lofty rhetoric: "A man's reach must exceed his grasp or what's Heaven for?" But it is also likely to lead to personal conflict. There may be conflict between immediate and long-term needs or conflict between various long-term goals, such as a happy family life and a high-level executive position.

Even if the needs or goals are not in conflict, the mere act of continuously seeking to fulfill needs may produce conflict. For example, there may be a conflict between an individual's desire to feel satisfied or content and the desire to meet new needs, and there is also a conflict whenever the individual encounters barriers that prevent continuous need satisfaction.

Frustration

When a person perceives barriers to satisfaction, the result is frustration. The barriers may be real or imagined. Examples of real barriers are lack of education, inadequate skills, and discriminatory hiring or promotion policies. Imagined barriers include the belief that one is unable to play a certain role or acquire a certain skill or the fear of trying something new.

Some people handle barriers by refusing to become discouraged. A police detective who has failed the sargeant's exam several times may continue to study and retake the exam as often as possible until a passing grade is achieved. Another way of handling a barrier is to find some other way over it. The detective might move to another city where qualifications for the position of sargeant are less rigorous. A third method of handling barriers is to change goals and adopt one that is more attainable. The detective could give up the goal of becoming a sargeant and instead apply for a position on a hostage negotiation team where he could learn new skills, acquire additional prestige, and earn a larger salary even though he will still be limited to the rank of detective.

PSYCHOLOGICAL REACTIONS TO CONFLICT

Conflict creates tension within the individual. Among the means by which people try to reduce inner tensions are:

1. Defense mechanisms
2. Aggressions
3. Substitution reactions
4. Avoidance mechanisms

Defense Mechanisms

Originally, the concept of a defense mechanism was applied to behavior that ensured physical survival, such as hiding from predators or freezing at the sound of a loud noise. By extension, it can also be applied to behavior that protects the individual's psychological well-being. For example, a man who is criticized for poor performance on the job may react by assuming an attitude of indifference toward his work. By demonstrating to others that he is not trying to succeed, he protects his self-image from the destructive impact of failure to achieve a goal.

In the business organization, the union is probably the most tangible form of group defense mechanism. It serves the dual purpose of providing the workers with protection from organizational exploitation and of serving as a social basis for psychological security. But many other forms of defense mechanisms are present in the organization. A defensive employee who seems to distrust the motives of his or her superiors, the organization, or fellow workers is displaying a personal form of defense mechanism. He or she may be reacting to real or imagined threats to security and is attempting to minimize any forseeable source of conflict.

Aggression

"Unbridled aggression can create havoc in the organization."

Another form of relieving tensions is aggression, when the individual takes direct or indirect action against a source of conflict or frustration. A familiar example of this reaction is a person physically attacking an opponent in a conflict-arousing argument. Subtler forms of the aggressive reaction are more common in most organizational conflicts.

Verbal in-fighting and "power plays" within an organization are a form of aggression in which some individuals try to eliminate or displace the influence of others. According to insiders, this kind of situation occurred at Ford in the late 1960s, when Simon E. Knudsen was brought in over the heads of several career Ford executives to take the position of president. The top executives at Ford were disappointed and frustrated by their own failure to win the position. Therefore, they reacted extremely aggressively, initiating a power struggle in the executive suite. Within nineteen months, Knudsen was out and Lee A. Iacocca, the leader of the aggressive reaction, became president.

Substitution Reactions

Another form of reducing the tension that comes from conflict is a substitution reaction. One example is adopting substitute or lowered goals to replace the thwarted original goals. The unsuccessful concert pianist who turns to pop music is experiencing a substitution reaction, as is the executive who realizes he will never reach the goal of becoming chief executive officer and decides instead to be the best sales manager the company has ever had.

Overcompensation is a form of substitution reaction. People with real or imagined shortcomings try to lower personal conflict by overreacting. A middle manager who fears she lacks mathematical ability may devote so many hours to learning to work with figures that she eventually becomes outstanding at such manipulations. In doing so, she attempts to mask her feelings of inadequacy and gain acceptance among those to whom she feels inferior.

Another substitution reaction—identification—occurs when an individual with blocked goals derives vicarious pleasure from observing another person succeed. The "armchair quarterback" fits into this category as he becomes more involved in supporting a team player than in participating in a sport himself. Identification also appears in politics, and candidates try to be indentifiable to gain votes. In fact, most of us tend to identify with our candidate in an emotional way even though on a purely conscious level our support usually is based on the candidate's policies, programs, and promises.

A final substitution reaction is commonly referred to as *rationalization*. When a person rationalizes about a conflict, he reaches acceptable conclusions about himself and others by creating reasons for his failure or difficulty. In short, an individual reaches the conclusions he wants to believe and hopes others will accept as truth. For instance, suppose our aspiring concert pianist is playing at a cocktail lounge when he encounters an old classmate from the conservatory. To a question about his past plans and goals, the musician might rationalize that he decided classical music was too stuffy. He could continue by pointing out the low pay, the frustrating years of preparation required, and the disadvantages of a traveling musician's life-style. Somewhat like a salesperson, the musician probably could be persuasive and sound sincere because he would be attempting to both reinforce his own belief in the correctness of his decision and convince his old classmate to approve of his action.

Avoidance Mechanisms

There are also psychological mechanisms by which a person may escape or avoid personal conflict. One form of avoidance is regression. It is noticeable among individuals who display immature or childish behavior when faced with conflict. Psychologists hypothesize that such a behavioral reaction is an attempt on the part of the individual to return to his or her less complex childhood. For example, a salesperson who is summoned to talk to the sales manager about her failure to meet her monthly quota might interrupt the manager by telling one joke after another or making inappropriate comments about a co-worker.

"Many people handle conflict by simply trying to avoid it."

Another type of avoidance is referred to as *repression*. This reaction occurs when a person excludes negative, conflicting thoughts that might endanger his or her emotional comfort. Employees sometimes have reason to feel unkindly about their boss or colleagues, yet for any number of economic or psychological reasons they will not openly voice their feelings. Instead, they may repress this conflict altogether and express their feelings in an unrelated area. A man who is lectured by the boss on his faults may not retaliate against the direct source of conflict. Repressing his anger against the boss, he goes home and snaps at his wife. She, in turn, vents her frustration by rebuking their son for a minor infraction.

The son then runs out into the backyard, picks up a twig, and swats his dog. Taking the example to its conclusion, we could assume that even the dog would redirect its frustration by biting a passing mailcarrier (thus, starting the cycle all over again when the mailcarrier gets home). This example may seem farfetched, but it does point out the sometimes irrational, subjective manner in which we attempt to resolve personal conflicts.

Personal Styles of Handling Conflict

Each of us has a personal behavioral style of dealing with conflict with another individual. Five of the major styles are (1) avoidance, (2) smoothing or accommodating, (3) forcing or win-lose, (4) compromising, and (5) collaborative or problem solving.

The avoidance style of handling conflict is displayed when an individual blocks out the conflict completely, refusing to deal with it like an ostrich that hides its head in the ground when threatened. Avoiders can be recognized by such phrases as "I don't want to get involved" or "It's not worth it to get upset." They always prefer neutrality or withdrawal when conflict arises. Attempting to force colleagues who have adopted an avoidance style to take sides on some office conflict will only produce more ingenious evasions.

Individuals who feel most comfortable with a smoothing or accommodating style also find conflict uncomfortable. When they encounter conflict with another person, they try to gloss over the problem. The real reasons for the conflict are not mentioned. Instead, an attempt is made to maintain surface harmony and act as if everything is all right. They can refer to a fist fight as a "little disagreement" and tend to believe that even the most serious organizational conflicts can be resolved if everyone concerned will "just be nice."

Accommodating is a style based on compromise. The accommodator tries to reach workable solutions by giving up his or her most difficult demands and trying to persuade others to do the same. This approach may achieve surface resolution of the conflict, as each party agrees to settle for what they can get. But it usually does nothing to resolve the underlying conflict, and it's only a matter of time until the tensions build up again and a new conflict breaks out.

The forcing style places the conflicting parties in a win-lose situation, in which the individual with the greatest power is likely to be the ultimate winner. This is the "him or me" approach taken by the young employee in the vignette that opened the chapter. His threat of quitting was intended to force the owner of the gas station into taking his side in his conflict with his manager. This approach is risky because people frequently overestimate their own power in a given situation; they force a confrontation and then are surprised to find that they lose. If Peter Richter really succeeds in forcing Al to choose, Al is much more likely to support his experienced night manager than a young employee who's been on the job less than a year. Even if Peter does win, the conflict wouldn't be over. Hank naturally would be resentful at being forced into a position of losing Al's support, and he would be sure to do everything he could to make life miserable for Peter. He might tell his friend the day manager that Peter is a troublemaker, or he might spread malicious rumors about Peter's personal life. When conflict is turned into a win-lose situation, everyone loses in the end.

The ideal style of handling conflict is the problem-solving or collaborative approach. Conflicts are confronted and openly discussed between parties. Both sides work through the issues, attempting to look objectively at the other's claims. Ultimately, a win-win or King Solomon type of solution is sought—one that is creative and at the same time maximizes the outcomes for both sides.

Henry Kissinger pointed out that this is the strategy of the good statesman. You cannot trick or persuade the other side into signing a treaty that is against their best interests. If you do, they will simply ignore the treaty as soon as they realize what's happened. The only way to win a lasting agreement is to get all the issues out on the table and then negotiate an agreement that all parties feel is fair and in their own best interests. The same principles that apply to peace in the Middle East also govern settlement of disputes in an appliance store over the way walk-in customers are allocated to salespeople.

"The best way to handle conflict is to find a way to let everyone win something."

CONSEQUENCES OF CONFLICT

Conflict, however it arises, creates tension for individuals within the organization. These tensions can have both bad and good effects. One manager who has given a lot of thought to both aspects is Norman Weldon, president of Cordis Corporation and the subject of the Managerial Dialogue on pages 329–330.

Negative Effects

Regardless of how it begins, conflict tends to create confusion within the organization. Cooperation and group goal orientation are diminished. If

Managerial Dialogue

"You can always disagree on issues."

Norman R. Weldon, Ph.D., president of Cordis Corporation

Cordis Corporation manufactures a variety of medical devices and is particularly noted as one of the leaders in pacemaker technology.

Norm Weldon thinks it takes teamwork to build a successful organization—and it's tough to create that team spirit in an atmosphere of internal conflict. Weldon has a Ph.D. in industrial economics from Purdue University. He also has more than thirty years of experience as a manager in electronics-oriented firms. Since 1979 he has been president of Cordis Corporation, which makes a variety of medical devices. "I believe that you have a problem with the definition of the word *conflict,*" Weldon says. "To me it connotes fairly serious disagreement about policy. If management is reasonably agreed on direction, you don't run into conflict in the popular sense."

Weldon believes serious conflict erupts in an organization when management cannot agree on goals or when the executives who move up the corporate ladder are not the most able. "At Cordis, we've found the best way to reduce conflict is to focus on goals—both short and long. You can usually get people to agree on goals." On the other hand, agreement on goals does not mean an end to discussion or disagreement. "You can always disagree on issues," Weldon believes. "That's healthy." Internal conflict is increased by poor performance at the executive level. "This creates tremendous conflict. Major conflict is caused by someone's refusal to accept leadership of the persons who have authority. One of our competitors just lost a key employee because he was better than his boss."

Weldon thinks there often is more internal conflict in a successful, established organization than in a striving new one. In an up-and-coming company, for instance, top management knows it must pull together to survive and prosper. In a mature organization, however, there may be fundamental differences between the old guard and the Young Turks over basic goals.

One theory of management speaks of the virtues of "creative tension"—where a dozen salespeople might compete for a single major account, or a half dozen architects might be told to sketch a new building, but only one design will be selected. Weldon calls that approach to management "a disaster." Weldon believes that it takes teamwork for an organization to achieve a useful goal. "I used to run a company with twenty subsidiaries," Weldon explains. "I used to encourage some conflict between subsidiaries as to who would achieve higher profits. At that level, I think it was beneficial—at least I hope so. But you don't want to encourage that kind of climate within an operating unit." Weldon has some advice on managing conflict in two areas where disagreement is almost bound to occur: during meetings and performance appraisals.

Meetings, which are often called to iron out a policy or deal with a management problem that transcends departments, often breed organizational conflict. How does Weldon deal with that conflict? "We encourage critical remarks, but each speaker must close with humor," Weldon says. "We've found this to be an effective way of reducing tensions." Even conflict during the highly emotional process of performance appraisals and salary reviews can be reduced. "Employees will accept a bad review if you behave as if you have their interest at heart." As a manager, Weldon believes you have to work with the employees to put the negative appraisal in the past and work together in the present. Ultimately, there is always employee termination as a means of reducing conflict. "Who you fire and for what reasons is more important in eliminating conflict than who you hire. You should wait about six months too long to fire someone—but less than six years!"

Weldon believes that most management traits are established by the age of 8 years and that some managers' personalities may actually promote conflict. "Let me on a playground with a bunch of third graders, and I can tell which ones will make managers. You can teach and improve techniques, but first you have to select the right people. I hire relatively new people. I think that shared experience is one of the keys to keeping conflict down."

In the area of management succession, Weldon has some firm ideas on reducing conflict. "The idea of having three executive vice presidents competing for the top job is lunacy!" Weldon exclaims. "You avoid that kind of competitive conflict by open communications. You don't build expectations."

Conflict, in its many forms, may never be banished from an organization. But in Weldon's view, there is one general method of keeping conflict under control. "You need lots of honest, one-on-one communication."

the research and development team has one general set of goals and the sales department another, then each group will be prone to pursue its own self-interests at the expense of the other's.

Conflict has the added advantage of being long-range and self-perpetuating in nature. Forgive and forget is a laudable motto, but unfortunately, most of us find it hard to adhere to either admonition. When fellow employees disagree, each tends to regard the other in a negative manner long after the original issue is past. For instance, think of a production director who is at odds with the head of the marketing department over the manner in which quality control information is handled. If the conflict between these two is prolonged and bitter, then it is quite possible that the production director will always regard the marketing department negatively, even if the director leaves the organization. The fact that the direct cause of conflict is removed—in this instance the marketing supervisor—does not preclude the possibility that the production manager will continue to feel hostile toward anyone involved in marketing.

The negative effects of this type of interpersonal conflict obviously can be detrimental to the organization's goals. They are likely to handicap the efforts of individual employees to achieve their own personal goals. Many of the mechanisms by which people cope with conflict involve behavior that can damage a career. The employee who gets into a slugging match with a colleague or regresses into childish behavior or hides in his or her office to avoid a conflict is not likely to win raises and promotions and may not even be able to keep the job.

Positive Effects for the Individual

Conflicts need not be entirely negative. Debates, negotiations, diversity, consultations—all of these may be positive forces for both the individual and the organization. From a psychological standpoint, conflict may help a person learn to cope with his or her environment. It is admittedly frustrating to meet with opposition, but those who experience it may learn from it. Most of us are in the process of learning that conflicts are situational, that they vary in intensity, and that different people involved in the conflict must be dealt with in different ways. All of these learning experiences help us cope with future conflicts. We have gained the ability to exert some control over our physical and emotional reactions. We may still lose our tempers, make rash statements, and sometimes react unreasonably, but even these lapses can provide insights into ourselves and others. In the course of conflicts, we gain an understanding of the reasons that others hold certain beliefs, and in turn, we tend to analyze, justify, or discard our views.

Conflicts also serve as a restraint on goal aspirations. All of us probably have passing fantasies about attaining great wealth, power, prestige, or status. These aspirations are tempered by our knowledge of the direct and indirect conflicting forces. A person who has encountered conflicts in his or her goal striving has some indications as to which goals are attainable and which goals are not. These experiences may help that person to analyze his or her strengths and weaknesses and then make the best of those capabilities. The person's choice of goals becomes more realistic, and therefore his or her chances of reaching them are improved.

Conflict may also serve as a means of personal growth. It helps a person learn how to cope with his or her own emotions and how to interact more successfully with others. In the long run, this is likely to make that individual more effective in all his or her personal relationships, both on and off the job.

Positive Effects for the Organization

Perhaps the most positive aspect of conflict is that it can help to eliminate the major problem of *group think*. This type of problem occurs when a very cohesive group of individuals fails to adequately evaluate the risks involved in their decisions. One research identified specific characteristics associated with group think, including[3]:

1. *Invulnerability.*   Group members feel that they cannot possibly fail. As a result, they tend to ignore risks associated with their decisions and are overly optimistic in formulating action plans.

2. *Inherent morality.*   Participants in the group believe that, since they are all working for the good of the group, anyone who opposes their strategies and decisions is evil or immoral.

3. *Pluralistic ignorance.*   Members who disagree with a view expressed by the group are unwilling to express their ideas because they recognize they are a clear minority. This leads to the belief that the group is in unanimous agreement when it almost certainly is not.

4. *Pressure on dissenters.*   Groups suffering from group think may apply pressure to any member who seems to rock the boat. Different ideas and different behaviors will be repressed, which robs the organization of new ideas and much needed criticism.

"A dose of conflict can help shake up a company that is becoming too sure of its own wisdom."

The danger of group think is that the group may undertake to implement decisions that are risky and perhaps even dangerous to the organization's survival. Consider a company trying to decide when to put a new toothpaste on the market. If the decision-making group is affected by group think, the product might be marketed before all the research results and risks have been tabulated. A few years down the road, the company may find that the toothpaste, advertised for its ability to whiten teeth, also causes erosion of tooth enamel.

Group think can be prevented by conflict. When conflict is stimulated within a group, it forces group members to consider the viability of alternative courses of action. Sometimes group leaders will even play devil's advocate (that is, urge the opposition to the group's major views) in order to stimulate thinking about both sides of a decision. Obviously, good decisions are those that take into consideration all the consequences, both positive and negative, that may occur when they are implemented. Group think prevents this from happening, whereas conflict encourages such evaluations.

ON THE JOB REVISITED . . .

As Richter's boss, you appear to be in an unpleasant situation. You either lose Richter because of his anger with Crowley or appease Richter and end up angering Crowley because you have failed to take his side of the conflict.

But are those the only options you have? Take a moment and list the possible ways that you could respond to Richter's comments. You should be able to come up with half a dozen alternatives. Then, pick the one that offers the best chance for a win-win situation and justify your answer.

SUMMARY

Conflict refers to any situation in which two mutually exclusive goals are sought and cannot be obtained simultaneously. Conflicts arise within the organization because the organization itself is inherently inflexible and cannot change policies to satisfy all individuals. They also arise when pragmatism and productivity are adopted at the expense of personal needs and when expectations about group or organizational goals are inconsistent with reality.

Conflict emerges from conflicting personal and organization goals as well as within the individual. Personal conflict occurs as the result of frustrated goals or role strain. Frustration refers to the perception of barriers to satisfaction, and people react to this conflict in a variety of behaviors. Each individual also has a personal style of managing conflict when it occurs between themselves and others.

Negative consequences of conflict in the organization are the tendency to create confusion and the fact that conflict is long-range and self-perpetuating. Positive consequences occur in helping people to cope with their environment, setting checks on unreasonable aspirations, helping people to deal with their own emotions, and minimizing the effects of group think.

HUMAN RELATIONS APPLICATIONS

Conclusion 1: People deal with conflict in a variety of ways including avoidance, accommodation, forcing a win-lose outcome, compromise, or collaboration.

Application: The best way to handle conflict is through collaboration or joint problem solving. Understanding another's method of approaching conflict situations can sometimes suggest the way to a solution.

Conclusion 2: Conflict situations can have both positive and negative effects.

Application: The effective manager needs to be aware of both the negative and positive consequences of conflict to be able to decide whether it is advantageous to stimulate or defer it.

DISCUSSION QUESTIONS

1. What are the major causes of conflict within an organization?
2. What are the four major psychological reactions to conflict? Describe each.
3. What do you think is your personal style of handling conflict? What are the other major styles that people use? Which style is the most effective?
4. Explain the positive and negative aspects of conflict.
5. What is group think, and how can it be avoided?

NOTES

1. Robert Townsend, *Up the Organization.* New York: Alfred Knopf, 1970, p. 39.
2. Marvin D. Dunnette and John P. Campbell, "Laboratory Education: Impact on People and Organizations," in *Concepts and Controversy in Organizational Behavior,* Walter Nord (ed.). Pacific Palisades, CA: Goodyear Publishing Co., 1972, pp. 456–457.
3. I. L. Janis, *Victims of Group Think.* Boston: Houghton Mifflin, 1972.

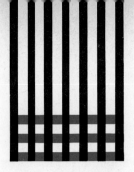

IMPROVING THE QUALITY OF WORKING LIFE

CHAPTER 13

ON THE JOB . . .

WHAT DOES "QUALITY OF WORKING LIFE" MEAN?

THE FIRST CONCERN ABOUT QWL

FINDING OUT WHAT QWL REALLY IS

ORGANIZATIONAL STRESS

    Organizational Stressors

    Consequences of Excessive Stress

COPING WITH JOB STRESS

    Organizational Methods

    Individual Methods

PROMOTING THE HEALTH AND SAFETY OF EMPLOYEES

OTHER QWL PROGRAMS

ON THE JOB REVISITED . . .

SUMMARY

HUMAN RELATIONS APPLICATIONS

DISCUSSION QUESTIONS

NOTES

MANAGERIAL DIALOGUE: Mary Kay Ash

ON THE JOB . . .

The Maxwell Company, located in a midsized industrial city in New England, manufactures a variety of specialized electronic cables used by telecommunications and computer companies in the manufacture of their products. Because of the nature of their work, Maxwell maintains a large research and development (R&D) department—twenty-five professional staff and fifteen assistants and clericals. The R&D department has been quite successful in developing innovative cable materials that can be used in phone switching systems and computers. In the company's ten-year history, the R&D department has compiled more patents than many firms twice Maxwell's size.

Maxwell has been highly profitable to its owners. The R&D, manufacturing, and sales operations are all housed in a rundown downtown warehouse, which the company picked up for a song and then renovated. Recently, however, Maxwell faced some personnel difficulties, primarily in the R&D department. A rival company in a Boston suburb had hired away three of the best engineers. That kind of raiding didn't trouble the company executives as much as the reasons the engineers gave for leaving. When they gave notice, Maxwell offered to match their new salaries, but received a unanimous refusal. The engineers left because their new employer offered them a brand-new building and state-of-the-art laboratory facilities, along with a gymnasium, jogging paths, and tennis courts just outside the plant. As one engineer put it, "Who wants to work in a slum, when you can work for a first-class outfit?"

When Maxwell's personnel director began screening candidates for the vacant positions, she ran into difficulty. Many job seekers liked the job description and Maxwell's leading position in the industry but had reservations about working in what they perceived to be an unsafe, unpleasant area. "You'd have to pay me $5,000 more a year just to put up with this location," said one applicant.

Maxwell's executive committee realized it had a major problem. The company would lose its technological edge and sales would probably drop if it couldn't attract first-rate engineers. On the other hand, Maxwell simply couldn't afford to put up a new building and move to the suburbs. The corporate treasurer had run through the figures for land acquisition and construction of a new plant in a suburban industrial park, and it was obvious that the company was stuck for at least five years. Not until then would the debt amassed by the renovation of the downtown warehouse be reduced to the point where Maxwell could even consider a move.

If you were Maxwell's president, what would you do now?

WHAT DOES "QUALITY OF WORKING LIFE" MEAN?

"A good quality of working life lets employees achieve their personal goals at the same time that organizational goals are furthered."

When you think about having a high quality of life, what do you imagine? Do you picture yourself jet-setting around the country with unlimited financial resources, or do you view yourself enjoying the work you do and the time you spend with your family and friends?

Each of us defines the quality of life in very different ways. Even researchers have had problems generating acceptable descriptions of what the quality of working life (QWL) really means. The best working definition of *QWL* is an attempt to integrate employee needs and well-being with organizational desires for higher productivity. The quality of working life has become an important topic. Organizations have been concentrating on specific areas in order to improve the quality of life for their employees: organizational stress and how it can be managed; improving the health and safety of workers.

Some of the particular questions and issues we will examine in this chapter are:

Why has there been a recent emphasis on improving the QWL?

What are the major elements associated with stress in organizations?

How are companies helping their employees cope more effectively with stress?

What are the major reasons for accidents and safety hazards in organizations, and how can they be alleviated?

THE FIRST CONCERN ABOUT QWL

The expression "quality of working life" started to become popular during the 1960s, when it became evident that such quality was not always present within organizations. During this decade, a number of governmental regulations were passed to encourage companies to take active steps in improving employment conditions for their workers. The Equal Pay Act (Fair Labor Standards Act of 1963), Title VII of the Civil Rights Acts, the Age Discrimination in Employment Act (1967), and the creation of equal opportunity guidelines (EEOC) were all aimed at assisting minority group members and women in improving their work status. The Occupational Safety and Health Act (1970) was also passed to ensure that every working person had safe and healthful working conditions. Out of this legislative activism grew a concern for learning more about the relationship between employees' attitudes and their performance. Also, an interest began to emerge in the social responsibility of organizations to provide their workers with employment situations that would yield greater life satisfaction. Such concerns were additionally fostered by new information about the improvements Europeans were making in work environments.

A number of specific developments in this country during the 1970s widened the appeal of and interest in QWL. Organizations such as the Gaines Pet Food plant in Topeka, Kansas, and the General Motors project at Tarrytown, New York, emerged into the limelight with their highly successful QWL programs. In 1974, Congress established the National Center for Productivity and Quality of Working Life. This group was charged with launching studies on improving productivity, supporting the growth of labor-management committees, and investigating other QWL activities. At about the same time a variety of nonprofit institutions were established to encourage collaborative efforts among management, labor, and the community in improving work experiences for employees. Some of these notable centers include the National Quality of Work Center, the Work in America Institute, the Center for Productivity at Texas Tech University, the Quality of Working Life Program at the University of California in Los Angeles, and the Massachusetts Quality of Working Life Center.

During the 1980s further interest in the quality of work life has emerged due to increased international competition faced by many organizations and a fascination with alternative management styles. Japanese management concepts have become particularly popular with the publication of such books as Ouchi's *Theory Z*. In fact, Japanese quality control circles, discussed earlier in the text, have been widely cited as excellent tools for improving the QWL. Peters' and Waterman's *In Search of Excellence* (New York: Harper and Row Publishers, 1983) has furthered the trend by attempting to pinpoint the ways successful U.S. firms have generated high levels of commitment and enthusiasm for their organization's mission. Finally, a number of companies such as Procter & Gamble, Cummins Engine, and General Foods have publicized their own successful attempts at improving the quality of the manufacturing environment. The box on page 339 details IBM's policies for improving QWL.

IBM'S POLICIES FOR IMPROVING QWL

In the course of his keynote address IBM Vice President Walton E. Burdick commented on a number of specific policies IBM is using to manage its U.S. work force, now numbering about 200,000.

Compensation

". . . everyone employed by IBM is salaried. All employees were placed on salary in 1958 and at the same time, all time clocks in the company were removed. . . . Today, employees fill out weekly time sheets that are verified by their managers."

Benefits

"All of IBM's benefit programs are non-contributory. . . . The benefit programs provide wide-coverage and we try to be as innovative as possible."

The Line Manager

"We try to maintain a very close employee and manager relationship. We give the manager full human resource responsibility, including merit evaluation and salary."

Training for Managers

"To enable managers to function well in this environment, we provide them with a broad base of management training. In addition, we require all managers, at all levels, to have 40 hours of specific management training each year."

Opinion Surveys

"Opinion surveys routinely conducted about once a year in most units are an anonymous process that allows employees to express their opinions on anything about the business, including top management."

Performance Appraisal

"There is a long tradition of individual treatment in IBM. I mentioned the merit system earlier. . . . The appraisal and counseling program is an integral part of that. This program requires that managers and employees sit down and develop objectives, and that employees be evaluated against these objectives at least annually."

Flexible Hours

"We announced in 1981 that individualized work schedules—popularly known as flextime—would be extended to the entire IBM Corporation—about 200,000 in the U.S. . . . Employees are enthusiastic, and management and employees both have seen this program as a current and tangible manifestation of our commitment to respect for the individual."

Quality Circles

"At present, we have in operation over 1,000 excel circles—commonly known as quality circles. Their numbers are increasing, consistent with the company's continuing emphasis on quality. This approach is an excellent way for employees to participate in job-related decisions that affect them."

Manager's Expense Fund

"Our managers are expected to be concerned with their people. To support their human relations efforts, managers are provided with funds for personalized gestures or recognition—or concern—such as a gift for a hospitalized employee."

Source: Reproduced with permission from *Ideas and Trends in Personnel* (newsletter), October 15, 1982, page 188. Published and copyrighted by Commerce Clearing House, Inc., Chicago, Illinois 60646.

FINDING OUT WHAT QWL REALLY IS

Most scholars think of QWL as having two distinct characteristics: a concern for the well-being and overall health of employees as well as for organizational effectiveness and a willingness to promote employee participation in work-related problems and issues.[1] Some of the specific criteria involved in improving and assessing the QWL include:

1. *Adequate compensation.*   How sufficient are the pay, benefits, and other forms of compensation in terms of helping workers maintain an acceptable standard of life?

2. *Safe and healthy environment.*   Are physical conditions hazardous? What job conditions affect employees' psychological and physical health?

3. *Development of human capabilities.*   To what extent does a job enable an employee to use and develop skills and knowledge and take part in work that is personally important?

4. *Growth and security.*   What career potential exists from maintaining the current job assignment?

5. *Social integration.*   Is there an opportunity to relate to others? Is advancement based on merit? Does equal opportunity exist?

6. *Constitutionalism.*   How much dignity and respect exists for employees? Can employees give honest opinions and be treated like mature adults? What are the employees' rights, and how are they protected?

7. *The total life space.*   Does a balance between work and life away from work exist? Is there an absence of high levels of job stress?

8. *Social relevance.*   Do employees perceive the organization as socially responsible? Does the organization take into consideration societal values in its waste and pollution policies, in its employment practices, and in the ways it deals with consumers and competitors?

"The organization benefits when employees believe the quality of their working lives is high."

An organization that fosters a high QWL for its employees will rate well on these eight dimensions. One example of such an organization is Mary Kay Cosmetics, whose founder, Mary Kay Ash, has some strong opinions on the quality of working life. She is profiled in the Managerial Dialogue on pages 341–342. To achieve such ratings, there has been a recent emphasis on developing methods and approaches to improve the nature of work and working conditions. The use of quality control circles, autonomous work groups (such as the Volvo plant in Kalmar, Swe-

Managerial Dialogue   ///   *"Make me feel important."*

Mary Kay Ash, founder of Mary Kay Cosmetics

Mary Kay Cosmetics is an international manufacturer and distributor of premium skin, body, and hair care items, cosmetics, and fragrances.

May Kay Ash thinks every person is special. "Whenever I meet someone, I try to imagine him wearing an invisible sign that says: Make me feel important! I respond to this sign immediately, and it works wonders." The founder of Mary Kay Cosmetics, the highly profitable Texas-based company, believes in improving the quality of working life through her "golden rule management." Every employee—at every level and at every position—should be treated with the same fairness and consideration, Ash says, because the true assets of any company are its people.

Founded in 1963, Mary Kay Cosmetics is now an international manufacturer and distributor of premium skin, body, and hair care items, cosmetics, toiletries, and fragrances. In a little over two decades, the company has grown from a single Dallas store to a worldwide force in the cosmetics industry with $323.7 million in sales in 1983 by more than 194,000 beauty consultants.

"We were filling a void in the industry when we began to teach skin care and makeup artistry, and we're still doing that today," says Richard Rogers, company president and son of Mary Kay. "Our marketing system, through which proficient consultants achieve success by recruiting and building their own sales organization, was a stroke of genius because the by-product has been management. In other words, we didn't buy a full management team—they've been trained one by one."

For Mary Kay Ash, improving the QWL within her organization has paid off. The following are some of the specific approaches she advocates:

1. Recognize the value of people. When you treat them as you would like to be treated yourself, everyone benefits.
2. Praise your people to success. Even criticism can build confidence if it's sandwiched between layers of praise.
3. Tear down that ivory tower. To be a good manager, you must be a good listener—and that means an open door policy.
4. Be a risk taker. Allow room for error and encourage suggestions and innovations.
5. Be sales oriented. Be sensitive to your customer's needs and wants, and remember nothing happens in business until somebody sells something.
6. Be a problem solver. Identify the real problems and take some action to solve them.
7. Create a stress-free work place. Fear of the boss, unreasonable deadlines, and so on can lower individual productivity.

8. Develop and promote people from within. Loyalty to a company is built on upward mobility.
9. Keep business in its proper place. At Mary Kay Cosmetics, the order of priorities is faith, family, and career, and these aspects can be balanced successfully.

Mary Kay Cosmetics is well known for its emphasis on sales and its rewards for top saleswomen. Every year, the company holds a three-day bash that is part inspiration, part recognition, part education, and all party. Top saleswomen win jewelry, trips, even pink Cadillacs. The Mary Kay program offers housewives a chance to earn a few extra dollars, and it offers aggressive full-time saleswomen a chance to get rich. That range of options undoubtedly contributes to the company's success. It was an early version of what has been dubbed *flextime,* giving the employee control over her time and the chance to balance "faith, family, and career."

The company is always searching for potential saleswomen, and it's common for regular customers to join the sales force. Even Mary Kay Cosmetics' annual report doubles as a recruiting brochure, headlined "Offering today's woman an unparalleled career opportunity."

Training is one of the keys to keeping the working climate at Mary Kay Cosmetics upbeat and focused on sales. The other key is upward mobility, with sales directors and managers coming from the ranks. "At Mary Kay Cosmetics we believe in promoting people from within the company," Ash says. "Such opportunities for individual growth create a healthy climate that encourages employees to think in terms of a long career with the company. In our sales organization, every person starts out equal as a beauty consultant. With our field people there are never any exceptions."

den, discussed in Chapter 8), and participative management techniques are three methods currently advocated by QWL proponents. Since these ideas were covered in previous chapters, this chapter will focus on other ways to improve QWL. Two important areas that affect employees' perceptions of work life quality are the level and types of stressors in the organization and the health and safety hazards that they are exposed to on the job.

ORGANIZATIONAL STRESS

A high QWL usually implies an atmosphere free from harmful levels of stress. *Stress* may be defined as occurring whenever "an environmental situation is perceived as presenting a demand which threatens to exceed the person's capabilities and resources for meeting it."[2] Each of us is probably all too familiar with the feeling of stress and its emotional effects. Consider some of the following examples:

> You're stuck in a traffic jam on your way to an important job interview.

> Your boss calls to inform you that unless your sales increase by 10 percent this month, you're out of a job.

> Your spouse claims to be in love with someone else.

> You have just received your sixth rejection letter from M.B.A. graduate programs.

> Your dentist explains that you need extensive periodontal surgery, which will cost $3,000.

The reactions to such stressors vary from person to person. They can include such things as profuse sweating, accelerated heart rates, a quick race to the nearest bar, insomnia, and depression. Obviously, such stressors, and the reactions we have to them, affect our overall quality of life and satisfaction levels.

In this section of the chapter we will identify common work stressors, their effects, and the ways in which they can be managed. It should be noted at the outset that there are a variety of individual differences in the levels of stress people can successfully manage. Although we will not be highlighting such differences here, you might want to review material from Chapter 2 on personality types A (more prone to stress-related disorders) and B to refresh your memories of some of these characteristics.

Organizational Stressors

There are many potential sources of stress within organizations. These stressors, in conjunction with events outside work (marital problems, family illnesses), interact to affect the total quality of one's life. Table 13.1 illustrates some of the major types of life events that can affect one's quality of life. This chart displays a social readjustment rating scale of stress-related disorders. Different types of life events are ranked according to the degree of stress they cause. Eight of these events relate to work situations:

1. Fired at work
2. Retirement
3. Business readjustment

TABLE 13.1 Social Readjustment Rating Scale		
Rank	Life Event	Mean Value
1	Death of spouse	100
2	Divorce	73
3	Marital separation	65
4	Jail term	63
5	Death of close family member	63
6	Personal injury or illness	53
7	Marriage	50
8	Fired at work	47
9	Marital reconciliation	45
10	Retirement	45
11	Change in health of family member	44
12	Pregnancy	40
13	Sex difficulties	39
14	Gain of new family member	39
15	Business readjustment	39
16	Change in financial state	38
17	Death of close friend	37
18	Change to different line of work	36
19	Change in number of arguments with spouse	35
20	Mortgage over $10,000	31
21	Foreclosure of mortgage or loan	30
22	Change in responsibilities at work	29
23	Son or daughter leaving home	29
24	Trouble with in-laws	29
25	Outstanding personal achievement	28
26	Wife begins or stops work	26
27	Begin or end school	26
28	Change in living conditions	25
29	Revision of personal habits	24
30	Trouble with boss	23
31	Change in work hours or conditions	20
32	Change in residence	20
33	Change in schools	20
34	Change in recreation	19
35	Change in church activities	19
36	Change in social activities	18
37	Mortgage or loan less than $10,000	17
38	Change in sleeping habits	16
39	Change in number of family get-togethers	15
40	Change in eating habits	15
41	Vacation	13
42	Christmas	12
43	Minor violations of the law	11

Source: Thomas H. Holmes and Richard H. Rahe, "The Social Readjustment Rating Scale," *Journal of Psychosomatic Research* 2(1967), pp. 213–218.

"Even a good change at work, such as a promotion or a big raise, can lead to increased stress."

4. Change in responsibilities at work
5. Change to a different line of work
6. Outstanding personal achievement
7. Change in work hours or conditions
8. Trouble with boss

Note that one of these stress elements—outstanding personal achievement—has very positive connotations. Despite the fact that some of these events may be happy ones, they still require a modification of an individual's typical way of life and can therefore be stressful. For example, when you have achieved major recognition for a job well done, there is added pressure on you to keep up the good work.

The work-related elements incorporated into the social readjustment rating scale are not the only stressors in the work environment. Emotionally induced stressors involve time pressure, expectations regarding future events, and problems of interpersonal relationships. Time pressures occur when people feel the need to make every minute of the day count. Some of this pressure may be external, and part of it can be self-created. Workers may feel that they must do "something right now," even when no deadlines are imposed on them.

Emotionally induced stress ensues when employees experience high levels of anxiety about impending events. Anxiety mounts over how a supervisor will view a report they've written or how a boss will react to a request for a personal day off. Such anticipation may be accompanied by a conviction that the worst possible events will occur. There is a classic story of such a self-fulfilling prophecy about a young man whose tire goes flat on an old country road. When he checks his trunk, he finds that his tire jack is missing. As he begins walking down the road to the nearest farmhouse to ask to borrow a tire jack, he begins to anticipate the farmer's response: "No, there's no way I'll let a city boy like you borrow my jack"; "I don't have a tire jack, I lent mine out to someone else." By the time he finally reaches the farmhouse, knocks on the door, and sees the farmer, he blurts out, "Keep your jack! I didn't want it anyway!"

A third type of emotionally induced stress occurs when a worker must deal with an individual he or she finds particularly unpleasant. The co-worker who insists on telling ethnic jokes, who makes belittling comments, or who expects an audience for stories of marital discord can definitely induce a rising level of stress.

There are a variety of other types of stressors in organizational characteristics and processes, job demands and role characteristics. Table 13.2 summarizes these stressors. Organizational characteristics and pro-

TABLE 13.2 Job Stressors

Organizational Characteristics and Processes	Job Demands and Role Characteristics
Organizational policies	**Working conditions**
Inequitable or inadequate performance evaluations	Crowding
Pay inequities	Lack of privacy; poor spatial arrangements
Ambiguous or arbitrary policies	Noise
Rotating work shifts	Excessive heat or cold
Frequent relocation	Lights: inadequate, glaring, or flickering
Idealistic job descriptions before hiring	Presence of toxic chemicals
	Safety hazards
Organizational structure	Air pollution, including radiation
Centralization; low participation in decision making	
Low opportunity for advancement or growth	**Interpersonal relationships**
Size	Inconsiderate or inequitable supervisors
Excessive formalization	Lack of recognition or acceptance
Excessive specialization and division of labor	Lack of trust
Interdependence of organizational units	Competition
	Difficulty in delegating responsibilities
Organizational processes	Conflict within and between groups
Poor communication	
Poor or inadequate feedback on performance	**Job demands**
Ambiguous or conflicting goals	Repetitive work
Ineffective delegation	Time pressures and deadlines
Training programs	Low skill requirements
	Responsibility for people
	Underemployment; overemployment
	Role characteristics
	Role conflict
	Role ambiguity
	Role underload/overload
	Role-status incongruency

Source: From Arthur P. Brief, Randall S. Schuler, and Mary Van Sell, *Managing Job Stress,* pp. 66–67. Copyright © 1981 by Arthur P. Brief, Randall S. Schuler, and Mary Van Sell. Reprinted by permission of Little, Brown and Company.

cesses include such elements as company policies, organizational structure, internal organizational characteristics, such as poor communication and lack of feedback. Job demands and role characteristics that can become potential irritants for employees include poor working conditions, problematic relationships with co-workers, excessive job demands, and role problems.

Role-related stress has been studied extensively. Role conflict was discussed in Chapter 9. Role ambiguity occurs when employees are not clear about the requirements, responsibilities, and duties associated with their jobs. In other words, their role has not been clearly defined. New employees and employees who fill recently developed jobs typically experience some level of role ambiguity. *Role overload* refers to having too many role-related demands placed on you. Students may experience this type of stress toward the end of an academic semester, with several projects due and final exams coming up. They often exhibit such adverse reactions as minor illnesses and absent-mindedness. Surprisingly, role underload can also produce stress. When employees find themselves in positions in which they are asked to do too little, monotony and boredom set in. They may begin to feel that they have little to contribute to the organization and begin to vegetate. Idleness may threaten an employee's self-esteem and other higher-level needs.

Consequences of Excessive Stress

Stress has been linked to a number of dysfunctional medical, behavioral, and organizational outcomes. For example, Senator Edward M. Kennedy reported a case before a congressional subcommittee of an employee who shot three foremen in a Detroit plant. The employee had been continuously exposed to excessive dangers and noise associated with the plant. When the employee went to trial and pleaded temporary insanity because of the stressful conditions of the work environment, the judge and jury (who visited the plant) gave a unanimous verdict of acquittal.[3] This example represents an extreme case of the potential effects that environmental stressors can have on behavior. It is unlikely that most employees will go to the length of killing their bosses, but there are some more common consequences associated with work stressors.

"One jury agreed that on-the-job stress could cause temporary insanity and acquitted a worker who shot three of his foremen in a noisy and dangerous plant."

Behavioral and psychological consequences.   A number of behavioral and psychological changes have been linked to consistent exposure to stressors. Among the more serious psychological problems are sleep disorders (insomnia), sexual problems, depression and something that has recently been labeled *burnout.* This phenomenon is said to occur when employees put considerable effort into a job that yields limited paybacks in terms of satisfaction or other sorts of rewards. Despite the lack of rewards, employees continue to devote more and more of their time to work activities until they finally reach a state of personal exhaustion and burnout. The specific symptoms of this phenomenon are listed in Table 13.3.

Two of the more serious behavioral consequences that have been linked to excessive stress levels are alcoholism and drug abuse. Together these two problems cost industry over $20 billion a year in wasted mate-

TABLE 13.3   Burnout Symptoms

1. Early stages
   a. Work performance
      Decline in efficiency
      Dampened initiative
      Diminished interest in work
      Progressively lessened ability to maintain work performance in times of stress

   b. Physical condition
      Exhaustion, fatigue, run-down physical condition
      Headaches
      Gastrointestinal disturbances
      Weight loss
      Sleeplessness
      Shortness of breath

   c. Behavioral symptoms
      Changing or dampened moods
      Quickness to anger and increasing irritability
      Diminished frustration tolerance
      Suspiciousness
      Feelings of helplessness
      Increased levels of risk taking

2. Later stages
   a. Attempts at self-medication (tranquilizers, alcohol)
   b. Increased rigidity (thinking becomes closed, attitudes become inflexible, negativistic, or cynical)
   c. Questioning of abilities of self, co-workers, and organization
   d. Increase in time spent working, with dramatic decline in productivity

Source: Leonard Moss, *Management Stress,* © 1981, Addison-Wesley, Reading, MA, p. 67, Table 5.1. Reprinted with permission.

rials, absenteeism, accidents, premature death, and rehabilitation programs.[4] Some of the specific findings related to alcoholism are:[5]

Each alcoholic worker costs a firm over $2,500 in unnecessary extras.

Alcoholic workers are 2 1/2 times as likely to be absent as are their fellow employees.

Compared to other employees, 12.8 percent of alcoholic workers are disabled for thirty days or more a year (6.5 percent for other workers).

Thirty-six million work days are lost due to excessive drinking.

The accident rate for alcoholic workers is 3.6 times that of fellow workers.

Alcoholic workers have twice the rate of heart disease, three times the incidence of digestive and muscular problems, and twice the incidence of high blood pressure, as compared with nonalcoholic workers.

Alcoholic workers collect over three times the amount of sickness payment as do other employees.

There are a number of reasons that an individual becomes an alcoholic or a drug addict; job stress is just one possible precipitating factor.

Medical and physical consequences of job stress.   According to experts in the field of stress research, there is a confirmed relationship between numerous work stressors and several types of physical diseases. Perhaps the clearest relationship found to date concerns the link between prolonged exposure to stress and heart disease. Other studies have indicated that stressful events may also precipitate such illnesses as peptic ulcers, asthma, headaches, cancer, back pains, and strokes. Obviously, however, genetic predispositions and a variety of additional factors are also related to such physiological difficulties. Stressors seem to increase the risk of medical problems when other contributors (e.g., family history, lack of exercise, poor diet) are present.

"No organization can function well when its employees are under stress."

Organizational consequences of stress.   We have already alluded to some of the organizational costs associated with such problems as alcoholism and drug abuse—two stress-related behavior patterns. When employees are exposed to high levels of stress on the job, we would also expect them to avoid their jobs as frequently as possible, resulting in high levels of absenteeism. Some recent research has shown that job performance also drops significantly when job stress rises to high levels. Finally, there is some indication that stress may be linked to employee sabotage attempts and aggression. Table 13.4 summarizes the organizational consequences of improperly managed stress.

COPING WITH JOB STRESS

If organizations are truly concerned about improving the QWL for their employees, managing stress levels is crucial.

Organizational Methods

Because companies are beginning to take note of the costs associated with job stress, they have been active in developing programs to help

TABLE 13.4 Organizational Consequences of Mismanaged Stress

Direct Costs	Indirect Costs

Participation and membership
  Absenteeism
  Tardiness
  Strikes and work stoppages
  Turnover
	Loss of vitality
	  Low morale
	  Low motivation
	  Dissatisfaction

Performance on the job
  Quality of productivity
  Quantity of productivity
  Grievances
  Accidents
  Unscheduled machine downtime
    and repair
  Material and supply
    overutilization
  Inventory shrinkages
	Communication breakdowns
	  Decline in frequency of contact
	  Distortions of messages
	Faulty decision making
	Quality of work relations
	  Distrust
	  Disrespect
	  Animosity

Compensation awards	*Opportunity costs*

Source: J. C. Quick and J. D. Quick, *Organizational Stress and Preventive Management*. New York: McGraw-Hill, 1984, p. 76.

ease it. Typically, three strategies have been pursued: offering stress management training programs, developing physical fitness facilities, and changing policies and organizational structures.

Stress management training programs involve a spectrum of activities ranging from helping employees assess the stressors in their lives to teaching them personal coping techniques. Examples of programs include some of the following:

New York Telephone Company uses "clinically standardized meditation" training for its employees to help them manage stress.

Equitable Life Insurance Company uses biofeedback techniques to ease their employees' tension levels.

B. F. Goodrich Tire's Group Learning Center offers a nine-hour program called "Manage Your Stress" for its employees to help them learn to alter their responses to stress.

Psychotherapist and dream analyst Dr. Joe Dillard conducts "dream incubation" workshops to teach top executives how to handle stress though their dreams. (See the box on page 351 for a discussion of handling stress through dreams.)

Other companies interested in alleviating harmful stress have developed physical fitness programs for employees. Regular and consistent

HOW TO HANDLE STRESS THROUGH DREAMS

The legend goes that inventor James Watt, the Scottish engineer who fathered the Industrial Revolution, was having a dream one night. In the dream, he was on top of a tall building, and the sky was raining molten lead. As he peered over the side of the building, he could see the drops of lead hitting a stream of water, whereupon they would solidify. When Watt awoke, he realized that the same principle could be applied in a factory—and thus he invented a process for producing lead shot.

The story may be apocryphal, but Dr. Joe Dillard likes to tell it nevertheless, to illustrate his view that dreams can be useful tools for businesspeople.

Dillard is a psychotherapist and dream analyst at the Association for Research and Enlightenment Clinic in Phoenix, and he believes that dreams affect the way people handle problems during their waking hours. "The stress management process occurs in dreams," he says. "If you don't handle that stress well, it colors your waking life. It's a basic pyschological law."

This phenomenon, he argues, has important implications for people in business. "If a CEO is agonizing about, say, whether or not to issue new stock, he may become worried and frustrated. This affects his decision-making. But he can do a lot of problem-solving while he is sleeping."

As an example, he cites the case of William Sechrist, a founder of Budget Rent-a-Car, who had been mulling over the question of incentive bonuses for employees. One night, he dreamed that he was putting quarter after quarter into a slot machine, with nothing to show for it. Then he inserted a gold coin—and promptly hit the jackpot.

Upon awakening, Sechrist concluded that the dream was telling him to provide big bonuses if he wanted to get results.

Of course, all dreams are not so easy to interpret, nor all problems so easy to solve. To facilitate the process, Dillard has developed a technique that he calls "dream sociometry," wherein a person analyzes a dream by—in effect—interviewing the dream characters.

"It's sort of like Gestalt role playing," he explains. By practicing dream sociometry, chief executive officers can learn how to sleep more creatively and handle stress more effectively, according to Dillard.

Dillard plans to teach CEOs to do just that at a series of "dream incubation" workshops beginning in November and plans to do further consulting in the future—assuming, that is, he can find CEO's who sleep at all."

Source: *INC.* (November 1983), pp. 29–33. Reprinted with permission, INC. magazine (November 1983). Copyright © 1983 by INC. Publishing Company, 38 Commercial Wharf, Boston, MA 02110.

forms of exercise are said to reduce tensions. Weyerhauser Company, PepsiCo, Exxon Corporation, Kimberly Clark, and Tenneco, among others, have invested major amounts of money to develop health and fitness facilities for their workers.

Finally, some firms have attempted to analyze their current organizational and structural policies to pinpoint areas of change in managing stress. For example, Schuler points out that when employees face a lack of participation, poor communications, lack of opportunities for advancement, and inequities in pay and evaluation policies, organizational structure targets can be changed to reduce stress. Among those advocated are:[6]

1. Clarification of policies regarding transfer and promotions.
2. Decentralization and increased participation.
3. Change in the selection and placement policies.
4. Change in the communication procedures and networks in the organization.
5. Change in the reward systems.
6. Utilization of training and development programs.
7. Statement of the performance evaluation system.
8. Development and utilization of permanent and temporary work groups.
9. Change in shift patterns and job rotation policies.
10. Changes in retirement policies.

HOW TO PROMOTE CORPORATE WELL-BEING

Integral Data Systems Inc. of Milford, N.H., is a healthy business. The $30-million manufacturer of computer peripherals offers its 350 employees a discount of at least 20 percent on membership fees at a local health club by making the initial payment. Participants then reimburse the company through payroll deductions. So far, 25 percent of the work force has joined the program. Most employees visit Hampshire Hills Racquet & Health Club during lunch breaks and before or after work shifts.

"We consider it a preventative-health benefit," says Sarah Joyce, Integral's personnel director. "It helps our people keep fit and relieves their job-related stress and frustration. It makes them more healthy and, consequently, more productive."

Nondiscounted memberships for a single adult range from $165 to $765, depending on the facilities used. These include tennis, squash, and racquetball courts; saunas, swimming pools, and weight rooms.

Integral's discount program cost about $10,000 in 1982. "That's a relatively small price to pay for what we get in return," says Joyce, adding that health club benefits are an effective recruiting tool.

"Highly trained people are attracted to these kinds of benefits," she says. "Our engineers like to go over while they're on break to play a quick game of racquetball."

To find out how to shape up your company, contact a nearby health club and ask about corporate discounts. Most clubs will negotiate a plan and offer your employees a free orientation day.

Source: INC. (October 1983), p. 162. Reprinted with permission, INC. magazine (October 1983). Copyright © 1983 by INC. Publishing Company, 38 Commercial Wharf, Boston, MA 02110.

Individual Methods

A variety of techniques have been suggested to help individuals manage their own stress. Physical fitness programs, as noted, have been recommended by a number of experts as beneficial. (See the box on page 352 for an account of one company's attempt to make health club memberships available to employees.) A good deal of current evidence indicates that social support groups are also very beneficial. When we have people who care for us and are willing to listen to and help with our problems, managing stress is an easier task. Additionally, such strategies as learning to manage one's time effectively, relaxation training meditation, and in extreme cases, therapy have been recommended. Some of the guidelines for relaxation training are suggested in Table 13.5.

PROMOTING THE HEALTH AND SAFETY OF EMPLOYEES

In addition to understanding and managing stress in organizations, the QWL can be markedly improved by promoting a healthy and safe work

TABLE 13.5   Guidelines for the Relaxation Response

1. Sit quietly in a comfortable position.
2. Close your eyes.
3. Beginning at your feet and progressing up to your face, deeply relax all your muscles. Keep them relaxed.
4. Breathe through your nose. Become aware of your breathing. As you breathe out, say the word "one" silently to yourself. Continue the pattern: breathe in . . . out, "one," in . . . out, "one," and so on. Breathe easily and naturally.
5. Continue for ten to twenty minutes. You may open you eyes to check the time but do not use an alarm. When you finish, sit quietly for a few minutes, first with your eyes closed and later with your eyes opened. Do not stand up for a few minutes.
6. Do not worry about whether you are successful in achieving a deep level of relaxation. Maintain a passive attitude and permit relaxation to occur at its own pace. When distracting thoughts occur, try to ignore them by not dwelling on them and return to repeating "one." With practice, the response should come with little effort. Practice the technique once to twice daily but not within two hours after any meal, since the digestive processes seem to interfere with eliciting the relaxation response.

Source: "Eliciting the Relaxation Response," pp. 114–115 from *The Relaxation Response* by Herbert Benson, M.D., with Miriam Z. Klipper. Copyright © 1975 by William Morrow and Company, Inc. By permission of the publisher.

"Businesses are legally required to promote the health and safety of their employees."

environment. Indeed, one of the major stressors in organizations can be a work place that workers perceive as unsafe.

Promoting health and safety in the work place is not an option but a requirement. Organizations in both the United States and Canada are *legally* required to promote such environments. The major piece of U.S. legislation in this area is the Occupational Safety and Health Act (OSHA) of 1970. This act allowed safety and health hazard inspections to be conducted for all U.S. organizations. Additionally, it structured formal reporting procedures for organizations to follow in recording accidents and job-related illnesses. The act also gave OSHA inspectors the power to issue citations to organizations that violate industry safety and health standards.

Most research has found that there are two main causes for accidents in the work place: the physical environment and employee inattentiveness. Physical environmental factors include such elements as defective equipment, unguarded machinery, slippery flooring, poor lighting, and the presence of dangerous chemicals or gases. Once an organization has identified the causes of health and safety hazards, it can begin to develop strategies for dealing with them. The work environment can be designed to minimize the likelihood of accidents. Installing warning lights, placing safety guards on dangerous equipment, and making sure employees wear safety goggles are some specific possibilities.

Implementing safety programs and reinforcing them with contests and prizes can also be useful. One midwestern transit company reduced accident rates almost 25 percent by posting daily feedback on accidents and by placing teams in competition with one another. The team with the lowest accident rate each week was given $5 worth of gas or bus tokens for each team member.[7] Similarly, a number of organizations have instituted management by objectives programs to deal with safety and health issues. The steps associated with such programs are:[8]

Identifying the hazards associated with current working conditions.

Using personnel records for an evaluation of the severity and risk of such hazards.

Developing and implementing relevant programs to control, prevent, or reduce the likelihood of accidents and setting specific reduction objectives.

Objectively assessing improvement in hazards and giving appropriate feedback to individuals directly involved.

Monitoring and evaluating the programs of specific safety and health programs, making changes as necessary.

One of the key ingredients in truly improving the safety and health of employees is management's commitment to safety goals and programs. It is particularly essential for supervisors to act as examples for their employees and to instill in them a desire for accident prevention.

OTHER QWL PROGRAMS

Companies interested in improving the QWL for their employees use many different techniques. Some have been discussed earlier in the text: flextime, quality control circles, and job enrichment (or as it is now called, "autonomous work groups"). Many of the attempts to improve QWL have involved increasing worker participation in decision making. Other attempts have encouraged more worker autonomy in their own job sphere.

Other organizations have instituted career counseling and planning programs as QWL techniques for employees. For example, General Electric offers assistance to their employees in assessing their specific career needs and in developing plans for achieving them. Additionally, their system provides a workbook guide for managers to use in coaching and counseling employees in career-related decisions. Career planning programs ultimately improve the QWL by better meshing individual employee needs with organizational goals.

"An increase in worker participation and autonomy usually leads to a noticeable improvement in the QWL."

ON THE JOB REVISITED . . .

Faced with stiff competition for top employees and stuck in an undesirable location, Maxwell's president decided to examine other ways of improving the quality of life for company employees.

First, Maxwell conducted a survey of senior engineering students at top schools throughout the nation to determine which factors they considered most important in choosing an employer. The survey results showed that salary and prestige, while important, were ranked below intangible factors such as company spirit, first-rate supervision on the job, and a sense of pride in their work. Quality of life factors, such as flexible hours and access to athletic facilities, also were highly ranked.

As a result of the survey, Maxwell began an internal campaign to promote corporate togetherness through regular "rah-rah" meetings, company-sponsored sporting teams, and Friday afternoon "beer blasts" on the roof (the safest spot in the neighborhood). It also made arrangements for employees to use the nearby downtown YMCA.

Six months later, when two engineers left for another company, Maxwell's personnel director promptly found two replacements who said they couldn't wait to work for the most employee-oriented company in the business.

SUMMARY

Improving the quality of work life involves showing a genuine concern for the well-being of employees while at the same time improving organizational effectiveness. A number of elements affect our perceptions about our working environment, including organizational stress and health and safety considerations. Organizational stressors include such things as role overload and underload, role ambiguity, role conflict, ineffective or inequitable policies, and excessive work demands. Additionally, employees experience emotionally induced stress when they have negative expectations concerning the outcome of certain organizational events. All of these stressors can be managed on an individual level through relaxation tactics or support groups. Companies have also helped to manage stress by offering stress management training and physical fitness programs and by altering organizational policies to alleviate harmful stress levels. Such intervention programs are important because stress is often associated with absenteeism, reductions in productivity, and serious mental and physical health problems.

Improving the health and safety of organizational environments is another way in which companies have tried to improve the quality of working life. The federal government has particularly encouraged programs in this area by enforcing such legislation as the Occupational Safety and Health Act.

Finally, a number of other programs have been designed to enhance quality of working life. Several of these techniques, such as quality control circles, flextime, and job enrichment/autonomous work groups, were discussed in earlier chapters. In this chapter, we noted that career planning programs can also assist in improving employee perceptions about their working life.

HUMAN RELATIONS APPLICATIONS

Conclusion 1:   Organizations have a social and, in some instances, a legal obligation to provide employees with a good QWL.

Application: Improving the QWL involves establishing equitable compensation; providing a safe, healthy environment; treating employees with respect and dignity; being responsive to societal needs; and allowing employees the opportunity to develop and satisfy their individual capabilities and needs.

Conclusion 2:   Excessive levels of stress may lead to lowered productivity, absenteeism, acts of aggression, and a variety of physical and psychological ailments.

Application: It is in an organization's best interest to monitor and assist employees in coping with high levels of stress. A variety of programs such as stress management training, biofeedback, and physical fitness facilities help to alleviate harmful stress symptoms.

Conclusion 3:   Effective organizations are committed to eliminating safety and health hazards in their environment.

Application: Promoting and ensuring the safety and health of employees may be done in a variety of ways: (1) establishing rewards/contests to minimize accidents, (2) soliciting employee input in order to initiate safety programs and (3) carefully monitoring existing programs.

DISCUSSION QUESTIONS

1. Name six major criteria that could be used to assess an organization's QWL.

2. Describe the major types of organizational stressors that affect an employee's QWL. Give an example of each.

3. What is meant by burnout, and what can be done to minimize such symptoms?

4. Describe some of the coping strategies that people can use to help manage their own stress levels.

5. What are the two major causes of work place accidents? How can organizations prevent such problems?

NOTES

1. E. F. Huse and T. G. Cummings, *Organization Development and Change*, 3rd ed. New York: West Publishing Co., 1985, Chapter 9, pp. 197–229.

2. J. E. McGrath, "Stress and Behavior in Organizations," in M. D. Dunnette (ed.), *Handbook of Industrial and Organizational Psychology*. Chicago: Rand McNally, 1976, p. 1352.

3. A. P. Brief, R. S. Schuler, and M. Van Sell, *Managing Job Stress*. Boston: Little, Brown and Co., 1981.

4. C. J. Francis and C. Milbourn, *Human Behavior in the Work Environment: A Managerial Perspective.* Glenview, IL: Scott, Foresman and Company, 1980, p. 134.

5. J. Follman, *Alcoholics and Business.* New York: American Management Association, 1976.

6. A. P. Brief,, R. S. Schuler, and M. Van Sell, *Managing Job Stress,* p. 120.

7. R. S. Haynes, R. C. Pine, and H. G. Fitch, "Reducing Accident Rates with Organization Behavior Modification," *Academy of Management Journal* 25; 2 (1982), pp. 407–416.

8. R. S. Schuler, *Personnel and Human Resource Management,* 2nd ed. New York: West Publishing Co., 1984, p. 479.

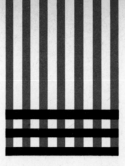

MANAGING THE ORGANIZATION
IN A CHANGING SOCIETY

PART 4

CHAPTER 14
Managing Change

CHAPTER 15
Corporate Culture

CHAPTER 16
Social Responsibility and the Organization

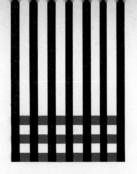

MANAGING CHANGE

CHAPTER 14

ON THE JOB . . .

CHANGE CAN BE THREATENING

RESISTANCE TO CHANGE

    Why Resistance Occurs
    Reducing Resistance to Change
    Diagnosing Obstacles to Change

THE STAGES OF CHANGE

    Unfreezing Stage
    Changing Stage
    Refreezing Stage

SELECTING A CHANGE APPROACH

    Top-Down Change
    Bottom-Up Change
    Shared Responsibility
    The People Who Make the Changes

THE ORGANIZATIONAL DEVELOPMENT APPROACH TO CHANGE

ON THE JOB REVISITED . . .

SUMMARY

HUMAN RELATIONS APPLICATIONS

DISCUSSION QUESTIONS

NOTES

MANAGERIAL DIALOGUE: Jane Campbell Cousins

ON THE JOB . . .

Davina Wolfe is the 34-year-old owner and manager of Ragtime, a clothing store in California. The store, open seven days a week, does its best business on Fridays and Saturdays; Sundays are generally very slow.

Ten salespeople work the various shifts and are paid a standard wage plus commission. Wolfe herself works almost every day. By keeping close tabs on the sales records for the months of April, May, and June, Wolfe came to the conclusion that Sunday was the worst day of the week for business. After some computation of costs, Wolfe figured that she was actually losing money on Sundays.

Further analysis showed that peak business occurred on Saturday evenings from 5:00 to 8:00 P.M., when the store closed. From these data, Wolfe concluded that the smartest thing for her to do would be to rearrange Ragtime's business hours. Wolfe decided that she would keep the store closed on Sundays, but stay open for an extra two hours on Saturday nights, until 10:00 P.M. This way, she figured that she could benefit from all angles. She would have more time to catch the late Saturday shoppers and would avoid the money-losing proposition of staying open on Sundays. Wolfe was pleased with the decision, and the next morning she called all the employees over to tell them about the change of plans.

The workers' immediate reaction was one of silence. When Wolfe asked for opinions, she got two reactions from her salespeople. In the first place, they didn't think it was fair for Wolfe to ask them to stay late on Saturday nights. Most of the employees, people in their twenties, wanted to have the freedom of spending Saturday nights as they pleased. The second complaint was slightly different. They all felt that they needed Sunday's work for the added money it brought in. They realized that Sunday was a slow day but thought it was a nice change of pace to be able to relax a little in the store. The meeting ended with Wolfe saying that she would give the change more thought.

Two days later, Wolfe called everyone together again and told them she had decided to go ahead with the new plan. This time the workers were furious. One yelled that Wolfe had no regard for her employees. Another screamed that she shouldn't be obsessed with the "almighty buck." By the time the meeting cooled off, Wolfe had given each of them the opportunity to leave. All the employees chose to stay.

The new schedule went into effect the following week, and Wolfe immediately began another study of sales. She was, of course, most curious about how the change would affect her profit margin. When she studied the results after three months, she was amazed. Sales had remained more or less constant through the week, but Saturday sales had dropped almost 30 percent. Between the hours of 8:00 and 10:00 P.M., Wolfe discovered she was actually losing money.

If you were Wolfe, what would you do?

CHANGE CAN BE THREATENING

Why do people fear and resist change? Sometimes they have an understandable reason, as when a change threatens to upset their prestige, comfort, or security. But often changing conditions pose no real peril other than the inconvenience of making people change their behavior.

Changes in our society, our cultural patterns, and our economy now occur at an unprecedented rate and are reflected in all American business organizations. Social and cultural changes affect us whether we like it or not. Internal changes in policy and procedure, however advantageous in the long run, always bring short-term disruption that is uncomfortable or downright threatening to employees.

This chapter focuses on the process of change as it affects members of the organization, attacking such questions as:

Why did the accelerating social change of the 1960s encounter so much resistance among business people?

Why do people resent change within the organization, even when it is designed to benefit them?

What are some managerial methods for overcoming resistance to internal change?

How can a supervisor be an effective change agent?

What is organization development, and what specific programs does it offer to help an organization change?

Most change can be accepted if the threatening aspects are removed through practical human relations. We all know the cliché that change is a fact of life, but many people have difficulty accepting that fact. Often change is resisted simply because people have become comfortable doing things in an established way and the need for a new mode of behavior requires some adjustment on their part. But once the adjustment is made, the new way of doing things becomes the norm. Future attempts to change it will also be greeted with resistance.

RESISTANCE TO CHANGE

Imagine that your instructor for this course is called away suddenly, midway through the semester, and a new instructor appears on Monday morning to finish the term. Immediately you will notice personality differences between the departed instructor and his replacement. Whereas the first professor winked at reasonable tardiness, the new instructor greets late arrivals with pointed remarks about D's and F's for the course. The professor who began the course expected healthy participation from everyone based on careful study of the text, but your new professor expresses a distrust of textbooks in general and sends her copy hurtling in the wastebasket. She believes strongly that students should develop an intuitive approach to management, which she will instill through selected anecdotes from her own experience as consultant to a corporation. Tests will henceforth cover the substance of her lectures rather than the material you have already absorbed from the text.

You have a sickening sensation that you will not be able to use any of the knowledge you have gained so far; your now-useless text hangs limp in your hand. You worry about your grade on the next test, and you realize you will now have to leave your previous class while the professor is in midsentence to avoid this instructor's vocal dislike of people who cannot arrive on the stroke of the hour. What you are experiencing is a reaction to change—a need to adopt a new set of behaviors to perform the job at hand, which is completing the course. You are probably also feeling a bit of resistance, and perhaps, insecurity since you are not sure how your efforts will meet the new professor's expectations. You sense a loss of stability. There will certainly be a change in status relationships in the class; the students who performed well under the old instructor may not shine so brightly under the new course management.

Why Resistance Occurs

This example helps you understand some of the feelings people have when they are forced to cope with changes in the organization. The most difficult changes are those that are imposed on us without our participation in the decision. You have to accept a new professor for the course, for example, if you want to finish the course and get the credits. Similarly, employees must often accept changes with no outward manifestation of their resistance. Internally, however, they may undergo a tremendous amount of stress that could have long-term consequences for the organization.

"Change can make people feel insecure and uncertain."

The classroom example brought to light a few of the common reasons for resistance to change: the inconvenience of change, the insecurity and uncertainty about how the change could affect things, and the alteration in relationship status. There is another, much more obvious reason that workers fear change. How many of you still have milk delivered to your home each morning by a milkman? How many of your towns have blacksmiths? The answer to both questions is probably zero or close to it. Such occupations and many others have disappeared because of changes in technology and in social customs. Milkmen and blacksmiths had sound economic reasons for resisting such changes. Many workers fear that automation and other advances in technology will phase them out of their occupations. Naturally, they—and their unions—will do whatever is necessary to prevent this from happening.

There are other economic rationales for resisting proposed changes. Employees sometimes fear that work place changes could lead to a reduction in wage levels or the demand to work harder for the same wage rates. Imagine how you would feel if your boss told you that the company only needs to have you work three days a week because the new equipment they have purchased will save two days per week in production schedules. Thus, you will only be paid wages for three days, rather than five, in spite of the fact that output is exactly the same. When such situations occur because of technological advances, management will sometimes find out that output is not as high as it should be. Workers may express their resistance to change by restricting output.

There is still another reason that employees may resist changes. We noted in Chapter 4 that people are motivated on the job by a number of different needs, including the desire to form friendships with co-workers. People therefore fear that valued relationships will be disrupted by work place changes. Work groups may be split up, causing members to lose not just friends, but allies. Change threatens valuable personal relationships.

Managerial Dialogue

"I wanted what I had to be here forever."

Jane Campbell Cousins, president of Merrill Lynch Realty/Cousins

Merrill Lynch Realty/Cousins is a unique real estate agency with over 300 realtor associates.

If you spent twelve years working for a small, family-owned real estate company that was suddenly swallowed up by a financial giant, you'd expect a few jolts. You might expect to be faced with new bosses, new policies, new paperwork, new everything. In the mid-1980s wave of corporate mergers and acquisitions, such experiences have become common. Yet the story of Jane C. ("Casey") Cousins shows that even such dramatic changes can be managed successfully, without the turmoil, discontent, and turnover often associated with such situations. Ask Cousins how she managed to minimize the effects of a merger with Merrill Lynch Realty and her thriving real estate organization, and she'll tell you it was because she did her homework. "I investigated Merrill Lynch far more closely than they investigated me," Cousins says. "I wanted what I had to be here forever." Since founding Cousins Realty in 1967, Jane Cousins has run an unusual real estate agency. "I was working for a company owned by a friend of mine with six to eight associates. These were other women, like me, who came from the volunteer sector and liked doing this. We were getting very busy and I enjoyed it so much that my friend said to me, 'How about you taking the company and I'll work for you.' "

From a small firm in 1967, Cousins Realty grew to 300 realtor associates in 1981, but it remained an unconventional company. "I have never had a traditional real estate office with many branches and managers. We were very, very selective as to who joined the company as associates, and 60 percent have never worked for another real estate agency." In September 1981, Cousins Realty became part of the national Merrill Lynch Realty company. "I saw Miami growing rapidly, with multinationals moving here and the financial sector becoming important. There were a growing number of transfers here, particularly from the Northeast," Cousins explains. "Yet few people understand it's a small town with lots of tradition. We were extremely profitable, and I did not need capital. What I wanted was another dimension to the real estate business, including more training and financial expertise."

At the time of the merger, Cousins had already looked over—and rejected—other possible partners. "There is a great mistake made sometimes that just because a company is acquired, everything changes. That would have been the case with Coldwell Banker, and I wasn't interested in selling to a real estate company that had a well-established residential business here."

When the deal with Merrill Lynch was signed, Cousins told her staff and it was back to business as usual. "There was no management change, no new rules or regulations." But Cousins herself has had some adjustments to make: sharing ownership of the firm, talking to Merrill Lynch officials in Atlanta, and filing a lot more reports. Change has deliberately been minimized for the realtor associates who make up the bulk of the organization. They have been able to take part in new training programs and take advantage of Merrill Lynch's extensive contacts to sell more homes, but they still feel like they're working for a small, family-owned firm. "The company in Miami is run like no other company in Merrill Lynch, and they're perfectly content with that. This company is perfect for this town. We've had some toe-to-toe fights and they've made mistakes, but they admit it and go back and try something new."

An example of a change that was carefully managed to avoid these adverse effects is discussed by Jane C. Cousins in this chapter's Managerial Dialogue on pages 366–367.

Not all resistance to change is bad. Many times, when employee resistance is encountered, it forces top management to take a hard look at proposed changes. As a result, changes—when and if they are initiated—will be more thoroughly thought out.

In some instances, people actually seek change. This may occur when (1) it's apparent that there's more to be gained than lost from the process, (2) the changes contribute to their level of need satisfaction, and (3) the proposed changes have occurred through their own efforts.[1] If, for example, a company offers a new flexible benefit program that allows employees to participate in choosing their own benefits, minimal resistance to the change is likely to occur. Most employees will feel they stand to gain more than they lose from the change.

Reducing Resistance to Change

When it is likely that resistance to change will occur and could be detrimental to the organization's goals, managers may need to work to reduce the inevitable resistance. Perhaps the first step is to make sure that everyone understands the rationale for the change. A supervisor must use his or her communication skills to reduce employee resistance. As Cicero in 46 B.C. said, "Nothing is so unbelievable that oratory cannot make it acceptable." Six other techniques of reducing resistance to change are widely used:[2]

1. Education and communication
2. Participation and involvement

"Resistance to change is inevitable, but with good management it can be reduced."

3. Facilitation and support
4. Negotiation and agreement
5. Manipulation and cooperation
6. Explicit and implicit coercion

Perhaps one of the most effective ways to reduce resistance to a desired organizational change is to allow employees to get involved and participate in decisions concerning the change. Such involvement helps employees understand the specifics of the change, as well as the rationale for it. People who are involved in making decisions usually become more committed to carrying them out.

Resistance to change frequently may be lessened simply by lending a sympathetic ear to employees' concerns about the impending changes. For example, when organizations decide to adopt a computerized system, many employees feel insecure about their abilities to learn computer skills. Managers can significantly reduce such feelings by coaching employees in the necessary skills and giving them encouragement. Table 14.1 summarizes the communications steps for reducing resistance to change.

The negotiation and agreement strategy gets employees to endorse change by working out a desirable exchange. If a change in technology means that employees on a piecerate system could lose wages in the short run, the company could pay them a temporary bonus while they learn to master the new technology. Such an offer will reduce the resistance employees are experiencing due to fear of smaller paychecks.

A supervisor might also use ingratiation tactics to get a change accepted. From past experience, it may be obvious that one particularly vocal em-

---

TABLE 14.1 Communication Steps for Reducing Resistance to Change

1. Make clear the *needs* for change, or provide a climate in which group members feel free to identify such needs.
2. Permit and encourage relevant group participation in clarifying the needed changes.
3. State the *objectives* to be achieved by the proposed changes.
4. Establish broad *guidelines* for achieving the objectives.
5. Leave the *details* for implementing the proposed changes to the group in the organization or to the personnel who will be affected by the change.
6. Indicate the *benefits* or rewards to the individuals or groups expected to accrue from the change.
7. Materialize the benefits or rewards: i.e., keep the promises made to those who made the change.

Source: Goodwin Watson and Edward M. Glaser, "What We Have Learned About Planning for Change," *Management Review*, American Management Association, November 1965, pp. 34–46. Used by permission.

ployee is likely to oppose change and influence others to do the same. To sidestep such powerful opposition, a manager might try to convince the dissident that the change is partly his or her idea. If all else fails, a supervisor may use explicit or implicit coercion to repress resistance to a change. Companies planning to undertake major changes sometimes have to make it clear to employees that those who cannot adapt will be forced to go elsewhere. All of the major strategies for handling resistance to change, along with their advantages and drawbacks, are shown in Table 14.2.

TABLE 14.2   Major Methods for Dealing with Resistance to Change

Approach	Commonly Used in Situations	Advantages	Drawbacks
Education and communication	Where there is a lack of information or inaccurate information and analysis.	Once persuaded, people will often help with the implementation of the change.	Can be very time-consuming if lots of people are involved.
Participation and involvement	Where the initiators do not have all the information they need to design the change, and where others have considerable power to resist.	People who participate will be committed to implementing change, and any relevant information they have will be integrated into the change plan.	Can be very time-consuming if participators design an inappropriate change.
Facilitation and support	Where people are resisting because of adjustment problems.	No other approach works as well with adjustment problems.	Can be time-consuming, expensive, and still fail.
Negotiation and agreement	Where someone or some group will clearly lose out in a change, and where that group has considerable power to resist.	Sometimes it is a relatively easy way to avoid major resistance.	Can be too expensive in many cases if it alerts others to negotiate for compliance.
Manipulation and cooperation	Where other tactics will not work, or are too expensive.	It can be a relatively quick and inexpensive solution to resistance problems.	Can lead to future problems if people feel manipulated.
Explicit and implicit coercion	Where speed is essential, and the change initiators possess considerable power.	It is speedy, and can overcome any kind of resistance.	Can be risky if it leaves people mad at the initiators.

Source: Reprinted by permission of the *Harvard Business Review.* An exhibit from "Choosing Strategies for Change" by John P. Kotter and Leonard A. Schlesinger (March/April 1979), p. 111. Copyright © 1979 by the President and Fellows of Harvard College. All rights reserved.

Diagnosing Obstacles to Change

One of the best ways to understand the various obstacles to change is through *force field analysis*.[3] This science fiction term refers to a concept of change as a process involving a number of different forces working both for and against the change. Some forces in an individual's life will push him or her to improve or change his or her condition, while other forces operate against changes and try to maintain the status quo. (See Figure 14.1 for an illustration of force field analysis.) Generally, these forces can be categorized into three major types: (1) those that have to do with one's self, (2) those that concern other people or groups, and (3) those that are nonpersonal or environmental. Understanding the forces impinging on an individual helps to identify ways that change can be fostered.

To pinpoint obstacles to change in an organization as a whole, a number of other issues need to be considered. Specifically, the following questions should be carefully addressed[4]:

1. To what extent are key people in the organization ready to change?

2. How important and necessary is the change?

3. Do people have the capability, in terms of relevant skills and knowledge, to change their behavior?

4. How much political support—and from whom—will the change effort have?

After these questions have been answered, the manager responsible for effecting the change should do some self-diagnosis.[5] Key questions are:

1. What changes in my own attitudes, assumptions, and behaviors are required if I am to fit in with the emerging organization?

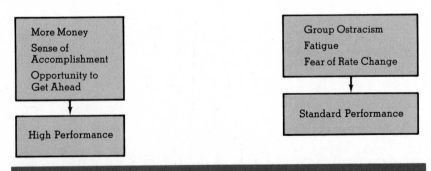

FIGURE 14.1 Forces That Increase and Decrease Performance

2. What skills and resources do I already have that mesh with the change?

3. What new knowledge, skills, attitudes, and behaviors do I need to learn?

4. Do I want to make these adjustments?

5. If the answer to question 4 is yes, how do I go about changing myself?

6. If the answer to question 4 is no, what are my options and how do I go about exercising them in a responsible way?

THE STAGES OF CHANGE

Kurt Lewin, a renowned social psychologist, suggests that there are three major stages of change in business organizations:

1. The unfreezing stage
2. The changing stage
3. The refreezing stage

Unfreezing Stage

"People won't change until they see what's wrong with things as they are at present."

For people or organizations as a whole to change, there must be some dissatisfaction with the status quo. If your study habits continually lead you to get A's on exams, the chances are good that you won't see a need to change your studying behavior. If you suddenly start to get a number of C's or, worse yet, failing grades on exams, however, you probably will start to panic and wonder how you should change. The panic and anxiety you feel represent the unfreezing stage. Something is wrong, and you realize you have to change in some way to rectify the situation.

Similarly, top-level executives in organizations begin to feel a need for change when they start getting information, internally or externally through market conditions, that something is not quite right. A company may begin to lose market share, or its turnover levels could skyrocket. These are the signals that lead to unfreezing in organizations.

Changing Stage

Two key conditions are required for change to take place. First, individuals or organizations must have some idea of a better way to function. For example, if you find that after years of getting A's, you are now getting C's, you need to be exposed to different study habits. Perhaps you will ask one of the top students in your class to help you study. Thus, you will have a new model to use in studying by yourself for future exams. One of the key ingredients in the changing stage is being aware of new options or courses of direction to pursue.

A second element necessary for change to occur is that the new options or behaviors must be seen as achievable and preferable to doing nothing at all. An employee whose skills have become obsolete has two major choices: learn a new skill or go on unemployment. Only if learning a new skill seems like a reasonable goal will that option be chosen.

Refreezing Stage

Once an individual has learned new behaviors, they must be reinforced in some way if they are to become permanent. Taking appropriate steps to maintain new behaviors is the essence of the refreezing process. According to one change expert, there are four major ways that individual, group, and organizational change can be made more permanent: (1) through formal structural systems, (2) through formal authority, (3) through new group norms, and (4) through cultural emergence.[6] The organization's formal structural systems can reinforce newly learned and desired behaviors through personnel policies and rules, compensations, benefits, and performance appraisal devices. If a company wants to encourage supervisors to develop their subordinates, for example, one way to refreeze this behavior is to make this criterion an important part of job appraisal for supervisors. The way in which superiors exercise their formal authority can also help to cement newly learned behavior patterns. Many training programs have failed to yield desired results because employees returned to an organization that did not reinforce their new behavior patterns. Take the example of a supervisor who goes to a seminar in human relations and learns to be more considerate and supportive of his subordinates' needs. When he returns to the organization, however, his boss expects him to be a hard-nosed disciplinarian. Therefore, his newly acquired behaviors will soon disappear.

"Change will not last unless group norms and values are altered to reflect the change."

A third way to support changed behavior is to develop group norms that foster and support the new changes. For example, to encourage more safety-conscious behavior in its employees, an organization might decide to start an accident-reduction contest between departments. The department with the best safety record over a three-month period would receive a departmental bonus, distributed equally among all department members. In such a situation, there will be a great deal of pressure to maintain safety records. Such norms are perhaps the most powerful sources in an organization for reinforcing desired behaviors. Finally, maintaining change in an organization depends on cultural emergence, or the perception that the organization's values and identity have changed. The manager as communicator has to help the staff see that change has occurred and that things are now different.

SELECTING A CHANGE APPROACH

The process of change in an organization is never easy, no matter how carefully planned. Experts say there are three major patterns of implementing change: top-down change, bottom-up change, and a shared approach to change. The three approaches are summarized in Table 14.3.

Top-Down Change

Top-down change uses formal authority to bring about change. The decision to change may be made by formal announcement through memos, speeches by top executives, policy statements, or other impersonal means. By throwing the formal weight of the organization behind the change, top management hopes that employees will change their outward behavior to comply, even if they disagree with the proposal.

TABLE 14.3 Three Different Approaches to Change

Top-Down Approach	Shared Approach	Bottom-Up Approach
Rapid change	Slow changes	Slow changes
Minimal involvement from employees	All levels of organization involved (top, middle, lower)	High levels of employee involvement
High power and expertise needed from change initiators	Lower level employees must avoid manipulation and cooptation	May be sabotaged at the top of the organization
Attempts to overcome resistance come later	High levels of commitment	Minimal resistance from employee groups and high commitment

Another top-down approach is to change the way in which employees perform their work. Computerizing operations might be one example. The change to a new technology is assumed to bring with it new ways of doing things and new attitudes on the part of employees, but only the technological change need be formally announced.

When top-level executives want change to take place very rapidly, they sometimes expedite the process by replacing key managers and personnel. Individuals who are supportive of the changes are then hired to fill their places. This often happens when a new top manager is hired. Rather than trying to persuade existing key personnel to accept new goals, new procedures, and new attitudes, the manager simply brings in new people (often those he or she has worked with in a previous job) who have no commitment to the status quo.

Another form of top-down change occurs when jobs, departments, or other forms of organizational structure are altered to accommodate a change. Management may decide, for example, to create new departments or change some of the lines of authority. Such structural changes are likely to bring other changes in relationships and attitudes as well.

Top-down strategies have the advantage that they can be instituted quickly. When the person initiating a change has high power, good relationships with employees, and clear expertise in the specifics regarding the change, a top-down approach can be used effectively. But it also has the potential to generate a tremendous amount of resistance from employees affected by the change.

Bottom-Up Change

In a bottom-up change, the major responsibility for change is given to people at lower levels in the company. Top-level management may not be involved and may know little about the change strategies. This ignorance can sometimes undermine the long-term effectiveness of a change approach. Incentives, job appraisals, and other company policies may not support the bottom-up change.

Bottom-up change can take place in a number of different ways. One of the more common is through training and management development programs. These programs may be selected by middle managers or even the personnel department. For example, a department head may arrange for weekend seminars on winning by negotiation. The supervisors who attend begin to change their behavior to make negotiation the most frequently used managerial strategy. Soon the entire department is using negotiation as a problem-solving technique, and any manager who uses another style of leadership, such as coercion or Machiavellianism, is severely criticized.

For the change to be permanent, it must have the support of top management. Job appraisal forms must emphasize negotiation skills; company directives should endorse the negotiation approach; and most importantly, the organization must stand behind negotiated settlements with workers. Without such support, negotiation skills gradually will fall into disuse.

Shared Responsibility

A third major approach to implementing change sets a course between top-down and bottom-up strategies. The shared responsibility approach involves employees from all levels of the organization in pinpointing problems and developing ideas for change. Organizational task forces are typical examples of this approach. They may, for example, be appointed by a firm's president to research a particular problem (e.g., how can we improve communication?) and then generate various alternative action steps. Since employees from all levels of the organization are included in such a group, there are typically high levels of commitment to the changes ultimately approved. Like the bottom-up approach, however, the shared responsibility for change procedure can take a tremendous amount of time.

The People Who Make the Changes

Ultimately, someone in the organization decides that it is time for a change and thus selects the approach to change that will be used. These choices will be related to the individual's personality and values. Managers who choose to bring about change through human relations are likely to focus on employee motivation, job satisfaction, and productivity. They may initiate creative incentive programs, job enrichment, management by objectives, and so on. Research shows that such managers tend to have liberal political views and range in age from 35 to 40 years. One of their high-priority goals is to equalize power relationships within organizational systems.

"Change is brought about by people, not the impersonal organization, and so change will occur in the way those people choose."

Other managers mainly are concerned with information flow and control systems within organizations. Typically, their backgrounds are in the area of operations research, and they tend to advocate technological innovations such as computerization of operations. Usually, such individuals are older and more politically moderate than the managers who focus on human relations.

A third type of manager works to improve organizationwide participation in decision making. These managers typically select change programs dealing with team development, improvements in interpersonal skills, and reorganization of the company's structure. Most have moderate to liberal political orientations and range in age from 40 to 50 years.[7]

THE ORGANIZATIONAL DEVELOPMENT APPROACH TO CHANGE

One of the more effective ways to manage change is through the process known as *organizational development.* Although the field of organizational development is only a few decades old, most practitioners and researchers agree that it can be defined as "a complex educational strategy intended to change the beliefs, attitudes, values, and structure of organizations so that they can better adapt to new technologies, markets, and challenges and to the dizzying rate of change itself."[8]

Companies interested in organizational development programs typically employ an outside consultant to help them get such programs off the ground. Such consultants are responsible for analyzing a company's current position, pinpointing key improvement areas, and then designing a series of change strategies to assist an organization in becoming more effective.

"In most large corporations, planning for future change is the full-time job of a group of employees."

Because organizational development is a relatively young field, there is little consensus about what works best. Typically, however, three major phases are involved: (1) the analysis period, (2) the intervention stage, and (3) the follow-up period. Figure 14.2 illustrates this process.

During the analysis phase, a consultant attempts to gather as much information about the company as possible. Interviews might be conducted with key executives or employees to find out their perceptions of key problems or potential change areas. Personnel files, annual reports, and other documents also might be used. Once the analysis is completed, interventions or change strategies are selected for each of the issues identified in the analysis. During this stage, a consultant generally will try to encourage as much participation as possible by organization members. Such participation helps to ensure commitment to the change strategies. Some of the more commonly used interventions are:

1. Training or educational techniques, such as leadership training methods, sensitivity training, team building

2. Confrontation strategies that bring together units of an organization that have had considerable conflict or communication problems.

3. Survey feedback techniques that disseminate and analyze survey data

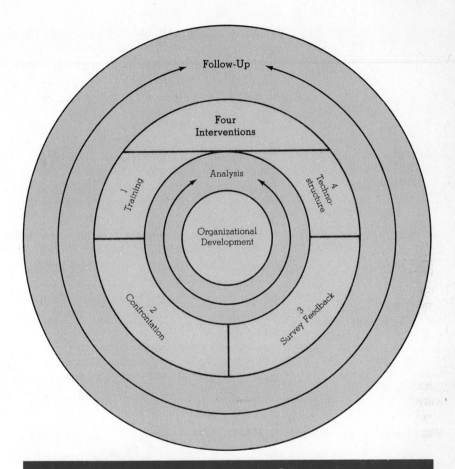

FIGURE 14.2 Organizational Development Process

that are then reported back to organizational departments as a basis for problem solving and planning activities.

4. Technostructural interventions that focus on changing an organization's structure or the way in which work is being performed.

The actual selection of these strategies depends on the specific needs of the organization, the preferences of key individuals within the firm, and the extent to which organizational participation is desired and feasible. Generally, a combination of several strategies is chosen.

After the change strategies have been implemented, follow-up, the third phase of organizational development, occurs. For best results, the effects of changes should be monitored and adjustments made as necessary. In some instances, outside consultants will cultivate "guardians" within the organization who are responsible for planning and implementing future organizational changes. Such guardians are usually members of the organization's personnel or human resources department.

ON THE JOB
REVISITED . . .

In studying the sales figures for her store, Davina Wolfe realized that her employees were the critical factor in determining the profitability of her store. Under the old schedule, Saturdays were the busiest days, in part, Wolfe reasoned, because her employees were excited about the week and passed that enthusiasm on to the customer. On Sundays, when the employees wanted to relax, sales were slow. The late-night Saturday hours under the new system, which Wolfe had expected to be her most profitable, were money losers because her employees didn't want to work them.

Wolfe decided to go back to the old hours—closing earlier on Saturdays and reopening on Sundays. But Wolfe decided on a new tactic to turn Sundays into a winning proposition: she would double the commission on all Sunday sales above a certain minimum. That would certainly encourage her employees to sell. When Wolfe told her employees about the new hours and the Sunday bonus, she was greeted with a loud cheer. Wolfe couldn't wait to see the results of her next sales study.

SUMMARY

Change occurs within our social, cultural, and economic systems at an extremely rapid rate. Organization members must learn to cope and adapt to such processes. This chapter described some of the major reasons why people resist change. We noted that alterations in familiar behavior patterns lead to insecurity and uncertainty about how the changes will affect the individual. In some instances, changes also lead to an alteration in interpersonal relationships and a disturbance of the status hierarchy. Resistance can be managed and anticipated, however. Effective communication about impending changes, getting employees involved in implementing aspects of the change, and showing how changes may be beneficial to employees are just a few ways of managing resistance.

This chapter also described the necessary ingredients for changing individual behavior—unfreezing, change, and refreezing. Diagnosing obstacles to change by using force field theory also helps facilitate alterations in behavior patterns. These patterns can be changed through several approaches: top-down, bottom-up, and a shared responsibility. The choice of any particular strategy or approach to change depends on the personality and values of the person selecting the change.

Finally, this chapter described organizational development, a program aimed at increasing the overall health of an organization. Such strategies usually use an outside consultant to give advice on how an organization can best adapt to the changing environment.

HUMAN RELATIONS APPLICATIONS

Conclusion 1:   Resistance to most organizational changes is inevitable, but it can be minimized.
Application: Supervisors can help to alleviate resistance by explaining the rationale for changes and by getting likely resistors involved in the change process. Occasionally, negotiation tactics, manipulation, and in extreme cases, coercion must be used to handle severe forms of resistance.
Conclusion 2:   Change may be implemented in three major ways: top-down approach, bottom-up strategy, or shared responsibility approaches.
Application: The choice of a particular implementation strategy usually depends on a change agent's personality and his or her values concerning the change process.

DISCUSSION QUESTIONS

1. Name some of the major reasons why resistance to change occurs in organizations.
2. How could a manager use negotiation as a tactic for alleviating resistance to change?
3. What is force field analysis, and how can it help us to understand the barriers to change in an organization?
4. Describe and give an example of each of the stages involved in the change process.
5. When would a manager use a top-down change approach rather than a bottom-up strategy?
6. What is organizational development?

NOTES

1. R. W. Reber and G. Van Gilder, *Behavioral Insights for Supervision.* Englewood Cliffs, NJ: Prentice-Hall, 1982.

2. J. P. Kotter and L. A. Schlesinger, "Choosing Strategies for Change," *Harvard Business Review* (March–April 1979), p. 11.

3. M. S. Plounick, R. E. Frye, and W. W. Burke, *Organization Development: Exercises, Cases and Readings.* Boston: Little, Brown and Co., 1982, pp. 14–19.

4. *Ibid.*, pp. 14–19.

5. M. Beer, *Organization Change and Development: A Systems View.* Santa Monica, CA: Goodyear Publishing Co., 1980, p. 64.

6. *Ibid.*, p. 64.

7. N. M. Ticky, "Agents of Planned Social Change: Congruence of Values, Cognitions, and Actions," *Administrative Science Quarterly* 19; 2 (1974), pp. 164–182.

8. Warren G. Bennis, *Organization Development: Its Nature, Origins, and Prospects.* Reading, MA: Addison-Wesley Publishing Co., 1969, p. 2.

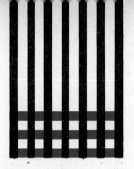

CORPORATE CULTURE

CHAPTER 15

ON THE JOB . . .

WHAT IS CORPORATE CULTURE?

CORPORATE CULTURE DETERMINES PRODUCTIVITY

BUREAUPATHOLOGY: A CORPORATE ILLNESS

MATCHING YOUR PERSONALITY TO A CORPORATE CULTURE

   Dress Codes
   Status Symbols

TYPES OF CORPORATE CULTURE

   IBM
   PepsiCo
   J.C. Penney
   Looking for a Way to Classify Corporate Cultures

IS THERE AN IDEAL CORPORATE CULTURE?

   The Japanese System
   What Creates Excellence?
   A Closer Look at Successful Corporate Culture

HOW TO CHANGE THE CORPORATE CULTURE

   Role Modeling
   Positive Reinforcement
   Make Employees Feel Important

ON THE JOB REVISITED . . .

SUMMARY

HUMAN RELATIONS APPLICATIONS

DISCUSSION QUESTIONS

NOTES

MANAGERIAL DIALOGUE: Thomas J. Peters

ON THE JOB . . .

Ramon Perez was perplexed. After three highly successful years as a waterbed salesman, the 24-year-old Perez had just taken a new job as customer relations manager for the main branch of the Watertown County Public Library. Perez enjoyed meeting the public and thought his years of sales had given him insights into customers' personalities. Perez wanted to move up from what he considered a "pushy" sales job into one that had "more class," as he once described it to his wife.

In his first three months on the job at the library, Perez was often frustrated by how long it took to get things done. In selling waterbeds, if a customer had a complaint or some other problem developed, Perez could go to his boss and get an immediate yes or no. But in the library, complaints from patrons or requests for new books, magazines, or newspapers seemed to Perez to take forever to resolve.

First he had to fill out a form, which in turn was given to a committee. The key committees with which Perez dealt were Acquisitions, which decided how to increase the library's holdings, and Patron Policy, which decided such matters as library hours and number of books to be checked out.

Perez thought he knew a way to speed up the process. He could join the Patron Policy committee, be selected chairperson, and push through the procedural changes needed. With the new year fast approaching—and the selection of new committees with it—Perez began to campaign. He set up posters in the employee lounge. He took several co-workers to lunch. He telephoned others at home.

Perez felt good about his chances. Nobody else was actively campaigning. Everyone told him they liked his ideas. But on that

January day when the fifty staff members voted, Perez got only a single vote for the Patron Policy committee. After he trudged home that night, all he could do was ask his wife, "What did I do wrong?"

WHAT IS CORPORATE CULTURE?

If a lifelong resident of New York City were to move to a small town in Nebraska, it wouldn't be surprising if he discovered some great differences between the culture of his old and new hometowns. The same behavior that would have been considered perfectly normal in Brooklyn would instantly brand him as being eccentric, if not an outright lunatic, in Grand Island. If the New Yorker wanted to be accepted there, he would have to change some of his behavior. For example, he would have to speak slower and more softly. He would have to learn to wait to be served in stores rather than pushing to the front. When he met people on a sidewalk, he would need to look them in the eye, rather than avoiding eye contact, as is the rule in New York.

The cultures of corporations vary like the cultures of different cities. Some companies are run in an intensely competitive fashion. Their employees must produce results in order to hold on to their jobs. Each supervisor tries to run the department so as to create more profits than rival departments and to make sure that no one is allowed to feel secure in any position. Other companies stress cooperation rather than competition. The working environment is relaxed, and even management and the labor union are able to pull together without serious disagreement. Employees are encouraged to feel secure, and no one is fired without plenty of warning.

Corporate culture is the pattern of attitudes and expectations shared by the members of a company. These beliefs work to shape the employees' behavior and to set the organization's policies. Based on how they are treated and how they are expected to behave, employees form a concept of the kind of organization they are working for.

A corporate culture generally is deeply rooted and capable only of slow change because many of the individual members of the company have a substantial stake in keeping things as they are. After all, anyone who has been promoted in the organization has received the promotion because he or she has refrained from violating the norms of behavior of the company.

This chapter investigates both the positive and negative aspects of corporate culture:

How does corporate culture affect employees' productivity?

Is it possible to match your own personality to the culture of the corporation for which you work?

What are some of the status symbols that express corporate culture?

Is there any one type of corporate culture that helps a company achieve excellence?

How can a corporate culture be changed?

CORPORATE CULTURE DETERMINES PRODUCTIVITY

Many experts believe that the corporate culture is one of the most significant factors involved in determining the productivity of a company. Howard Schwartz and Stanley M. Davis argue that:

> *These mundane routines buried deep in companies' culture (and subcultures) may be the most accurate reflections of why things work the way they do, and of why some firms succeed with their strategies where others fail. And if we can get at the way in which these minutiae determine an organization's ability to create and to carry out strategy—[then] we can learn a great deal about how to manage an organization through a period of strategic change.*[1]

A successful firm usually has some sort of distinctive company philosophy and way of doing things that are well matched to the goals of the organization. In many cases the members of the corporation may not even be aware of this social glue that holds their organization together; an outsider or newcomer might be in a position to observe the corporate culture more objectively. But even though the corporate culture may seem to be invisible, a good supervisor or employee should train himself or herself to observe how the corporate culture operates and how it is helping or hindering the organization. The proper corporate culture can serve to make people want to work harder because they feel it is in their interest to do so. A corporate culture may also permit the organization to respond to change more effectively. If innovation is totally discouraged, for instance, the corporation ultimately may pay the price for being too conservative.

"The corporate culture influences employees whether or not they are aware of the fact."

Larry J. B. Robinson, head of a Cleveland-based chain of jewelry stores, reports that corporate culture has been the central factor involved in the growth of his business from two to seventy-four stores. "If you want to improve profitability," Robinson says, "you should base your corporate culture on the Golden Rule." He says that his employees are urged to "do unto others as you would have them do unto you," and that because of this, customers feel confident they are not being cheated when they buy an expensive ring or necklace.[2]

BUREAUPATHOLOGY: A CORPORATE ILLNESS

Just as having the appropriate corporate culture can be an invaluable help in achieving the organizational goals, having the wrong corporate culture can often be the underlying cause of a firm's difficulties. Richard Hodgson argues that several clearly identifiable signs indicate that a "poisonous" organizational climate exists. Some of the signs of what he calls *bureaupathology* are:[3]

1. At all levels in the organization, significant numbers of people do not know what they should be doing, how to do it, or why.

2. Even among the competent, there are many who cannot be bothered to do well what they really know how to do.

3. People who are doing really well are not being adequately rewarded.

4. Leaders have disappeared into their jobs. They are buried in paperwork. They are hidden behind their desks. They are burdened by technocracy, hampered by rules and regulations, disoriented by change. At the top, they have often disappeared behind the mahogany curtain, sometimes with private elevators and chauffeured limousines, so that almost no one in their organizations ever sees them.

Although the cures for bureaupathology may be complex, it is often easy to see what has caused the disease. The pattern is fairly common. Often, a company will initially flourish under its founder, who may have been personally responsible for creating some of the products or concepts that won a sizeable share of the market for the firm. As the company grows rapidly in its early years, the corporate culture is vigorous and flexible. After the founder retires, the company may go on making money because of the support of loyal customers, but the corporate culture may become more rigid. Executives may become too cautious in their thinking. They may stress avoiding risks and holding on to what the company already has. The firm may promote mediocre employees who are unimaginative and who can do little except follow orders. People with innovative ideas may be ignored or even discouraged.

One firm that apparently fell victim to this syndrome is the Walt Disney Productions Company. In recent years many of the employees at Disney became so intent on keeping alive the wholesome, clean-cut values of its founder's movies of the 1930s, 1940s, and 1950s that the Disney Co. lost touch with contemporary, young filmgoers. The firm's executives were reported to be sharply divided on the issue of whether to make the film *Splash,* which turned out to be the studio's first hit in years.

Another way that many companies have gone wrong recently is that they have come to overemphasize numbers. Every aspect of the business is evaluated in terms of results that can be expressed numerically and analyzed by computer. This approach, though useful in some areas, can lead the firm to concentrate on short-term gains at the expense of long-term goals.

Hodgson maintains that finding a cure for bureaupathology begins with initiating real communication between executives and subordinates and with a willingness to take a long-range view of the situation:

> *The dialogue between boss and subordinate should not start with a backward look at evaluation of past performance, should not start with setting of isolated goals, should not even start with a review of individual job responsibilities. Instead, the dialogue starts with a knowledgeable conversation between boss, subordinates, and subordinates' peers as to the problems and prospects that exist for their business, now and in the forseeable future.*[4]

MATCHING YOUR PERSONALITY TO A CORPORATE CULTURE

"Before taking any job, you should ask yourself how comfortable you feel in that corporation's culture."

In searching for the elusive perfect job, a would-be employee needs to understand that the first step of the matching process is learning about a particular company's values, policies, and traditions. The corporate culture often plays a major role in determining how successful workers will be at a particular job and how much they will enjoy (or not enjoy) doing that job.

Even within one type of industry or business, companies may operate quite differently. For instance, a disc jockey at an easy listening radio station in a small town may find that the company does not appreciate his loud manner, bad puns, and off-color jokes. On the other hand, a top-forty station in a metropolitan area may value those same qualities a great deal and show it by raises and promotions. At one high-tech company, a salesperson may be expected to be part of a team, with each person making one part of a joint sales presentation. Another firm, however, may value a salesperson who does it all single-handedly. Some companies actively seek women for high management positions; others avoid placing women in decision-making positions, even though the companies' executives may officially accept affirmative action.

If the values of the corporation match those of the employee, the worker has a head start toward success. If not, then the employee may be struggling uphill throughout his or her career there. Employees must be prepared to be adaptable, however. If a worker holds out for the ideal firm for which he or she feels perfectly suited, the individual may be faced with an endless job search. Many small compromises, especially in superficial matters of conduct, may be necessary. An employee who feels that a corporation is solid and that the job offers good opportunities may be wise to accept the limitations of the firm's corporate culture. For example, on joining a certain advertising firm you might be surprised to discover that all of your colleagues claim they work virtually twenty-four hours a day, seven days a week. If they leave the office before 10 P.M., it's only because they're taking the work home with them. If they're traveling out of town for the weekend, they always say that it's a business trip (even though the "business" may be conducted at poolside with a cool drink). After a while it becomes clear that everyone cannot possibly be doing *that* much work and remain sane. Thus, you conclude that this particular corporate culture requires an employee to pretend to be a hopelessly addicted workaholic.

Dress Codes

Perhaps the most obvious aspect of corporate culture is the way that people at any given job usually dress. If you apply for a job on Wall Street dressed in a T-shirt, jeans, and sneakers, or if you apply for a job at a car wash dressed in a three-piece suit, you aren't likely to be hired, much less accepted by other workers. But many executives say there is much more to choosing the right clothes than simply avoiding such obvious errors. Such apparently trivial decisions as whether or not to wear a button-down collar may actually be of considerable importance.

Executive recruiter Gerry Roche of Heidrick and Struggles argues that "Dress is a very, very critical key one looks at in an executive." He reports that he once sent a man to Europe to be interviewed for the presidency of a multinational firm. After the transatlantic flight it was only natural that the candidate would be a bit haggard, but Roche says he was surprised to receive a phone call from an official of the conglomerate angrily complaining, "You sent me a guy with sagging socks."

In general, the most important piece of advice to keep in mind in deciding what to wear is to observe carefully how your colleagues dress and then dress likewise. Keep in mind that one should strive to copy those people who are on one's own level of status within the company. Different standards may apply to those higher up or lower down. Don't overdress (no display handkerchiefs, for instance), and never, *never* attempt to dress better than your boss.

"It's up to you whether you dress for success or failure."

For those who would like to read more specific suggestions on what to wear to work, the bible of millions of young professionals is *Dress for Success* (Chicago: Follet Company, 1977) by John T. Molloy. Molloy has also written a sequel, *The Woman's Dress for Success Book.* For men who aspire to managerial positions, Molloy prescribes a blue or gray two-piece suit of conservative cut, a white or light pastel shirt with long sleeves, a neatly patterned tie darker than the shirt, dark over-the-calf socks, and wingtips or other plain, laced shoes. For women, Molloy suggests a two-piece suit—skirt and blazer-style jacket—worn with a blouse analogous to a man's shirt.

Since the publication of *Dress for Success* in 1975, Molloy reports that dress codes, especially at the higher managerial levels, are becoming much more strict. In 1983 he said:

> *Five years ago when I talked to companies about how they wanted recruits to dress, the message was, "We'd like the young man to wear a suit, but won't hold it against the women if they don't." Today I hear, "We have so few jobs and so many qualified applicants, we're looking for ways to eliminate candidates. Those who won't dress appropriately we'll eliminate."*[5]

One other point for men to keep in mind: although it's important to be concerned with dressing properly, a man shouldn't talk too much with male co-workers or (more important) male supervisors about the question of what to wear. As Lois Fenton, a consultant for Executive Wardrobe Engineering of Mamaroneck, New York, points out, "Men are very suspicious about a man who is too interested in clothes." She says, "A man who sits next to me on a flight may ask what I do. When I tell him he'll say, 'I'm not interested in clothes,' and then for the duration of the flight he'll pump me for information on how to dress."[6]

Status Symbols

Another aspect of corporate culture that employees should be advised to observe closely is the use of status symbols. Such signs of success as a spacious office or the key to the executive washroom serve an important purpose. They show employees where they and others belong in the corporate hierarchy. The rewarding of status symbols can also serve to boost the egos of those who receive them, and the desire to obtain status symbols can serve to drive workers to achieve more. James Polczynski identifies six categories of status symbols:

1. Position titles
2. Office accouterments
3. Office space
4. Private secretaries
5. Position accouterments (such as special parking places, country club memberships, and expense accounts)
6. Position prestige (subtle status symbols such as being consulted frequently by top management)

Office space and trappings are probably the most easily identifiable status symbols, and experts say that an employee's office tells a great deal about how he or she fits into the corporate culture. A survey by the American Society of Interior Designers found that the boss's office usually occupies a corner location, is the biggest in the firm, and is filled with such accessories as original artwork (67 percent), oriental rugs or custom carpeting (51 percent), or custom-built furniture (36 percent). Of the chief executives surveyed, 62 percent had private washrooms and 45 percent had private waiting rooms.

A great deal of careful planning often goes into such details as office space, location, and furnishings. Union Carbide once assigned office space in its fifty-three-story headquarters so that the employees working on any one given floor ranked higher than all the employees working on floors below them.

Another aspect of great importance is the location of offices within a floor. The closer a manager's office is to the chief executive's, the more power that manager possesses. Another sign that a manager is important is having an office located as far as possible from the main entrance to the corporation's offices. As more and more status symbols are awarded, firms have begun to publish elaborate and extremely specific charts that show each employee exactly what perks he or she is due. The Ford Motor

Company, for example, has established twenty-seven different levels of rank, from clerk to chairman of the board, each with its own set of status symbols.

Status symbols have acquired so much importance that Polczynski writes about one executive "who suffered acute anxiety and whose performance tapered off considerably after being given a one-drawer instead of a two-drawer desk in his new office. In his opinion, his position necessitated a two-drawer desk."[7] This story of the anxious executive illustrates another important point about status symbols. Employees should learn to be aware of the significance of status symbols, but fighting battles with other colleagues to see who can one-up the others and get the most perks is usually counterproductive for both the executive and the company. At some businesses more energy seems to be expended by workers in these petty rivalries than in finding ways of improving the competitive position of the corporation as a whole. When the corporate culture is too dependent on the manipulation of such symbols, little real work gets done.

TYPES OF CORPORATE CULTURE

Although the process of forming a culture may be much the same in all corporations, the actual culture itself differs widely. Such factors as the competitiveness of the industry, the original location of the firm, and the personality of the founder may all be significant influences. To illustrate the wide range of attitudes and values that a corporate culture may endorse, we will look at three very different corporate cultures: IBM, PepsiCo, and J.C. Penney.

IBM

The company most notable for its emphasis on the importance of corporate culture is IBM. Company founder Thomas J. Watson said, "The basic philosophy, spirit, and drive of an organization have far more to do with its relative achievement than do technology or economic resources, organizational structure, innovation, and timing."[8] Long before it became a major force in its industry, IBM established a corporate culture aimed at treating employees with consideration and providing courteous service to customers. IBM policy states that:

1. All employees should be respected and treated with dignity.
2. The company should aim to accomplish every task in a superior way.
3. The customer should be given the best service possible.

Top management at IBM says that every aspect of the company has been developed in such a way as to meet these goals. For instance, neither time clocks nor layoffs are ever used at IBM. IBM executives maintain that it is this employee-oriented policy that has been responsible for the company's extraordinary success story. Experts outside the company point out that IBM has had a tradition of stressing excellence and innovation. In their book *In Search of Excellence* (New York: Harper & Row, 1982), Peters and Waterman hold up IBM as the model for an effective corporate culture.

PepsiCo

The key value at PepsiCo is competitiveness. In contrast to a company like IBM, where cooperation is paramount, Pepsi stresses competition in every aspect of an employee's working life. Just as Pepsi executives are jointly determined to surpass arch rival Coca-Cola, they must also be individually determined to surpass rival executives at PepsiCo.

The atmosphere at Pepsi is aimed in many different ways at rewarding employees who display aggressiveness and the competitive spirit. Supervisors are continually pressured to improve market share; a decline of a mere fraction of one percentage point can lead to a supervisor's dismissal. A policy of "creative tension" is maintained by frequently shifting employees to different positions. Because of this policy, employees are often willing to go to great lengths to keep their jobs. Further, PepsiCo policy demands that executives be in good physical shape if they wish to be promoted. Four physical fitness instructors are on the staff of the company headquarters.

The example of PepsiCo is important because of the sharp difference between its corporate culture and that of IBM and other firms that stress cooperation among employees. This difference reminds us that there are many ways to organize a thriving enterprise and that there is no one sure fire formula for success.

J.C. Penney

J.C. Penney aims to be supportive of its employees to the point that even those workers who are considered to be "marginally competent" are not fired. Instead, the company seeks to place them in other jobs within the firm. For this reason the J.C. Penney staff is especially loyal to the corporation. Executives feel that this makes employees likely to do more to please customers.

Founder James Cash Penney established the following seven principles, which still underlie the basic culture of the organization:

1. To serve the public, as nearly as we can, to its complete satisfaction.

2. To expect, for the service we render, a fair remuneration and not all the profit the traffic will bear.

3. To do all in our power to pack the customer's dollar full of value, quality, and satisfaction.

4. To continue to train ourselves and our associates so that the service we give will be more and more intelligently performed.

5. To improve constantly the human factor in our business.

6. To reward men and women in our organization through participation in what the business produces.

7. To test policy, method, and act in this manner: "Does it square with what is right and just?"

Above all, J.C. Penney stresses fairness, just as PepsiCo stresses competitiveness and IBM stresses excellence.

Looking for a Way to Classify Corporate Cultures

A number of systems for classifying the various types of corporate cultures have been developed. Two of the most noted of these systems were discussed in Chapter 6: Douglas McGregor's Theory X and Theory Y and Rensis Likert's classification system. Theory X and Theory Y reflect two distinctive points of view on corporation management. Theory X assumes that employees dislike work and must be coerced into performing their tasks well. Decisions are always made at the top, and orders are given out to subordinates. Theory Y, however, is based on the idea that members of today's better-educated work force want to be given a chance to express their ideas and to take part in decision making. A corporation that operates according to Theory Y would allow for collaboration and self-control and would spurn the "carrot and stick" approach of Theory X. Rensis Likert's classification system emphasizes many of the same factors considered important by Douglas McGregor. Likert contrasts two types of corporate cultures, System I and System IV. System I is

"Businesses, like people, have distinct personalities, and businesses in trouble may need a corporate psychiatrist."

an authoritarian kind of organization in which employees are motivated by the fear of punishment and control is concentrated in the hands of the top executives. In a System IV company culture, on the other hand, Likert says that workers are motivated by participation and involvement in decision making and by the fact that they share the organization's goals. By accomplishing its goals they also accomplish their own.

Psychologist Harry Levinson says he believes that all organizations have personalities, just as individuals do. General Motors, for example, he diagnoses as being powerful, aggressive, and defensive. IBM has a high energy level. Eastern Airlines is masculine and aggressive. Most of the major banks used to be stuffy, conservative, and autocratic, but many now are becoming more competitive and innovative. Levinson argues that organizations, like individuals, sometimes have moods of depression and crises in which they need help.

When Levinson is called in to diagnose an ailing corporation, he assembles genetic data (facts of financial conditions), historical data (the background of company crises and complaints), and interpretive data. The last item includes the "emotional atmosphere," which is assessed on the basis of such items as whether workers leave their jobs on the dot of quitting time, clerks' civility or rudeness, and the writing style used in bulletin board notices. What Levinson calls the interpretive data also includes the "masculine-feminine quotient" of a group. For instance, a feminine organization may provide an atmosphere of warmth and support, but it may fail to produce as much as a more masculine organization. But Levinson also points out that a tough, hard-headed masculine corporation may lose good personnel by not being sensitive enough to the needs of its people. Another important element of the emotional atmosphere is the "energy level," which concerns the speed and vigor with which a company reacts to changing market conditions.

Social psychologist Roger Harrison has developed a theory of what he calls *organizational ideologies,* or the systems of thought that are central determinants of the character of organizations (their corporate cultures). Harrison reports that organizational ideologies are designed:[9]

1. To specify an organization's goals and values and consequent measures of success and worth.
2. To prescribe suitable relationships between individuals and the organization, or what each can expect from the other.
3. To indicate what kinds of control of behavior in the organization are legitimate and illegitimate.
4. To determine which qualities or characteristics of members should be valued and how these should be rewarded or punished.

5. To show members how to treat each other—whether to compete or to collaborate.

Harrison's work has identified four basic types of organizational ideologies: power orientation, role orientation, task orientation, and person orientation. An organization with a power orientation ideology is ruthlessly competitive, jealous of its territory, and exploitative of weaker organizations. It exercises tight, internal control in a hierarchical structure. Although it lets a few aggressive people claw their way to the top, it offers little security to the average employee. A power-oriented corporation may use too much of its resources and energy in policing its own employees, and reliance on simple rewards and punishment tends to create superficial compliance that thinly masks a desire to rebel.

An organization that aspires to be as rational and orderly as possible is considered to have a role orientation. Its managerial emphasis on agreements, rules, legality, procedures, and responsibilities contrasts sharply with the management practices of the power-oriented companies. Rights and privileges are made clear, and predictability is valued. These organizations change slowly. Banks, public utilities, and insurance companies usually fall into this category.

The highest value for firms with a task-oriented technology is achievement. Such an organization permits nothing to stand in the way of reaching a given goal. Employees are retrained or replaced if they do not change appropriately, as are roles, rules, and regulations. Authority is derived mainly from knowledge and competence rather than from position. Internally, such an organization is collaborative and flexible, not competitive or rigid. Smaller organizations (such as research laboratories, high-risk businesses, social service groups, and some of the new high-tech firms started by computer whiz kids) frequently have this ideology. A conflict that often occurs comes from the attempt to plug role-oriented people into a task-oriented system. Another difficulty with task-oriented corporations is that individuals who don't have the knowledge or skills for the work at hand must be replaced by those who do.

Authority is discouraged in an organization dominated by person-oriented ideology. Members are expected to influence and instruct each other, to share unrewarding or unpleasant tasks equally, and to enjoy working with their colleagues. Some consulting companies and some small groups of researchers work this way. Many signs of social change point to a movement in the direction of person-oriented ideology even at large organizations in the future.

IS THERE AN IDEAL CORPORATE CULTURE?

■ ▪ ■ ▪ ■ ▪ ■ ▪ ■ ▪ ■ ▪ ■ ▪ ■ ▪ ■ ▪ ■ ▪ ■ ▪ ■

"A sure way to attract attention is to come up with a new way of recognizing the best corporate culture."

As soon as researchers began to set up classification systems for corporate cultures, some people began to ask, "But which one is the best?" Most scholars agree that there is no simple answer to this question. It depends on the competitive situation of the organization, on its goals, and of course, on the people who make up the organization. Yet the search goes on to identify the corporate culture that can help an organization achieve its goals. What are some of the characteristics of a successful corporate culture? Different experts give different answers.

The Japanese System

The extraordinary advances made by Japanese firms in recent years have been widely reported in the press and carefully observed by business experts in the United States. Many authorities believe that corporate culture has been an important factor in the Japanese success story.

The key difference between corporate cultures in America and in Japan is that U.S. firms tend to stress individuality and competitiveness, while the Japanese stress teamwork and cooperation. An executive of the Mitsubishi Corporation says, "There is pride and even sibling rivalry in our company, but there is a family consciousness. Everyone believes that his colleagues and superiors care about his welfare." In Japan promotions are based more on seniority and teamwork than on individual achievement. Workers are often guaranteed lifetime employment with a firm. It is very rare, virtually a social disgrace, for an employee to be fired.

The Japanese believe that their use of quality control circles has given them an edge over U.S. companies. But, as was discussed in Chapter 8, quality control circles work only in a corporate culture marked by cooperation and a high degree of employee participation. Many American firms are moving to organize their own versions of quality control circles, designed to give employees more input into decision making, but it remains to be seen whether they will truly be effective in American corporate cultures. Lawrence Miller, president of the Tarkenton Company, warns:

> *We should not try to turn our culture upside down and imitate the Japanese model. . . . The Japanese work well in teams, are willing to sacrifice immediate self-advantage for the advantage of the group, and demonstrate a loyalty and commitment to their groups*

that is unmatched in this country. Their group orientation is a foundation for the many management practices, such as quality circles, that many U.S. corporations are trying to emulate. The problem in doing this is that those practices cannot successfully be implemented outside of the greater cultural context which serves as their foundation.[10]

What Creates Excellence?

The Japanese challenge was certainly one of the factors that helped to make *In Search of Excellence: Lessons from America's Best-Run Companies,* by Thomas Peters and Robert Waterman, a bestseller in 1982. Peters and Waterman argue that American businesses can regain their competitive edge by treating people with respect—both workers and customers—and by developing healthier corporate cultures.

Peters and Waterman visited dozens of prosperous firms and interviewed hundreds of employees and executives. Their research led them to conclude that:

Excellent companies were, above all, brilliant on the basics. Tools didn't substitute for thinking. Intellect didn't overpower wisdom. . . . These companies listened to their employees and treated them like adults. . . . They allowed some chaos in return for quick action and regular experimentation.[11]

Peters and Waterman compiled a list of forty-three companies as examples of excellence in management and corporate culture. They cited eight attributes of excellence that most of these firms possessed:

1. *Bias for action.*   A preference for doing something—anything—rather than sending an idea through endless cycles of analyses and committee reports.

2. *Staying close to the customer.*   Learning his or her preferences and catering to them.

3. *Autonomy and entrepreneurship.*   Breaking the corporation into small companies and encouraging them to think independently and competitively.

4. *Productivity through people.*   Creating in all employees the awareness that their best efforts are essential and that they will share in the rewards of the company's success.

5. *Hands-on, value-driven.*   Insisting that executives keep in touch with the firm's essential business and promote a strong corporate culture.

6. *Stick to the knitting.*   Remaining with the businesses the company knows best.

7. *Simple form, lean staff.*   Few administrative layers, few people at the upper levels.

8. *Simultaneous loose-tight properties.*   Fostering a climate where there is dedication to the central values of the company combined with tolerance for all employees who accept those values.

Despite the acclaim for *In Search of Excellence* (Peters is currently making about $1.5 million annually in lecture fees; he is the subject of the Managerial Dialogue on page 398), some business experts are having second thoughts about the book's prescriptions for success. There does seem to be general agreement that *In Search of Excellence* was right in stressing the importance of people at a time when many companies were overstressing the importance of numbers, but one consultant charges that Peters and Waterman ignored the importance of technology and government policy. A *Business Week* study reports that strict adherence to the eight commandments, which do not emphasize reacting to broad economic and business trends, may actually hurt a company. *Business Week* also notes that some of the forty-three excellent firms, such as Atari and Texas Instruments, have recently run into serious difficulties.

"Even 'excellent' firms can run into trouble."

A Closer Look at Successful Corporate Cultures

Several of the other theories regarding the ideal corporate culture have been subjected to some of the same criticisms aimed at *In Search of Excellence.* In brief, these theories, though useful in many ways, turn out to be somewhat academic and remote from reality. The study of corporate culture is not an exact science. Some general statements can be made, but definite conclusions are hard to come by.

The real business world usually is based more on the survival of the fittest than on the Golden Rule. Although many corporations do stress that employees should be treated with respect, most executives are concerned primarily with bottom-line results. American businesses are often ruthlessly competitive environments.

It is also important to remember that the corporate culture is not necessarily what the top executives say it is. Corporate culture is what actually occurs, on a day-to-day basis. If the reward system is not changed, for example, it doesn't matter that official policy says that behavior is supposed to change. Take the case of the head of the sales department at a camera store who calls a meeting of the staff and tells them, "We don't want any high-pressure sales presentations. Don't push people to buy

Managerial Dialogue

"Wield a scalpel, not a pickax."

Thomas J. Peters, author, lecturer, and entrepreneur

Peters has divided his enterprise into four companies. Skunkworks, Inc., is the holding company; the other companies are the Palo Alto Consulting Center, a Center for Management Excellence, and Not Just Another Publishing Company.

Thomas J. Peters, co-author of the runaway bestseller *In Search of Excellence* and its sequel, *A Passion for Excellence,* believes corporate culture can determine whether or not a company ever achieves excellence. In an interview from his California-based Center for Management Excellence, Peters says a corporate culture that seeks excellence in performance starts with top management and how they treat their employees. "If you expect your people to treat your customers with courtesy, you must treat your employees with courtesy." Peters believes that a corporation that values its employees is the starting point for many good things. "Our simpleminded but not so simplistic approach is that there are only two ways to make money: treat your customers decently and innovate constantly. And you don't get superb service without people; therefore, the third leg of the stool is respect for the individual."

One example of a corporation that has achieved this kind of corporate culture is Publix Supermarkets, based in Lakeland, Florida. For decades Publix chairman George Jenkins instilled that philosophy in his company. Publix was one of the last supermarket chains to open for business on Sundays—a day that had been reserved for employees to spend with their families. In turn, that intense concern for employees led to a perceived caring about the customer, an attitude that propelled Publix to decades of growth and success in Florida.

Not all corporations have such a corporate climate, however. Some are ruled by fear, which stifles innovation—a factor Peters sees as crucial in today's competitive business environment. Other corporations accept mediocre output or fail to hold nonachievers accountable for their failing.

A leader who wants to improve his or her company's internal culture must realize, though, that there are no overnight turnarounds. "You can read our book and start tomorrow," Peters says. "But your employees will be appropriately skeptical. The only way to earn their respect is to demonstrate it day in and day out, particularly when times get rough. You will see strides in months, but it takes a dozen years to a lifetime to make it stick." There is no magic formula for changing a corporate culture. No policy manual will do the trick. "There is little doubt that anyone who wants to change the corporate culture has to remove some people, but you've got to go at it with the attitude that management has got talented people—they just haven't been led right," Peters says.

Get rid of the "one or two turkeys" that everybody agrees has to go, "but that's it." Otherwise the manager is looked at as a threat to the organization. "Wield a scalpel, not a pickax."

A true climate of excellence shows up most in the little things, the casual conversations down the hall. "You live it in the small stuff, not the big stuff. Start with senior management, then it's contagious."

equipment. Just tell them about the products, and let them make up their own minds about purchases. Don't worry about how many sales you get." Despite this official policy, however, employees may discover that raises and promotions are still based exclusively on sales figures. In that event, salespeople may realize that regardless of what they are told by management, they have little choice in practice but to continue to press hard for sales, perhaps even to the extent of misrepresenting their products, if they want to be rewarded by the store.

Even within a single industry, there are many cases of competing firms with opposing corporate cultures. Nowhere is this more dramatic than in the sports world. Some coaches, like the late Vince Lombardi of the Green Bay Packers, have run their teams almost like military units, insisting on a fanatical devotion to winning at almost any cost. Other managers, like Don Shula of the Miami Dolphins, have a looser, more person-oriented approach. Since both coaching styles have won championships, one can conclude that different approaches may work better for different people and organizations.

The work of Terence Deal and Allan Kennedy attempts take into account the complexities of the real business world. Deal and Kennedy argue that what is most important is not the particular type, but that a corporate culture is strong, coherent, and well suited to its goals. They make the point that in a company with a strong culture, beliefs and patterns lend support to the company's basic principles. According to Deal and Kennedy, "Many business problems occur because corporate cultures are weak. A company's culture may be based on contradictory principles that don't help employees understand what is expected of them or what will insure success in business."[12] They take the position that the guiding principles of successful companies can vary widely, although people in strong cultures normally consider their basic principles to be universal.

What a company must do, then, is to select the kind of corporate culture that will work best for it. The most difficult task, say Deal and Kennedy, is to change the corporate culture in the direction that executives have decided is advantageous: "Most meaningful change—for example, developing a market orientation or becoming more cost effective—involves cultural transformations."[13]

HOW TO CHANGE THE CORPORATE CULTURE

A firm may gradually develop an unhealthy corporate culture, which slowly drains away its vitality. A long time may elapse before people in the organization realize that there are serious problems with the old patterns of corporate culture. We will discuss the three major ways of reversing these trends: role modeling, positive reinforcement, and making employees feel important.

Role Modeling

One of the most effective means of changing the corporate culture is through *role modeling*. Managers must behave in such a way as to serve as a model for employees. If a manager at a large department store decides that his or her company needs to be more courteous and responsive to the public, then he or she must be courteous and responsive to his or her employees. The manager must be willing to listen to suggestions and complaints from subordinates. Even if he or she believes that some of the suggestions are poor ones, the manager should respond politely and indicate that he or she is genuinely interested in what they have to say. Many executives makes the mistake of saying they want to hear comments from workers and then go on to ignore every suggestion they receive; they may even tell the workers just how dumb their ideas really are.

> *"The executive who serves as a role model can be an effective agent of change in the corporate culture."*

The secret of good role modeling is to avoid falling into the situation of telling workers, "Don't do as I do, do as I say." If one wants employees to behave in a certain way, an executive must be prepared to do likewise. For example, if a PepsiCo executive tells subordinates that they ought to stay in good physical shape, then that executive ought to be in at least as good a shape as most of his or her employees.

Role modeling isn't limited only to face-to-face encounters with employees. Dee d'Arbeloff, president of Millipore, Inc., an industrial filter manufacturer, uses fifteen-minute videotapes to give talks to those employees he can't meet with regularly. Any executive of a large company who gives a speech to hundreds of his or her workers in an auditorium can use the occasion to convey important cultural signals to subordinates. If, for instance, he or she wishes to foster a corporate culture that is vigorous, the executive needs to present himself or herself as energetic and dynamic.

Positive Reinforcement

The main point about positive reinforcement is that management must reward (usually by promotions or salary increases) the behavior it seeks to encourage. When employees discover that management says one thing in its official policy, yet rewards something else, it creates cynicism among workers. They will then tend to distrust anything management tells them in the future. Many top executives make the mistake of informing employees that concentrating on long-term goals, such as developing better relations with customers or coming up with innovative ideas, is most important, and then they chiefly reward those workers who produce short-term gains. Such a policy is doomed to foster an unhealthy corporate culture.

Positive reinforcement need not be strictly financial. A member of top management may reward many employees effectively simply by thanking them, if not in person, then at least by sending them a note of appreciation. The few minutes required of the executive to notice subordinates' good work may be time that's spent very productively.

Make Employees Feel Important

Changing the corporate culture at a particular firm is essentially a matter of changing the behavior of the people who work for that corporation. Many of the same skills that a person needs to get along with people in other areas of life are also important in the supervisor-subordinate relationship. If a supervisor can convince subordinates that he or she truly values their contributions, he or she is at a great advantage in motivating them to change or improve. One way that a supervisor can emphasize employees' importance is by coaching and helping them to develop new skills. Many organizations have instituted career counseling and development programs for their employees. On the other hand, the supervisor or organization that denigrates employees' work or makes them feel that they could be easily replaced may have trouble getting cooperation from subordinates when changes are required.

What is most important for managers to remember about corporate culture is not any one particular rule or theory. Instead, a manager should train himself or herself to pay attention to how the corporate culture works (or fails to work) at the firm. Without an understanding of employees' beliefs and expectations, a manager may find it impossible to improve his or her company.

ON THE JOB
REVISISTED . . .

Ramon Perez was unaware of the wide differences in corporate culture between a waterbed factory and a public library. While his aggressiveness had been rewarded in his job as a waterbed salesman, the same quality was punished in library setting.

Perez can succeed at the library, however, if he studies the "rules of the game" and plays by them. On the other hand, he might find the organization's culture so alien to his basic personality that he may switch to a more congenial corporate culture.

SUMMARY

Every corporation develops its own distinctive culture that shapes the behavior of its employees. A healthy corporate culture encourages productivity, but a corporate culture that is too weak or too rigid can undermine a company's health and imperil its very existence.

Managers can expect to be most effective within a corporate culture whose value and beliefs they share. Cultural values will be expressed in such areas as dress codes and the use of status symbols. Corporate cultures vary widely in these areas, and scholars have created classification systems for corporate cultures. Some are based on the formal structure of the corporation, some on the methods of motivation, and some on the corporate beliefs and values.

The search goes on for the "best" corporate culture, and there seems to be as many theories as there are best-selling authors. The truth of the matter is that many different kinds of corporate culture can be effective, depending on the physical and economic environment and employees' acceptance of the culture. Corporate culture can be changed by the people who work for the corporation through role modeling, positive reinforcement, and a focus on the needs of employees.

HUMAN RELATIONS APPLICATIONS

Conclusion 1:   An appropriate corporate culture can be an invaluable asset in achieving organizational goals, while an inappropriate culture can lead to major difficulties.

Application: Good supervisors or employees should train themselves to observe how the corporate culture operates and how it is helping or hindering the organization.

Conclusion 2:   Unhealthy corporate cultures can be changed over a period of several years.

Application: Changing an organization's culture is a difficult task but one that can be done through role modeling, positive reinforcement of new corporate values, and active efforts to show employees that their contributions are important to the company.

DISCUSSION QUESTIONS

1. Describe what is meant by bureaupathology and discuss some of the major signs indicating that it exists.
2. Using Polczynski's six categories of status symbols, indicate what a highly successful executive might have in each category.

3. Compare and contrast the corporate cultures represented by IBM, PepsiCo, and J.C. Penney. Which one would you feel most comfortable working in and why?

4. According to Harrison, what are the four major organizational ideologies? Give an example of a company that would fit into each type.

5. What are the major characteristics of those American firms that Peters and Waterman describe as showing excellence in how they are managed?

NOTES

1. Howard Schwartz and Stanley M. Davis, "Matching Corporate Culture and Business Strategy," *Organizational Dynamics* (Summer 1981), p. 31.

2. Robert C. Wood, "Rituals and Stories, Heroes and Priests," *Inc.* (December 1982), p. 105.

3. Richard Hodgson, "Organizational Bureaupathy and How to Cure It," *The Business Quarterly* (Autumn 1979), p. 5.

4. *Ibid.*, p. 7.

5. Walter Kiechel III, "The Managerial Dress Code," *Fortune* (April 1983), p. 194.

6. *Ibid.*, p. 193.

7. James J. Polczynski, "Status Symbols: Signs on the Road to Success," *Management World* (July 1982), p. 29.

8. Edwin L. Baker, "Managing Organizational Culture," *Management Review (July 1980), p. 8.*

9. Roger Harrison, "Understanding Your Organization's Character," *Harvard Business Review* (May–June 1972), pp. 119–128.

10. Lawrence M. Miller, "Managing the New Corporate Culture," *National Underwriter* (September 3, 1983), p. 28.

11. Thomas J. Peters and Robert H. Waterman, *In Search of Excellence.* New York: Harper & Row, 1982. See also Thomas J. Peters and Nancy Austin, *A Passion for Excellence: The Leadership Difference.* (New York: Random House, 1985).

12. Terence E. Deal and Allan A. Kennedy, *Corporate Cultures: The Rites and Rituals of Corporate Life.* Reading MA: Addison-Wesley, 1982.

13. *Ibid.*

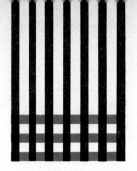

SOCIAL RESPONSIBILITY AND THE ORGANIZATION

CHAPTER 16

ON THE JOB . . .

WHAT DOES A BUSINESS OWE THE COMMUNITY?

DEFINING SOCIAL RESPONSIBILITY

PURSUING PURELY ECONOMIC GOALS

THE CASE FOR THE SEPARATION OF BUSINESS
   AND SOCIAL WELFARE

THE PRAGMATIC APPROACH TO SOCIAL RESPONSIBILITY

   Can Companies Be Both Socially Responsible and Profitable?
   Deregulation and Social Responsibility
   How Can Social Responsibility Be Measured?

AN ACTIVIST VIEW OF CORPORATE RESPONSIBILITY

SOCIAL RESPONSIBILITY AND PEOPLE IN THE ORGANIZATION

ON THE JOB REVISITED . . .

SUMMARY

HUMAN RELATIONS APPLICATIONS

DISCUSSION QUESTIONS

NOTES

MANAGERIAL DIALOGUE: James W. McLamore

ON THE JOB . . .

Andrea Andrews, new director of community relations at Amalgamated Chemical, faced a dilemma. Three months ago, Amalgamated Chemical had hired Andrews to improve its public image. The New Jersey pesticide manufacturer had been criticized for several years by environmental groups and local TV commentators who pointed out that birds and fish were dying in great numbers downstream from the chemical plant. Then a report discovered that residents of the city where the plant was located had a significantly higher rate of liver cancer than the rest of the state. Editorials in a dozen papers called for the shutdown of Amalgamated Chemical until health officials determined whether the plant's residues were causing the cancer.

Andrews, a veteran public relations professional, worked with a companywide task force to determine how Amalgamated could weather the storm. The task force, which included Amalgamated's chief executive officer, marketing director, plant manager, and staff official, came up with three widely different courses of action:

1. Amalgamated could make a large pledge to the American Cancer Society, reap the favorable publicity, and then take its time sending in the actual donation. This was the alternative favored by the marketing director.

2. Amalgamated could assemble a handpicked team of cancer experts and researchers to examine the liver cancer data. Their mission would be to deny the suggested link between the disease and Amalgamated's plant. The plant manager favored this idea.

3. Amalgamated could "tough it out." With press releases providing information about the number of people the plant employed and the total value of its economic contributions to the community, the company would issue an implicit threat: unless the criticism stopped, it would close the plant and move operations to the Sunbelt. The chief executive officer liked this idea a lot.

If you were Andrews, what would you do?

WHAT DOES A BUSINESS OWE
THE COMMUNITY?

As the twentieth century draws to a close, what do most people view as the obligations of business organizations to the society at large? Should a corporation do nothing more than try to create the best life for its owners and employees by maximizing profits and wages, or does a corporation have a responsibility to the community in which it is located and to the nation as a whole? Are these dual concerns in conflict, or can an organization successfully deal with both?

The question of social responsibility often varies with the type of organization discussed. A hospital, for instance, may be privately owned and profit-generating, but the community is likely to believe it still has a social responsibility to treat sick people whether or not they can pay the full rates. Yet no one expects Macy's to allow poor people to have winter coats whether or not they can pay the full price. What is the essential difference?

Other questions arise when it comes to philanthropic activities of profit-seeking corporations. Why should a paint manufacturing company help a "little theater" group in the community? What benefit does a major oil refiner gain by offering college scholarships to lower-class high school students? Are such corporate philanthropies truly social responsibilities, or are they an irresponsible squandering of profits that should go to the workers who created them and to the company stockholders? This chapter will deal with the role of profit-seeking organizations in our society and questions such as:

What is the argument against corporate responsibility for improving social conditions?

How does the public think organizations are behaving toward the questions of social responsibility?

Why do conservative economists cringe at awards to business organizations for contributions to the arts?

Why is the doctrine of "enlightened self-interest" gaining credence among corporate executives?

How can an organization's degree of social commitment be empirically measured?

How does an organization relate social responsibility to the interaction of its own co-workers?

DEFINING SOCIAL RESPONSIBILITY

■■■■■■■■■■■■■■■■■■■■

"We don't all mean the same thing when we talk about the 'good life.' "

What does it mean for a corporation to be socially responsible? One business publication asserts that since business functions by public consent, its basic ethic must be "to serve constructively the need of society—to the satisfaction of society."[1] This interpretation implies that when society shifts its needs or satisfactions—say, from a desire for one car per family member to a yearning for clean air and bicycle trails across the city—business should respond. But does this require a moral commitment, or does it merely describe the mechanism of a marketplace?

In the past, most people agreed that businesses met their social obligations by producing a supply of both necessities and luxuries in goods and services, by providing jobs and hence purchasing power, and by being the primary creator of most of the wealth of the nation. If "the good life" is defined in materialistic terms, then it would appear that American business has indeed met its responsibilities. Real disposable income has more than tripled per person over the last eighty years, while work time has declined by a third. Business has also provided pecuniary benefits to over 30,000,000 Americans who hold stocks and to some 100,000,000 people who have life insurance policies, mutual fund shares, and pensions. Growth in business translates directly into appreciation of increase in their personal fortunes. As the Committee for Economic Development stated in 1971:

> *Business has carried out its basic economic responsibilities to society so well largely because of the dynamic workings of the private enterprise system. The profit-and-loss discipline continually spurs businessmen to improve goods and services, to reduce costs, and to attract more customers. By earning profit through serving people better than their competitors, successful business concerns have been able to contribute importantly—through taxes and donations—to the financial support of public and private organizations working to improve the quality of life. By operating efficiently, business concerns have been able to provide people with both the means and the leisure to enjoy a better life.*[2]

Undoubtedly, a better life is the general goal of every human being. But what makes a given person's life better? Isn't it possible that, once a satisfactory standard of economic security is achieved, the things that make life "better" will be defined in terms beyond the strictly monetary?

Over the last fifteen or so years, American society has become increasingly vocal about new priorities. As more and more people have enough living space, cars, appliances, clothes, and trips to satisfy them, they are remembering the large number of people in the world who don't have even minimal necessities. Moreover, life with traffic jams, gray air, mud-colored water, and stripped mountains does not look so good. Fundamental changes are taking place in certain social attitudes, with greater emphasis going toward human rather than economic values. Ecologists now challenge economists; health is becoming a goal as important as wealth. We are learning new ways of thinking about what makes both individual and societal life "better."

Current expectations seem to be for a high level of social responsibility from corporations. For example, when federal programs in many areas were cut back in the mid-1980s, President Reagan urged individuals, states, and especially businesspeople to pick up the slack. With social improvement programs losing an estimated $33 billion, a federal study estimated that businesses would have to increase their corporate donation to 15 percent, instead of the historic 1 percent of pretax earnings.[3]

The Reagan administration's admonitions to American business are but the latest reflections of a decades-long trend of expecting business to respond to the community's desire for a better quality life, including such features as good health care and the elimination of poverty; equal opportunity for individual self-fulfillment, regardless of race or sex; training and education for full and rewarding participation in modern society; career opportunities and jobs in all sectors of society; communities with decent housing, safe streets, efficient transportation, clean environment, cultural and educational opportunities; and mutual respect and civility among people.

A 1970 study by Opinion Research Corporation revealed that about 60 percent of the electorate consider it a primary responsibility of business to keep the environment free of pollution, 38 percent believe that corporations should take responsibility for training and hiring racial minorities, 46 percent feel that corporations should make massive financial contributions to support public education, health, and charities, and 29 percent would like to see corporations cooperate in cleaning up and rebuilding inner-city ghettos. Yet many corporate leaders disagree with these views. A three-year study in the 1980s found that only 14 percent of top executives and 15 percent of middle management think their companies place much importance on improving the quality of life.[4] This conflicting set of expectations compels a greater awareness of broad social problems on the part of the corporate employees.

The question of corporate social responsibility then grows out of a background of societal values that have gradually shifted from simple economic well-being of the individual to complex total society and environmental well-being. But the answer to the question of how a corporation best fulfills its social responsibility is not simple. Moreover, there are different schools of thought about what a corporation must do to meet its responsibilities. Three of these approaches are shown in Figure 16.1.

1. Traditional View of Business Responsibility

Example 1: If a manager makes a decision to invest in a new product line, his or her only concern is whether the new product line is profitable.

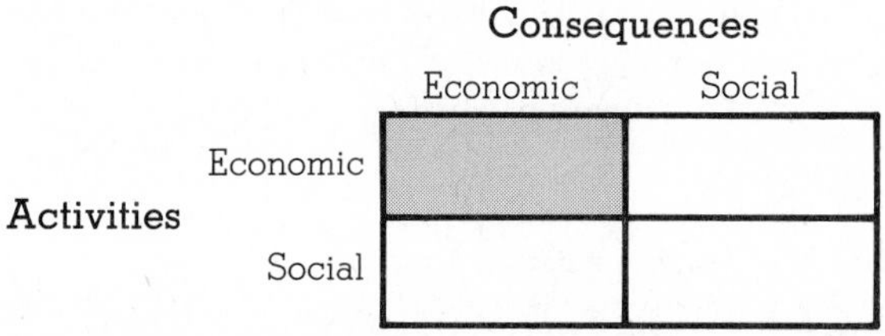

2. Philanthropic View of Business Responsibility

Example 2: If a firm gives monetary contributions to the United Way campaign (a social activity), it is concerned that these contributions have the intended social impact and consequences.

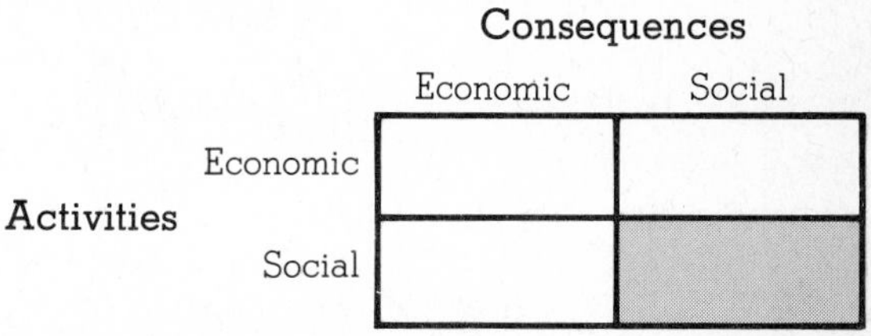

3. Contemporary View of Business Responsibility

Example 3: Business is attentive to the social consequences (e.g., pollution, discrimination, unsafe products) of its economic activities. In short, business is creating negative side effects that must be prevented or ameliorated.

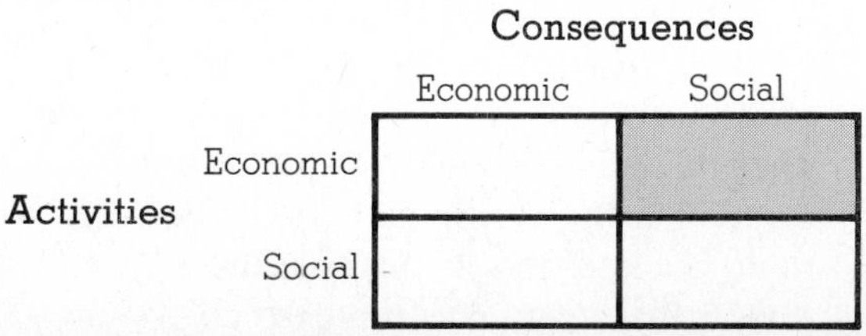

FIGURE 16.1   Business Responsibility: Three Approaches

Source: James J. Chrisman and Archie B. Carroll, "Sloan Management Review's Forum: Corporate Responsibility—Reconciling Economic and Social Goals," Sloan Management Review (Winter 1984), pp. 60–61.

PURSUING PURELY ECONOMIC GOALS

"Some theorists believe that the money businesses spend on social programs is stolen from stockholders."

A strong argument can be made that corporations have no right to be philanthropic. Milton Friedman and other neoclassic economists hold that a business organization's basic responsibility is to its stockholders—to maximize profits for their benefit. Money spent in social programs is not only wrongly stolen from them but also may result in economic inefficiencies. For instance, a machinist hired solely because he is a member of a minority group could ruin thousands of dollars of parts and hold up an entire assembly schedule.

A similar argument asserts that before a business can seek social goals, it must first be economically productive. Successful business involvement in social issues cannot be realized independently from high performance in terms of profits. In other words, corporations should not necessarily eschew all social contributions, but it is impossible for business to finance even the smallest such moves without, first and foremost, being profitable.

THE CASE FOR THE SEPARATION OF BUSINESS AND SOCIAL WELFARE

The Friedman position is the most emphatic statement of the separation of business and social welfare. Friedman believes that once society has established a framework of laws, "rules of the game" that punish fraud or deception and promote open and free competition, it is the duty of business only to use its resources to increase profits. The sole social responsibility of business is to stay within the rules of the game. In fact, Friedman seems to believe that society has more of a responsibility to business than business has to society.

Friedman's next argument is that if the powerful people who run big corporations begin to decide what they should do for society, they will undermine everyone's freedom. He poses a question: If businesspeople do have a social responsibility other than to make as much money for their stockholders as possible, how shall they determine what it is? He doubts that tough corporate executives are suited to being moral arbiters for society.

Even if they are, Friedman continues, they have no right to make their stockholders serve the social interest. Spending company profits (which might be returned to the shareholders as dividends or used to raise the value of the company's stock by being invested in capital improvements) is equivalent to taxing the shareholders. He asks, "Is it tolerable that these public functions of taxation, expenditure, and control be exercised by the people who happen at the moment to be in charge of particular enterprises, chosen for those parts by strictly private groups."[5] He calls a policy that encourages corporations to make contributions for social purposes by allowing deductions for tax purposes a step in the direction of separating ownership and control of business, as well as undermining the basic nature and character of our society. It is a step away from an individualistic society and toward the corporate state.

Friedman calls corporate spending of profits for social purposes reprehensible, not only because of the dangers to a free democratic system, but also because many stockholders desperately need the dividend income. An elderly woman whose dividends do not keep up with inflation may find she is unable to afford a comfortable nursing home, while money that could have been paid out in dividends goes instead to support a local art museum. Other theorists have criticized corporate programs designed to hire and train minorities. Since trainees usually are paid more than they are actually worth in terms of their productive capacities, such programs are unfair to experienced employees, who are not rewarded for their greater productivity. In addition, the inefficiency pushes prices up, thereby decreasing sales and adversely affecting the company's profitability.

It has also been pointed out that measures taken by corporations to prevent pollution can cut deeply into corporate profits. For example, General Motors, which generally earns close to 20 percent on its net worth, made only 15.2 percent during the five-year period from 1967 to 1971, when General Motors made major antipollution investments. (See Table 16.1.)

TABLE 16.1 Year-End Statistics for General Motors Corporation		
Income Category	Net Income Before Taxes	Net Income After Taxes
1966	$3,270,791,691	$1,793,391,691
1967	3,013,376,076	1,627,276,076
1968	3,524,814,777	1,731,914,777
1969	3,453,995,164	1,710,695,164
1970[a]	778,486,848	609,086,848
1971	3,719,809,493	1,935,709,493
1972	4,222,606,765	2,162,806,765

[a]During 1970, operations were affected by a nine-week strike.

Source: *Moody's Industrial Manual*. New York: Moody's Investors Service, 1973, Vol. 1 A–1.

THE PRAGMATIC APPROACH TO SOCIAL RESPONSIBILITY

Another point of view sees the corporation as a permanent and powerful institution in society. Like other institutions, large corporations operate within intricate networks of obligation—to employees, stockholders, suppliers, customers and consumers, community neighbors, and government. The larger the organization, the greater its power, and sooner or later society will demand accountability for that power.

Modern businesspeople are prepared to act within the framework of laws that require advertising honestly, treating employees fairly, and so on. Moreover, they are often enlightened enough to trade off short-run profits against qualitative improvements in the organization that contribute to long-run profit growth. They do this because they understand that the corporation functions in the whole of society, not only the marketplace. Yet a manager is still rated by how well he or she maintains steady earnings improvement while making increasingly sophisticated, even subtle trade-offs to enhance his or her company's public image.

The doctrine of enlightened self-interest contains negative and positive aspects. On the one hand, a company that invests in its local area's educational, medical, and cultural assets may well be able to attract workers with superior skills who would not move to a sterile or inconvenient suburb. High technology workers want their children to have better-than-average schooling; they value a lively recreational and cultural scene. A business forced to operate in an ugly and dangerous urban area may find that it makes economic sense to put some of its revenue into housing rehabilitation, day care centers, and drug clinics. In the broadest sense, good neighbors make good consumers.

> "A business that acts like a good citizen may be trying to prevent government intervention."

On the other hand, what many corporate executives may really be trying to do is prevent government intervention. The role of government in guiding, if not actually forcing corporations toward acting for the good of society started in 1935. Adam Smith's "unseen hand" began to become visible when an amendment to the Internal Revenue Code permitted corporations to deduct up to 5 percent of pre-tax income for charitable contributions. In a landmark case in 1953, the New Jersey Superior Court held that it was not merely a right, but a duty of businesses to support higher education (in this case, Princeton University) in the interest of the long-term welfare of the company's stockholders, because a corporation could not possibly operate efficiently in a malfunctioning society.

It is also true that the definition of *stockholder* has changed over the years. Friedman's view seems based on an individual stockholder whose investment is limited to a few carefully chosen companies. But nowadays, most investors hold equities in many companies. A huge proportion of investment is done through pension trust, insurance companies, mutual funds, and so on, which means that stockholders' interests ride with the corporate sector as a whole, rather than with any specific company.

Can Companies Be Both Socially Responsible and Profitable?

During the 1970s, four social responsibility funds were founded based on the philosophy that businesses could be both socially responsible and profitable. Analysts for the Third Century Fund made investments only in companies with the highest record of pollution control, product purity and safety, and minority relations. The Pax World Fund provided religious groups with an investment plan that enabled them to avoid holdings in firms that profited from the Vietnam War. The Social Dimensions Fund used the research services of the Council on Economic Priorities to invest in firms with priorities of pollution control, product quality, and equal opportunity hiring. First Spectrum Fund took a slightly different approach, rewarding by investing in those companies willing to adopt socially responsible policies. One of the members of the First Spectrum group answered the Friedman argument against such tampering with the free market system this way:

> *Our fund's basic assumption is that for this decade the companies that are the most enlightened in dealing with their social problems will, in fact, be the most profitable, too. Enlightened management is a sign of good management and good management usually means profits.*[6]

But that investing attitude vanished during the recession of the early 1980s, and such funds took a nose dive. No longer did investors care what products a company manufactured or what its policies on hiring were. Instead, stock market analysts, financiers, and investors tried to find companies that could hold their own during the economic downturn. Thus, the stock market's concern with social responsibility appears to depend on the business cycle—a luxury item to be considered during good times and jettisoned during a recession.

Corporations also adapted to the changing economic climate. Programs to help transferred employees find affordable housing at their new location quietly disappeared. Minority hiring and affirmative action became secondary to the question of avoiding layoffs. Donations to the arts and social programs fell off across the country. This experience seems to lend support to Friedman's arguments that there is an inherent conflict between the obligation to be a profitable company and the obligation to be responsive to the community needs.

Yet for many companies, the two objectives go hand in hand. One such company is Burger King, founded by James McLamore, the subject of the Managerial Dialogue on pages 414–415. Another case in point is the Campbell Soup Company. "Good citizenship is vital to corporate success, and basically it's demonstrated in two ways," said retired president and chief executive officer, William B. Murphy.

> *First, the company must treat its employees fairly. Second, it must participate in the life of the community through such activities as hospital drives, community chest, youth programs—the opportunities are as diverse as our nation itself.*[7]

Campbell's commitment to its community, the blighted city of Camden, New Jersey, went far beyond rhetoric. During the 1960s and 1970s, the

Managerial Dialogue   *"Being a good social citizen is essential."*

James W. McLamore, director, co-founder, and chairman emeritus of the Burger King Corporation

For James McLamore, founder of Burger King, social responsibility and corporate profits go hand in hand. "Being a good social citizen is essential," McLamore emphasizes. "And the benefit to you and your business is substantial. What's good for the company is good for the community." McLamore, who opened the first Burger King is 1954 (a year before Ray Kroc founded McDonald's), has an impressive string of civic and professional accomplishments to match his words: national restauranteur of the year in 1979; Boy Scouts of America good scout award in 1975; Junior Achievement hall of fame in 1978; United Way campaign chairman in 1974; American Heart Association campaign chairman in 1970; Chairman of the board of a major university in 1980. "I have always in my business career—and that goes back to when I was 21 and opened my first restaurant—gotten involved in community affairs. Understanding the environment has given a tremendous advantage to me personally."

Early in his restaurant career, before the days of Burger King, McLamore got involved with his area's fledgling restaurant association. "It was invigorating and enriching—and fun. I wouldn't have gotten that experi-

McLamore serves as a director on various boards: the Pillsbury Company, Southeast Banking Corp., Ryder System Inc., Storer Communications, and the National Restaurant Association.

ence inside my head," McLamore says. "I have no doubt that the perspective they gave me contributed to my success. I recommend industry participation to all the young fellows."

One of McLamore's proudest examples of corporate social responsibility is Burger King's program to allow minorities to open their own restaurant franchises. "Long before it was stylish to consider helping black minorities, I initiated a model minority franchise program in the late 1960s. I felt at the time that even though it was a high-risk situation—they didn't have equity capital—that it was important to bring minorities in. Ours may be one of the oldest minority franchise programs in the country."

McLamore thinks it somewhat ironic that Burger King became a target in 1984 of the Reverend Jesse Jackson and Operation Push's campaign to hire more minority workers. Jackson was "a tough negotiator with his boycott threats. I don't think we had to do as much as we did. I'm very proud of what we did." The present management of Burger King has given considerable emphasis to the hiring of minority employees, McLamore adds.

While Burger King's size and visibility may have made it a target for Jackson, it also allowed McLamore to take the lead in civic activities. Burger King has been a leader in giving to social and cultural causes. A newspaper survey of major corporations in South Florida in 1984 found Burger King's $4,000,000 in contributions twice that of any other corporation giver. McLamore headed that regional United Way campaign in 1974. "Because Burger King Corporation is very visible, it attracted the attention of many smaller businessmen. If you have size and position, you have to be wise to use that power—that's leadership." McLamore has traveled a great deal in his business career, leaving him little time for Rotary, Kiwanis, or other service clubs, but he firmly believes that businesspeople need to expand their horizons. "I know too many businesspeople who are so myopic. They never leave the desk or factory. There's a big world out there that impacts on them and their company. Unless you're out there, you don't really sense what is happening." Being an advocate, a joiner, helped McLamore develop his marketing sense. "I'm a believer in the old Christian virtue that if you cast bread on the waters, you get a lot in return. I found it paid high dividends. It has enabled me to envision how I should change the environment of the company and avail myself of marketing sense." But McLamroe believes his sense of social responsibility was not fueled simply by the fact that he was in the restaurant business, a service industry. All corporations share similar concerns. "If business people in this world don't have a sense of the world—and other institutions—then they can't make sense of their own institution. Businesspeople are viewed as leaders. They have the stature and responsibility that go along with it. They *must* concern themselves with the best interest of the community. I have no use for businessmen who are so selfish that they don't strive to contribute to their community."

company spent more than $6,000,000 to help improve the city through programs such as park construction, summer youth job programs, urban housing, and financial aid to minority-owned businesses. "We know that if your enterprise is to prosper over the long term, it must have a favorable environment," Murphy said. "This means, of course, that we must help solve the community's pressing social and economic problems because we are affected by those problems."[8]

Another approach to social responsibility was taken by American Express in the early 1980s. American Express makes a donation to a designated "local cause" each time its famous credit card or traveler's check is used in that particular area. The Atlanta Arts Alliance, for example, receives $0.05 each time the card or traveler's check is used, $2.00 for each new card issued, and $5.00 each time travel arrangements valued at more than $500 are made in a fifteen-county area surrounding Atlanta. In 1982, American Express began a new customer information service called *Consumer Cards*. These brochures carry no advertising messages but contain information on credit rights and mail order rights—both areas of keen interest to American Express. It is hoped that such programs will benefit not only the public but also American Express, by establishing an image of the kind of consumer-sensitive company many consumers want to patronize.

Deregulation and Social Responsibility

During the 1970s and 1980s, the federal government moved broadly to deregulate a number of basic industries—communication, transportation, and financial services. The goal was a return to free market conditions in which the strongest, best managed companies would survive. Although the results of deregulation may be beneficial in the long run, in the short run companies use resources that once went toward meeting social responsibilities to help them battle their new competition.

The Federal Communications Commission (FCC) formerly exerted broad authority over the nation's television and radio stations. When it came time to renew its license, each station had to list the socially responsible activities it had performed. On occasion, the FCC would strip the station's license and award it to a minority group or other party that demonstrated its ability to use the public airwaves for greater public good. The FCC now takes a more limited view of its authority. Television stations may broadcast political debates in which some candidates are excluded without worrying about the FCC's once powerful "fairness doctrine." Radio stations that once carried newscasts every half hour to satisfy FCC demands for community service now play nothing but music

"Thanks to deregulation, money that some businesses used to spend on social programs now goes to fighting the competition in the marketplace."

twenty-four hours a day. It's a different environment—one in which broadcasters worry more about competition and less about social responsibility.

Deregulation in the airline industry has created new airlines and cut-rate fares. Thanks to the pressures of competition for the most profitable routes, a city away from an airline's hub system—such as Bakersfield, California, or Jacksonville, Florida—may find its major air carrier suddenly reducing flights or pulling out altogether, to the detriment of area residents.

Financial institutions once offered the same basic services to rich and poor alike: passbook savings. Banks offered checking accounts and commercial loans, while savings and loans lent home mortgage money. It's not that simple anymore. As the financial services industry emerges from its regulatory era, banks and savings and loans find themselves competing with stock brokerage firms, money market funds, venture capitalists, and even retailers like K mart and Sears. There is intense competition for savings dollars and for the making of consumer and commercial loans, and customers are finding that in this new era, it is better to be rich than poor.

Customers with $100,000 or more to invest are being courted by "private" bankers and the best financial advisers. The poor, on the other hand, must pay higher service charges on their checking accounts and may get no interest at all on small-balance savings accounts. The trend toward electronic banking services—the convenience of banking from the home or office—is useful only to the middle and upper classes, as only they can afford the computer. Automatic twenty-four-hour tellers are located only in prosperous neighborhoods, never in poor ones.

The contrast between regulated and deregulated industries is perhaps most clearly shown by the utility industry. A recent study on corporate planning shows that utilities are probably the leading industry in forecasting emerging social and political trends and in bringing those social issues to management's attention.[9] Why are utilities so concerned about their surrounding social environment? They exist in a regulated environment in which political whims and social trends determine the price of their services and the profits of their shareholders. An extreme example occurred in Miami in 1982 when Dade County commissioners voted to require Southern Bell maintenance and repair crews to add a "manhole watcher" to make sure that no unsuspecting citizen fell into an open manhole. The Southern Bell accounting department determined that the cost to the company of this regulation was 11 cents per customer each month—a figure that was added to each customer's monthly phone charge.

How Can Social Responsibility Be Measured?

In the Southern Bell case, the cost of social responsibility was measured exactly—11 cents a month—but measurement is often difficult. One method for measuring social responsibility was developed by David Bronheim for the Third Century Fund. To measure a company's ecological impact, his staff evaluates the effects of each stage of its operation: extraction, manufacturing, transportation, and whatever stages of operation are appropriate. Each phase of production is then ranked on a twelve-point scale. With regard to discriminatory hiring practices, companies are graded on the percentages of Indians, blacks, or Hispanic workers employed relative to the size of those minority groups in the company's geographical area and on the numbers of minority group members and women in managerial positions. Of course, a high rating on social responsibility does not necessarily make a company a good investment from a financial point of view.

A more detailed and technical approach to measuring social responsibility uses standard accounting procedures. The Corporate Social Audit, developed in 1972, is a four-step program for social auditing. It inventories activities with a social impact, explains the circumstances that led to the adoption of the activities, evaluates the activities, and then assesses the way they fit into broad corporate as well as social goals. An example of a social balance sheet can be seen in Table 16.2.

The audit, with its dollar figures certified by authorities external to the company, appeals particularly to businesspeople and managers who have a highly developed cost-benefit sense. The attempt to measure the

TABLE 16.2　How One Company Measures Its Social Contributions

Abt Associates, Inc. Social Balance Sheet
Year ended December 31, 1983 with comparative figures for 1984

Social Assets Available

Staff	1984	1983
Available within one year	$ 2,594,390	$ 2,312,000
Available after one year	6,368,511	5,821,608
Training investment	507,405	305,889
	9,470,306	8,439,497
Less accumulated training obsolescence	136,995	60,523
Total staff assets	9,333,311	8,378,974

TABLE 16.2   *(continued)*

Organization		
Social capital investment	$ 1,398,230	$ 1,272,201
Retained earnings	219,136	—
Land	285,376	293,358
Buildings at cost	334,321	350,188
Equipment at cost	43,018	17,102
Total organization assets	2,280,081	1,932,849
Research		
Proposals	26,878	150,090
Child care research	6,629	—
Social audit	12,979	—
Total research	46,486	15,090
Public services consumed net of tax		
payments	152,847	243,399
Total social assets available	11,812,725	10,570,312
Social Commitments, Obligations, and Equity		
Staff		
Committed to contracts within one year	43,263	81,296
Committed to contracts after one year	114,660	215,459
Committed to administration within		
one year	62,598	56,915
Committed to administration after		
one year	165,903	150,842
Total staff committments	386,424	504,512
Organization	1987	1986
Working capital requirements	60,000	58,500
Financial deficit	—	26,814
Facilities and equipment committed to		
contracts and administration	37,734	36,729
Total organization commitments	97,734	122,043
Environmental		
Government outlays for public services		
consumed, net of tax payments	$ 152,847	$ 243,399
Pollution from paper production	1,770	770
Pollution from electric power production	2,200	1,080
Pollution from automobile commuting	10,493	4,333
Total environmental obligations	167,310	249,582
Total commitments and obligations	651,468	876,137
Society's equity		
Contributed by staff	8,946,837	7,874,462
Contributed by stockholders	2,182,347	1,810,806
Generated by operations	32,023	8,907
Total equity	11,161,257	9,694,175
Total commitments, obligations, and equity	$11,812,725	$10,570,312

impact of a corporation's social programs in terms of costs, benefits, performance, or even profits gives managers a way to make decisions in this area.

AN ACTIVIST VIEW OF CORPORATE RESPONSIBILITY

A number of economists, social scientists, philosophers, and citizens take an activist view of corporate duty. While Friedman fears the shift of social power from the elected government to private corporation, John K. Galbraith has praised the new industrial state, which he believes already exists. The view of Galbraith and others of like mind is that it is precisely the size and power of large corporations, coupled with their generally wide profit margin, that gives them not only the capability but the obligation to assume wide-ranging social responsibility. This activist philosophy differs from both of Friedman's arguments that the corporation has no overriding civic duty and the pragmatists' belief that civic duties should be undertaken only when they contribute to corporate ends. This position holds that it is the duty of businesses to use their power to promote moral and social goals.

"Activists say that businesses, like people, have an obligation to the community in which they function."

One of the most important areas of social responsibility for the business organization is minority hiring. The proponents of corporate responsibility point to the disadvantages for all of society caused by economics of discrimination. Discrimination maintains higher salaries for white men; thus, they are paid more than they should be, and those higher wages are passed along to consumers in the form of higher prices. Moreover, the low salaries paid to minorities (and the scarcity of job opportunities) make them virtually unable to participate in the economy except as a drain (welfare checks). Those who have studied "the economics of discrimination" conclude that the costs of such a policy include a rise in consumer prices, reduction in productive output, decrease in the return on (white, predominantly male) capital, and tax increases.

How do those who take an activist's view of corporate duty answer Friedman's charge that they are not only depriving shareholders of the individual freedom to spend "their" money as they wish, but also are acting as unelected rulers of us all? They point out that our elected government does determine the nation's goals and priorities. Passage of laws (equal employment, open housing) and creation of agencies (Environmental Protection Agency, Equal Employment Opportunities Commission) are the expression and manifestation of those objectives. They can be achieved, however, only through massive cooperative efforts of all our institutions, including business—the so-called private sector. The fact that the government has allowed tax advantages to the public good means that it is the will of the people that the private sector should be involved in public policy.

SOCIAL RESPONSIBILITY AND PEOPLE IN THE ORGANIZATION

A major aspect of corporate social responsibility is the probable effects upon members of the organization themselves. On the one hand, if profit maximization is subordinated to social goals, employees may be concerned that they will suffer economically. On the other hand, employees of corporations are part of the general public and share in the benefits. There is no good reason to believe that employees' needs and social goals are mutually exclusive.

Aggressively hiring minority employees and establishing nondiscriminatory policies toward female employees are two ways in which organizations may practice social responsibility in their own backyards. A fast food chain that hires large numbers of teenage workers might make regular contributions to high school vocational education programs. The newspaper industry has been active in fighting illiteracy and sponsoring current events programs for elementary school students. Packagers of beer and soft drinks, recognizing that their containers wind up as litter, have pledged considerable resources to cleaning up the environment. Liquor companies actively promote safe driving campaigns. These are just some of the ways organizations have found to involve their members in constructive social projects.

The image that an organization presents to the public has a lot to do with the way its employees perceive their jobs and personal contributions. Corporations vary widely in their desire to present a public-spirited appearance. Some organizations express little interest in social service. Conversely, Mobil Oil has earned a public reputation as an enlightened, progressive corporation. This is reflected in Mobil's long-running advertising campaign for highway safety, which carried the tag line, "We

"A business that doesn't prosper won't make a social contribution."

want you to live." The degree to which an organization gets involved with social goals also helps to determine the kinds of employees it will attract.

Finally, a corporation's involvement in the problems of society depends upon its leadership. The importance of top management's commitment to civic goals was stressed by Carl Gerstacker, chairman of Dow Chemical during the 1970s when the company's military-oriented products were under attack. A decade later, Dow executives said they recognized the importance of the climate within an organization in achieving social responsibility in the outside world. Gerstacker outlined the following principles:

1. Social responsibility must be a firm, deep-seated belief of management. It must start with top management and continue down.

2. Management must be consistent in its support of social responsibility. When times get tough, the tough keep giving.

3. Social responsibility programs must be a long-term commitment. One doesn't give to the United Way one year and not the next.

4. Management cannot preach one thing and do another. A corporation that disregards this policy may create a credibility gap.

5. Always frame your approach in terms of the carrot, not the stick. You must change people's minds and convince them of the desirability of social responsibility.

Gerstacker concluded:

> *The business community's efforts to solve social problems must be integrated with long-term profit growth. If done properly, solving social problems is both good business and good citizenship, for those two goals are wholly compatible.* [10]

ON THE JOB REVISITED . . .

Andrea Andrews was in a difficult situation. She could propose an image-building campaign with the American Cancer Society, knowing that her superiors would immediately sabotage any actual donations; or she could order a fraudulent clean bill of health from a team of experts who would do no investigating; or she could deny that Amalgamated Chemical had any social responsibility to its community beyond providing jobs and wages.

Andrews knew the company's top management had no interest in public relations, community donations, or social responsibility. She resigned from Amalgamated the next day and was soon offered a job by the Bipartisan Commission on Social Responsibility.

SUMMARY

There has always been debate over the social responsibility of business organizations. Traditionally, American businesspeople have discharged this responsibility by supplying necessities and luxuries, by providing jobs and hence purchasing power, and by being the primary source of most national wealth. But fundamental changes in national priorities have taken place. Ecology has stolen much attention from economics, health is surpassing wealth as a goal, and new factors account for what makes individual and society life worthwhile. The goals of business are now the subject of new controversy.

Classical economists like Milton Friedman argue that the only real social responsibility of corporate officials is to make as much money for their stockholders as possible. Pragmatic managers often take a second point of view known as enlightened self-interest, seeking profits inextricably tied to a healthy society. This point of view has found more favor since the Reagan administration's moves to scale down federal funding for social programs, coupled with the deregulation of many basic industries.

Some business observers feel that organizations can be both profitable and responsible, such as investment firms that invest only in companies that have exhibited social responsibility. Other critics feel that the philosophy is wrong and that business has a responsibility to take an active role toward solving society's problems. John Kenneth Galbraith believes that the sheer size, power, and profitability of large corporations incur obligations in the public interest. In this view, corporations have a responsibility to raise the quality of life in the social environment, regardless of profitability.

These three approaches may be summed up in the following manner: (1) the requirements of business are only to compete fairly and maximize profits; (2) business should maximize profits, but take a more responsible view of the best way to do so; and (3) business should use its power and resources to promote social ends.

HUMAN RELATIONS APPLICATIONS

Conclusion 1:   Friedman and other economists argue that an organization's major responsibility is to its stockholders, not to society at large.

Application: According to this view, business should not spend profits to improve societal conditions. It is the duty of business only to use its resources to increase stockholders' returns on their investments.

Conclusion 2:   The pragmatic approach to social responsibility views organizations as intricately interwoven with the society in which it operates.

Application: According to this view, organizations may trade off short-term profits against qualitative improvements in the organization and community at hand in order to foster long-term profitability.

Conclusion 3:   The activist approach concerning social responsibility stresses the obligation of organizations to help solve society's problems.

Application: According to this view, organizations should take leadership roles in alleviating discrimination, wage inequities, pollution problems, and so on by clearing up their own backyards first and then helping the rest of society clean theirs.

DISCUSSION QUESTIONS

1. What is the doctrine of enlightened self-interest and how does it relate to social responsibility?
2. How can we measure the extent to which a company displays social awareness and responsibility?
3. According to Gerstacker, what principles should a company follow to become more socially responsive?

NOTES

1. Committee for Economic Development, *Social Responsibilities of Business Corporations.* New York: CED Research and Policy Committee, 1971, p. 11.
2. *Ibid.,* p. 12.
3. James J. Chrisman and Archie B. Carroll, "Sloane Management Review's Forum: "Corporate Responsibility—Reconciling Economic and Social Goals," *Sloan Management Review* (Winter 1984), p. 60.
4. Alan Cox, "The Cox Report on the American Corporation," cited in James A. Files, "How Executives Perceive the Corporate Social Role," *Public Relations Journal* (January 1983), p. 7.
5. Milton Friedman, *Capitalism and Freedom.* Chicago: University of Chicago Press, 1962, p. 134.
6. Harvey Shapiro, "Wall Street's New Social Responsibility Funds," *Saturday Review* (August 26, 1972), p. 44.
7. "Gantt Medalist 'Bev' Murphy: How to Mix Business with Civic Responsibility," *American Management Association's Management Review* (March 1980), p. 36.

8. *Ibid.,* p. 36.

9. Robert B. Dickie, "Influence of Public Affairs Offices on Corporate Planning and of Corporations on Government Policy," *Strategic Management Journal* 5 (1984), pp. 15–34.

10. D. R. Stephenson, "Internal Public Relations Efforts Further Corporate Responsibility: A Report from Dow Canada," *Public Relations Quarterly* (Summer 1983), p. 8.

CASES FROM THE CONSULTANT'S IN-BASKET

The following twelve cases may be used as supplementary material; there are three cases for each of the four parts of the text. The following are general guidelines to obtain the maximum benefit from the case study method.

1. List and discuss the main issues of the case. Do not merely present a summary of the case, focus instead on the incidents in the case that precipitated the problems. The problems themselves are the main issues of the case. For example, the issue is insubordination in a case in which a worker refuses to obey an order from a superior. To understand how the problem developed, list the steps that led up to the problem.

2. Write down general observations and impressions of the human relations event.

3. Look for the theoretical framework. Because the text covers many of the points raised in these cases, you can check relevant chapters and make note of page numbers that can be used as references for theory.

4. Arrive at a decision. The decision must be action oriented. The decision should incorporate specific recommendations for action to be taken in regard to all parties to the problem. Since every employee is considered a valuable resource, the best decisions are those that make all the involved parties willing to be productive workers who help the organizations achieve its goals.

Source: Cases from the Consultant's In-Basket are copyrighted © and reprinted by permission of Harold W. Berkman, Inc.

5. Note what the expected reaction to the decision might be. As the laws of physics tell us, for every action, there is a reaction. The most successful decisions are those that have foreseen the reactions and provided for them.

6. Summarize what has been learned. The student should understand not just the meaning of the case but also its significance to a future manager.

CASES FOR PART 1

Next Step Mars

SYNOPSIS

Alice Jorgenson, 25, had just received her masters degree in astrophysics when she went out looking for a job. She found work with a government subsidized organization called *Next Stop Mars*, a company involved in the construction of rocket ships to be used for space travel. When she began working, she discovered that her job was not as important as she had expected it to be.

Ever since she was a youngster, Alice Jorgenson had watched with intense fascination the launching of rockets on television. As a child, her parents had always kept her well-supplied with toy rockets to play with. As she grew out of adolescence, Jorgenson always said that she had only one career in mind—she would settle for nothing less than working for the space program, where she would have a chance to construct "real" ships.

Throughout high school and college, Jorgenson spent most of her time and energy in studying astronomy and physics. When it came time for her to do graduate work, she studied astrophysics, thereby preparing herself for a future job in the space travel field. She had been an excellent student, and her advisors told her that she would have no difficulty finding a rewarding job in the area of her interest.

With the help of her college placement service, Jorgenson was able to schedule an appointment with director of personnel at Next Stop Mars. The company, subsidized by the government, conducted research into the never-ending possibilities of space travel, as well as attempting to put theory into practical use. Jorgenson was thrilled at the prospect of working with such a well-known and important organization.

The interview for Jorgenson was set up with a Mr. Quentin of the personnel department. When Jorgenson arrived at the company offices, she was immediately impressed with the displays in the lobby. A secretary asked Jorgenson to fill out the employment application, and shortly thereafter, Mr. Quentin himself poked his head out the door and motioned for Jorgenson to enter. Jorgenson took a deep breath and went into the office in an expectant mood.

Mr. Quentin shook Alice's hand and told her to sit down and make herself comfortable. He then began the interview by asking:

Quentin: It says here on your application, Alice, that you've studied astrophysics quite thoroughly. Is space travel something you've always been interested in?

Jorgenson: Yes. That's why I'm so anxious to work with this company. I firmly believe that space travel is the most important trend of the future.

Quentin: I agree, Alice. The way we run things around here shouldn't discourage you, I hope.

Jorgenson: What do you mean?

Quentin: Well, a new member of the company immediately begins working on what we call first stage projects. Now a lot of the young people here like yourself feel that as soon as they begin working, they should start in on projects of the utmost importance. Patience is the name of the game in this organization.

Jorgenson: What kind of a job did you have in mind for me?

Quentin: Usually, our new employees spend their first week just strolling around getting the feel of what we do here. After that, we run you through a series of tests that help us to determine exactly what type of work you're best suited for. That way, we don't waste time in the trial and error period with you. In the past, the tests have almost always revealed the best possible spot for each new employee. Once you have found your niche, promotion is up to you. If you're a hard worker, then you'll find your time here most rewarding.

Jorgenson: I understand.

The following week, Jorgenson underwent the series of tests and was placed in the painting department of the first stage program. Her duties included painting various parts of the aircraft with special paint as well as pasting decals on certain parts of the vehicle. Jorgenson could not understand how the tests could have revealed that she was best suited for painting since she had never taken an art course in her life. Nevertheless, she did her work carefully, keeping in mind the words of Mr. Quentin that promotion was up to herself. After six months of painting, a job which Jorgenson considered boring and tedious, her work began to decline. One day, in near despair, Jorgenson went up to Mr. Quentin's office and asked if it were possible for her to be retested.

On the Campaign Trail

SYNOPSIS

The following case is a report on Hugh Dickson, campaign manager for John Billingsley, candidate for the office of state attorney general. Of course, everyone in the campaign organization is there on a voluntary basis. Dickson and the others really believe in their candidate and have been working extremely hard for the last six months to get him elected. Dickson, however, has encountered some problems in getting through to some of the workers.

"I can't believe the grief I've been getting from some of the people who are working on this campaign. We've been together for six months, and now that election day is only two weeks away, these people are beginning to lose interest. For my part, I find that I'm more excited now than ever before. It looks like our candidate for state attorney general, John Billingsley, is going to win the office. At least that's what the polls are leading us to believe. Everyone must think that the election is all sewed up, so they don't bother doing their work anymore. No one seems to believe me when I tell them that more votes are won and lost in the last two weeks of an election than during any other period."

These were the words of campaign head Hugh Dickson to his close friend, Roger Altman. Altman had commented that Dickson had a worried look on his face and wanted to know what the problem was. Altman went on to ask Dickson if he had any specific incident in mind that was particularly troubling. Dickson answered that he had, and proceeded to tell Altman the story of what happened that afternoon:

"I was sitting in my office, when, all of a sudden, the press relations man, Foster, comes barging in. He was yelling something about two of our leaflet distributors. As he told it, these two teenagers, Doug and Lisa, weren't working all that hard. Now, ordinarily we have our canvassers assigned to a particular area of the city where they are to hand out leaflets, remind the voters about Election Day, and be prepared to answer any questions the voters might have about John Billingsley. Well, for some reason, these two were sitting on the curb, holding their leaflets and not doing too much of anything else. Foster said that when he saw them in the street, he told them to get up quickly, because there was still a great deal of work to be done. Apparently, the two kids then answered that they had done enough for the day and that it was obvious that Billingsley was going to win the election anyhow. They also said that they were tired of working for such a thankless cause. They complained that they've never even so much as met the man they're working for. The discussion between Doug, Lisa, and Foster concluded with Doug saying that he was ready to quit working for our organization. Foster said that he wouldn't have to bother quitting because he was already fired. Doug and Lisa stood up simultaneously and threw their remaining leaflets in Foster's face. Foster became enraged and screamed at them as they walked away down the street.

"So after Foster gave me this bit, I was quite upset. Doug and Lisa have always been two of the best teenagers we've had in this organization. Right from the start six months ago, they were anxious to do whatever they could do to help the cause. Even though they hadn't discussed matters with Billingsley personally, they had read his opinions and stands in the local newspapers and found themselves agreeing with his point of view for the most part. I'm really worried that this run-in with Foster is somehow symbolic of the fact that we might have lost touch with the young voters whose support we were counting on to take this election."

"A couple of hours after Foster left my office, Doug and Lisa came in to say they were sorry but they couldn't see themselves working for this organization any longer. They said that they resented taking orders from men like Foster—men who, in their eyes, tried to throw their weight around a bit too much. They added that they thought he was a very weak man, one who had just jumped aboard a winning bandwagon. They were afraid that Billingsley must have promised him some favor in return for his work during the campaign. Doug and Lisa agreed that if that were the case, they were going to get out."

"I told them that that was far from the truth. I even tried to defend Foster (even though I don't particularly care for him either) by saying that he was probably a bit strung up from all the pressures of the election. When they didn't seem all that impressed by what I was saying, I told them that I hadn't realized that they had never actually met Billingsley and that I would be glad to arrange a get-together."

Altman: Well, it certainly sounds like you went a long way to please these kids. I don't understand it. How important can they be?

Dickson: It's not the kids per se. It's what they symbolize—the youth vote. We need that vote, Bob. If we can really publicize Billingsley's concern for the youth, we'd be in good shape.

Altman: So what did they say to your offer?

Dickson: Basically, thanks but no thanks. They said that it was good working for the organization for a while, but they now found themselves not really caring one way or another who won the election.

Plumbing the Depths of the Problem

SYNOPSIS

The Olson Plumbing Company, located in Chicago, has been in business for over seventy years producing various plumbing supplies that they wholesale to department stores. Recently, there has been some dissension in the organization among the employees as a result of what they have called "poor leadership," as well as a decided lack of motivation. To better understand and deal with the problems, the company heads have called a meeting to discuss just what can be done to rectify the troubles.

Lately, there has been some trouble at the Olson Plumbing Company. The organization, a rather large one, has been in business for many years and has acquired a reputation as one of the finest in its field. The company has always taken great pride in pleasing its clients. As a matter of fact, upon entering the company offices, the first thing one notices is a large sign hanging over the receptionist's desk which reads "Keep the Customer Satisfied."

The difficulties that have arisen in recent months are strictly internal. There has been visible dissension among the employees as well as a clear ill feeling of the workers toward their supervisors. The organization's executives have been having a difficult time understanding the root of these troubles since they have never encountered anything quite like it before. They have never really experienced a strong display of employee dissatisfaction, and they have certainly never had to deal with the relatively large employee turnover they have witnessed of late.

The company employees are divided between a union and a nonunion employment force. The nonunion work force is made up of the managers, the supervisors, the engineers, and nonunion employees who punch the time clock. The working conditions at the company's base are decent as working conditions go, although they are by no means head and shoulders above the rest of the field. The benefits provided by the company are not particularly good. Hospitalization costs are handled by the company as are tuition refunds for educational classes that relate to the job.

The workers at the Olson Company don't want to get lost in their job and become little more than a computer number. Many of them are in positions where they anticipate promotion and higher salary. Many people on the work force use their time within the company as a stepping stone to further their career. It is vital for an employee to make certain that his work is recognized by "the brass."

The company maintains a quality control department which consists of an administrator, three engineers, three researchers, four secretaries, and a dozen union employees. All of these people, with the exception of the administrator, punch the time clock. The work load at the company is highly demanding—in order to accomplish the required work, approximately fifty to fifty-five hours per week are required of the nonunion workers. Although the work is generally done on time, the workers themselves rarely get the credit they deserve. Ordinarily, it is the department head who gets the pat on the back for the work that is done under his supervision. Thus, the only way the employees know how good a job they are doing is by indirect compliment from the department head. And compliments from that direction often do not make it all the way down the line to the union workers.

Recently there has been a wave of transfer requests in the company. Already, a couple of engineers and a researcher have left the plant, and the pile of transfer requests has begun to grow on the personnel director's desk. As a result of this turn of events, the personnel director has requested a meeting with the quality control supervisor and several of the more severely affected department heads to find out just what's going on. Some of the problem areas to be discussed were listed on the agenda for the meeting as follows:

1. The large turnover within the department.
2. The slowdown in total production and lack of willingness on the part of the employees to work overtime.
3. The general employee dissension.

At the meeting, the personnel director informed the quality control manager that he had already heard "through the grapevine" of several problem areas in his department:

1. Most of the nonunion employees feel that they should be salaried and taken off the clock.
2. All of the employees feel that they are not receiving sufficient recognition for the work that they are doing. They want to know when

they are doing a good job, and want to hear about it for themselves, not from their department head.

3. The pay increases are not proportional with the increases in the work load.

4. The responsibility for each person's work load is not clearly defined, thereby leaving numerous questions in the air.

There is, in addition, substantial pressure upon the management to replace the quality control manager. The heads of the company are faced with the alternatives of replacing the manager and starting anew, or trying to reorganize their way around the problems while retaining existing employees.

CASES FOR PART 2

Preparations for a Visitor

SYNOPSIS

Frank Mills and Gus Johnson are a skilled team chosen to work on a prestigious assignment for the Wilkins Company. Despite their careful preparations, they are unable to complete the job on time. Even though their supervisor is aware that they are not at fault, she refuses to back them up. As a result they are fired.

The Wilkins Glass Manufacturing Company is one of the largest of its kind in the country. In addition to producing many types of glasses for different purposes, the company maintains a team of laboratory-trained scientists for research into various possibilities of advances and innovations in the production of glass. One item in particular that has brought them much fame is a new type of bullet-proof glass. Articles in several national magazines have indicated products coming out of Wilkins Company are both revolutionary and safe.

Early in the year, a great deal of excitement began circulating around the factory. Word was that a highly distinguished public figure would be making his first visit to the United States. And Wilkins Company had been selected to supply their new form of bullet-proof glass for the automobile the visitor was to use. The government wanted to avoid all risks with a visitor of such stature, so when the final confirmation came that Wilkins Company was the choice, preparations were made. It was decided that the guest would be chauffeured around in one of the large American luxury cars; therefore, the people at Wilkins would be responsible for supplying eight windows.

The men chosen by Gonzales, supervisor of the relevant department, to perform the custom cutting and fitting were Frank Mills and Gus Johnson. Mills and Johnson had worked as a team for fifteen years. They were thought to be highly responsible and most competent men. Naturally, both were quite excited to be working on a job of such importance. The word got around the plant that the foreign visitor might even pay a visit to express his thanks to the Wilkins Company.

Finally the day arrived for Mills and Johnson to install the new glass windshields. The car was delivered windowless from the automotive company, and Mills and Johnson prepared to get under way. Ordinarily, a job of this sort would take about six hours, but in this very special case, the two had figured that they'd better allow themselves eight. When they arrived at the stockroom, they picked up the custom-cut glass (they had done this part of the work earlier in the week after securing the precise measurements of the car from its makers) and filled out a requisition form for a Number 9 lever. This particular lever was the only one that would work with the high-quality, extremely hard glass. The stockroom clerk took the order and went into the back room to get the tool, as Mills and Johnson went over the procedure for installation once more. After fifteen minutes the clerk returned with a bewildered look on his face, and said, "I don't know what happened, but the Number 9 is missing. We only had one in stock, and someone must have taken it out without filling out the proper forms or at least without letting me know. I'm sorry, guys, but there's really nothing I can do for you." Mills and Johnson were highly upset at this turn of events because they knew full well that only the Number 9 lever was sturdy enough to handle the glass. They decided that they had better speak with Gonzales at once.

When they got to Gonzales's office, the supervisor seemed more than a little harried. "A rotten day all around," she said. "I hope you have some good news for me."

"Sorry," said Mills. "More bad news is on the way. The tool we need to install the windows in the car, the Number 9 lever, is missing. The clerk in the stockroom says he hasn't seen it for days."

"Well, use something else then. Use your imagination. I don't care how you do it, but that car had better be ready by tomorrow. I'm not gonna take the blame for this. If you think I'm gonna face Wilkins and tell him at the last minute, we can't do it; you're crazy."

Mills and Johnson left the office in a state of anxiety. They well knew that the Number 9 was the only tool that could accomplish the job and that using anything else would be dangerous. Nonetheless, they went back to the stockroom and picked up a Number 8 lever and a hammer with which they were planning to drive the less durable lever into place. The clerk, aware of their difficult situation, just said, "good luck."

The two workers returned to the garage where the car was waiting and awkwardly began their task. It became even more clear to them that using the hammer and the wrong lever was a risky operation. Gonzales, making her rounds in the meantime around the various shops, stopped by and observed Mills and Johnson at work. After watching for a couple of minutes, she moved along. Shortly thereafter, Johnson's hand slipped as he was attempting to knock the lever into place and broke the tool. With this, they went back to the stockroom only to find that there were no more Number 8 levers to be found. It was now obvious that there was no possible way that the car would be ready in time for the dignitary's arrival. When the men told Gonzales about the accident and the ensuing predicament, she cried, "Now you're gonna have to face Wilkins. I'm not gonna take the blame for any of this. You will be in big trouble for not using the proper equipment. Just don't try to put the blame on me!"

Mills and Johnson, trying to keep their cool, proceeded to the office of George C. Hiram, vice president of the Wilkins Co., and told him that Gonzales was trying to "screw them." Hiram said he understood their situation and he promised the men that he would speak to Mr. Wilkins personally. He also assured them that he would make all efforts to free the men of any of the blame that might be cast upon them.

As a result of the hearing that took place in the president's office with Gonzales, the two workmen, Mills and Johnson, were relieved of their jobs at the Wilkins Glass Manufacturing Company.

A "Special" Group of Workers

SYNOPSIS

The Carswell Sheet Metal Company has been in business for around fifty years and employs a work force of over 300 employees. They carry a standard line of products and only under special circumstances do any custom production. At the beginning of December, they were asked by the governor's office to produce a special (and large) order of custom-cut sheet metal. To accommodate the governor, the president of the company, Mr. Carswell, asked plant manager Jack Pine to assign a special force of twenty workers to devote their full time and effort for two months to handle the special request. Pine did this, but discovered that these special assignment workers wanted extra compensation for their work.

Voice on the telephone: Mr. Carswell? I'm calling from the governor's office. The governor has asked me to ask you if it would be possible for your company to produce a custom order. He said that he realizes that you don't ordinarily fill such orders, but he also mentioned that this is really quite important.

Carswell: Yes, I have already received a letter from the governor explaining the importance and urgency of his order. In fact, I was ready today to write him a letter explaining that we will somehow find a way to handle his request even though this is our busy season.

Voice: Thank you, Mr. Carswell. I'm going up to his office shortly and I'll inform him of your decision.

With the governor's request fresh in his mind, Carswell went over to the metal shop where his manager, Jack Pine, was watching over his workers. Carswell called Pine aside and explained the immediate importance of the special situation. Pine promised Carswell that he would somehow find a way to handle it, and Carswell went back to his office feeling assured that things would work out just fine. After all, Pine had been with the organization for a good number of years and had always been considered a good and trusted employee. Pine always seemed to get things done no matter now impossible they appeared.

In going over his employee records, Pine discovered that he had about twenty men who were skilled enough to handle the particular type of cutting job the governor had requested. The whole job would take about two months of steady work. When Pine had settled upon his choice of workers for the project, he called the men into his office to explain the situation and its great importance. They agreed to do the work required and subsequently elected Elmer Wheeling as the project captain. Wheeling would be their immediate supervisor as well as liaison between the workers and Pine.

The following day, Pine and Wheeling organized their force and the workers got under way. All had been promised a bonus by Mr. Carswell for their effort in this special project. This pleased them and gave them added incentive to do a good job. But after a week on the job, they decided that they wanted something more. Not only did they want the bonus, but they wanted a specially marked-off area in which they could work. The general feeling among these workers was that since they were doing something special and of great importance, they should be treated in a special and favored manner. No longer did they see the project as merely an extension of their regular work, but rather they viewed it as a sort of testimony to the fact that they were the most highly skilled workers in the plant. This, they felt, entitled them to preferential treatment.

One afternoon, the special force got together for a meeting to discuss their feelings with their representative, Wheeling. They explained that they wanted the special area, the bonus, and the right to eat lunch in the cafeteria that was ordinarily used solely by the managers and supervisors of the various departments. Wheeling felt that these requests were not unreasonable, so he approached Jack Pine the following morning:

Wheeling: Jack, I'm speaking for all the men on the special work force now. We've decided that since we're involved in a special project, we should get some kind of special treatment. (He goes on to list the requests of the men.) I believe that if you think about what we're saying you'll agree that it's only fair.

Pine: I don't understand this, Elmer. I picked you guys to do this work because I trusted you to do it and do it well. I wasn't bargaining for any of this nonsense . . .

Wheeling: This is no nonsense, Jack. We're completely serious about these requests. I'll tell you something else; if something isn't done about them real soon, you may just find yourself without anyone who has the proper training to do this work for the governor. And knowing Carswell, you'll get the blame pinned on you. So either you speak up for us, and things'll be fine, or you don't and you'll end up suffering more than we will.

Pine: Let me think about it, Elmer. I'll get back to you in a day or two.

As Pine considered his options in the matter, he realized that he was in a very precarious position. If the men left work, he indeed would be blamed. He didn't see how he could really arrange to answer all their requests without setting off all the other employees into groups organizing requests of their own. On the other hand, he had a sneaking suspicion that maybe Wheeling was just using big and threatening talk. Pine found it a little hard to believe that twenty men who had invested so many years of their lives at Carswell would be willing to walk off the job over these petty requests.

The Grass Is Always Greener . . .

SYNOPSIS

The Swensen Envelope Company prints and produces business envelopes for many of the large establishments in the area. The work force consists of typesetters, designers, printers, and assembly line workers who take care to see that each envelope is properly folded and glued. Lately, there have been a number of complaints from the assembly line workers regarding such matters as low pay and uncomfortable working conditions. When some of these complaints were answered, workers in the other departments began to feel as if they had a right to complain as well—they too felt that their situations could be improved.

William Hardy, head of employee relations at Swensen Envelope Company, has recently been beseiged with a flood of problems. Most of his worries originate in the assembly line department. There, the employees have been complaining that their working conditions are not quite what they should be, and what is more, they feel that their pay is not up to par either.

Fundamentally, this is the way Swensen Envelope works:

1. A prospective customer comes into the office and meets with one of the salespeople regarding an order of custom-designed envelopes. Swensen has about half a dozen different basic styles upon which variations are often made.

2. Once the order is placed, a designer plans out the way in which the envelope is to be made.

3. The designer then brings "blueprints" to the typesetting department where a printing plate is constructed.

4. The plate is brought to the printing department where several sample envelopes are made up. These are then sent to the customer for final approval. Once the go-ahead is received, printers begin the mass production of envelopes. The average order at Swensen Envelope is for approximately 2,000 envelopes.

5. As the printed envelopes come down the assembly line, the sixty or so workers there fold and glue each one by hand.

The assembly line workers have recently begun to feel that they are the neglected part of the operation. They are the lowest paid workers in the organization. Also, general opinion in the department is that both the lighting and ventilation are poor. Most workers say that they leave the end of the day with a throbbing headache as a result of these two factors. Because of these complaints, there has been a large turnover in the assembly line department the last several months. Hardy doesn't really understand this, and he asks himself why these people had never raised such complaints before.

In an effort to quell some of the trouble, the company (upon Hardy's recommendation) hired a new supervisor to head the assembly line department. Phyllis Lawrence had worked for various other mass production companies in the past.

The first thing Lawrence did when she arrived on a Monday morning was to call a general meeting of all assembly line workers to give them the opportunity to voice their dissatisfactions. By the time everyone had spoken their piece, two hours had elapsed, and Lawrence was left in her office with the realization that she had a big job on her hands. Nonetheless, when the lunch whistle blew, and all the assembly liners went to the cafeteria, the general consensus was that they were pleased to have a new supervisor who seemed to be interested in what they had to say. Most of them firmly believed that Lawrence would be able to do something to aid them.

About two weeks later, all assembly line workers were given the day off so that a new air conditioning system could be installed. A week after that electrical engineers came into the building to replace the lighting system for the assembly line. Needless to say, the workers were happy about both their new conditions and their new supervisor.

The work rate picked up tremendously in the assembly line department from there on in. But another problem soon arose. Having witnessed what Lawrence had done for the assembly liners, the printers now began to complain that they needed new and modern equipment. Thus, as the printers' level of disenchantment rose, their production level fell. And of course, without printed material to fold, the assembly liners found themselves with a lot of free time. Consequently, their wages declined because they all worked on an hourly basis.

Hardy was perplexed. He wondered if Lawrence hadn't spoiled the assembly liners and therefore planted the seed of discontent in the organization. His conflict, simply put, was this: Should he transfer Lawrence to the printers' department? Should he try hiring another supervisor like Lawrence to deal with the printers? And if he did that, who would file the next complaint? Or perhaps should he just tell the printers that they've no grounds for complaint, that their equipment is good enough?

CASES FOR PART 3

Pack Up Your Troubles

SYNOPSIS

Located in Florida, the Pomerantz & Sons Packing Company deals strictly in sending fresh Florida fruit in cases to northeastern states. The president of the company, Jean Pomerantz, has recently named her son, Larry, supervisor of the warehouse. This move was effected with the idea of freeing Jean Pomerantz for control over the paper work and "business end" of the operation, while it was expected that Larry would best learn the fine points of the business working at it firsthand. After his appointment, Larry came up with new ideas, some of which did not meet with unanimous approval from the other employees.

Jean Pomerantz, president of the Pomerantz & Sons Packing Company of Florida, in an effort to lead her 24-year-old son into an executive position with the organization, recently appointed Larry supervisor of the warehouse. Larry's duties include making sure that only good, ripe fruit is sent up north, keeping a close eye on the employees, and checking that the correct amount of fruit is sent in each shipment. Jean Pomerantz attends to the overall functioning of the company in addition to handling sales.

Larry has been in the job for about six months, and although he has a pretty good idea of how to run the warehouse, some of the employees who have been with the company for many years have not fully accepted their new supervisor. They usually follow his instructions, but at times, they question his judgment among themselves.

The chief packer, Basil Blakely, has been with Pomerantz & Sons for nineteen years. Ordinarily, he gives the orders in the packing room, and everybody listens to him without question because they realize that he's experienced and knows what he's talking about. Blakely has always been a tough character. When he sees that something is not being done exactly the way he ordered it, he is not reticent about expressing his anger. Although some of the employees working under him fear him to some degree, they all respect him and think he is the best person for the job. Blakely never received any formal education beyond high school, but as he puts it, "I learned all I need to know just by keeping my eyes open.

And if people think they're so smart that they can argue with me, I'll show them that they're not so smart after all."

Early in April, in preparation for the summer season, the busiest time of the year for Pomerantz & Sons, Larry Pomerantz devised a new process for ensuring the accuracy of orders. According to his plan, each employee in the warehouse would be required to fill out a requisition form for each piece of fruit needed before placing it into the shipping crate. Although the work might be slowed down a little until the workers got used to the new operation, Larry believed the itemizing process would eventually help cut down on order mistakes and lead to a more efficient way of packing.

When Larry told Blakely about his proposition, Blakely became enraged.

Blakely: What the hell's the reason for that? Everything's been going fine here. We don't need new ideas here. I got everyone working just as hard as they can. They know just what they're supposed to do and they do it. So why don't you take your ideas somewhere else and leave us to our work!

L. Pomerantz: Okay, Arnie, if that's the way you want it. I'm the supervisor here and I give the orders. So if you don't like the way I run things, you can just get out of here. Employees like you are a dime a dozen. Besides, you're the only one around here who thinks you're so special.

Blakely: All right, kid. You can be the big boss if you want. I've got enough experience so I can work in any of the packing plants around here. You get your wish. I'm leaving! Let's see what you can do now with the big season. Let's see how well the others listen to your ideas. See ya later.

Without another word, Blakely left the warehouse. Undoubtedly, Larry was a bit surprised that Blakely had reacted so quickly and so harshly. When Larry told his mother about what had happened, she was more than mildly upset.

J. Pomerantz: I don't know what we're going to do now, Larry. Blakely was the best.

L. Pomerantz: Don't worry, I know this business well enough by now. I can take care of the warehouse by myself. I guarantee you we'll get through the summer with flying colors. The way I have it planned, starting today everything in the warehouse is going to have some rhyme and reason to it for the first time. Blakely was more talk than action anyhow. I watched him as he worked. He didn't do a thing that I couldn't do.

J. Pomerantz: You're forgetting one thing, Larry. And unfortunately, what you're forgetting is the most important thing of all.

L. Pomerantz: What's that?

J. Pomerantz: The employees in the warehouse all liked and got along with Blakely. They're going to be mighty upset when they hear that you fired him.

The Fire Station

SYNOPSIS

The following case is drawn from a letter written by a young fireman trainee working in Lincoln, Nebraska, to his father in Kansas City. The letter relates to an incident wherein the decision of a fire rescue squad leader is questioned by his subordinates at the scene of an emergency.

Dear Dad,

Yesterday, something happened which was of great importance to me and my life, and I felt it would be the best idea for me to share it with you. Keep in mind that while I shall essentially stick to the facts in relating the story, every now and then, I'll probably find it impossible to refrain from interjecting some of my own opinions and feelings about the incident.

Here in Nebraska, the hot and dry climate make this area quite susceptible to fire. Now, of course, none of us here at the station particularly enjoys just sitting around and playing cards all day long, but there is a unanimous sentiment that we would prefer to play cards for the rest of our lives and never have to face a fire. I say this not because we are cowards—that is a long way from the truth of the matter. It's just that we know better than anyone of the horrible destruction a fire can cause, as well as being acutely aware of the danger each and every one of us prepares to face whenever that alarm rings. What happened yesterday was something I'll never forget and is something I pray never happens again.

Here is the story: We were sitting around playing gin rummy, when the alarm went off. Quickly, we donned our fire-fighting attire and sped off to the scene of the emergency. When we arrived (the fire was going on in a field about three miles from our station), an old barnhouse was up in blazes. There were five of us there at the time including our captain, (Fred Isaacson), three other firefighters, and myself. By the time we had readied all our equipment, the barn was about halfway down. Well, naturally, we started hosing down the barn, but at one point Isaacson thought he heard a moaning sound coming out of the barn. It seemed impossible that it could have been a child since the barn has not really been in use for quite some time. More likely was the possibility that a young animal might have been trapped amidst the flames. None of us heard any sound whatsoever, but Isaacson said he was certain. He then made the crucial tactical decision—in a loud (and strangely nervous) voice, he ordered Craig Porter to go into the barn and see who or what was in there, and if possible to pull it out. Some of us questioned this move for a moment, but Isaacson screamed, "Come on, quit arguing. We've got to get in there and rescue whatever living thing is trapped!" Porter, a veteran fireman, reluctantly entered the barn. In the meantime, of course, the rest of us continued the hosing process. After two minutes we had not heard anything from Porter, and I must confess, I more than anyone else (Porter was quite a good friend of mine), grew extremely frightened. A moment later, my fears were confirmed. The fire had burnt right through one of the beams holding up the roof of the barn, and the entire structure collapsed. As much as it pains me to tell you this, Craig Porter's last act was one of trying to save a living thing.

At the funeral, perhaps only Isaacson felt worse than I did. Imagine, he's got to live with this for the rest of his life. The chief of the department, along with all the other firemen, told him not to let this destroy him. They said that he made his decision in the line of duty; it was a split-second move with the obviously good intention of saving a life. There was no way that Isaacson could possibly have foreseen what would happen to Porter.

All of this, including the funeral, happened yesterday. I've had a night to sleep on the events of yesterday, and a full day's worth of thought to arrive at my own conclusions about the matter. Sure, Isaacson felt deep sorrow about what had taken place and he apologized till he was blue in the face. But somehow, that doesn't seem like enough to me. The incident itself is bad enough, but it's what's behind it, the principle, the theory, that for me is most troublesome. I mean, here's this guy, Captain Isaacson, in a position of high authority and responsibility, and I have the impression that he just couldn't keep his cool in the emergency situation. I question whether or not he should remain on the force. On the other hand, he showed that he was a man made of strong stuff in that he didn't try to shirk any of the responsibility. He admitted all along that the mistake was his. Not once did he put the blame on "extenuating circumstances." This, I have to admit, impressed me. The one thing that still worries me greatly about all this, is: Would I follow Isaacson's orders? Now, who's the poor public servant, Isaacson or me?

Sincerely,
Your son,
Robert

A Hidden Defect

SYNOPSIS

Stan Farber, an ex-marine, had just begun working for the ABC Transit System after having been honorably discharged from the service just over a year ago. Starting out as a ticket clerk, he had made rapid progress in learning the ropes of the business and was offered a promotion if he could pass the company physical. He did well on the test except for one area, which prohibited him from taking on the new position. As a result, his work suffered.

The ABC Transit System ran all the bus lines in and around a large southeastern city. Stan Farber, an ex-marine, had just begun working for ABC after receiving his honorable discharge from the service just over a year earlier. Farber was looking forward to his work, since he had become quite accustomed to working with people. The fact that he was going to be employed by a public transportation system pleased him greatly.

Farber was initially hired as a ticket clerk. His job consisted of selling bus tickets to the commuters and keeping an account of exactly how many tickets he had sold for each destination during the day. Two other people worked as ticket clerks at Farber's station, and he got along with them famously. The station at which Farber worked was located conveniently—only a three-block walk from his home. There was one disadvantage to working at the particular station, however, as Farber soon realized. Centrally located, it was one of the busiest if not the busiest station on the entire system. At many of the other stations, there were lag periods, usually between the rush hours, where the ticket clerks could take a break. In his location, Farber was not afforded the opportunity to take breaks to read the newspaper or talk with the other employees. From the minute Farber entered the station at 7:00 A.M. until the moment he left at 4:00, he was kept busy.

Nonetheless, Farber was so used to hard work from his experience in the Marines that the heavy volume of sales did not particularly bother him. He felt that the constant presence of ticket buyers helped make the time pass quickly and kept him from being bored with his work. Farber saw his job as a challenge because of this.

In a little over six months, Farber handled the work quite smoothly. This was clearly recognized by his supervisor, George Bentley. Bentley felt that it was remarkable that with only six months experience, Farber was handling the job as well as any of the other clerks who had been with ABC for a number of years. It seemed as if everything came naturally to Farber, and his good relationship with his fellow employees was something Bentley was quite excited about.

The next step up the ladder at ABC was the position of ticket agent. The work in that position was much more difficult and required greater responsibility, but the pay scale was adjusted accordingly. Essentially, the job consisted of being in charge of five to seven stations. The ticket agent made sure that all the stations were functioning properly, and that all operational problems were solved. It was standard policy at ABC that nobody gets promoted to ticket agent until they have had five years experience with the organization. It was felt that it generally took that much time for a person to gain the respect of co-workers as well as to learn the ins and outs of the business. Bentley felt that after only six months on the job, however, Farber had proven himself worthy of the promotion. He exhibited confidence and poise at the ticket office and related to the customers as well as anyone ever had before at ABC.

When Bentley asked Farber if he would be interested in a change, he answered that he most certainly would. Farber was attracted by the additional money that he would make as well as the higher status in the company. The new job had two disadvantages, however, in that Farber would be required to make daily trips to each of the stations he was to oversee and his time off would now be Tuesday and Wednesday instead of Saturday and Sunday. This meant perhaps less time to spend with his family. Nevertheless, after discussing the situation with his wife, he agreed that it would be a chance that he really shouldn't pass up and he informed Bentley of his decision.

To be promoted to the position of ticket agent, Farber would have to pass a physical examination given by the company doctor. Farber wasn't worried about that since he knew he was still in excellent shape. The physical was scheduled for the following Monday.

Over the weekend, Farber told his family and friends about his promotion. They were all quite happy for him and in his honor, a small party was thrown. Farber was quite proud.

Farber reported for the physical on Monday and he felt most confident. He passed most parts of the examination with flying colors, but when it came to the last section of the test, a test for color blindness, he failed. Farber hadn't realized that this was a qualification for the ticket agent's job. He returned home depressed and had to tell everyone that he didn't get the promotion after all.

From that day on, Farber's work as a ticket clerk went downhill. His co-workers found him wholly disagreeable. Even some of the commuters whom he had befriended now preferred to avoid him because when they did speak to him he was gruff with them. Farber's absenteeism and tardiness increased.

CASES FOR PART 4

City Hospital

SYNOPSIS

City Hospital employs a large staff of doctors and nurses as well as maintaining an internship program for medical students. The supervisor of the intern program, Raymond O'Malley, spends most of his day giving lectures to the students and demonstrating practical applications of theories. His former assistant, Jane Burton, has just been transferred to another division within the hospital and has been replaced by Carlos Random. O'Malley has been confused lately regarding the different tone of the reports he has received from each.

The internship program at City Hospital for young medical students has been in operation for eight months. The director of the program, Dr. Raymond O'Malley, delivers daily lectures to the students as well as demonstrates various techniques. Each intern does a year's service at City Hospital and is then transferred to another institution in the area for a final year of experience-gathering.

First thing in the morning, interns meet as a group with the assistant supervisor. Here, they discuss what went on the previous day, what problems were encountered, and how they could be solved. They then proceed to the lecture hall where Dr. O'Malley gives a lecture for about an hour, which is followed by more discussion. After lunch, the interns return and begin floor duty. They visit with the patients, hear complaints, and occasionally administer various medical procedures such as blood pressure tests. At the end of the day, they meet once more with the assistant supervisor to raise any questions they might have. It is rare that they see Dr. O'Malley in the afternoon because he is usually occupied with business of his own. The bulk of their time is spent in dealings with the assistant.

The new assistant to Dr. O'Malley is Carlos Random, a diligent worker who has been employed elsewhere in the hospital for eleven years. He replaces Jane Burton, a young woman who was transferred to another assignment within the hospital after serving as assistant to O'Malley for seven months. It was arranged that Burton would stay on for the first week Random was on the job. O'Malley is perplexed by the conflicting reports from his two assistants. They read as follows:

Report of Jane Burton

> This week, things have gone smoothly as usual. Each of the interns has displayed a real interest in the work and seems willing to work hard to become a doctor. The very few absentees have been noted on a separate form. Several of the patients have asked me to thank particular interns for their display of interest and concern with their situations. I have done that, and the interns all seemed quite pleased with the fact that the patients are recognizing and appreciating their efforts.

Report of Carlos Random

> This being my first week on the job as assistant supervisor for the intern program, I may be under some misconceptions as to exactly what's supposed to be going on. Throughout the week, the mornings have proceeded normally (at least what I assume to be normally—time will tell just what really is the usual state of affairs). I was a bit irritated, however, at what went on during the afternoons. I was led to believe that each intern is given an hour for lunch after which he or she is supposed to return to work and assume floor duty. Strangely, only about half of the interns seemed interested in being precise about their timing. Not everyone returned from lunch on time, and even those who did seemed to delay beginning their afternoon duties. When they finally did get under way, it didn't strike me that they were spending enough time with each patient they visited. Perhaps later in the week, you, Jane Burton, and I could get together to discuss just how the interns are supposed to organize their day. It seems to me that they're wasting a lot of their valuable time.

O'Malley placed the two reports on his desk and decided to hold the suggested meeting with Jane Burton and Carlos Random. He immediately summoned them both to his office, where the following conversation took place.

O'Malley: I want you to read each other's report of the week on the intern program. [He hands them the reports and they read them.] What do you think?

Random: I don't know what you call "normal," Jane, but they were not working as hard as they should have been, it appeared to me.

Burton: Well, I'll tell you the story. Those kids are all good kids. Whenever I need any one of them for a special assignment, I have no hesitation about asking them for a favor or a little extra work. The reason that they appeared to you to be loafing, Carlos, was that I always allowed them to use their own discretion as to how to occupy their afternoons. They're all mature and intelligent; I don't believe that any of them would want to waste time. I saw no reason to hold an iron hand over them. I told them what had to be done and I let them do it however they thought proper. Of course I supervised them in their activities, but I rarely gave direct orders if I could possibly avoid it.

O'Malley: Did they seem to expect the same from you, Carlos?

The Reincarnation of Clark Kent

SYNOPSIS

Ronald Bunnette was a reporter with the *Granville Journal*, a local paper in a small midwestern town. The newspaper rarely covered stories of national importance but rather dealt principally with happenings of interest to the residents of the town that it served. Another reporter on the paper's staff, Ellen Fielding, was always called upon to cover "the big story" whenever an important local event came up. Bunnette after a while became discontent with his position as small-time reporter and made inquiries into the possibility of being assigned to stories which were more "relevant." When he finally got his chance, a series of misunderstandings thwarted his effort.

The *Granville Journal*, a local newspaper in a small midwestern town, puts out one edition per week—on Tuesdays. Reporter Ronald Bunnette worked for the paper for seven years but never had the opportunity to cover what he deemed "a big story." When his family and friends asked him about this, he merely replied that "big things just don't happen in Granville." From the view in his office, however, he knew that in reality, things were happening; it was just that he was never assigned to cover them.

Bunnette had studied journalism in high school and had been assistant editor of his school paper, but financial strains had made it impossible for him to attend college. Thus, when he had applied for a job at a big city newspaper seven years ago, he was promptly turned down. Although he was a bit discouraged at the time, Bunnette was not completely defeated. He had spent the greater portion of his life struggling, so he was used to defeats. He found his way to Granville and landed a job.

The top reporter on the *Granville* staff, Ellen Fielding, had been with the paper for twelve years and was widely considered to be one of the finest reporters in the entire area. Kravitz, the editor, had always taken good care to see to it that Fielding was assigned the top stories to cover. As he explained it, "If I've got a big news item, I'm going to give it to Fielding. She's so damn good, better than anyone else I've got—although the rest of my staff is of high quality—but why should I have to play Mr. Nice Guy and risk poor coverage of a big story by assigning it to someone else? I run a paper here, but it's also a business. And my business is to sell papers. So it makes perfect sense, at least to me, that if there's some big happening, Fielding gets the assignment. It's my job to please the readership and keep them as customers." So Bunnette, although experienced, always found himself covering stories and local events of what he considered to be of somewhat lesser importance.

One day, Bunnette went into Kravitz' office with the notion of telling the editor that he would very much appreciate the chance to expand his range and cover events of greater significance. The conversation between the editor and the reporter took place as follows.

Kravitz: What can I do for you, Bunnette?

Bunnette: Well, Mr. Kravitz, I've got a problem that's been bothering me for quite a while now. I've been working here for seven years now, and I just feel as if I haven't made any real progress. I mean I'm covering the same kind of stories that I was doing when I first got here, and seven years is a long time.

Kravitz: I see. What's your assignment for this week?

Bunnette: In one sense, I'm almost embarrassed to say. Remember that fire last Friday over at the playground? Well, I'm supposed to do a kind of social welfare piece on that. I mean that's all well and good for some kid coming out of college for a first assignment, but I've been here a good while.

Kravitz: Alright Bunnette, I'll tell you what . . . I'm certain that you're aware that the governor is coming to Granville on his reelection campaign route in June, about a month from now. I plan on having Fielding cover the story, but if your work maintains a good level between now and then, your assignment will be to go along with Fielding and provide whatever assistance she may need in the course of interviews, the actual composition of the piece, or both.

Bunnette: That sounds great to me. I assure you, Mr. Kravitz, you won't regret this decision. In fact, I think you'll see that I'll do such a good job that you won't have any reluctance about giving me assignments like this in the future. Thanks a lot.

Toward the end of May, Kravitz began interviewing several college students for various positions with the paper. Of the eight that were interviewed, three were hired. In the meantime, Bunnette was busy preparing for his big chance, boning up on the governor's political record and dreaming up provocative questions to pose to the distinguished guest.

A week before the governor was due to arrive, Ellen Fielding became seriously ill and had to be hospitalized. Kravitz and staff were quite worried because they had planned on having Fielding write what was probably to be the most important article of the year. Word began to get around the office that Bunnette would therefore cover the big story. Kravitz himself assured Bunnette that this would be the case.

But two days before the big day, Bunnette noticed Kravitz walking into his office with his arm around the shoulder of one of the new young members of the staff. Bunnette heard the editor tell the new reporter that he would have to familiarize himself with the ins and outs of the visiting politician. The reporter replied that it would be no trouble since he had studied politics at the university and was well versed in the governor's activities. Kravitz added that he would have only two days to prepare himself.

The next day, Bunnette heard from some of his co-workers that Kravitz was planning to have his new reporter cover the big story. At first heartbroken, but later furious, Bunnette left the office of the *Granville Journal* for the last time with a word to no one.

The young reporter did, in fact, get to cover the story, and his family and friends were quite surprised when he told them that up until the last minute, Kravitz had planned to use him as an assistant to the more seasoned reporter, Ronald Bunnette.

The Real Cost of Building a Highway

SYNOPSIS

The Chung Construction Company, an East Coast–based outfit, specializes in the building of highways. Their latest project involves the construction of a new four-lane highway running parallel to Interstate 95 through Maine. The company has met with resentment on the part of the area's residents.

One trend in the road construction field has been the move toward new and larger highways. In northern New England, one of the largest companies to handle this type of work is the Chung Construction Company, owned and operated by Peter Chung. Chung has earned the reputation of fulfilling his contracts on time and is not averse to pushing his workers to the fullest degree to accomplish a mission.

Last spring, the Chung Company was given a contract to build a new four-lane highway running parallel to Interstate 95 from Portsmouth, New Hampshire, to Portland, Maine. Except for a few miles at the southerly end of the proposed roadway, the road would be constructed entirely within the state borders of Maine. The deal was arranged by the Chamber of Commerce of the State of Maine and the Chung Company. There was a specified period of time in which the work had to be completed, and all terms of the contract had been deemed fair and reasonable by both parties.

The residents of Maine were informed of the proposal about two months before construction was due to begin. Initially, the reaction was minimal—people did not feel as if they were being pressured until they saw the steam shovels and other equipment right in front of their eyes. As the day when work was scheduled to commence drew closer, some of the citizens began to protest. They felt that it was unfair for the state and the Chung Company to "destroy their beautiful land with another anonymous superhighway." They argued that it had been done before with Interstate 95. They saw no need at all for another road of this type to tear up their forests and drain their streams. They resolved that this time, they weren't going to let any big organization push them around. Their logic, as it was phrased, was that the land belongs to the people and it is the people who had the right to decide just what should be done with it. It seemed only fair to them that if they didn't have any use for another large highway, then the highway simply should not be built.

A town meeting was held for the purpose of discussing what actions the citizens could take prior to the week before work was scheduled to begin. At the meeting, one of the community leaders, Roberta R. Dixon, took the initiative to lead the others in a calm discussion of what action could be taken. After several ideas were tossed around, it was decided that Dixon would be sent (as a representative of the people) to speak in a joint meeting of the Chamber of Commerce and the lawyer for the Chung Company. Dixon was set to inform them that the people of the area were not about to sit back and watch a new highway destroy the serenity of their homes. It was further resolved that if this attack drew no response, the citizens would initiate a sit-down strike on the land to be excavated. This action would delay Chung Construction Company's efforts.

At the joint meeting held two days later, Dixon expressed the views of her "constituents" as follows. "We the citizens of this area have decided that it is wholly unfair for you to engage in the construction project you have planned. It seems to us that you, as large organizations, have a certain responsibility to us, and we overwhelmingly feel that by going ahead with your plan, you would be neglecting that responsibility. We can sympathize with your reason for building the highway, but you as well must be able to sympathize with our reasons for not wanting it. The noise and pollution that would come as a result of the proposed construction would surely make our living situation intolerable. True, you have another sort of responsibility to the tourists who travel through our state, but there is already a superhighway, Interstate 95, that they can use. We don't believe that it's necessary for you to engage in another project of this type. We'd like to act in a responsible manner, but if you refuse to honor our requests, we have decided by unanimous vote to initiate a sit-down strike on the land to be used for the highway, thereby preventing the construction workers from beginning work. We sincerely hope that you'll take our argument into consideration."

The representatives of both the Chamber of Commerce and the Chung Company promised to think about what Dixon had said and promised that they would postpone construction on the site for another week while they thought about alternative plans. A week later, Dixon received a letter from the representative for the Chamber of Commerce that said, in effect, that the department had considered all the possibilities and had decided that no alternative route was feasible. They announced that they were going ahead with their original plans. That evening, Dixon called a meeting of the town residents to discuss the procedure for commencing a sit-down strike. A lawyer was on hand to make sure that everything the citizens planned was within their civil rights.

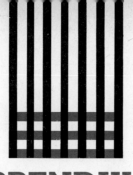

APPENDIX A
JOURNAL/MAGAZINE REVIEW

The Academy of Management Journal, Walter B. Newsom, Business Manager, College of Business, Mississippi State University, Mississippi State, MS 39782.

Uniformly rated among the top two scholarly journals in the field in the behavioral side of management. Publishes current empirical research by management scholars from the fields of business policy and strategy, careers, health care administration, management education, managerial consultation, organizational behavior, management theory, organizational development, personnel and human resources, production and operations management, public sector management, social issues, and women in management. The content is primarily scholarly in tone, with numerous statistical tables and charts. However, practical implications of findings are also discussed. Articles are written by scholars and go through a rigorous review process; less than 15 percent of those submitted are published. Target audience is educators, serious students, staff experts, educated managers. Published quarterly (March, June, September, December) by the Academy of Management.

The Academy of Management Newsletter, Rose Knotts, Editor, Department of Management, North Texas State University, P.O. Box 13677, Denton, TX 76203-3677.

Articles appearing in the *Newsletter* contain information about members in the Academy of Management and current management trends. The emphasis is on informational affairs, and the focus covers national and international trends and events. Articles are written primarily by key people in the Academy and edited by the Newsletter editor. The target audience is membership in the Academy of Management (which is primarily academicians). The publication reports on books, conferences, scholarly events, and so on but does not contain book reviews, scholarly articles, nor research projects.

The American Review of Management and Inventiveness Report, The American Classical College, American Institute for Management and Inventiveness, P. O. Box 4526, Albuquerque, NM 87196, (505) 843-7749.

The success of a company is not predicated on the economic conditions the country and world are in, but on the competence of its management. It is management that makes profits, just as it is management that rules countries. Further, the science of management is changing all the time. New discoveries in management are made constantly. The managerial ideas of yesterday are supplanted by the new managerial ideas of today. The American Classical College and its research organization, the American Institute for Management and Inventiveness, issues monthly management studies under the general title of *the American Review of Management and Inventiveness Report.* Each issue discusses a single supremely important topic. The studies are easy to read, direct, to the point, readily applicable, and highly informative. We never forget our goal—which is your goal—the better, more profitable functioning of a human institution that is devoted to the acquisition of profits and power.

Business and Society Review, 870 Seventh Avenue, New York, NY 10019, (212) 977-7436.

In the vanguard of controversial business issues, this one-of-a-kind journal focuses on the most basic questions of business economics, philosophy, and ethics; airs critical new ideas; and records the latest developments. In each issue, top experts and thinkers share their insights and opinions in lively, up-to-date articles on matters of special interest to the corporate community. The *Review* consistently presents opinions from all sides of the political spectrum, from business executives to public interest activists; from Marxists to Libertarians. In addition, each issue contains regular features such as company performance roundup (which reports on both the successes and failures of American business in areas of public concern), symposia on controversial issues, and reviews of new books of interest.

D & B Reports, Dun and Bradstreet Corporation, 299 Park Avenue, New York, NY 10171, (212) 593-6723.

Deals with management issues of interest to entrepreneurs and small-business owners in a style both colorful and practical. The lively, brightly illustrated format addresses the common interests of both start-ups and mature but still growing small companies (with sales under $12 million). Feature articles often take the form of how-to stories based on the experiences of a variety of businesses and cover such subjects as raising money, managing growth, stimulating innovation, computerizing the small operation, shopping for services, and marketing products. In-depth profiles of small-company managers are also a staple, as are regular features on sales, automation, government, exporting and importing, tax issues and money management. A highlight each year is the wide-ranging survey of small-business presidents drawn from Dun & Bradstreet's data base of more than 7,000,000 companies.

Harvard Business Review, Soldier's Field Road, Boston, MA 02163.

Publishes articles on all areas of management, including finance, technology, business-government relations, strategy, human relations, education, and law. Articles are written for top executives and shed new light on management problems. Examples from corporate experience illustrate or enhance the main theme or argument. Most articles are written by businesspeople or professors. The audience consists primarily of executives who want practical but original and in-depth information on management issues.

The Journal of Education for Business, Heldref Publications, 4000 Albemarle Street, N.W., Washington, DC 20016, (202) 362-6445.

Formerly *The Journal of Business Education,* this publication is a valuable resource for those who teach and train personnel for the business world. The *Journal* features practical articles on business fundamentals, career education, consumer economics, distributive education, management, and trends in communications. Regular departments cover visual aids, new books, and research to create an information network for all business trainers and educators. The *Journal* is published monthly, October through May.

Nation's Business, U. S. Chamber of Commerce, 1615 H Street, N.W., Washington, DC 20062, (202) 463-5650.

A major information resource of particular value to the owners and/or managers of smaller to medium-sized businesses. Editorial features keep readers up-to-date on Washington developments that affect business, on contemporary management techniques that help them do a more effective job of running their own businesses, on case histories of successful entrepreneurs who explain the innovative techniques they used, and on trends in technology, marketing, franchising, finance, and other areas of interest to businesspeople. The publication is particularly well tuned into the world of the entrepreneur, and its editorial content is selected on the basis of relevance and usefulness to those individuals.

Research Management, The Industrial Research Institute, Inc., 100 Park Avenue, Suite 3600, New York, NY 10017, (212) 683-7626.

An international journal dedicated to enhancing the effectiveness of industrial research, *Research Management* is for managers of research, development, and technology and for students of the subject. Contributed articles deal with such subjects as planning and budgeting, invention and innovation, project selection and management, modes of organizing for technological innovation, human resource development, technology marketing, and technology policy. Every issue carries three departments that keep practitioners up-to-date on news of the current science and technology scene; new books, reports, and other information resources; and managerial techniques and problems.

SAM Advanced Management Journal, M.H. Abdelsmad, Editor, SAM-AMS, c/o Virginia Commonwealth University, Richmond, VA 23284, (804) 257-1741.

The Society for Advancement of Management, publisher of the *Journal,* was established in 1912 by the father of scientific management, Frederick W. Taylor, and his associates. The *Journal* is subscribed to by various managers, academicians, and libraries in the United States and over sixty countries around the world in addition to regular SAM members and students. The *Journal* is a quarterly, refereed publication, especially designed for the general manager. Areas of interest include all areas of management, such as human relations and organizational behavior, strategic management, international management, planning, productivity improvement, time management, and using computers in top managerial decisions.

Sloan Management Review, Sloan School of Management, MIT, 50 Memorial Drive, Cambridge, MA 02139, (617) 253-7170.

The nation's second largest general management journal providing managers with the latest tools and information needed for effective problem solving and decision making. Articles focus on original concepts, new research trends, innovative management techniques and practical applications, and case studies. A regular feature is the SMR forum, a lively section devoted to advocacy and thought pieces dealing with controversial subjects such as economic forecasts, management ethics, and business-government relations. The *Review* also features book reviews and an annotated list of recent management publications. Readers are primarily middle and top management: over 40 percent are corporate officers and directors. Material is presented in a clear, straightforward manner, making use of graphs and charts. The *Review* is a quarterly publication.

Supervisory Management, American Management Association, 135 W. 50th Street, New York, NY 10020, (212) 586-8100.

A magazine for first-line and second-line managers that provides practical, commonsense solutions to the difficult supervisory problems that make the task of managing and motivating people seem like the world's most thankless job. Articles are written by management practitioners, theorists, and educators and deal with such issues as how to get the staff working together as a team, the proper disciplinary actions, how to train, how to screen applicants, and how to level with employees about performance. Regular features include a real-life case drawn from the files of the American Arbitration Association, a knotty problem frequently encountered by managers to which readers can offer solutions, and advice on how to deal with after-five personal concerns. Graphs and charts supplement the text.

Training: The Magazine of Human Resources Development, Lakewood Publications, 50 S. Ninth Street, Minneapolis, MN 55402, (612) 333-0471.

The leading publication in the field of job-related training and human resources development. Its coverage of issues, trends, techniques, and how-to information is designed to appeal to training professionals in all types of organizations and to managers for whom employee development is a concern. Articles by staff members, free-lance writers, and practitioners delve into subjects ranging from the psychology of human motivation to specific principles of instructional design, from management and sales training to computer-assisted instruction and technical training. Monthly features include book reviews, staff and guest editorials, and a profile of training activity in a specific company, including the training budget. *Training* Magazine's Industry Report, released annually in the October issue, is the most comprehensive research-based analysis available of training and development activity in the United States.

The Wall Street Review of Books, Redgrave Publishing Company, South Salem, NY 10590.

The only professional journal devoted exclusively to reviewing works of interest and importance to the business, financial, and economic communities and to libraries serving their informational needs. *The Wall Street Review of Books* is designed by editorial policy to guide readers with business, financial, and economic interests to intelligent choices coincident with their needs. Good in-depth reviews guide selective and particular readers to titles that must be read and provide insights into ones that can be bypassed. *The Wall Street Review of Books* reviews trade and professional books in the fields of economics, business, finance, banking, and economic and business history. Novels dealing directly with finance and business will be considered, as well as textbooks.

Across the Board
(formerly: *Conference Board Record*)
845 Third Avenue
New York, NY 10022
(Monthly)

Administrative Science Quarterly
Graduate School of Management
Cornell University
Ithaca, NY 14853
(Quarterly)

Akron Business and Economic Review
College of Business Administration
University of Akron
Akron, OH 44325
(Quarterly)

American Behavioral Scientist
Sage Publications, Inc.
275 South Beverly Drive
Beverly Hills, CA 90212
(Bimonthly)

Arbitration Journal
American Arbitration Association
140 West 51st Street
New York, NY 10020
(Quarterly)

Arkansas Business and Economic Review
University of Arkansas
College of Business Administration
Fayetteville, AR 72701
(Quarterly)

Association Management
1575 Eye Street N.W.
Washington, DC 20005
(Monthly)

Baylor Business Studies
Hankamer School of Business
Baylor University
Box 6278
Waco, TX 76706
(Quarterly)

Business and Economic Review
Division of Research
College of Business Administration
The University of South Carolina
Columbia, SC 29208
(Bimonthly)

Business and Society
Business Research Center
Roosevelt University
430 S. Michigan Avenue
Chicago, IL 60605
(Semiannual)

Business Horizons
Graduate School of Business
Indiana University
Bloomington, IN 47405
(Bimonthly)

The Business Quarterly
School of Business Administration
The University of Western Ontario
London, On N6A 5B9, Canada
(Quarterly)

*Business: The Magazine of Managerial Thought
    and Action*
College of Business Administration
Georgia State University
Atlanta, GA 30303
(Quarterly)

California Management Review
Graduate School of Business Administration
University of California
Berkeley, CA 94720
(Quarterly)

Canadian Business Review
The Conference Board in Canada
Suite 100
25 McArthur Road
Ottowa, ON KIL 6R3, Canada
(Quarterly)

The Columbia Journal of World Review
Columbia University
814 Uris Hall
New York, NY 10027
(Quarterly)

Directors and Boards
The Journal of Corporate Action
229 S. 18th Street
Philadelphia, PA 19130
(Quarterly)

Employment Relations Today
Executive Enterprises Publications
33 West 60th Street
New York, NY 10023
(Quarterly)

Equal Opportunities International
MCB University Press
P.O. Box 10812
Birmingham, AL 35201
(Quarterly)

Health Services Manager
American Management Association
135 West 50th Street
New York, NY 10020
(Monthly)

Human Relations
Plenum Publishing Corporation
233 Spring Street
New York, NY 10013
(Monthly)

Human Resource Management
Graduate School of Business Administration
University of Michigan
Ann Arbor, MI 48109
(Quarterly)

INC.
38 Commercial Wharf
Boston, MA 02110
(Monthly)

Industrial and Labor Relations Review
New York State School of Industrial
    and Labor Relations
Cornell University
Ithaca, NY 14853
(Quarterly)

Industrial Relations
Institute of Industrial Relations
University of California
Berkeley, CA 94720
(Triannual)

International Management
McGraw-Hill House
Shoppenhangers Road
Maidenhead, Berkshire
SL6 20L, England
(Monthly)

The Journal of Applied Behavioral Science
NTL Institute for Applied Behavioral Science
36 Sherwood Place
P.O. Box 1678
Greenwich, CT 06836
(Quarterly)

Journal of Applied Social Psychology
7961 Eastern Avenue
Silver Spring, MD 20910
(Eight times a year)

Journal of Business
University of Chicago Press
P.O. Box 37005
Chicago, IL 60637
(Quarterly)

Journal of Business Research
Elsevier North-Holland, Inc.
52 Vanderbilt Avenue
New York, NY 10017
(Quarterly)

Journal of Economics and Business
School of Business Administration
Temple University
Philadelphia, PA 19122
(Quarterly)

Journal of Employment Counseling
American Association for Counseling
    and Development
5999 Stevenson Avenue
Alexandria, VA 22304
(Quarterly)

Journal of International Business Studies
Academy of International Business
University of South Carolina
College of Business Administration
Columbia, SC 29208
(Triannual)

Journal of Labor Research
Department of Economics
George Mason University
Fairfax, VA 22030
(Quarterly)

Journal of Management
Southern Management Association
Texas Technical University
College of Business Administration
Lubbock, TX 79409
(Triannual)

*Journal of Organizational Behavior
    Management*
The Haworth Press
28 East 22nd Street
New York, NY 10010
(Quarterly)

Journal of Small Business Management
International Council for Small Business
Bureau of Business Research
P.O. Box 2065
West Virgina University
Morgantown, WV 26506
(Quarterly)

Management Review
American Management Associations
Subscription Services
Box 319
Saranac Lake, NY 12983
(Monthly)

Management World
Administrative Management Society
AMS Building
2360 Maryland Road
Willow Grove, PA 19090
(Monthly)

Monthly Labor Review
Superintendent of Documents
Government Printing Office
Washington, DC 20402
(Monthly)

National Productivity Review
33 West 60th Street
New York, NY 10023
(Quarterly)

Organizational Dynamics
American Management Associations
Subscription Services
Box 319
Saranac Lake, NY 12983
(Quarterly)

Personnel
American Management Associations
Subscription Services
Box 319
Saranac Lake, NY 12983
(Bimonthly)

The Personnel Administrator
American Society for Personnel Administration
606 N. Washington Street
Alexandria, VA 22314
(Monthly)

Personnel Psychology
929 Harrison Avenue
Columbus, OH 43215
(Quarterly)

Public Administration Review
American Society for Public Administration
1225 Connecticut Avenue N.W.
Washington, DC 20036
(Bimonthly)

Public Personnel Management
International Personnel Management
   Association
Suite 870
1850 K Street N.W.
Washington, DC 20006
(Quarterly)

Quarterly Review of Economics and Business
Bureau of Economic and Business Research
University of Illinois
1206 S. Sixth Street
Champaign, IL 61820
(Quarterly)

*Successful Business: The Magazine For
   Independent Business*
505 Market Street
Knoxville, TN 37902
(Quarterly)

Training and Development Journal
American Society for Training and Development
P.O. Box 1443
1630 Duke Street
Alexandria, VA 22313
(Monthly)

Urban and Social Change Review
McGuinn Hall
Room 202
Boston College
Chestnut Hill, MA 02167
(Semiannual)

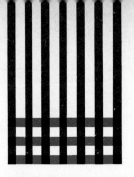

APPENDIX B
SUGGESTED READINGS

CHAPTER 1

Anderson, Andy, "Step Inside with Me: The Automated Office of the 1990s," *Credit and Financial Management* 87 (January–February), 1985, pp. 14–17.

Best, Fred, "The Nature of Work in a Changing Society," *Personnel Journal* 64 (January 1985), pp. 36–42.

Blake, Robert R., and Mouton, Jane S., "Out of the Past: How to Use Your Organization's History to Shape a Better Future," *Training and Development Journal* 37 (November 1983), pp. 58–65.

"The Changing Shape of Offices," *Modern Office* (Australia) 24 (February 1985), pp. 8–9.

Galitz, Wilbert O., "What the Office of the 1990s Will Be Like," *Journal of Forms Management* 10 (May–July 1985), pp. 4–7.

Goddard, Robert W., "The Rise of the New Organization," *Management World* 14 (January 1985), pp. 7–11.

Hoyt, Leeza L., "Preparing for the Office of the Future," *Journal of Property Management* 50 (March/April 1985), pp. 10–11; 13.

"Informatics," *Worklife* (Canada) 4; 2 (1985), pp. 8–9.

Mueller, Robert K., "Renaissance Managers: A New Breed for Tomorrow's Electronic Office," *Today's Office* 19 (March 1985), pp. 32–36.

Oyer, Paul D., "An Integrated Office in the 90's? Start It Now!" *Office* 101 (January 1985), p. 146.

Russel, Robert Arnold, "The Office of the Future," *Executive* (Canada) 27 (May 1985), pp. 61–62.

Springer, T.J., "Workplace Integration: A Human-Centered Approach," *Office* 101 (January 1985), p. 99.

"Westinghouse Opens Its 'Ultimate Workplace,' " *Office Administration and Automation* 46 (February 1985), pp. 40–42, 76.

CHAPTER 2

Arsenault, Andre, and Dolan, Shimon, "The Role of Personality, Occupation and Organization in Understanding the Relationship Between Job Stress, Performance and Absenteeism," *Journal of Occupational Psychology* (UK) 56 (September 1983), pp. 227–240.

Comer, J.M., "Machiavellianism and Inner vs. Outer Directedness: A Study of Sales Managers," *Psychological Reports* 56;1 (1985), pp. 81–82.

Cunningham, Mary E., "Prejudice: A Luxury Corporate Society Cannot Afford," *Marketing Times* 29 (July–August 1982), pp. 24–26.

Dolecheck, M.M., and Dolecheck, C.C., "How Do Male and Female Employees with Business Degrees Perceive Discrimination on the Job?" *Akron Business and Economic Review* 14; 2 (1983), pp. 12–15.

Firth, M., "Sex-Discrimination in Job Opportunities for Women," *Sex Roles* 8; 8 (1982), pp. 891–901.

Golson, Hodges L., "The Technically-Oriented Personality in Management," *IEEE Transactions on Engineering Management* EM-32;1 (February 1985), pp. 33–36.

Grant, Charles T., "Blacks Hit Racial Roadblocks Climbing Up the Corporate Ladder," *Business & Society Review* 52 (Winter 1985), pp. 56–59.

Hollon, C.J., "Machiavellianism and Managerial Work Attitudes and Perceptions," *Psychological Reports* 52; 2 (1983), pp. 432–434.

Margerison, Charles, "The Vocational Preference of Chief Executives," *Management Decision* 21; 3 (1983), pp. 34–43.

McNatt, Robert J., "Pride and Prejudice: The Story of Black Employee Associations," *Black Enterprise* 14; 9 (April 1984), pp. 63–65.

Micou, Ann McKinstry, "The Invisible Hand at Work in Developing Countries: Seven Prejudices Against Multinationals," *Across the Board* 22 (March 1985), pp. 8–17.

Miles, Mary, "Charm Your Way to Success," *Computer Decisions* 17; 8 (April 23, 1985), pp. 154, 156.

Shea, M.T., and Beatty, J.R., "Measuring Machiavellianism with MACH-V: A Psychometric Investigation," *Journal of Personality Assessment* 47; 5 (1983), pp. 509–513.

Sterns, Laura, Alexander, Ralph A., Barrett, Gerald V., and Dambrot, Faye H., "The Relationship of Extraversion and Neuroticism with Job Preferences and Job Satisfaction for Clerical Employees," *Journal of Occupational Psychology* (UK) 56; 2 (1983), pp. 145–153.

Wakin, Edward, "The Impressive Step to the Top: Will You Make It?" *Today's Office* 17; 8 (January 1983), pp. 44–50.

CHAPTER 3

Bell, George R., "Listen and You Shall Hear," *Association Management* 36 (March 1984), pp. 103–107.

Brodigan, Julia, "Silence Isn't Golden," *Supervision* 47 (January 1985), pp. 14–16.

Brownell, Judi, "Listening: A Powerful Management Tool," *Supervisory Management* 29 (October 1984), pp. 35–39.

Crow, Porter J., "How to Change Their Minds: Preparing a Persuasive Presentation," *Vital Speeches,* 51; 14 (May 1, 1985), pp. 439–441.

Currie, Catherine, "Communicating in an Automated Environment," *Canadian Banker* (Canada) 91; 6 (December 1984), pp. 18–21.

De Mare, George, "Communicating: The Key to Establishing Good Working Relationships," *Price Waterhouse Review* 28; 2 (1984), pp. 27–32.

Denton, D. Keith, "A Manager's Toughest Job: One-on-One Communication," *Supervisory Management* 30 (May 1985), pp. 37–43.

Figel, Marge, "The Art of Productive Listening," *American Salesman,* 29 (August 1984), pp. 3–6.

Fitzgerald, Paul E., "How to Play Catch—and Be a Better Communicator," *Supervisory Management* 30 (January 1985), pp. 26–31.

Lederer, Jerome, "Human Factors in Operational Communications," *Professional Safety* 30 (April 1985), pp. 14–18.

Main, Jeremy, "How to Sell by Listening," *Fortune* 111;3 (February 4, 1985), pp. 52–54.

Palmroth, Bill, "Improve Your Listening I.Q.," *American Salesman* 30 (May 1985), pp. 13–15.

Pasanetti, JoAn, "When the 'Boss Lady' Speaks, It's Worth a Listen," *Advertising Age* 55; 15 (April 2, 1984), pp. M-12, M-16.

CHAPTER 4

Anderson, A.J., "Managing Deadwood: Three Dangerous Assumptions," *Journal of Library Administration* 5; 3 (Fall 1984), pp. 2–6.

Brookhart, Smith W., III, "If You're Really Serious About Employee Motivation. . .," *Bank Marketing* 16 (September 1984), pp. 43–46.

Cudworth, E.F., "Delta Air Lines President Ronald W. Allen Discusses Company's Highly Successful Employee Motivation Program, Long-Range Strategic Thinking," *Industrial Engineering* 16 (October 1984), pp. 84–87, 99.

Demirdjian, Z.S., "A Multidimensional Approach to Motivating Salespeople," *Industrial Marketing Management* 13; 1 (February 1984), pp. 25–32.

Di Bari, Nick, "Compensation vs. Motivation," *Sales and Marketing Management* 133; 5 (October 8, 1984), pp. 48–49.

Ellman, Edgar S., "Write Your Own Personnel Policy Manual," *Industrial Distribution* 74 (May 1985), pp. 237–238.

Fitzgerald, Paul E., Jr., "Worker Perceptions: The Key to Motivation," *Health Care Supervisor* 3; 1 (October 1984), pp. 13–18.

"Flex Comp Viable for Meeting Varying Needs," *Employee Benefit Plan Review* 39; 11 (May 1985), pp. 105–106.

Furnham, Adrian, and Schaeffer, Rosemary, "Person-Environment Fit, Job Satisfaction and Mental Health," *Journal of Occupational Psychology* (UK) 57; 4 (December 1984), pp. 295–307.

Gilliam, Les, "Diversity, Not Intensity, the Best Approach to Staff Motivation," *Computerworld* 18; 33 (August 13, 1984), pp. 55, 74.

Hollman, Robert W., "Creating a Climate for Employee Self-motivation," *Montana Business Quarterly* 22; 4 (Winter 1984), pp. 5–8.

Langemo, Mark, "Motivating Toward Excellence and Productivity," *ARMA Records Management Quarterly* 19; 2 (April 1985), pp. 24–26.

Lawrence, Kathy, "Motivating Staff," *Data Processing* (UK) 26; 9 (November 1984), pp. 17–19.

Michalski, Richard, "Decentralized Decision-making: Motivating Managers to Look at the 'Big Picture,' " *Cost and Management* (Canada) 58 (March–April 1984), pp. 55–59.

Miles, Mary, "Fighting that Losing Feeling," *Computer Decisions* 17; 11 (June 4, 1985), pp. 64, 111.

"Money Isn't the Best Tool for Motivating Technical Professionals," *Personnel Administrator* 30 (June 1985), pp. 63–78.

"Motivation and Training," *Credit Union Magazine* 51 (February 1985), pp. 74–78.

Seelig, Pat, "Employee Motivation: Counter Attacks," *Incentive Marketing* 159 (May 1985), pp. 94–98.

Taylor, Thayer C., "MCI Mixes Computers and Motivation," *Sales and Marketing Management* 132; 8 (June 4, 1984), pp. 42–46.

"Tell Your Employees, 'We Care,' " *Business Insurance* 18; 22 (May 28, 1984), p. 8.

Walton, Richard E., "From Control to Commitment in the Workplace," *Harvard Business Review* 63 (March–April 1985), pp. 76–84.

CHAPTER 5

Anderson, A.J., "On the Importance of Recognition," *Journal of Library Administration* 5; 3 (Fall 1984), pp. 7–15.

Ernest, Robert C., and Baenen, Leonard B., "Analysis of Attitude Survey Results: Getting the Most from the Data," *Personnel Administrator* 30 (May 1985), pp. 71–80.

Godkin, Lynn, "Anticipated Job Satisfaction: Attitudinal Bias Among Women," *Arkansas Business & Economic Review* 17; 3 (1984), pp. 7–11.

Gordon, Judy A., "Releasing Energy and Enthusiasm: An Interview with Robert Townsend," *Credit and Financial Management* 87; 2 (March 1985), pp. 16–22.

Hackett, Rick D., and Guion, Robert M., "A Reevaluation of the Absenteeism-Job Satisfaction Relationship," *Organizational Behavior and Human Decision Processes* 35; 3 (June 1985), pp. 340–381.

Henning, Jo-El, "The Necessity of Support Systems," *Training and Development Journal* 39 (June 1985), p. 14.

Hobson, Charles J., Hobson, Robert B., and Hobson, John J., "Why Managers Use Criticism Instead of Praise," *Supervisory Management* 30 (March 1985), pp. 24–31.

Ivancevich, John M., "Predicting Absenteeism from Prior Absence and Work Attitudes," *Academy of Management Journal* 28; 1 (March 1985), pp. 219–228.

Johnson, K.L., "Praise: More Precious than Money," *Managers Magazine* 59 (November 1984), pp. 16–18.

Latack, Janina C., and Foster, Lawrence W., "Implementation of Compressed Work Schedules: Participation and Job Redesign as Critical

Factors for Employee Acceptance," *Personnel Psychology* 38; 1 (Spring 1985), pp. 75–92.

Lucas, George H., Jr., "The Relationships Between Job Attitudes, Personal Characteristics, and Job Outcomes: A Study of Retail Store Managers," *Journal of Retailing* 61; 1 (Spring 1985), pp. 35–62.

Micolo, Anthony M., "Gaining Acceptance as a New Supervisor," *Supervisory Management* 30 (June 1985), pp. 5–7.

Shapiro, K.P., "New Programs Reward 'Key Contributors,'" *Business Insurance* 19; 7 (February 18, 1985), p. 48.

York, David R., "Attitude Surveying," *Personnel Journal* 64; 5 (May 1985), pp. 70–73.

Zahra, Shaker A., "A Comparative Study of the Effect of Role Ambiguity and Conflict on Employee Attitudes and Performance," *Akron Business and Economic Review* 16; 1 (Spring 1985), pp. 37–42.

CHAPTER 6

Bartunek, Jean M., "How Organization Development Can Develop Organizational Theory," *Group & Organization Studies* 8; 3 (September 1983), pp. 303–318.

Cohn, Steven F., and Turyn, Romaine M., "Organizational Structure, Decision-Making Procedures, and the Adoption of Innovations," *IEEE Transactions on Engineering Management* EM-31; 4 (November 1984), pp. 154–161.

Drazin, Robert, and Howard, Peter, "Strategy Implementation: A Technique for Organizational Design," *Columbia Journal of World Business* 19; 2 (Summer 1984), pp. 40–46.

Frederiksen, Lee W., Riley, Anne W., and Myers, John B., "Matching Technology and Organizational Structure: A Case Study in White Collar Productivity Improvement," *Journal of Organizational Behavior Management* 6; 3, 4 (Fall–Winter 1984), pp. 59–80.

Gresov, Christopher, "Designing Organizations to Innovate and Implement: Using Two Dilemmas to Create a Solution," *Columbia Journal of World Business* 19; 4 (Winter 1984), pp. 63–67.

Hall, Roger I., "The Natural Logic of Management Policy Making: Its Implications for the Survival of an Organization," *Management Science* 30 (August 1984), pp. 905–927.

John, George, and Martin, John, "Effects of Organizational Structure of Marketing Planning on Credibility and Utilization of Plan Output," *Journal of Marketing Research* 21; 2 (May 1984), pp. 170–183.

Mackenzie, Kenneth D., "Design of a Supermarket Chain," *Human Systems Management* (Netherlands) 5; 1 (Spring 1985), pp. 56–65.

Mackenzie, Kenneth D., "The Organizational Audit and Analysis Technology for Organizational Design," *Human Systems Management* (Netherlands) 5; 1 (Spring 1985), pp. 46–55.

Mackenzie, Kenneth D., "A Strategy and Desiderata for Organizational Design" *Human Systems Management* (Netherlands) 4; 3 (Spring 1984), pp. 201–213.

Masuch, Michael, "Vicious Circles in Organizations," *Administrative Science Quarterly* 30; 1 (March 1985), pp. 14–33.

McGinnis, Michael A., "The Key to Strategic Planning: Integrating Analysis and Institution," *Sloan Management Review* 26; 1 (Fall 1984), pp. 45–52.

Sherman, J. Daniel, and Smith, Howard L., "The Influence of Organizational Structure on Intrinsic Versus Extrinsic Motivation," *Academy of Management Journal* 27; 4 (December 1984), pp. 877–885.

Stevenson, William B., Pearce, Jone L., and Porter, Lyman W., "The Concept of 'Coalition' in Organization Theory and Research," *Academy of Management Review* 10; 2 (April 1985), pp. 256–268.

Stillman, Richard J., II, "The Romantic Vision in American Administrative Theory: Retrospectives and Prospectives," *International Journal of Public Administration* 7; 2 (June 1985), pp. 107–148.

Telem, Moshe, "The Process of Organizational Structure," *Journal of Management Studies,* 22 (January 1985), pp. 38–52.

CHAPTER 7

Albanese, Robert, and Van Fleet, David D., "Rational Behavior in Groups: The Free-Riding Tendency," *Academy of Management Review* 10; 2 (April 1985), pp. 244–255.

Gladstein, Deborah L., "Groups in Context: A Model of Task Group Effectiveness," *Administrative Science Quarterly* 29; 4 (December 1984), pp. 499–517.

Krantz, James, "Group Process Under Conditions of Organizational Decline," *Journal of Applied Behavioral Science* 21; 1 (February 1985), pp. 1–17.

Menninger, Roy W., "A Retrospective View of a Hospital-wide Group Relations Training Program: Costs, Consequences and Conclusions," *Human Relations* 38 (April 1985), pp. 323–339.

Podsakoff, Philip M., and Todor, William D., "Relationships Between Leader Reward and Punishment Behavior and Group Processes and Productivity," *Journal of Management* 11; 1 (Spring 1985), pp. 55–73.

Raelin, Joseph A., "An Examination of Deviant/Adaptive Behaviors in the Organizational Careers of Professionals," *Academy of Management Review* 9; 3 (July 1984), pp. 413–427.

Spillane, R., "Authority in Small Groups: A Laboratory Test of a Machiavellian Observation," *British Journal of Social Psychology* 22 (February 1983), pp. 51–59.

Van De Vliert, Evert, "Escalative Intervention in Small-Group Conflicts," *Journal of Applied Behavioral Science* 21, 1 (February 1985), pp. 19–36.

CHAPTER 8

Allen, Cheryl D., Howell, Jerry D., and Pavlik, Alan, "Managing Your Organization's Quality Circles," *Quality Circles Journal* 8; 2 (June 1985), pp. 10–12.

Allen, John, "It Really Works: Company Comments on Quality Circles," *Quality Circles Journal* 8; 1 (March 1985), pp. 8–9.

Allen, John T, "Distributors . . . Think Quality Circles!" *Industrial Distribution* 74 (May 1985), pp. 63–65.

Burtch, Susan, "Quality Circles at Aetna Canada," *Quality Circles Journal* 7; 4 (December 1984), pp. 40–41.

Collard, Ron, and Dale, Barrie, "Quality Circles: Why They Break Down and Why They Hold Up," *Personnel Management* (UK) 17 (February 1985), pp. 28–31.

Connelly, Sharon L., "Work Spirit: Channeling Energy for High Performance," *Training and Development Journal* 39 (May 1985), pp. 50–54.

Haskew, Michael, "Management and Quality Circles: Communicating and Cooperating," *Quality Circles Journal* 8; 2 (June 1985), pp. 16–19.

Heinzlmeir, Larry A., "What Is Productivity?" *Canadian Manager* (Canada) 9; 4 (December 1984), pp. 8–10.

"Labor-Management Cooperation and Worker Participation: Elements of Program Development," *Arbitration Journal* 40; 2 (June 1985), pp. 67–73.

Meyer, Gordon W., and Stott, Randall G., "Quality Circles: Panacea or Pandora's Box?" *Organizational Dynamics* 13; 4 (Spring 1985), pp. 34–50.

Middleton, Rupert, "Team Briefing and Quality Circles Prove Their Value," *Management World* 14 (June 1985), pp. 36–37.

Steel, Robert P., Mento, Anthony J., Dilla, Benjamin L., Ovalle, Nestor K., II, and Lloyd, Russell F., "Factors Influencing the Success and Failure of Two Quality Circle Programs," *Journal of Management* 11; 1 (Spring 1985), pp. 99–119.

Tate, William C., "Measuring Our Productivity Improvements," *Business Quarterly* (Canada) 49; 4 (Winter 1984/1985), pp. 87–91.

Towler, John, "Develop the People Factor in Productivity," *Industrial Management* (Canada) 9; 5 (June 1985), p. 20.

Wada, Takuya, and Vecchio, Robert P., "Quality Circles at Mitsubishi," *Quality Circles Journal* 7; 4 (December 1984), pp. 33–34.

Youker, Robert B., "Ten Benefits of Participant Action Planning," *Training* 22 (June 1985), pp. 52–56.

CHAPTER 9

Connolly, James, "The Communications Manager: Born Again," *Computerworld* 18, 19; 53 (December 31, 1984/January 7, 1985), pp. 85–90.

Frost, Taggart F., "The Sick Organization; II. The Manager's Role in Treatment," *Personnel* 62 (June 1985), pp. 44–49.

Grindlay, Andrew, "The Information Systems Manager as Statesman," *Business Quarterly* (Canada) 49; 4 (Winter 1984/1985), pp. 6–10.

Hornig, Lilli S., "Women in Science and Engineering: Why So Few?" *Technology Review* 87; 8 (November–December 1984), pp. 30–36, 38–41.

Lynn, Laurence E., Jr., "Manager's Role in Public Management," *Bureaucrat* 13; 4 (Winter 1984/1985), pp. 20–25.

Margerison, Charles, and McCann, Dick, "The Managerial Linker: A Key to the High Performing Team," *Management Decision* (UK) 22; 4 (1984), pp. 46–58.

Nienburg, R.E., and Steele, M.C., "So Now You're a Manager," *Computerworld* 19; 21 (May 27, 1985), pp. 35–41.

Numerof, Rita E., "The Manager as Conflict Negotiator," *Health Care Supervisor* 3; 3 (April 1985), pp. 1–15.

Raimondi, Donna, "Salary Gap Pervades DP: Job Agencies Offer Pointers to Aspiring Women Workers," *Computerworld* 19; 6 (February 11, 1985), pp. 1, 6.

Ryan, Gerald P., Lezotte, Frank, and Jordan, Bebe, "The Communications Manager: Describing the Job/Doing the Job," *On Communications* 2(February 1985), pp. 43–49.

Washing, Harry A., and Boveington, Kurt W., "Are Data Processing Managers Neglecting the Career Development of Their Employees?" *Personnel Administrator* 30 (June 1985), pp. 191–200, 215.

CHAPTER 10

Adair, John, "Leadership: Be Helmsman and Navigator, but Stay Out of the Engine Room," *International Management* (UK) (European Edition) 40 (June 1985), p. 73.

Adair, John, "Leadership: The Special Talents that Set a Leader Apart," *International Management* (UK) (European Edition) 40 (April 1985), p. 78.

Alexion, John C., "The Decision Maker: Leadership and Responsibility," *Review of Business* 6; 3 (Winter 1984), p. 1.

Bass, Bernard M., "Leadership: Good, Better, Best," *Organizational Dynamics* 13; 3 (Winter 1985), pp. 26–40.

Behling, Orlando, and Rauch, Charles F., Jr., "A Functional Perspective on Improving Leadership Effectiveness," *Organizational Dynamics* 13; 4 (Spring 1985), pp. 51–61.

Calloway, D. Wayne, "The Straw that Stirs the Drink: Leadership at PepsiCo," *Planning Review* 13; 3 (May 1985), pp. 8–13.

Derven, Ron, "Professional Detachment is Operating Philosophy at Landauer Under John White's Leadership," *National Real Estate Investor* 27 (June 1985), pp. 140–144.

Kets De Vries, Manfred F.R., and Miller, Danny, "Narcissism and Leadership: An Object Relations Perspective," *Human Relations* 38 (June 1985), pp. 583–601.

Lampton, William, "Ten Positive Signs Ahead: Leaders as Agents of Change," *Fund Raising Management* 16; 4 (June 1985), pp. 112, 126.

Meindl, James R., Ehrlich, Sanford B., and Dukerich, Janet M., "The Romance of Leadership," *Administrative Science Quarterly* 30; 1 (March 1985), pp. 78–102.

Middleton, Ava, "Leadership for One Minute Managers," *Association Management* 37 (May 1985), pp. 103–106.

Miskin, Val D., and Gmelch, Walter H., "Quality Leadership for Quality Teams," *Training and Development Journal* 39 (May 1985), pp. 122–129.

Strawhecker, Paul, "The Process of Developing Innovation and Leadership," *Fund Raising Management* 16; 1 (March 1985), pp. 26–33.

Townsend, Robert, "Townsend's Third Degree in Leadership," *Across the Board* 22 (June 1985), pp. 48–52.

Wright, Norman B., "Leadership Styles: Which Are Best When?" *Business Quarterly* (Canada) 49; 4 (Winter 1984/1985), pp. 20–23.

CHAPTER 11

"Bottom-Up Management," *Inc.* 7 (June 1985), pp. 33–48.

Brown, Barbara A., "Performance Appraisals: How to Make Them Work," *Employment Relations Today* 12; 1 (Spring 1985), pp. 39–42.

Critchley, Barry, "Four Hours Under the Gun Testing Job Selection Tests," *Rydge's* (Australia) 57 (May 1984), pp. 86–87.

Edwards, Mark R., Borman, Walter C., and Sproull, J. Ruth, "Solving the Double Bind in Performance Appraisal: A Saga of Wolves, Sloths and Eagles," *Business Horizons* 28; 3 (May–June 1985), pp. 59–68.

Grove, Andrew S., "Employee Appraisal: When You're the Judge," *Computer Decisions* 16; 6 (May 1984), pp. 190–196, 246–250.

Lee, Cynthia, "Increasing Performance Appraisal Effectiveness: Matching Task Types, Appraisal Process and Rater Training," *Academy of Management Review* 10; 2 (April 1985), pp. 322–331.

Linnen, Beth M., "Employee Reviews Should Be Tailored to the Institution," *Savings Institutions* 106 (June 1985), pp. 114–115.

Litecky, Charles R., "Better Interviewing Skills," *Journal of Systems Management* 36 (June 1985), pp. 36–39.

Oliver, John E., "Performance Appraisals that Fit," *Personnel Journal* 64 (June 1985), pp. 66–71.

Owen, Darrell E., "Profile Analysis: Matching Positions and Personnel," *Supervisory Management* 29 (November 1984), pp. 14–20.

Pelissero, John P., "Personnel Evaluation and the Military Manager: Contrasts in Performance Appraisal Systems," *Public Personnel Management* 13; 2 (Summer 1984), pp. 121–132.

"Self-Appraisals: A Participative Technique for Evaluating and Improving Employee Performance," *Small Business Report* (February 1984), pp. 37–40.

CHAPTER 12

Caffarella, Rosemary S., "Managing Conflict: An Analytical Tool," *Training and Development Journal* 38 (February 1984), pp. 34–38.

Coombes, Paul, "The Union Path to Conflict Resolution, Partnership, and Prosperity," *Rydge's* (Australia) 57 (November 1984), pp. 30–31.

Duff, James C., "The Quantitative Monitoring of Absenteeism: Do 'No-Fault' and Just Cause Standards Conflict?" *Arbitration Journal* 40; 1 (March 1985), pp. 61–62.

Fahs, Michael I., "Communication Strategies for Anticipating and Managing Conflict," *Personnel Administrator* 27 (October 1982), pp. 28–34.

Numerof, Rita E., "The Manager as Conflict Negotiator," *Health Care Supervisor* 3; 3 (April 1985), pp. 1–15.

Phillips, Ronald C., "Project Conflict: Cost, Causes and Cures," *Public Utilities Fortnightly* 115; 10 (May 16, 1985), pp. 35–39.

Rahim, M. Afzalur, "A Strategy for Managing Conflict in Complex Organizations," *Human Relations* 38 (January 1985), pp. 81–89.

Shockley-Zalabak, Pamela S., "Current Conflict Management Training: An Examination of Practices in Ten Large American Organizations," *Group & Organization Studies* 9; 4 (December 1984), pp. 491–507.

Smith, Roger B., "A Working Partnership for Managing Change: Company, Unions and Employee Relationships," *Vital Speeches* 51; 5 (December 15, 1984), pp. 146–148.

Walton, Matt S., III, "When Incentive Goals Clash," *Sales and Marketing Management* 134; 5 (April 1, 1985), pp. 66–68.

CHAPTER 13

Bernacki, E.J., and Baun, W.B., "The Relationship of Job-Performance to Exercise Adherence in a Corporate Fitness Program," *Journal of Occupational Medicine* 26; 7 (1984), pp. 529–531.

Davidson, M.J., and Cooper, C.L., "Occupational Stress in Female Managers: A Comparative Study," *Journal of Management Studies* (UK) 21; 2 (April 1984), pp. 185–205.

Dotson, Beth, "Spending Money to Save Money: Can the Investment in an Employee Fitness Plan Work for an Independent Agency?" *Rough Notes* 128 (June 1985), pp. 38–39, 47.

Horne, W.M., "Effects of a Physical Activity Program on Middle-aged, Sedentary Corporation Executives," *American Industrial Hygiene Association Journal* 36 (March 1975), pp. 241–245.

"How Company Health Plans Cut into Absenteeism," *Rydge's* (Australia) (November 1983), pp. 168–170.

Jacobs, Sally, "The Spouse's Demand to the Corporation," *New England Business* 6; 7 (April 16, 1984), pp. 68–71, 78.

Kendall, Rick, "Business Joins the Nation's Fitness Room," *Occupational Hazards* 47 (May 1985), pp. 97–100.

Kondrasuk, Jack N., "Corporate Physical Fitness Programs: The Role of the Personnel Department," *Personnel Administrator* 29 (December 1984), pp. 75–80.

"Measuring the Shape of Corporate Fitness Plans," *Employee Benefit Plan Review* 38; 10 (April 1984), pp. 10–14.

Morgan, Philip I., Patton, John, and Baker, H. Kent, "The Organization's Role in Managing Midlife Crisis," *Training and Development Journal* 39 (January 1985), pp. 56–59.

Pehanich, Mike, "Health Clubs Zero in on Corporations," *Advertising Age* 53; 6 (February 8, 1982), pp. M-18–M-19.

Perham, John, "Executive Health Audit/How Busy CEOs Keep in Shape/ Fitness Programs Down the Line/Check-Up Centers for Physical Exams," *Dun's Business Month* 124; 4 (October 1984), pp. 88–112.

Porter, Nelson D., "Union Endorses Quality of Working Life," *Canadian Business Review* (Canada) 11; 4 (Winter 1984), pp. 10–12.

"Reduced Costs, Increased Worker Production Are Rationale for Tax-Favored Corporate Fitness Plans," *Employee Benefit Plan Review* 38; 5 (November 1983), pp. 20–22.

Shephard, R.J., Morgan, P., Finucane, R., and Schimmelfing, L., "Factors Influencing Recruitment to an Occupational Fitness Program," *Journal of Occupational Medicine* 22 (June 1980), pp. 389–398.

Stevens, A.G., Marchal, C., and Miles, D.S., "Body-Composition Changes Following a Corporate Employee Fitness Program," *Medicine and Science in Sports and Exercise* 17; 2 (1985), p. 246.

Williamson, Arthur R., "Ergonomics . . . Changing the Workplace to Fit the Worker," *Words* 13; 5 (February–March 1985), pp. 19–22.

CHAPTER 14

Alvarez, Joan, "Change Management," *Journal of Information Management* 6; 2 (Winter 1985), pp. 39–50.

Atkinson, Philip E., "Who Should Manage Change?" *Management Services* (UK) 29 (February 1985), pp. 14–15.

Berardo, Donald J., and Everly, George S., Jr., "Stop — I Want to Get Off! Coping with Change in Corporate DP: Managing Change Demands Three Simple, Personal Steps," *Data Management* 22 (September 1984), pp. 18–24.

Boyle, Richard J., "Why Wrestle with Jellyfish?: Lessons in Managing Organizational Change," *National Productivity Review* 4; 2 (Spring 1985), pp. 180–183.

Comfort, Louise K., "Integrating Organizational Action in Emergency Management: Strategies for Change," *Public Administration Review* 45 (Special Issue; January 1985), pp. 155–164.

Hedin, Anne, "Management: Smoke on the Winds of Change," *Small Systems World* 12 (November 1984), p. 55.

Lynn, George, and Lynn, Joanne Barrie, "Seven Keys to Successful Change Management," *Supervisory Management* 29 (November 1984), pp. 30–37.

McGowan, Robert P., and Stevens, John M., "Coping with Change: Urban Issues and Management Strategies," *International Journal of Public Administration* 7; 1 (1985), pp. 67–81.

Pereira, Cesar L., "Managing Change: Is Top Management Really Committed to Innovation?" *Industrial Engineering* 17 (June 1985), pp. 12–14.

Smith, Barry, "Management Development: 'An Island of Change,' " *Journal of Management Development* (UK) 3; 3 (1984), pp. 26–38.

Smith, Roger B., "A Working Partnership for Managing Change: Company, Unions and Employee Relationships," *Vital Speeches* 51; 5 (December 15, 1984), pp. 146–148.

Sobczak, James J., "Managing Technological Changes," *Telecommunications* 19 (April 1985), pp. 66r–66x.

Stephenson, Blair Y., "Managing Systems Change Hinges on the Human Element," *Data Management* 22 (September 1984), pp. 10–17.

CHAPTER 15

Bryman, Alan, "Leadership and Corporate Culture: Harmony and Disharmony," *Personnel Review* (UK) 13; 2 (1984), pp. 19–24.

Burton, Kathleen, "End-User Computing Varies with Corporate Culture," *Computerworld* 19; 18 (May 6, 1985), p. 26.

De Frank, Richard S., Matteson, Michael T., Schweiger, David M., and Ivancevich, John M., "The Impact of Culture on the Management Practices of American and Japanese CEOs," *Organizational Dynamics* 13; 4 (Spring 1985), pp. 62–76.

Ernest, Robert C., "Corporate Cultures and Effective Planning," *Personnel Administrator* 30 (March 1985), pp. 49–60.

Gardner, Meryl P., "Creating a Corporate Culture for the Eighties," *Business Horizons* 28; 1 (January–February 1985), pp. 59–63.

Gordon, George G., and Haegele, Monroe J., " 'Corporate Culture' in Financial Services," *Bankers Monthly* 101; 12 (December 15, 1984), pp. 16–18.

Hughes, Holly, "Defining Corporate Culture with Meetings," *Successful Meetings* 34 (March 1985), pp. 27–30.

MacLeod, Jennifer S., "Changing Power Relationships Within Corporations: A Challenge," *Employment Relations Today* 12;1 (Spring 1985), pp. 31–35.

McPherson, Joseph, "Inspiring Creativity While 'Wandering Around,' " *International Management* (UK) (European Edition), 39 (April 1984), p. 77.

"New Business Mavericks: Let 'Em Loose!" *Marketing Communications* 10; 5 (June 1985), pp. 23–26.

Nicholls, John R., "An Alloplastic Approach to Corporate Culture," *International Studies of Management and Organization* 14; 4 (Winter 1984/1985), pp. 32–63.

Pascale, Richard, "The Paradox of 'Corporate Culture': Reconciling Ourselves to Socialization," *California Management Review* 27; 2 (Winter 1985), pp. 26–41.

Smith, Wayne, "Infusing Quality in the Corporate Culture," *Computerworld* 19; 4 (January 28, 1985), pp. 33–34.

Tolentino, Arturo, "Incorporating Quality Control Circles in the Corporate-wide Productivity Improvement Program," *Quality Circles Journal* 8; 2 (June 1985), pp. 6–9.

"Tom Peters' Formula for Supervisory Excellence," *Supervisory Management* 30 (February 1985), pp. 2–6.

Walter, Stephanie K., "Top Techies Anguish Over the New Corporate Culture," *Management Technology* 3; 2 (June 1985), pp. 71–72.

Zemke, Ron, "Stalking the Elusive Corporate Credo," *Training* 22 (June 1985), pp. 44–51.

CHAPTER 16

Baker, James C., "The International Infant Formula Controversy: A Dilemma in Corporate Social Responsibility," *Journal of Business Ethics* (Netherlands) 4; 3 (June 1985), pp. 181–190.

Bell, K.D., "Accountability in the Private Sector," *Practising Manager* (Australia) 5; 1 (October 1984), pp. 12–16.

Boulanger, Robert, and Wayland, Donald, "Ethical Management: A Growing Corporate Responsibility, I," *CA Magazine* (Canada) 118 (March 1985), pp. 54–59.

Corbett, Harold J., "The Best of Thieves: Restoring Trust in Business," *Vital Speeches* 51; 11 (March 15, 1985), pp. 349–352.

Filios, Vassilios P., "Corporate Social Responsibility and Public Accountability," *Journal of Business Ethics* (Netherlands) 3; 4 (November 1984), pp. 305–314.

Jones, Peter T., "Sanctions, Incentives and Corporate Behavior," *California Management Review* 27; 3 (Spring 1985), pp. 119–131.

Logan, John E., Logan, Sandra P., Mille, Jean M. Edouard, "Corporate Social Responsibility," *Business and Economic Review* 31; 2 (January 1985), pp. 25–27.

Maitland, Ian, "The Limits of Business Self-regulation," *California Management Review* 27; 3 (Spring 1985), pp. 132–147.

Moskowitz, Milton, "The Corporate Responsibility Champs . . . and Chumps," *Business and Society Review* 52 (Winter 1985), pp. 4–10.

GLOSSARY

Attitudinal consistency (5) Occurs when the cognitive, affective, and action tendency components of each individual attitude are consistent with one another.

Authority (10) Having the capability to perform an action.

Behaviorally anchored rating scale or BARS (11) An evaluation device that combines the critical incident technique with a rating scale to assess an employee's performance.

Beliefs (5) What a person holds to be true about some object, without any particular response, to the object indicated.

Bureaupathology (15) A type of corporate illness that involves such characteristics as a large number of employees not knowing what they should be doing, a lack of rewards for good performance, leaders who are overburdened with paperwork, and so on.

Burnout (13) A serious physical/emotional problem linked to excessive, long-term stress that leads to a state of personal exhaustion.

Centralization (6) An organization in which authority is concentrated at the top of the hierarchy.

Comparison person (5) An individual, similar to ourselves, against whom we compare our job situation in terms of what we put into our job and what we receive for our efforts (from equity theory).

Computer phobia (1) A fear of computer technology.

Conflict (12) Arises out of the differences within and among people and groups in terms of their goals, needs, experiences, and outlooks on life.

Continuous reinforcement schedule (4) Linking a reward to desired behavior every time such behavior occurs.

482

Critical incident technique (11)   An evaluation method that involves having a supervisor record on-the-job situations that the employee either handled well or poorly.

Cue (2)   Any stimulus found in an individual's environment that can trigger a drive.

Cybernation (1)   The combination of computers and automation to assist in a more efficient manufacturing process.

Decentralization (6)   Contains several centers of authority and responsibility.

Defense mechanism (12)   Behavioral thoughts that attempt to protect an individual's psychological well-being.

Delegation (6)   The assignment of specifically stated duties, responsibilities, and authority from one group member to another.

Deviance (7)   Behavior that does not conform to society's norms.

Discrimination (2)   Actions that are taken against the object of prejudice.

Drive (2)   An arousal mechanism that causes an individual to act (e.g., hunger, thirst).

Ego (2)   The reality component of personality, according to Freud. It attempts to balance the impulsive needs of the id with the moralistic desires of the superego.

Executive (9)   A decision maker in the business organization whose primary focus is on subordinates (e.g., how to motivate them, how to communicate with them, and how to achieve the organizations' goals through their efforts).

Executive function (10)   Occurs when a leader influences group behavior to conform to his or her conscious intentions.

Expectancy (4)   The subjective estimate made by an employee as to whether his or her effort will lead to particular levels of performance.

Folkways (7)   Define expected behavior, but failure to observe a folkway is generally considered to have only small moral or emotional significance.

Force field analysis (14)   A process through which an individual may begin to understand the factors in life that push him or her to change or maintain his or her behavior.

Group think (12)   A problem that occurs in a highly cohesive group and leads to the inability of the group to consider the risks involved in their decisions.

Halo effect (11)   Occurs when someone evaluating the performance of a subordinate allows one particular characteristic of the employee to bias all other aspects of the individual's performance rating.

Hedonism (1)   A philosophy of life that stresses the need for immediate satisfaction and pleasure for its own sake.

Horizontal loading (4)   Giving an employee new tasks that are supposed to enrich his or her job but actually just enlarge the number of tasks expected of the employee.

Horizontal specialization (6)   The division of labor, as typified by the various departments or bureaus of a large organization, each of which is responsible for a different phase of the organization's work.

Hygiene factors (5)   According to Herzberg, these are elements in an employee's work environment that may lead to job dissatisfaction (e.g., poor working conditions, poor relationships with co-workers).

Id (2)   According to Freud, this is the first element of personality to develop. It represents the personality's main energy source and constantly seeks immediate gratification of its needs.

Instrumentality (4)   The subjective estimate an employee makes concerning the likelihood that various levels of performance will lead to various outcomes, such as rewards.

Job descriptive index (5)   A questionnaire that attempts to measure job attitudes.

Leniency bias (11)   Occurs when an evaluator gives inflated performance assessments.

Linking pin (6)   An individual who serves as a coordinating link or liaison between his or her department and another department/unit within an organization.

Locus of control (2)   A personality concept associated with Fulcon Rotter that deals with the extent to which an individual feels he or she has control over his or her destiny.

Manager (9)   A person who achieves organizational goals by arranging for other people to perform necessary tasks.

Managerial Grid (10)   A leadership training device developed by Blake and Mouton that describes five distinct leadership styles.

Mores (7)   Social rules that have greater moral significance than folkways and that are subject to strict sanctions.

Motivator factors (5)   According to Herzberg, these are job situations that may lead to high levels of job satisfaction (e.g., responsibility, challenging work).

Norms (7)   The rules, both stated and unstated, that specify what a person should and should not do within a given culture.

Operant behavior (4)   A movement instrumental in changing an environmental condition.

Opinions (5)   The verbal expression of attitudes.

Organization (6)   A social group that has been deliberately formed in order to pursue certain definite goals.

Personality (2)   A unique combination of traits and personal characteristics that results in behaviors that are relatively stable over time.

Pluralistic ignorance (12)   The misperception on the part of individual group members that they should not voice a dissonant opinion because they are in a clear minority.

Power (10)   The ability to bend others to your will.

Prejudice (2)   Judging people and situations on the basis of already existing attitudes and opinions.

Projective technique (4)   A personality assessment technique that involves showing individuals ambiguous stimuli with the intent of having them project aspects of their personality onto them.

Quality of working life (13)   The degree to which employees are able to satisfy important personal needs through their work place.

Recency error (11)   Occurs when only the most recent behavior displayed by an employee is used in making a performance assessment.

Refreezing (14)   The last process in changing attitudes and behaviors, which involves reinforcing the newly learned behavioral patterns and attitudes.

Reinforcement (2)   Any event that follows a behavior and is designed to increase the behavior's frequency of occurrence in the future.

Reliability (11)   Deals with whether or not a measurement instrument (e.g., selection questionnaire or performance evaluation device) is stable and consistent.

Respondent behavior (4)   An organism's reaction to external stimuli.

Role (9)   A set of behavioral expectations associated with a specific position in a social system.

Role conflict (9)   Occurs when an individual must enact two different roles at the same time (e.g., friend and manager).

Sanctions (7)   The means society uses to enforce its norms.

Selective perception (3)   The tendency to listen only to selected parts of a message and to block out other information.

Self-fulfilling prophecy (3)   When people behave in the manner that they believe is expected by others.

Shaping (4)   The creation of new behaviors by successively reinforcing parts of the behavior until an individual can finally perform all aspects of the task.

Social balance sheet (16)   An inventory of corporate activities that have a significant social impact.

Socialization (9)   The process of passing on a group's culture, morals, values, and rules of behavior.

Span of control (6)   The number of employees a manager supervises.

Stereotyping (3)   Forming judgments about people based on impressions we have about a group to which they belong.

Substitution reaction (12)   One way of reducing tension arising from conflict by substituting or lowering goals to replace those that have been blocked.

Superego (2)   The moralistic component of personality, according to Freud. It seeks to do what is "morally and socially" correct.

System I-IV (15)   Label coined by Rensis Likert to describe different types of corporate cultures.

Theory Z (8)   A term used to describe characteristics of some Japanese companies, including lifetime employment, nonspecialized careers, and decisions by consensus.

Unfreezing (14)   The first process in changing attitudes/behaviors, which involves showing an individual that his or her existing beliefs and behavioral patterns are no longer effective.

Valence (4)   Employee's perception of the attractiveness of various outcomes or organizational rewards.

Validity (11)   Whether or not a measurement instrument (e.g., selection tool or performance evaluation device) is measuring what it is supposed to measure.

Values (5)   Larger beliefs or ideas regarding what is good and correct.

Vertical loading (4)   Involves increasing an employee's authority and autonomy, giving him or her a complete natural unit of work, and designing tasks that will enable an employee to develop specialized expertise.

Vertical specialization (6)   The division of power by which authority is distributed throughout the company.

Voluntary simplicity (1)   A value orientation that stresses the need to get "back to the basics," particularly in buying decisions (e.g., generic products, inexpensive transportation means).

INDEX

Boldface page numbers are references to tables.

Accommodating style of handling conflict, 327
Achievement, need for, 96–99
Action-tendency component of attitudes, 121–122
Adams, Stacy, 124
Adjustment, attitudes and, 118
Affective component of attitudes, 121
Age Discrimination Act of 1967, 292
Age Discrimination in Employment Act, 7, **59** of 1967, 338
Aggression, relieving tension and, 325
Aging work force, 5, 7, **7**
Air Line Pilots Association, 316
Airlines, deregulation and, 417
Alcoholism, 347–349
Allen, Douglas M., 174
American Airlines, Inc., 315, 317
American Express, 74, 416
American Society of Interior Designers, 389

American Telephone and Telegraph, 32–33, 120
Ancker-Johnson, Betsy, 251–252
Apple Computer Inc., 98
Appraisals. *See* Performance appraisals
Argyris, Chris, 154, 161, 320
Ash, Mary Kay, 341–342
Atlanta Arts Alliance, 416
Attitudes
  changing, 120
  definition of, 117–118
  difference between opinions, beliefs, values and, 119–120
  effects on behavior, 122–130
  formation of, 120–122
  functions of, 118–119
  job satisfaction and, 124
  measuring, 130–134
  what causes positive and negative, 124, 126–129
Attitude survey
  administration of, 133
  design of, 131–132
  feedback of, 134
Attitudinal consistency, 123–124
Authority, leaders and, 277–278
Avoidance mechanisms, relieving tension and, 326–327

Avoidance style of handling conflict, 327

Bain & Company, 74
Balance theory, attitudes and the, 123
Barnard, Chester, 160–161
Becker, Howard, 187, 188
Behavior
  attitudinal effects on, 122–130
  deviance, 186–190
  effects of groups on, 183–186
  of leaders, 269–271
  modification, 111–112
  norms, 183–184, 185–186
  personality and, 51–56
  respondent, 100
  sanctions, 184–185
Behavioral consequences, stressors and, 347–349
Behavioral expectation scale (BES), 298
Behaviorally anchored rating scale (BARS), 298, **298**
Beliefs, definition of, 119
Bendix Corporation, 28
Bennis, Warren, 159–160
Berger, Judith, 290–291

Bethlehem Steel Company, 155
B. F. Goodrich, 112, 350
Birch, David, 29
Blake, Robert R., 279–280
Blake, William, 25
Blanchard, K., 281–283
Blau, Peter M., 142
Blue-collar jobs, decline of, 8–9
Boeing Co., 316
Boschert, Chris, 315, 316
Bottom-up change, **373**, 374–375
Boy Scouts, 211
Bronheim, David, 418
Burdick, Walton E., 339
Bureaucracy, 158
Bureaucratic relationship, leaders
    and, 270
Bureaupathology, 385–386
Burger King Corporation, 414–
    415
Burnout, 347, **348**
Burns, Anthony, 125–126
Business Week, 96, 397

Cafeteria incentive plans, 107–
    110, **108, 109, 110**
Campbell, John, 319–320
Campbell Soup Company, 414,
    416
Cathartic process, 306
Cattell, personality factors and, **50**
Centralization versus
    decentralization in
    organizations, 147
Central tendency bias, 302
Change(s)
    bottom-up, **373**, 374–375
    diagnosing obstacles to, 370–
        371
    force field analysis and, 370
    how to implement, 373–375,
        373
    organizational development
        approach to, 376–78

reducing resistance to, 367–369,
    368, 369
shared approach to, **373,** 375
stages of, 371–373
top-down, 373–374, **373**
who makes, 375–376
why resistance occurs to, 364–
    367
Changing stage, 371–372
Checklists for performance
    appraisals, 299
Chicago Tube & Iron Company, 74
Child-care arrangements, 19
Chrysler, 199
Chusmir, Janet, 180–181
Civil Rights Act, **59,** 248
    Title VII of the, 338
Classical organization theory, 154
    evaluating, 159–160
    Fayol and, 156–157, **157**
    Taylor and, 155–156
    Weber and, 157–159
Coercion, resistance to change
    and, 368, **369**
Cognitive component of attitudes,
    121
Cognitive dissonance theory,
    attitudes and the, 124
Collaborative style of handling
    conflict, 328
Columbia University, 96
Committee for Economic
    Development, 407
Communication(s)
    definition of, 65–66
    field of, 32–33
    formal, 68
    how to encourage effective, 83–
        84, 86
    informal, 68–70
    listening and receiving and, 79–
        81, **80**
    message sending and, 78–79
    nonverbal, 81–83, **82**
    patterns of, 67–70

perceptual barriers and, 71–73
physical barriers and, 73, 75
problems with, 71–78
process of, 66–67
semantics and, 75–76
sociopsychological barriers and,
    76–78
steps for reducing resistance to
    change, **368**
upward, 70
voice messaging, 74–75
Communist Manifesto, 25–26
Comparative evaluation tools,
    300–301, **301**
Competition
    cultural differences and, **47–48**
    negative linkage, 191
Computers
    advances in the field of, 22–23,
        27–28, **164**
    changing views of, 17–18, 32
Conflict(s)
    causes of, 317–322
    consequences of, 328–331
    definition of, 314, 317
    goals and, 318–322
    healthy, 313–314
    job assignments and, 321–322
    managers and, 241–244
    managers and outside work
        environment, 250, 252–253
    negative effects of, 328, 330–
        331
    personal nature of, 322–324
    positive effects of, 331–332
    psychological reactions to, 324–
        328
    roles and, 241
    satisfying needs and, 323
    small groups and organizational,
        191–192
    two-tier wage systems and, 315–
        317
    ways of managing, 327–328
Conglomeration, **165**

Congruity theory, attitudes and the, 124
Consultive management, 209
Consumer Cards, 416
Content theories of motivation, 91, 92–99
Continental Illinois National Bank & Trust Company, 128
Contingency approach to organizational design, 164
Contingency model of leadership, 275–276
Control(s)
  a leader's exercise of, 276–279
  delegating, 208–211
  for increased productivity, 200–202
  quality control circles, 215–218
Cooley, Charles H., 171, 230
Cooperation/positive linkage, 191
Cordis Corporation, 329–330
Corning Glass Works, 74
Cornnell, Susan, 93
Corporate culture
  bureaupathology and, 385–386
  classifying, 392–394
  definition of, **165,** 383
  dress codes, 387–388
  how to change, 399–401
  Japanese system, 395–396
  positive reinforcement and, 400–401
  productivity and, 384–385
  role modeling and, 400
  status symbols, 389–390
  types of, 390–392
  what creates excellence, 396–397
Corporate Social Audit, 418, **418–419**
Council on Economic Priorities, 413
Cousins, Jane Campbell, 366–367
Critical incident technique, 124, 297

Cues, 46
Cultural differences, personality and, **47–48**
Cummins Engine, 338
Cybernation, 28

Daily Camera, 180–181
d'Arbeloff, Dee, 400
Davis, Stanley M., 384
Deal, Terence, 399
Dean, Joel, 142–143
Decentralization versus centralization in organizations, 147
Decoding messages, communication and, 66
Defense mechanisms, 324–325
Dehumanization, work force and, 17–18
Delegation
  of control, 208–211
  in organizations, 147–150
Demassing, **165**
Democratic management, 210–211
Democratic relationship, leaders and, 271
Dependent-nurturant relationship, leaders and, 269
Deregulation
  future jobs and, 32
  social responsibility and, 416–417
Developer, manager's role, 237–239
Deviance, 186
  causes of, 187–188
  on the job, 189–190
  within the organization, 188–189
Dickens, Charles, 25
Dillard, Joe, 350, 352
Discrimination
  companies and, 59–60
  definition of, 58

legislation on, **59**
of women, 248–249
Diversification, **164**
Division of labor, 145–146
Donnelly Mirrors, 30
Donner, Frederic, 264
Dow Chemical, 422
Dowling, W. F., Jr., 202
Dream sociometry, 352
Dress codes, 387–388
Dress for Success, 388
Drives, 46
Drucker, Peter, 8, **164,** 295
Drug abuse, 347–348
Dubin, Robert, 182
Dunnette, Marvin, 319–320

Eastern Airlines, 199, 393
Eastman Kodak, 218
Education/communication approach, resistance to change and, 368, **369**
Ego defense, attitudes and, 118–119
Electronic voice mail, 74–75
Emery Air Freight Corporation, 112
Employees, dealing with problem, 307–308
Engels, Friedrich, 25
Environmental Protection Agency, 421
Equal Employment Opportunities Commission, 421
Equal Employment Opportunity Act, **59,** 248
Equal Pay Act, 248
  of 1963, 292, 338
Equitable Life Insurance Company, 350
Equity theory, attitudes and, 128–129
Erikson, Erik, **45**
Essay evaluations, 298–299

Etzioni, Amitai, 152–153
Evaluations. *See* Performance appraisals
Executive, manager's role, 236–237
Executive function of leadership, 266–268
Executive Order, **59**
Executive Wardrobe Engineering, 388
Exit survey, 131
Expectancy theory of motivation, 100–102
Experience curve, **165**
External control, personality and, 54, **55**
Exxon Corporation, 351

Facilitation/support, resistance to change and, 368, **369**
Fair Labor Standards Act of 1963, 338
Fayol, Henri, 144, 156–157, **157**
Fazio Supermarket, 315
Federal Communications Commission (FCC), 416
Federal Register, 292
Federal Reserve Bank (Atlanta), 22
Feedback
    performance appraisals and, 304–306
    rules for giving, **83**
Feinberg, Samuel, 264
Fenton, Lois, 388
Fiedler, Fred E., 275–276
Financial institutions, deregulation and, 417
First National City Bank, 30
First Spectrum Fund, 413
Fisher Foods Inc., 315
Flat versus tall structure of organizations, 146–147
Flextime, 110–111
Folkway, 185

Forced-choice statements, 299, **299**
Forced distribution method of evaluating, 301
Force field analysis, 370
Forcing/win-lose style of handling conflict, 327–328
Ford Motor Company, 73, 218, 325, 389–390
Formal communication, 68
Formal organization
    structure of, 144
    versus informal organization, 153–154
Formal versus informal leadership, 273–276
Formulation, communication and, 66
Fraser, Douglas, 20
French, R. L., 273
Freud, Sigmund, 42–46, 229–230
Friedman, Milton, 410–411, 413, 420
Fromm, Erich, **45**
Frustration, conflict and, 323–324
Fuchs, Victor R., 245
Fuggini, Frank, 305
Functions of the Executive, The, 160

Gains Pet Food, 338
Galbraith, John K., 420
Gamache, Ronald F., 316
Gangplank principle, 157
Geneen, Harold, 233–234
General Electric, 112, 303, 305, 355
General Foods, 338
General Mills, 30
General Motors Corporation, 393
    corporate profits and, 411, **411**
    Saturn plant and, 20–21
    skilled tradespeople and, 9
    at Tarrytown, New York, 338

Gergen, Kenneth J., 253
Gerstacker, Carl, 422
Glenn, John, 268
Goal-linkage, 191
Goals
    conflict and, 318–322
    organizations and, 141–142
    social responsibility and economic, 410
Goal setting, 102
Gore, Wilbert L., 162
Graves, J. P., 293
Groups (employee)
    effects on behavior by, 183–186
    high-performing system, 174
    how groups help individuals, 176–179
    how groups help larger organizations, 179–183
    informal, 170–176
    manager's role in small work, 191
    organizational conflict and small, 191–192
    peer, 171–172
    task-oriented peer, 172–176
Group think, 322

Halo effect bias, 302
Hardin, David, 42
Harrison, Roger, 393–394
Harwood Manufacturing Company, 107
Hayakawa, S. I., 81
Health care, field of, 33
Health of employees, promoting the, 352–355
Heidrick and Struggles, 387
Henning, Margaret, 249–250
Hersey, P., 281–283
Herzberg, Frederick, 103, 124, 126–128, 130
Hewitt Associates, 93
Hewlett-Packard, 218

High-performing system (HPS), 174
Hirsch, Don A., 315
Hodgson, Richard, 385, 386
Hoffmann-LaRoche, 75
Homans, George, 171, 175–176
Honeywell, Inc., 178
Horizontal loading, 103
Horizontal specialization, 145
Horney, Karen, 44–45
House, Robert J., 283
Hughes, Paula, 251
Human Equation Ltd., The, 42
Humanistic organization theory
  Argyris and, 161
  Barnard and, 160–161
  evaluating, 163–164
  Likert and, 161–163
Human needs, hierarchy of, 92
Hygiene factors, 126
Hynes, John, 75

Iacocca, Lee A., 325
IBM, 27, 218, 390–391, 393
  policies for improving quality of
    working life, 339
Idealistic relationship, leaders and,
  270–271
Independent linkage, 191
Individualism, importance of, 11
Individualization, 191
Industrial Revolution, 24–26
Informal communication, 68–70
Informal groups, 170–176
Informal leadership, formal
  versus, 273–276
Informal organization, formal
  versus, 153–154
Infotron Systems Corporation, 74
Inman, B. R., 22–23
Innovator, manager's role, 239
In Search of Excellence: Lessons
  from America's Best-Run
  Companies, 338, 391, 396–
  397

Instrumentality, motivation and,
  101
Insurgent-coercive relationship,
  leaders and, 269–270
Integral Data Systems Inc., 353
Interdependence, increase of, 11–
  12
Internal control, personality and,
  54, 55
International Association of
  Machinists, 316
International Labor Organization,
  8
International Telephone and
  Telegraph Corporation (ITT),
  233–234
Intrapreneuring, 165

Jackson, Reverend Jesse, 415
Japan
  corporate culture in, 395–396
  quality control circles in, 216–
    217, 338
Jardin, Ann, 249–250
J. C. Penney, 391–392
Jenkins, George W., 104–105, 398
Job Descriptive Index (JDI), 132,
  132
Job enrichment programs, 103–
  107
Job(s)
  conflict and job assignments,
    321–322
  decline of blue-collar, 8–9
  deregulation and future, 32
  deviance on the, 189–190
  of the future, 30–33
  technology and the creation of,
    29, 30, 32
Job satisfaction
  attitudes and, 124
  relationship between
    performance and, 130
Job stressors, 346

Johnson, George E., 262–263
Johnson Products Company, Inc.,
  262–263
Joyce, Sarah, 353
Jung, Carl, 45

Katz, Daniel, 118
Katz, Michael, 203
Kennedy, Allan, 399
Kennedy, Edward M., 347
Kennedy, John F., 264
Kimberly Clark, 351
Kmart, 417
Knowledge, attitudes and, 119
Knudsen, Simon E., 325
Kroger Co., 315

Labor unions, productivity and
  the role of, 207–208
Lawler, E. E., 130
Leadership
  behavior of, 269–271
  Blake and Mouton's Managerial
    Grid, 279–280
  bureaucratic relationship, 270
  contingency model of, 275–276
  definition of, 261, 263
  democratic relationship, 271
  dependent-nurturant
    relationship, 269
  development of, 265–266
  difference between
    management and, 263–265
  executive function of, 266–268
  exercising control and, 276–279
  formal versus informal, 273–
    276
  functions of, 266–268
  Hersey and Blanchard's
    situational model of, 281–283
  House's path-goal theory, 283
  idealistic relationship, 270–271
  insurgent-coercive relationship,
    269–270

learned or inherited, 260–263
manager's role and, 235–236
personal qualifications for, 271–272
situational factors that influence, 272–273
Learning theorists, 46–49
Legal aspects of performance appraisals, 292
Legislation
discrimination, **59**
performance appraisals and, 292
for quality of work, 338, 354
Leisure time, increase in, 11
Leniency bias, 302
Levering, Robert, 203
Levinson, Harry, 393
Levitt, Theodore, 264
Lewin, Kurt, 371
Likert, Rensis, 132, 161–163, 201, 202, 392–393
Line versus staff managers in organizations, 150–152
Listening, elements of effective, **80**
Listening and receiving, communication and, 79–81, **80**
Locke, Edwin, 102
Lombardi, Vince, 399
Lower expectations, effects on the work force by, 14–15
Lowy, Robert, 203

Mabe, Donald, 206
McClelland, David, 96–99
McCormick and Company, 211
McFadden, Betty, 251
McGregor, Douglas, **164,** 201, 247, 392
Machiavellianism
how to achieve power, 278
personality and, 54–56, **56**
McLamore, James W., 414–415

Maier, R. F., 306
Malotke, Joseph, 20
Management
addresses of publications dealing with, 462–465
case studies in, 429–456
consultive, 209
decision styles of, 213–215, **213**
democratic, 210–211
difference between leadership and, 263–265
journal/magazine reviews on, 457–462
multiple, 211
Management, productivity and supportive, 202–204
Management by objectives (MBO), 295–296
Management by walking around, **165**
Management theory, four decades of, **164–165**
Management training programs, 350
Manager, role of the
conflicts of, 241–244
definition of, 232–235
as developer, 237–239
as an executive, 236–237
as a human being, 239
as innovator, 239
as a leader, 235–236
Mintzberg model, 239–240
as negotiator, 237
outside work environment conflicts and, 250, 252–253
in small work groups, 191
women and, 244–250
Managerial Grid, **165**
Blake and Mouton's, 279–280
Managing, 233
Manipulation/cooperation, resistance to change and, 368, **369**
Manno, Eugene, 178

Marx, Karl, 25
Mary Kay Cosmetics, 341–342
Maslow, Abraham, 92–96
Massachusetts Quality of Working Life Center, 338
Matrix management, **165**
Matthews, Gordon, 74–75
Mayo, Elton, 188, 189–190, 319
MD Resources, Inc., 290–291
Mead, Margaret, 231
Medical consequences of job stress, 349
Meijer Inc., 316
Merrill Lynch Realty/Cousins, 366–367
Message sending, communication and, 78–79
Michigan Bell, 112
Microelectronics and Computer Technology Corporation (MCC), 22
Miller, Lawrence, 395–396
Millipore, Inc., 400
Mills, Theodore, 268, 269
Minnesota Satisfaction Questionnaire (MSQ), 132
Minority hiring, 420, 421
Mintzberg model, 239–240
Mitsubishi Corporation, 395
Mobil Oil, 120, 421–422
Molloy, John T., 388
Moral values, profile of, **15–17**
Moreno, J. L., 173
Mores, 185
Morgan, Dennis W., 315
Moskowitz, Milton, 203
Motivation
behavior modification and, 111–112
cafeteria incentive plans, 107–110, **108, 109, 110**
flextime, 110–111
incentives and, 93
job enrichment programs, 103–107

participation as, 107
scheduling reinforcement, 112
self-esteem, 94
Motivation, theories about, 91
content, 91, 92–99
expectancy, 100–102
goal setting, 102
McClelland's, 96–99
Maslow's, 92–96
process, 91, 99–102
stimulus-response, 99–100
Motivator factors, 126
Mouton, Jane Srygley, 279–280
Multiple management, 211
Murphy, William B., 414, 416
Murray, Mark, 93

National Center for Productivity
and Quality of Working Life,
338
National Quality of Work Center,
338
Nature versus nurture, personality
and, 50–51
Needs, conflict and, 323
Negative linkage, 191
Negotiation/agreement, resistance
to change and, 368, **369**
Negotiator, manager's role, 237
New York Telephone Company,
350
Nilles, Jack, 178
Nonverbal communication, 81–
83, **82**
Norms, 183–184, 185–186

Occupational Safety and Health
Act (OSHA) of 1970, 338, 354
Odiorne, George, 295
*100 Best Companies to Work for
in America, The,* 203

One-minute managing, **165**
Open door policy, communication
and, 70
Operant behavior, 100
Opinion Research Corporation,
408
Opinions, definition of, 119
Opportunity Act of 1972, 292
Organizational consequences of
stress, **349,** 350
Organizational development
approach to change, 376–378
Organizational ideologies, 393–
394
Organization(s)
centralization versus
decentralization, 147
classical theory of, 154–160
classification of, 142
conflict with small groups, 191–
192
definition of, 141
delegation in, 147–150
deviance within, 188–189
division of labor and, 145–146
factors that determine the
structure of, 143, 145–154
flat versus tall structure for,
146–147
formal structure of, 144
formal versus informal, 153–
154
goals of, 141–142
humanistic theory of, 160–164
line versus staff managers in,
150–152
productivity and the role of,
204–207
profits and, 142–143
regulatory activity in, 153
trends in, 17–19
Ouchi, William, 216–217, 338
Overcompensation, conflict and,
325
Owen, Robert, 26

Paired comparison method, 300,
301
Participation
definition of, 199
motivation and, 107
productivity and, 199–200,
211–215
quality control circles and, 215–
218
resistance to change and, 368,
369
Passion for Excellence, A, 206,
398
Path-goal theory, House's, 283
Pavlov, Ivan, 99, 100
Pax World Fund, 413
Peer groups, 171–172
task-oriented, 172–176
Penney, James Cash, 392
PepsiCo, 351, 391
Perception, communication and,
66
Perceptual barriers,
communication and, 71–73
Perdue, Frank, 205–206
Performance
how to measure employee,
294–299
relationship between job
satisfaction and, 130
Performance appraisals
behavioral expectation scale, 298
behaviorally anchored rating
scale for, 298, **298**
checklists for, 299
comparative methods of, 300–
301, **301**
critical incident technique for,
124, 297
dealing with problem
employees, 307–308
direct measures for, 294–295
employee resistance to, 303
errors and problems with, 301–
303

essay evaluations, 298–299
evaluation process, 288–289
feedback on, 304–306
forced-choice statements for, 299, **299**
how to improve, 303–304
legal aspects of, 292
management by objectives, 295–296
necessity of, 289–291
rating scales for, 296, **297**
reliability of, 293
structure of, 306–307
subjective procedures for, 296–299
validity of, 293
who conducts, 294
Personal biases, 303
Personality
  behavior and, 51–56
  cultural differences and, **47–48**
  definition of, 40–41
  development of, 42–46
  discrimination and, 58–60, **59**
  ego and, 43
  Freud and sociopsychoanalytic theory and, 42–46
  id and, 43
  internal/external control and, 54, **55**
  learning theorists and, 46–49
  Machiavellianism and, 54–56, **56**
  major factors of, **50**
  nature versus nurture and, 50–51
  prejudice and, 57–58
  relative stability and, 41
  structure of, 42–43
  superego and, 43
  theories on, influenced by Freud, **45**
  trait theorists and, 49–50
  Type A, 51, **53,** 54
  Type B, 54
  types of, 41
Person orientation, 394

Peters, Thomas J., 206, 338, 391, 396–397, 398
Phillips 66, 120
Photocircuits Glen Cove, 305
Physical barriers, communication and, 73, 75
Physical consequences of job stress, 349
Physical fitness programs, 351
Physio-Control Corporation, 203
Polaroid, 30
Polczynski, James, 389, 390
Porter, L. W., 130
Portfolio management, **165**
Positive linkage, 191
Positive reinforcement, corporate culture and, 400–401
Potter, Robert, 316, 317
Power, leaders and, 277–278
Power orientation, 394
Precision Castparts Corporation, 30
Pregnancy Discrimination Act of 1978, **59**
Prejudice
  causes of, 57–58
  definition of, 57
Prince, The, 55, 278
Principles of Scientific Management, 155
Problem solving style of handling conflict, 328
Process theories of motivation, 91, 99–102
Procter & Gamble, 218, 338
Productivity
  controls for increased, 200–202, 208–211
  corporate culture and, 384–385
  economics of, 197–198
  participation and, 199–200, 211–215
  quality control circles and, 215–218
  role of the labor union and, 207–208

role of the organization and, 204–207
supportive management and, 202–204
worker's reactions to, 201–202
Profits
  organizations and, 142–143
  social responsibility and corporate, 413–416
Projective technique, 96
Psychological consequences, stressors and, 347–349
Psychology Today, 249–250
Publix Super Markets, Inc., 104–105, 398
Puritan work ethic, 11

Quad/Graphics Inc., 106
Quadracci, Harry V., 106
Quality control circles (Q-C), 215
  in America, 218
  in Japan, 216–217, 338
Quality of working life (QWL). *See also* Stress
  appeal of, 338
  assessing, 340
  companies participating in, 338–339, 340–342
  definition of, 337
  legislation for, 338
  promoting the health and safety of employees, 352, 354–355
  quality control circles and, 338
  types of programs in, 355
Quantitative management, **164**

Ranking employees, 300
Rating scales, 296, **297**
Rationalization, relieving tension and, 326
Reagan, Ronald, 268, 408
Recency error, 302
Red Cross, 211
Refreezing stage of change, 372–373

Regression, relieving tension and, 326

Reich, Charles, 18

Reinforcement, 46
corporate culture and positive, 400—401
scheduling, 112

Relative stability, 41

Relaxation response, guidelines for, **353**

Reliability, performance and, 293, 294

Repression, relieving tension and, 326-327

Research laboratories, creation of, 27

Respondent behavior, 100

Restructuring, **165**

RoBards, Martine J., 42

Robinson, Larry J. B., 385

Roche, Gerry, 387–388

Rogers, Carl, 76, 79

Rogers, Richard, 341

Role modeling, corporate culture and, 400

Role players, born or made, 229–230

Role(s). *See also* Manager, role of the
conflict/strain, 241
cultural influences on, 231
definition of, 229
orientation, 394
overload, 347
socialization and, 229–232

Rosenberg, M. J., 123

Roszak, Theodore, 18

Rotter, Julian, 54

Ryder System, Inc., 125–126

Safety of employees, promoting the, 352–355

Saint-Simon, Claude Henri de, 26

Sanctions, 184–185, 278

Saturn plant, 20–21

Sayles, L. R., 202

Schaefer, William Donald, 148–149

Schuler, R. S., 351

Schwartz, Howard, 384

Scott, Sid, 199

Scott, W. Richard, 142

Sears, Roebuck, 133, 417

Sechrist, William, 352

Selective perception, 71–72

Self-fulfilling prophecies, 72–73

Self-fulfillment, value of, 12

Selznick, Philip, 153

Semantics, communication and, 75–76

Shaping, behavior and, 112

Shared approach to change, **373, 375**

Shell Oil, 120

Single adults, effects on the work force by, 10

Situational leadership model, Hersey and Blanchard's, 281–283

Skinner, B. F., 99–100

Smith, Adam, 26, 145–146, 314, 412

Smoothing style of handling conflict, 327

Social balance sheet, **418–419**

Social Dimensions Fund, 413

Socialization, 229–232

Social readjustment rating scale, **344**

Social responsibility
activist view of, 420–421
corporate profits and, 413–416
definition of, 407–409
deregulation and, 416–417
economic goals and, 410
effects on employees, 421–22
government intervention and, 412
measurement of, 418, **418–419,** 420
separation of business and social welfare, 410–411

Social trends
increase of singles in society, 10
postponement of marriage, 10
two-income families, 9–10

Social values, effects on the work force by changes in, 10
from conformity to individualism, 11
from independence to interdependence, 11–12, 14–15
from work to leisure, 11

Sociogram, 173, 175

Sociopsychological barriers, communication and, 76–78

Staff versus line managers in organizations, 150–152

Status symbols, 389–390

Stereotyping, 72

Stimulus-response theory of motivation, 99–100

Storer, Peter, 84–85

Stress
behavioral and psychological consequences of, 347–349, **348**
consequences of excessive, 347–350
coping with, 350–353
definition of, 342–343
guidelines for relaxation response, **353**
job stressors, **346**
management training programs, 350
medical and physical consequences of, 349
organizational consequences of, **349,** 350
physical fitness programs, 351
role overload and, 347
social readjustment rating scale, **344**
types of, 343–347

Strictness bias, 302

Subjective procedures for measuring employee performance
  behaviorally anchored rating scale, 298, **298**
  checklists, 299
  critical incident technique, 124, 297
  essay evaluations, 298–299
  forced-choice statements, 299, **299**
  rating scales, 296, **297**
Substitution reactions, relieving tension and, 325–326
Suedfeld, P., 123
Suggestion programs, 209–210
Sullivan, Harry Stack, **45**
Support managers, 202–204
Sweeney, Patrick J., 174
System I, 161, 163, 392–393
System IV, 163, 393
Systems approach to organizational design, 164
Szczesniak, Christine, 128

Tall structure of organizations, flat versus, 146–147
Tannenbaum, A. S., 201
Task orientation, 394
Task-oriented peer groups, 172–176
Taylor, Frederick W., 144, 155–156
Technology
  benefits of, 28, 30, 31–32
  computers, 27–28
  definition of, 19
  future of, 22–23
  historical background of, 23–24
  Industrial Revolution, 24–26
  innovation in, 26–27
  job creation and, 29, 30, 32
Tenneco, 351
Tennessee Valley Authority (TVA), 153–154

Texas Instruments, 30
Texas Tech University, Center for Productivity at, 338
T-groups, **165**
Thematic apperception test (TAT), 96
Theory X, 201, 392
Theory Y, **164,** 392
Theory Z, **165,** 216–217, 338
Theory Z corporations, characteristics of, **217**
Third Century Fund, 413, 418
Three-component attitude model, 120
  action-tendency component, 121–122
  affective component, 121
  cognitive component, 121
3M, 74
Tjosvold, Dean, 191
Topaz Travel Inc., 93
Top-down change, 373-374, **373**
Townsend, Robert, 313–314
Traits, definition of, 49–50
Two-income families, increase of, 9–10
Two-tier wage systems, 315–317
Type A personality, 51, **53,** 54
Type B personality, 54

Unfreezing stage of change, 371
Union Carbide, 389
United Air Lines Inc., 316
United Auto Workers (UAW), 20–21
United Parcel Service Inc., 315, 316
U.S.Bureau of Labor Statistics, 8
U.S.Postal Service, 316
University of California (Los Angeles), Quality of Working Life Program at the, 338
University of Michigan, Survey Research Center at the, 161
Upward communication, 70
Utilities, deregulation and, 417

Valence, motivation and, 101
Validity, performance and, 293–294
Values, definition of, 119
Values and life-styles (VALS), 12, **13–14,** 14–15
Vertical loading, 103
Vertical specialization, 145
VMX (voice message exchange), Inc., 74–75
Vocational Rehabilitation Act, **59**
Voice messaging, 74–75
Voluntary simplicity, 12
Volvo, 105, 107, 182, 340
Vroom, V. H., 100, 213–214

Wackenhut, George R., 52–53
Walt Disney Productions Company, 386
Warren, Alfred, Jr., 20
Waterman, Robert H., 338, 391, 396–397
Watson, Thomas J., 390
Weber, Max, 144, 157–159
Weiner, Norbert, 28
Weldon, Norman R., 329–330
Western Electric, 188, 189–190, 319
Westinghouse Electric, 74
Weyerhauser Company, 351
White-collar worker, increase in the, 8–9
W. L. Gore & Associates Inc., 162
Woman's Dress for Success Book, The, 388
Women in the work force, 8
Women managers
  discrepancies in earnings of, **248, 249**
  discrimination and, 248–249
  effectiveness of, 247
  full income of, 245
  guidelines for, 250
  role models, 251–252
  sexual harassment and, 249

stereotypes and the realities for, 244–245, 247

Work and Motivation, 100

Work force, trends in the
  aging, 5, 7, **7**
  changes in social values and, 10–12, **13–14**, 14–15
  dehumanization and, 17–18
  deregulation and, 32
  increase of the white-collar worker, 8–9
  single adults and effects on the, 10
  two-income families, 9–10
  women in the, 8

Work in America Institute, 338

Wozniak, Stephen G., 98

Wynn, William H., 316

Yamamoto, Craig, 203

Yetton, P., 213–214

Zaleznik, Abraham, 265

Zero-based budgeting, **165**